Understanding the Assault o

Understanding the Assault on the Black Man, Black Manhood and Black Masculinity

Wesley Muhammad, Ph.D.

Atlanta

A-TEAM PUBLISHING
PO Box 551036
Atlanta GA, 30355
www.ateampublishing.com

© 2017 by Wesley Muhammad, Ph.D.
Second Revised Edition

All Rights Reserved. No part of this book may be reproduced or transmitted in any form by any means, electronic, photocopying, mechanical, recording, information storage or retrieval system without permission from the publisher, A-Team Publishing. Brief quotations may be used in reviews or commentary.

Contents

*Plates 1-8*     101-104
*Plates 9-19*    145-149

PART ONE
**War on the Black Man: From Nixon to Clinton and Beyond**

1. Introduction                                          3-7
I. *Disappearing the Black Male*
II. *Still a Threat*
III. *Why this Book?*

2. 'Kill the Male, Spare the Female'                     9-26
I. *Today's Context: The Dying Whites*
II. *Kill the Male, Spare the Female*
III. *Spare the Female II*
IV. *Rise of the Black Matriarchy*

3. The Clintons: Super Predators and their Black Prey    27-51
I. *President Clinton, White Supremacy and the Crime Bill*
The Biden-Clinton Crime Bill
II. *Hillary's Young Black Super Predators*
III. *Global Super Predators*
Rwanda
Haiti

PART TWO
**Global Project: Feminizing the Black God**

4. The Global Strategy: The Samburu and the Zulu         55-75
   As Examples

v

I. *The Global Strategy*
II. *Killing and Feminizing the Black God*
III. *Neutralizing the Renowned Zulu Masculinity*
A Peculiar Masculinity
The Black God and Southern Cradle Patriarchy
The Church's Assault on Zulu Gender Culture
Killing the Black God (Again)
The Economic Uprooting of the Traditional Zulu Manhood

5. European Expansion and the Homosexual Enterprise     77-100
I. *Imperial Sodomy*
II. *America's Delectable Negro*
Ritual Cannibalism and Homosexuality Institutionalized in American Slavery
Jim Crow Lynchings and Sacrifice to the Christian God
Castration as a Transfer of Power
*Excursus:* Modern Example
III. *The Lady of the Races*
The "Man" and His "Boy": Why Saggin Is Faggin
IV. *Conclusion*

PART THREE
**The Esoteric Agenda: Killing the Black God**

6. The Black God, the Black Bull and the Black Man     107-130
I. *Who Is The Black God?*
II. *The Attribute Animal*
III. *Birth of the Black Man (God)*
The Cosmogonic Egg and the Primordial Atom
The Primordial Atom and the Birth of God
The Blue God (Lord of Sapphire)
IV. *The Great Ancestor and His Sons*

7. White Supremacy and the Black Gods     131-138
I. *War of the Gods*
II. *Indo-Aryan War Religion*

8. Killing Their Own Black God     139-144
I. *The Proto-Indo-European Black God*

PART FOUR
## Taming the Black Bull: War with the Black Male Mind

9. Operation Ferdinand: Creating Docile Black Males    153-168
I. *The New Rebellions and Their Aftermath*
II. *Mind Murder: Creating Black Zombies*
Dr. Ernst Rodin's Castrated Black Bulls of the Inner-City
Dr. José M.R. Delgado's Remote Controlled Black Bulls
Delgado's Experiments and the Black Matriarchy
III. *Shutting It All Down (But Not Really)*

10. Weaponizing Science Against Black Boys    169-179
I. *Super Predator: The XYY Study*
The White Super Predator
From Tall White to Young Black Super Predators
The Boston (Harvard) Project
The Maryland (Johns Hopkins) Project
Scientifically Demonizing Black Boys

11. The Pharmacological Assault on Black America:    181-200
    Keeping the Black Male Subordinate
I. *Dominance Hierarchy Studies*
II. *Sociopharmacology: The Scientific Roots of Urban Carnage*
III. *Serotonin: The Biochemical Key and the Magic Bullet*
IV. *The Pharmacological Assault on the Black Male Mind*

12. Mind Suppression and Behavioral Modification    201-208
    Of the Black Male
I. *Mind Fixing The Black Man*
II. *Criminalizing Black Boys from the Crib to the Womb*
III. *Criminalizing Black Male Fearlessness*

PART FIVE
## Creation of the Deadhead: Drugs and Social Controlling The Black Man

13. Jolly West: The CIA's Pivot from Psychosurgery    211-234
    To Crack Cocaine
I. *Dr. West and "Operation Ferdinand"*
II. *Dr. West and MK-ULTRA*

III. *Dr. West and the U.S. Government Target Young Black Men*
IV. *The CIA and Social Control Through Drugs*
The CIA and Aldous Huxley's Ultimate Revolution

14. Dope and Weed: Manufacturing the Deadhead     235-255
I. *The CIA, the Mafia, and Black America's Heroin Scourge*
II. *The Pot Plot: Weed and the Happy, Defective Slave*
Chemically Induced Euphoria
Your Brain on Weed
Weed and Reproduction
The CIA's Enhanced Marijuana Hits The Streets
The Government's Soma Pill
The CIA Imports The Streets' Marijuana
The Plot Deepens: George Soros

15. "Operation Ferdinand" and the War on Drugs     257-264
I. *War on the Black Male*
II. *War on Drugs I: Nixon's Prelude*
III. *War on Drugs II: Reagan's Crack Conspiracy*

16. Tailor-made Cocaine: How White Science Made Black Zombies     265-283
I. *The White Lady and the Negro*
Cocaine, Coca Cola and the Fear of the Super Negro
II. *The CIA's Tailor-made Cocaine Ravages Argentina*
III. *Prototype in Peru: The Zombie Test Run*

17. The Crack Conspiracy: The Confessions     285-305
I. *Who Created Crack?*
II. *Crack as a Legacy of Dr. Jolly West*
The Johnny Appleseed of Crack
Crack Confessions
III. *The White House and Black America's Crack Epidemic*
Rick Ross Did Not Introduce Crack
Black People Were Specifically and Exclusively Targeted, Again
*Excurses: Strawberry, The Crack Holocaust's Greatest Victim*

PART SIX
**Killing God in the Black Man's Brain, and Resurrecting Him**

18. Autism and the Chemical War Against     309-334

The Black Male Mind (God)
I. *From White Boys' Disease to Black Boys' Disease*
II. *Blowing the Whistle on the CDC's Conspiracy Targeting Black Boys*
The Thimerosal Conspiracy
The Thimerosal Cover Up
The Criminal Assault on the Mind of Black Boys and the Criminal Cover Up
III. *Autism and the Assault on Serotonin (Just What the Government Ordered)*
IV. *"Operation Ferdinand" and Autism: Creating Docile Black Males*
V. *Eli Lilly, Thimerosal and the Biomedical Control of Black Males*

19. Putting Out the Black God's Light               335-355
I. *The Light of God in the Body of Man*
II. *The Science of the Power of God in the Black Man's Brain*
III. *Melanin and the Power of God: The Black Man as Apex*
The Thimerosal Connection

20. Creating the "Lady of the Races": Science and Black   357-379
    Homosexuality
I. *The Black "Sissy"*
II. *A Horrendous Scientific Study of Sodomy and Black Boys*
Excurses: History of Johns Hopkins Nazi-like Experiments
III. *Lab Homo: The Scientific Manipulation of Sexuality*
Chemical Castration and the Feminization of the Black Male
IV. *Serotonin and the Scientific Spawning of Homosexuality*
V. *Chemically Feminizing the American Public*

21. Concluding Reflections: "Arise, O God!"         381-386

**Appendix:** "The Black Man and the White Fear"    387-397
Interview with Sis Ebony Muhammad and **Hurt2Healing**

*Select Bibliography*                                399-414

x

PART ONE

# War On The Black Man

## From Nixon to Clinton and Beyond

# 1   Introduction

> *Sadly, the real truth, which is a taboo to speak, is that this is a culture that does not love black males, that they are not loved by white men, white women, black women, or girls or boys. And that especially most black men do not love themselves. How could they, how could they be expected to love surrounded by so much envy, desire, hate? Black males in the culture of imperialists white supremacist capitalist patriarchy are feared but they are not loved.* bell hooks, **We Real Cool** (2004)

## I.   *Disappearing the Black Male*

Professor Michelle Alexander asks the question in 2010, "Where Have All the Black Men Gone?"

> A recurring question has surfaced in mainstream and ethnic media for more than a decade. The phrasing of the question differs depending on who's asking the question and why, but the question tends to boil down to this: Where have all the black men gone? They're missing in churches, missing from their families, missing from college campuses, and absent from work. Black women can't find a man to marry. Black children don't know where to find their father. Where are those guys? ...
>
> Here's a hint for all those still scratching their heads about those missing black fathers: Look in prison.
>
> The mass incarceration of people of color through the War on Drugs is a big part of the reason that a black child born today is less likely to be raised by both parents than a black child born during slavery. The absence of black fathers from families across America is not simply a function of laziness, immaturity, or too much time watching Sports Center. Hundreds of thousands of black men have disappeared into prisons and jails, locked away for drug crimes that are largely ignored when committed by whites.[1]

The Black male in America has been and remains the target of a concerted and ongoing war, but most of us perceive not. In October 1982 Pres. Ronald Reagan announced the War on Drugs. This War, Prof. Alexander documents in her important book, *The New Jim Crow*, had really nothing to do with concern

---

[1] Michelle Alexander, "Where Have All the Black Men Gone?" *The Huffington Post* April 24, 2010.

about the drug scourge on America and had everything to do with this government's concern about the *Black* Scourge on America, Black men in particular: "the drug war from the outset had little to do with public concern about drugs and much to do with public concern about race."[2] As a result of this fabricated war,[3] more Black men are under correctional control today than were enslaved in 1850, a decade before the Civil War began. But drugs were not just the false *pretext* of this war; drugs were also the *weapon* used in this War against Black America. In 1985 crack hit many of the streets and "blew through America's black neighborhoods like the Four Horsemen of the Apocalypse, leaving behind unspeakable devastation and suffering."[4] Thanks to the brilliant and courageous journalism of the late Pulitzer Prize-winning reporter Gary Webb of the *San Jose Mercury*, we now know for a fact that the rise of the crack epidemic in the Black communities along with the resultant gang violence that forced so many Black mothers to bury their sons and their daughters was connected to the CIA's active and tacit drug trafficking operations.[5] The Reagan administration's CIA spawned the ghastly drug problem in Black America on the *frontend* and Pres. Reagan's punitive but contrived War on Drugs then decimated and almost totally destroyed the ranks of productive Black men on the *backend*. The War on Drugs was a conscious and calculated assault on Black men in America, for reasons we shall detail below.

But the government agencies involved in this War against the Black male is not limited to the CIA under the Reagan Administration. CDC Senior Scientist Dr. William Thompson, who was granted official whistleblower status, along with Dr. Brian Hooker and Attorney Robert F. Kennedy Jr., have blown the whistle on the Center for Disease Control and Prevention in

---

[2] Michelle Alexander, *The New Jim Crow: Mass Incarceration in the Age of Colorblindness* Revised Edition (New York: The New Press, 2010, 1011) 49.
[3] On this fabricated war see below.
[4] Quote in Alexander, *The New Jim Crow*, 51
[5] Gary Webb, *Dark Alliance: The CIA, the Contras, and the Crack Cocaine Explosion* (New York: Seven Stories Press, 2004 [1998]); Nick Schou, *Kill The Messenger: How the CIA's Crack-Cocaine Controversy Destroyed Journalist Gary Webb* (New York: Nation Books, 2006). And see below.

Atlanta whose recommended MMR (measles, mumps and rubella) vaccine contains a potent brain killing mercury compound that has been linked to the development of autism in millions of American children, but has a most devastating impact on Black boys.[6] According to the whistleblower the CDC knew this and covered it up through widespread manipulation of scientific data and fraud. As we shall show, Black boys were specifically targeted. According to Robert Kennedy Jr., this is the New Tuskegee Experiment. So, while the government-complicit drug scourge and the government's contrived War on Drugs have neutralized a large portion of young adult and adult Black men by disappearing us into prisons, the CDC is neutralizing scores more by poisoning the brain while still in the cradle. And if that is not enough, the National Institute of Health is participating in the homosexualization of young Black males. We will look at all of these more deeply in the upcoming chapters.

II.   *Still A Threat*

But you have to ask yourself: why, after 400+ years of assault on the Black male through slavery, Reconstruction, Jim Crow, War on Drugs, etc.; after, by most objective measures, successfully disempowering and un-manning the Black male in American society, why is the Black male in America *still* the white man's chief threat such that he (the white man) remains obsessively preoccupied with his (the Black man's) destruction or at the very least social control? What is it about the Black male that this society fears so much, even today after 400+ years? We know for a fact that they are still targeting the Black male: the many Michael Browns and Tamir Rices attest to it. There is something about the Black male that even after 400 years of the best or the worst that this hostile culture (White America) has to offer, he is still a threat to be neutralized by any means necessary. What is it about the Black male in America? And also: if the white male has outlawed our Black manhood, what is the Black manhood that is actually outlawed in America? It's not machoism. He lets us have all the guns we want. In fact, he provides them to

---

[6] See discussion below.

us. He lets us fight and even kill, as long as we are killing someone Black. A reason we don't really adequately appreciate this assault on Black manhood is because we really don't comprehend what Black manhood is. The white male comprehends though. And he is hell-bent on no full, collective expression of Black manhood ever occurring in America.

But what is really behind White Supremacy's war against the Black Man? Is it racism? Well, that's a part. But it's deeper than that. White Supremacy is waring with the Black Man, *not* primarily because he is Black but because he is *God*. The War against the Black Man is White Supremacy's War against God.

### III. *Why This Book?*

You may ask and it would be a legitimate question: why Brother Dr. Wesley is another book on the assault on the Black male even necessary? By now, we all know that America is hostile to Black men. But that is precisely the problem. Too much familiarity breeds disrespect. We have become so familiar with the *fact* of the American assault on the Black male that we don't respect that fact like we should. This is why there is no real urgency to change the situation in the lives of individuals. We have the problem of simultaneously knowing both *too well* and *too insufficiently*. Black men know well that there is an assault but we don't know well enough about the plot to guard against falling prey to its many traps on a daily basis and Black women know their man is under assault but don't yet know enough of the architecture of the plot to keep from unwittingly becoming an aider and abettor to the plot, as he is an aider and abettor in the plot himself.

One of the reasons most people, Black and white, fail to grasp and take seriously the depth of the problem of this assault on the Black male is because we assume it to be an isolated historical American phenomenon restricted to antebellum America. And we believe that the feminization of the Black male is incidental to the white man's strategy of domination – a side show, so to speak. It is not. It is in fact *central* to his strategy. The American assault on the Black man – his manhood and his masculinity – from slavery till today was and is part of a Global Project, and only by understanding that Global Project and its methods repeated all over the world, can we fully appreciate what is going on here in America.

The white man feminized the Black man before a Black man was ever born in America. During the age of European expansion European Race Theory – their pseudo-scientific theories on the character and nature of the races of men – characterized the African as "The Lady of the (Human) Race," over and against the masculine Anglophone European, the true "Man" of the human race. Not because the white male really was convinced of that but because *his* masculinity was to be the *only* masculinity recognized and legalized in any areas under his power. Where ever the white man has set his boot his is the only manhood that is tolerable. So where he conquers on the earth he must neutralize the masculinity and manhood of the local men. It is part of his strategy of domination. And his methods are the same everywhere.

# 2    'Kill the Male, Spare the Female'

I.    *Today's Context: The Dying Whites*

On November 7, 2015 columnist Ross Douthat of ***The New York Times*** published an op-ed entitled "The Dying of the Whites."[7] The inspiration of this op-ed was a startling study published that month in the ***Proceedings of the National Academy of Sciences*** by Noble Prize winning economist from Princeton University Dr. Angus Deaton and his wife Anne Case.[8] The study documented a shocking white reality that right now white thinkers and policy-makers are scrambling to understand and to change: The whites are not just "dying," in the words of Douthat, they are *killing themselves* at an alarming rate through alcohol and drug poisoning, prescription drug abuse, and suicide.

For several decades in the wealthiest of the Western industrialized nations the mortality or death rate of whites has steadily declined. Western man's ill-gotten wealth has enabled him to live a little longer and make his quality of life better. In America, between 1978-1998 the mortality rate of Middle Aged Working Class Whites (MAWrCWh) declined by 2% on average each year, and in that twenty year period their death rate dropped by 1/3 overall. But in 1998 something dramatic happened. After falling sharply for two decades an abrupt reversal occurred. Between 1999 and 2013 the mortality rate for whites between the ages of 45 and 54 with a high school education rose dramatically. While in the other rich Western nations the steady decline of white mortality rates continued on pace, in America – the wealthiest nation on the planet - the mortality rate of MAWrCWh *ceased to decline* and between 1999-2013 the death rate remarkably and inexplicably reversed, *increasing a half percent each year*. For

---

[7] Ross Douthat, "The Dying of Whites," ***The New York Times*** Nov. 7, 2015.
[8] Anne Case and Angus Deaton, "Rising morbidity and mortality in midlife among white non-hispanic Americans in the 21st century," ***Proceedings of the National Academy of Sciences*** 112 (December 8, 2015) 15078-15083.

those two decades, the death rate of these whites increased by a total of 20%, resulting in 500, 000 extra white deaths over that time period. Outside of wartime, it is very unusual in advanced nations for a large group of the population to see such a jump in mortality rates, Joel Achenbach and Lenny Bernstein tell us.[9]

> In other advanced countries, such as the United Kingdom, the death rate among middle-aged people fell by about a third between 1999 and 2013. Here, in the United States, the death rates for Hispanics and blacks declined similarly. Middle-aged white Americans, particularly those with a high-school education or less, didn't share in these gains. Instead, their mortality rates rose, which is pretty shocking.[10]

How do we account for this "shocking" circumstance? These whites are not just falling over either: they are pushing themselves over. Soaring rates of drug and alcohol abuse due to heightened economic insecurity and frustration is considered a culprit. Between 1999 and 2013 epidemic drug poisoning increased six-fold in the white middle-aged demographic, especially with painkillers such as OxyContin.[11] But a purely economic explanation doesn't hold up. "[T]he shocks to the U.S. economy over the past few decades have effected poorly educated blacks and Hispanics just as much as they have affected whites – arguably, more severely. So why the death rise among whites?" asks John Cassidy.[12] Indeed, during this time the Black and Hispanic death rates were doing something *very different*: "the mortality rate for minorities in the U.S. continued to fall between 1999 and 2013, mirroring the trend in Europe, and the African-American death rate in particular *fell hugely* (emphasis added)."[13] Despite the cloud of death that this government and its agencies and that this society ensures hovers over every Black community in America and every Black life; despite the "six million ways to

---

[9] Joel Achenbach and Lenny Bernstein, "Prestigious medical journals rejected stunning study on deaths among middle-aged whites," *The Washington Post* November 3, 2015.
[10] John Cassidy, "Why did the Death Rate Rise Among Middle Aged White Americans?" *The New Yorker* November 9, 2015 .
[11] Cassidy, "Why did the Death Rate Rise."
[12] Cassidy, "Why did the Death Rate Rise."
[13] Douthat, "The Dying of Whites."

kill a Black man" that this government openly and clandestinely employs; despite all of the "Black Death" and carnage that *we* bring upon ourselves; despite all of this and in the midst of all of this the death rate of the Black man and woman *decreases* while the death rates of whites *increases*. So among whites, Hispanics and Blacks, the Black American population has the greatest decline in mortality rate, 2.6 % decrease per year, against 1.8 % decrease for Hispanics; for whites, their's go in the *opposite* direction: a half percent increase of death each year.

Also an enigma is the timing of this increased "White Death":

> And why did the death rate start to rise in 1999? The U.S. economy was booming at that time. The employment rate was under 4.5 per cent, and wages were rising. Far from being a period of economic trauma, the late nineties stand out as a period of growth and prosperity.[14]

So the researchers want to know: why are these whites in the richest White nation in the world killing themselves at such alarming rates through painkillers and alcohol and drugs and suicide? It is no doubt because they are seeing their world fall. This "epidemic of white pain," their feelings of "dispossession" that they are trying to relieve themselves of through painkillers and drugs is probably caused by the psychological trauma that has come from the realization that American White Supremacy is crumbling around them. The governor of Main, Paul LePage, very candidly told us why whites are mad and committing suicide. He complained about "D Money and dem" coming up from New York selling whites the heroin that they are overdosing on and then - the real problem - they knock up a young white girl before they leave! Mayor LePage suggested that *that* is the real problem, because whites' fear genetic annihilation as the late great Dr. Francis Cress-Welsing laid out for us, may Allah be pleased with her.

This White Fear is not mere speculation. The 2008 U.S. Census projected that by 2042 the national U.S. population will be majority Black, Brown and Asian. Whites will be a minority

---

[14] Cassidy, "Why did the Death Rate Rise."

(again). Northwestern University scholars Maureen A. Craig and Jennifer A. Richeson conducted research in 2014 on the impact that this information about America becoming a "majority-minority nation" had on whites.[15] Their research indicated that 31 percent of whites surveyed – Republican, Democratic, Catholic, Protestant – were bothered by this, perceiving it as a "group-status threat." This perception of threat increased racial bias among those surveyed and portended increased racial hostilities for the future. Indeed, these whites felt immediately threatened, even though the threat was not expected to manifest for three decades. These bothered whites therefore supported more "conservative," i.e. racially biased and even racist, political policy. The only thing that made the surveyed whites feel better, Craig and Richeson tell us, is the reassurance that, despite the demographic shift, "Whites are likely to remain at the top of the future racial hierarchy in a majority-minority America".[16]

What is the solution? The "Great White Hope," Thomas Edsall of *The New York Times* tells us, is this: "The trick for the Republicans in their quest to maintain white majoritarian hegemony is to allow this fusion of issues to do its mobilizing work at a subliminal level, without triggering widespread resistance to explicit manifestations of bias and race prejudice."[17] In other words, in order to maintain White Supremacy in America, policies must be only covertly rather than overtly racist. Edsall was (presumably) talking primarily about the Republican political strategy, but he perfectly describes also the U.S. Government's strategy to maintain White Supremacy in this country. It's a racist strategy but the average observer is none the wiser. For example: target Black boys with a brain poison, but make it look like a larger American autism epidemic. This is the

---

[15] Maureen A. Craig and Jennifer A. Richeson, "More Diverse Yet Less Tolerant? How the Increasingly Diverse Racial Landscape Affects White Americans' Racial Attitudes," *Personality and Social Psychology Bulletin* 40 (March 2014): 750-761; idem, "On the Precipice of a "Majority-Minority" America: Perceived Status Threat From the Racial Demographic Shift Affects White Americans' Political Ideology," *Psychological Science OnlineFirst*, April 3, 2014:1-9.
[16] Craig and Richeson, "On the Precipice," 7.
[17] Thomas B. Edsall, "The Great White Hope," *The New York Times* May 20, 2014.

strategy born from what Carol Anderson aptly and correctly describes as "White Rage":

> What was really at work here was *white* rage...White rage is not about visible violence, but rather it works its way through the courts, the legislatures, and a range of government bureaucracies. It wreaks havoc subtly, most imperceptibly. Too imperceptibly, certainly, for a nation consistently drawn to the spectacular-to what we can *see*. It's not the clan. White rage doesn't have to wear sheets, burn crosses, or take to the streets. Working the halls of power, it can achieve its end far more effectively, far more destructively...The trigger for white rage, inevitably, is black advancement. It is not the mere presence of black people that is the problem; rather, it is blackness with ambition, with drive, with purpose, with aspirations, and with demands for full and equal citizenship. It is blackness that refuses to accept subjugation, to give up. A formidable array of policy assaults and legal contortions has consistently punished black resilience, black resolve. And all the while, white rage manages to maintain not only the upper hand but also, apparently, the moral high ground."[18]

This White Rage is now just as it always has been directed at Black men in particular. In the words of Orlando Patterson: "It was always the case in America that 'superadded' to the burden of being a male slave or a male laborer was the burden of the assault on Afro-American men's integrity and identity as men...[R]acist oppressors were virulently obsessed with the maleness of the Afro-American male and brutally sought to extinguish any hint of manhood in him."[19] But contrary to what Patterson suggests, there is no real evidence of "remarkable changes in the attitudes of Euro-Americans" as it relates to Black manhood and masculinity, as we shall show.

So whites are pained, they are psychologically traumatized, they are *angry*, and they have guns. Those who don't kill themselves with drugs or by cliff-jumping prepare themselves to kill Black people, Black men in particular. These

---

[18] Carol Anderson, Ph.D. *White Rage: The Unspoken Truth of Our Racial Divide* (New York: Bloomsbury, 2016) 4-5.
[19] Orlando Patterson, "Broken Bloodlines: Gender Relations and the Crisis of Marriages and Families Among Afro-Americans," in idem, *Rituals of Blood: Consequences of Slavery in Two American Centuries* (New York: Basic Civitas, 1998) 8.

psychologically traumatized whites are in law enforcement, in the justice system, in politics, etc. and are unleashing their fury on the Black man in America today because they see us as their # 1 Enemy. The covert white strategy is thus easy to define: Kill the Male, Spare the Female.

## II. *Kill the Male, Spare the Female*

*It was always the case in America that 'superadded' to the burden of being a male slave or a male laborer was the burden of the assault on Afro-American men's integrity and identity as men...[R]acist oppressors were virulently obsessed with the maleness of the Afro-American male and brutally sought to extinguish any hint of manhood in him.* Orlando Patterson, "Broken Bloodlines" (1998)

"Kill the male, spare the female" is the draconian plot that Pharaoh hatched against the Children of Israel to keep them from growing in strength and power. We know what "Kill the male" looks like. It looks like Officer Darren Wilson gunning down Michael Brown while Brown is surrendering with his hands up. It looks like Officer Timothy Loehmann rolling up on 12-year old Tamir Rice while he was playing outside as 12-year old boys should do and immediately gunning him down with absolutely no provocation, and then the city blames the 12-year old Black boy for his own un-provoked murder. Wilson and Loehmann undoubtedly represent the tip of the iceberg of the "White Supremacist Infiltration of Law Enforcement" that the F.B.I.'s 2006 Unclassified Intelligence Assessment Report warned of. In particular, the Report showed concern over the infiltration of law enforcement by so-called "ghost skins," those who avoid overt displays of their beliefs in order to blend in while covertly advancing white supremacists causes.[20]

We thus know well what "Kill the Male" looks like, at least *one method* of "Kill the Male." But what does "Spare the Female" look like? It looks like Oklahoma City officer Daniel Holtzclaw using the power of his badge to rape 13 vulnerable Black women and girls. America is killing the Black male and sparing the Black female because the Black male is seen by White Supremacy as

---

[20] "(U) White Supremacist Infiltration of Law Enforcement," Federal Bureau of Investigation Intelligence Assessment 17 October 2006, pg.5.

enemy combatant and the Black female is seen as the Booty, and as the Booty they can have their way with her. We now know that Daniel Holtzclaw is just the tip of the iceberg. *The Huffington Post* reported in November 2015:

> In a yearlong investigation of sexual misconduct by U.S. law enforcement, The Associated Press uncovered about 1,000 officers who lost their badges in a six-year period for rape, sodomy and other sexual assault; sex crimes that included possession of child pornography; or sexual misconduct such as propositioning citizens or having consensual but prohibited on-duty intercourse.
> 
> The number is unquestionably an undercount because it represents only those officers whose licenses to work in law enforcement were revoked, and not all states take such action. California and New York - with several of the nation's largest law enforcement agencies - offered no records because they have no statewide system to decertify officers for misconduct. And even among states that provided records, some reported no officers removed for sexual misdeeds even though cases were identified via news stories or court records.
> 
> "It's happening probably in every law enforcement agency across the country," said Chief Bernadette DiPino of the Sarasota Police Department in Florida, who helped study the problem for the International Association of Chiefs of Police. "It's so underreported and people are scared that if they call and complain about a police officer, they think every other police officer is going to be then out to get them."
> 
> Even as cases around the country have sparked a national conversation about excessive force by police, sexual misconduct by officers has largely escaped widespread notice due to a patchwork of laws, piecemeal reporting and victims frequently reluctant to come forward because of their vulnerabilities - they often are young, poor, struggling with addiction or plagued by their own checkered pasts...
> 
> The AP's findings, coupled with other research and interviews, suggest that sexual misconduct is among the most prevalent type of complaint against law officers.[21]

The victims are targeted. They come from the "vulnerable" demographics: young, poor, drug addicts or those with criminal records. The victims largely come from underprivileged communities of color. These predatory police victimize juveniles like school children about one-third of the time.

---

[21] Matt Sedensky and Norman Merchant, "Hundreds of Cops Kicked Off Force For Committing Sex Crimes," *The Huffington Post* November 1, 2015.

This is not a new phenomenon. Calvin C. Hernton, in his important work, *Sex and Racism in America* (1965), reports:

> it is a common saying in the South among white males that 'a man is not a man until he has slept with a nigger'...[T]he white supremacist's (or racist's) concept of the Negro female is that all of them are sluts and prostitutes; at best, they are objects of open sexual lust. In the mind of the racist, the northern ghettos are viewed as jungles of smoldering black flesh against which the prejudiced white man can act out his lewd concept of the sex act...the white man, the white racist...exemplifies the more pornographic emotions when he thinks of or actually sees a Negro female...Down South, where racism is rampant, a common experience of all Negro males is the humiliation of hearing about and often witnessing Negro women being fondled, insulted, and seduced by white men.[22]

Hernton recounts an incident that was all too common then and now: in one southern town the police took a Black women away from her Black male companion and put her in the patrol car. They then drove her to the outskirts to the city and raped her in open daylight.[23]

This sexual advantage taking of the Black women by white men is also common in the work place. John Griffin, a white reporter who traveled through the South posing as a Black man, revealed a conversation he had with a white employer:

> He told me how all of the white men in the region crave colored girls. He said he hired a lot of them both for housework and in his business. "And I guarantee you, I've had it in every one of them before they ever got on payroll." "Surely some refused," I suggested cautiously. "Not if they want to eat – or feed their kids," he snorted. "If they don't put out, they don't get the job."[24]

Again, this is neither a new nor a specifically American phenomenon. When the Germans conquered the coastal and interior parts of Togo in West Africa, scholars argue, African women were forced to be concubines of the German men. "All unmarried (German) settlers naturally had a Herero[25] woman as a

---

[22] Calvin C. Hernton, *Sex and Racism in America* (New York: Grove Press, Inc., 1965) 6, 90-91.
[23] Hernton, *Sex and Racism in America*, 91-92.
[24] John Howard Griffin, *Black Like Me* (New York: Sugnet, 1963) XX.
[25] Of southern Africa.

table and bed companion. Here," the colonial officer admitted, "that is a matter of course, like drinking and eating..."[26] There was even an "African Harem" at the military post that ensured a ready supply of Black concubines.

In this regard I should like to introduce you to Joseph Thomson, Scottish explorer and geologist dispatched to Kenya by the British Royal Geological Society in 1883. In a semi-autobiographical novel that he wrote in 1888 after spending time among the Maasai people there and being smitten by the beautiful Maasai women, he wrote:

> To marry a negress for the sake of having something to care for besides one's self! Plenty of room for self-sacrifice there, I should fancy! I wonder, now, If I *could* care for a negress? After all, why not? A man grows fond of his dog, and even gets to have a certain feeling of companionship for him; I suppose it would be equally possible with [a Maasai] maiden some fresh, budding young child of nature, even though black and barbaric. *Ulu* (1888, 1: 36)

Indeed, white men don't genuinely love Black women, even those they marry, except in the way he can also love his dog.

Sexual violence was a tool of colonial control. It was political praxis.[27] European men established control over invaded territories through sex with indigenous women. "In the colonial setting sex, both metaphorically and literally, became a force for colonizing the non-Western world. Essentially, unrestrained male heterosexuality became an instrument for European conquest."[28] As Andrea Smith says as well: "U.S. colonizers view the subjugation of women of the Native nations as critical to the success of the economic, cultural, and political

---

[26] Daniel J. Walther, "Sex, Race and Empire: White Male Sexuality and the 'Other' in German Colonies, 1894-1914," **German Studies Review** 33 (2010): 52-53 [art.=45-71].
[27] David Kenosian, "The Colonial Body Politic: Desire and Violence in the Works of Gustav Frenssen and Hans Grimm," **Monatshefte** 89 (1997): 182-195; Andrea Smith, "Not an Indian Tradition: The Sexual Colonization of Native Peoples," *Hypatia* 18 (2003): 70-85.
[28] Walther, "Sex, Race and Empire," 45.

colonization...Symbolic and literal control over their bodies is important in the war against the Native peoples."[29] There could be no more illustrative example of this political use of sexual violence than in the report penned by Bartolomé de Las Casa, the 16th century Spanish historian who chronicled the first decades of the colonization of the West Indies. In his ***Devastation of the Indies*** he reported:

> The Christian attacked them with buffets and beatings...Then they behaved with such temerity and shamelessness that the most powerful ruler of the island had to see his own wife raped by a Christian officer.[30]

Thus, such institutionalized sexual terror is not peculiar to America. In fact, America's tactics grow out of a *global* strategy of domination employed by White Supremacy and its architects. US Law Enforcement executes Pharaoh's command to "Kill the Male," and US officers are given what's tantamount to a license to enjoy the spoils of war, the booty: "Spare the Female." When Black women are killed by cops, like Rekia Boyd, or Miriam Carey or Sandra Bland, it's because as booty the Black woman is not targeted, but is expendable and her life doesn't matter anymore than the Black man's does. If 'Kill the Black Male' means kill the Black man in six million ways or more, "Spare the Female" means keep the Black woman around but only for sexual use and abuse by the conquerors of the Black man, and when she gets out of line – out of her place - she can get it too. It is pathetically poetic that, the South Carolina officer Ben Fields who showed such indifference to the life of our little sister, was "dating" a Black woman at the time according to the police chief. The chief said "dating."

---

[29] Smith, "Not an Indian Tradition," 74.
[30] Bartolomé de Las Casa, ***Devastation of the Indies*** (Baltimore: John Hopkins University Press, 1992) 33.

## III.  Spare the Female II

> *White supremacist capitalist patriarchy's refusal to allow black males full access to employment while offering black females a place in the service economy created a context where black males and females could not conform to standard sexist roles in regard to work even if they wanted to.* bell hooks, ***We Real Cool*** (2004)

Orlando Patterson, the John Cowles Professor of Sociology at Harvard University, published an important essay in 1998 entitled "Broken Bloodlines: Gender Relations and the Crisis of Marriages and Families Among Afro-Americans." It is a lengthy essay and I have no intention here of engaging it fully. Rather, I want to cherry pick and highlight certain quotes that are most relevant to our discussion.

Using numerous stats and graphs Patterson documents clearly the profound difference in the quality of life in America for Black men and Black women. In practically every aspect of physical, social, economic, professional, and educational life Black women excel Black men.

> When current trends are projected, there is every reason to believe that Afro-American women will soon surpass Afro-American men in median income. Indeed, when we take account not just of median income but of the numbers and proportions of Afro-American women in desirable occupations, it is already the case that they have outperformed Afro-American men in absolute terms and Euro-American women in relative terms...On the whole, it is safe to say that ethnic differences in the economic experiences of Afro-American and Euro-American women have either disappeared or are on the verge of becoming insignificant. Afro-American women continue to suffer serious gender biases in the economy, but they suffer them equally with Euro-American women. Appearances to the contrary, there is no double-burden of race and gender in economic matters...[W]e find in almost every area of education and skills acquisition Afro-American women are far outperforming Afro-American men...Afro-Americans are the only ethnic group in which women outperform men in most of the hard sciences, especially physics, math, and computer science; engineering is an exception, but Afro-American women are fast catching up...[O]nly among Afro-Americans do we find men substantially below parity in the fields of medicine, dentistry, law, and business.[31]

---

[31] Orlando Patterson, "Broken Bloodlines: Gender Relations and the Crisis of Marriages and Families Among Afro-Americans," in idem, ***Rituals of Blood:***

Patterson documents that Black women surpass Black men in all top occupational categories. For example, among executive, administrative and managerial workers, there were in 1994 (the last data available to him) 127 Black women to every 100 Black men. Compare this to 64 white women for every 100 white men. Likewise, among professionals there were 151 Black women for every 100 Black men vs. 85 white women to every 100 white men.

This of course is only half of the story. In terms of vital statistics, the ultimate tests by which we can evaluate life's burdens according to Patterson, the picture is very, very disturbing.

> In 1994 (...) Afro-American male life expectancy at birth was 64.9 years, which was 8.4 years less than Euro-American men, 9 years less than for Afro-American women, and 14.7 years less than for Euro-American women. This figure is not only shocking for an advanced industrial society, it is, in fact, significantly lower than that for men of several Third World societies such as Cuba and the Afro-Caribbean states of Jamaica, Barbados, and Trinidad-all with populations that originated in exactly the same region of West Africa, and with almost identical Afro-European levels of miscegenation, as Afro-Americans...Equally distressing are the differences in expected death rates per year. For every 1,000 live male Afro-American births in 1990, almost 20 were expected to die by 1991, compared with 16 Afro-American females, between 8 and 9 Euro-American males, and between 6 and 7 European females. At age twenty the differences are even greater; 3.8 times as many Afro-American men as Afro-American women could expect to die within the year. A major factor contributing to both the low life-expectancy rates and the high death rates is the much higher rate of death from violence and accidents among Afro-American men...Afro-American men die from violence and accidental causes at disproportionally greater levels throughout all age categories. Note, in contrast, that the gap between Euro-American and Afro-American women is negligible for most age groups and virtually disappears after age sixty-five...Afro-American men committed suicide at 6.2 times the rate at which Afro-American women did. What is more, Afro-American men are the only group for whom the rate is rising steadily...the suicide rate for Afro-American women is among the lowest in the nation.[32]

---

*Consequences of Slavery in Two American Centuries* (New York: Basic Civitas, 1998) 9, 11-12, 16-18.
[32] Patterson, "Broken Bloodlines," 12-14, 15-16.

These facts are startling. There can be no question whether the Black male in America suffers a double burden – ethnic and gender – in America. He most certainly does. Patterson asks:

> How do we explain all of this? Why are the fortunes of Afro-American men declining so precipitously while those of Afro-American women are getting better? Why, in particular, are Afro-American women now poised to assume leadership in almost all areas of the Afro-community and to outperform Afro-American men at middle- and upper-middle-class levels of the wider society and economy?[33]

The answer is undeniable: kill the male, spare the female. American hostility to Black manhood never abated.

### IV. Rise of the Black Matriarchy

Jessie Bernard was an American sociologist and radical feminist scholar. Nevertheless, she had an important candid moment in her book, ***Marriage and Family Among Negros*** (1966):

> Negro men have been more feared, sexually and occupationally, than Negro women. In fact, Negro women have more often proved attractive to the white world...not only as sex partners but also as nurses or 'mammies.' As a result, Negro women have been less isolated from the white world; they have more intimate contacts with it; they have lived in the homes of white families; they have had greater opportunity to mingle with white people. More doors-back doors to be sure-have opened for them. They have, therefore, felt more at ease in the white world. Even in their contacts with social-work agencies and the world of bureaucracy, they have known their way around. Negro men and women have, in brief, tended to live in somewhat different worlds, both under slavery and after emancipation...

> [The] institution of slavery in the United States subverted the relations between the sexes. And in so doing it inflicted grievous wounds on the Negro man...*The Negro man had to be destroyed as a man [in order] to 'protect' the white world.* Unwittingly, unintentionally, even against her own will, the Negro woman participated in the process...The Negro man...was put in a situation in which *conformity to masculine norms was all but impossible*...One does not have to resort to psychoanalytic figures of speech to see that the Negro men were castrated by the

---

[33] Patterson, "Broken Bloodlines," 23.

white world-sometimes literally as well as figuratively (emphasis added).

Mrs. Bernard's candor here is appreciated. American White Supremacy had to castrate and destroy the Black male in order to protect itself. Masculinity itself was virtually proscribed for the Black male. As William H. Grier and Price M. Cobbs note:

> Whereas the white man regards his manhood as an ordained right, the Black man is engaged in a never ending battle for its possession. For the Black man, attaining any portion of manhood is an active process. He must penetrate barriers and overcome opposition in order to assume a masculine posture. For the inner psychological obstacles to manhood are never so formidable as the impediments woven into American society.[34]

Daniel P. Moynihan was the Assistant Secretary of Labor in Pres. Lyndon B. Johnson's administration. In 1965 he wrote and distributed a strictly in-house, non-public report to the President and his deputies entitled "The Negro Family: The Case for National Action." This Report was intended to motivate the President and his deputies to launch massive federal employment and anti-poverty initiatives directed at Black Americans. This strictly in-house Report fell into the hands of some governmental mischief makers who were not pleased with either the Report's conclusions or objective. They leaked small quotes torn from their context to the press and the public. A fire-storm ensued. Once the already scandalized Report was finally released to the public many, including American feminists, launched a campaign to discredit it and neutralize the Report's perceptive, candid observations and thwart its recommendations.[35] Having read the so-called Moynihan Report for myself, I am very clear on why white American conservatives and radical American feminists

---

[34] William H. Grier and Price M. Cobbs, **Black Rage** (New York: Basic Books, 1968) 49.
[35] See for example Kay S. Hymowitz, "The Black Family: 40 Years of Lies," **City Journal** Summer 2005; James T. Patterson, "Moynihan and the Single-Parent Family: The 1965 Report and its Backlash," **Education Next** Spring 2015: 6-13; Serena Mayeri, "Historicizing the 'End of Men': The Politics of Reaction(s)," **Boston University Law Review** 93 (2013): 729-744.

were both so bent on misrepresenting and neutralizing it, and I am clear on its relevance to us today in 2016. Moynihan wrote:

> the racist virus of America still afflicts us…(T)hree centuries of sometimes unimaginable mistreatment have taken their toll on the Negro people. The harsh fact is that, as a group, at the present time, in terms of ability to win out in the competitions of American life, they are not equal to most of those groups with which they will be competing. Individually, Negro Americans reach the highest peaks of achievement. But collectively, in the spectrum of American ethnic and religious and regional groups, where some get plenty and some get none…Negros are among the weakest…It is more difficult for whites to perceive the effect that three centuries of exploitation have had on the fabric of Negro society itself. Here the consequences of the historic injustices done to Negro Americans are silent and hidden from view. But here is where the true injury has occurred: unless this damage is repaired, all the effort to end discrimination and poverty and injustice will come to little…Of the greatest importance, the Negro male…became an object of intense hostility, an attitude unquestionably based in some measure on fear…Keeping the Negro "in his place" can be translated as keeping the Negro male in his place: the female was not a threat to anyone…The very essence of the male animal, from the bantam rooster to the four star general, is to strut. Indeed, in 19th century America, a particular type of exaggerated male boastfulness became almost a national style. Not for the Negro male. The 'sassy nigger' was lynched…(T)he Negro community has been forced into a matriarchal structure which…seriously retards the progress of the group as a whole, and imposes a crushing burden on the Negro male and, in consequence, on a great many Negro women as well.

The "Negro" community has been forced into a matriarchal structure. The Black Matriarchy in America is real. What did Moynihan mean by Black Matriarchy? He meant that either fathers were absent from the home, as were ¼ of the Black homes in 1965 or, while physically present, the lack of gainful employment forced a role reversal in the home, disempowering the Black father as head of his household. Moynihan rightly observed that, "At the heart of the deterioration of the fabric of Negro society is the deterioration of the Negro Family." You weaken the family, you weaken the nation. Moynihan documented his case with 24 pages of charts and tables. He suggested that, until Black men reclaimed their proper place as breadwinning heads of households, poverty, violence and dysfunction would mar the hard-won progress of the Civil Rights movement. So Moynihan urged in his Report a national effort of focusing government policy and resources on improving employment opportunities for Black men in particular with an eye toward reinstating them as primary breadwinners in the marital household. Feminists don't like that talk at all.

Despite all of the negative press the Moynihan Report received and still receives, while certainly not flawless, it *did* correctly identify the problem, its root, and the consequences. Erol Ricketts, sociologist-demographer with the Russel Sage Foundation, in a 1989 follow-up study disputed the Report's claim that the contemporary Black family formation emanated directly from slavery.[36] However, it is in fact the case that:

> In the plantation domestic establishment, the woman's role was more important than that of her husband. The cabin was hers and rations of corn and salt pork were issued to her. She cooked the meals, tended the vegetable patch, and often raised the chickens to supplement the rations. If there was a surplus to sell, the money was hers. She made the cloths and reared the children. If the family received any special favors it was generally through her efforts.[37]

Patterson rightly points to the "ethnocidal assault on gender roles" during slavery, particularly the "certain consequence of slavery," i.e. "it was most virulent in its devastation of the roles of father and husband."[38] He goes on to say: "While this male emasculation did not lead to a 'matriarchy,' it did change the position of women in relation to men."[39] It is to be conceded that 'Black Matriarchy' is not an apt description of the situation during slavery, nevertheless the post-slavery Matriarchy described by Moynihan perfectly comports with the data on Black male and female roles in society as presented by Patterson. And even Ricketts confessed: "the *Report* turned out to be an accurate piece of social forecasting in that it predicted rapidly increasing rates of female headed families among

---

[36] Erol Ricketts, "The origin of black female-headed families," *Focus* 12 (Spring-Sumer 1989): 32-37.
[37] Maurice Davie, *Negroes in American Society* (New York: McGraw, 1949) 207.
[38] Patterson, "Broken Bloodlines," 27.
[39] Patterson, "Broken Bloodlines," 32.

blacks."[40] Ricketts points out as well: "as black male labor force participation and employment have declined since World War II, the employment position of black women remained relatively stable."[41] The result is the total realization of Moynihan's prediction. Entrenched, multigenerational poverty is largely Black and is intricately intertwined with the collapse of the nuclear family. While 26% of American children were born into single parent homes in 2005, 72% of Black children were. At the time of Moynihan's Report (1965), 24% of Black children were born into single-family homes.[42]

In order for Black America to heal from our slavery-inflicted wounds, grow and genuinely progress as a people the Black Family must be reconstituted and strengthened. No strong Black Family, no strong Black Nation. And it is the case that in order for the Black Family to be strengthened the Black man *must* be re-constituted, empowered and re-integrated into the family in his proper role. Moynihan knew like we know today that, as long as the Black man is disempowered in the home, he can never go out and become empowered in this hostile society that has literally been at war with his manhood for over 400 years. Sisters, if you want your husband to be a man *out there* you must help him be *the* man in the home. You have to help place him on his throne in the home. But it doesn't start Brothers with her *letting* you be the man. It starts with you determining to be the man in your home whether she or anyone else likes it or not. In order to be treated as the man we have to *be* the man. But Moynihan also knew then as we know now that in order for the Black male to actually *be* the man in his home he must be able to perform the *duties* of the man of the home, and that requires gainful employment and/or access to resources. And so Moynihan appealed to the President to make the government resources available to help reconstitute the Black man as a Man in his home and thus in society. What was the government's response to this

---

[40] Ricketts, "origin of black female-headed families," 34.
[41] Ricketts, "origin of black female-headed families," 35.
[42] Kay S. Hymowitz, "The Black Family: 40 Years of Lies," *City Journal* Summer 2005.

accurate analysis and appropriate recommendation to empower the Black man in America in his home?

President Johnson acknowledged the truth of the Report, but then did nothing to implement its findings or recommendations. Instead, (covert) action on the Report was taken by his successor President Nixon who took the Report seriously and took the potential of the strong Black male in American society seriously as a *serious threat*. In 1968, three years after the Report was distributed, Nixon declared Black people, i.e. the Black male, his enemy and when he got into office in 1971 he launched an all-out War against the Black Male under the false pretense of a War on Drugs.[43] We shall elaborate on this point later. With Moynihan's analysis as a backdrop, instead of marshalling government policy and resources to improve the Black male's condition and thereby stabilizing the Black Family, Nixon marshalled government policy and resources to declare and wage a war against the Black male and further debilitate the Black Family. In 1982 President Regan re-initiated and expanded the War on Black Men disguised as a War on Drugs, and President Bill Clinton did the *most* damage. The Clintons are Super Predators and the Black male is their prey. Mass incarceration as a consequence of this four-decade long fabricated War on Drugs has decimated the Black male population. There are more Black Men under correctional control today than were enslaved in 1850, a decade before the Civil War. At the time Moynihan wrote in 1965 24% of Black households were absent a Black Father. Today, after four decades of a covert governmental war against the Black male, 70% of Black households are Fatherless. This did *not* happen by accident.

---

[43] See below.

# 3  The Clintons: Super Predators and Their Black Prey

Image from Roger Morris, *Partners in Power* (1996)

I. *President Clinton, White Supremacy and the Crime Bill*

In 1985 Arkansas Governor Bill Clinton joined political strategist Al From, Georgia Senator Sam Nunn, Virginia Governor Chuck Robb and Tennessee Senator Al Gore and together they established the Democratic Leadership Council (DLC). The aim of the DLC was to get the White House back from the Republicans by making the Democratic party more palatable to a key constituency: white males, Southern white men in particular. Taking a page from Nixon's Southern Strategy, the DLC would appeal to the Southern white male electorate by whistle-blowing the embrace of White Supremacy.[44] There is no clearer, more transparent display of the DLC's aim and agenda than the campaign event that they organized for presidential candidate Bill Clinton on March 1, 1992, a week before Super Tuesday. It was a press conference held at the Stone Mountain Correctional Institute in Stone Mountain, Georgia.

---

[44] Christopher Petrella, "On Stone Mountain: White Supremacy and the Birth of the Modern Democratic Party," *Boston Review* March 30, 2016.

The small state correctional facility was actually located at the base of the actual Stone Mountain, Georgia's most renowned historical marker. But the imposing Stone Mountain is also an iconic site for American white supremacists. The initial sculpting of the mountain, celebrating three Confederate soldiers, was by a Klansman named Gutzon Borglum, who also sculpted Mount Rushmore. The modern Ku Klux Klan was born during a rally atop Stone Mountain on November 25, 1915. For the next fifty years Stone Mountain would be the site of the annual Labor Day cross-burning. And as Nathan Robinson, editor of *Current Affairs* writes: "The town of Stone Mountain itself also became a 'white supremacist mecca'…perhaps no other location in the country has remained so closely associated with white supremacy for so long."[45] The state prison where this Clinton campaign event took place was at the base of this icon of white supremacy, located at 5500 Venerable Street. James Venerable, after whom the street is named, was a legendary local Klan leader.

The picture taken from this press conference (Plate 1) depicts Bill Clinton flanked by DLC leader Sam Nunn, behind him Georgia Governor Zell Miller, and opposite Nunn is Georgia Congressman Ben Lewis, outspoken defender of the Confederate flag. Behind all of these suited white men are suited young black males – suited in prison jumpsuits. The racist audacity of this photo op is stunning. As Christopher Petrella of *The Boston Review* points out:

> It is hard to imagine that the DLC would not have been aware of Stone Mountain's significance as a theater of white supremacy when it staged Clinton's campaign event at the prison there. In fact, the choice of that particular place as a campaign stop-arranging white political leaders in business suits in front of subjugated black male prisoners in jumpsuits-is illegible *except* in the light of this history.[46]

---

[45] Nathan J. Robinson, *Super Predator: Bill Clinton's Use & Abuse of Black America* (W. Somervillw, MA, 2016) 37-38.
[46] Christopher Petrella, "On Stone Mountain: White Supremacy and the Birth of the Modern Democratic Party," *Boston Review* March 30, 2016.

Robinson notes also that the photo, called an "iconic photo of 1992,"

> sent an unmistakable message. If President Clinton wanted to "signal to poor and working-class whites that he was willing to be tougher of black communities than Republicans had been," he could hardly have done better than stand in front of a shackled mass of black men at the base of Stone Mountain...only a year after its Klan picnics had finally stopped. For a clutch of white politicians to pose in front of black inmates would be mildly nauseating in the most innocuous of locales; that Clinton did it with a pair of open bigots at the entrance of the "Confederate Rushmore" should violently churn the stomach.[47]

This was a carefully tailored message indeed, to the DLC's target constituency: Southern white males. California Governor Jerry Brown got it right. He said Clinton and his cohorts looked "like colonial masters" signaling to white voters: "Don't worry, we'll keep them in their place." Governor Brown said the implications are clear: "Two white men and forty black prisoners, what's he saying? He's saying we got 'em under control folks."

This press conference and its iconic image inaugurated President Clinton's "tough on crime" campaign and presidency. It is my suggestion that this image perfectly illustrates and encapsulates President Clinton's whole approach to race and politics. He decided early to appeal to America's white supremacist instincts by politicizing race and criminalizing Black men, then imposing the harshest penalties on Black men – note Clinton's callous execution of mentally disabled Ricky Ray Rector. President Clinton's "tough on crime" presidency was appropriately launched in America's mecca of White Supremacy. His 1994 Crime Bill, I suggest, must be seen in this light.

### THE BIDEN-CLINTON CRIME BILL

The Violent Crime Control and Law Enforcement Act, signed by Clinton in 1994, was perhaps one of the harshest laws in this country's history: it was the "apotheosis of late-20th Century American draconianism."[48] Senator Joe Biden takes credit for

---

[47] Robinson, *Super Predator*, 40, 41.
[48] Robinson, *Super Predator*, 45, 52.

authoring it, even referring to it as the "1994 Biden Crime Bill."[49] The devastating impact on the Black community is certainly Clinton's legacy though:

> Clinton escalated the drug war beyond what conservatives had imagined possible a decade earlier. As the Justice Policy Institute has observed, "the Clinton Administration's 'tough on crime' policies resulted in the largest increase in federal and state prison inmates of any president in American history...Clinton-more than any other president-created the current racial undercaste.[50]

It is thanks to President Clinton that there are now more Black men under correction control than were enslaved in 1850. Racism and white supremacy drove the crafting, the signing and enacting of the 1994 Crime Bill. This is further indicated by perhaps President Clinton's most ignominious "tough on crime" action, which incidentally introduces us to the President's signature manner of dealing with any Black interests that he chooses to countenance in order to reap the political benefits: I call it the Clinton Double-Cross. The action is the upholding of the unambiguously racist crack cocaine 10-1 sentencing disparity.

In 1995 the United States Sentencing Commission, after studying the disparity, produced a recommendation that the sentencing be equalized, 1 - 1. The Commission's recommendations had always been accepted prior to this issue. Nevertheless, Congress passed a bill *blocking* the plan to equalize sentencing and correct the racial injustice inherent in the existing sentencing prescriptions. This move by Congress was unprecedented. Black leaders and lawmakers including the Congressional Black Caucus called on President Clinton to uphold the Sentencing Commission's recommendation and equalize the sentencing. President Clinton gave the Black activists and the whole world good reason to feel confident that the President understood and was sensitive to what's at stake and was prepared to do the right thing. On October 16, 1995 – the day

---

[49] Nicholas Fandos, "Joe Biden's Role in '90s Crime Law Could Haunt Any Presidential Bid," *The New York Times* August 21, 2015.
[50] Michelle Alexander, *The New Jim Crow: Mass Incarceration in the Age of Colorblindness* (New York: The New Press, 2011) 56-57.

of the Million Man March – President Clinton gave a speech at the University of Texas and declared: "Blacks are right to think something is terribly wrong...when almost one in three African American men in their 20s are either in jail, on parole or otherwise under the supervision of the criminal justice system." He acknowledged that it was unfair that a "disproportionate percentage" of Black men were in prison for drug crimes "in comparison to the percentage of blacks who use drugs in our society."[51] The President gets it.

A week after these remarks Clinton stunned everyone, especially the Black people he had just placated or, better, deceived. On October 27th he signed Congress's bill into law, nullifying the Sentencing Commission's recommendations. The racist 10 – 1 disparity was upheld. This is the Clinton Double-Cross. We see it over and over again.

II.     *Hillary's Young Black Super Predators*

I unapologetically hold Hillary Clinton culpable for the murder of Tamir Rice. Of course I'm not claiming that the Democratic Presidential Nominee had any direct involvement with or *responsibility* for those tragic events that occurred at Cleveland's Cudell Recreation Center on November 22, 2014. That would be foolish. I most definitely am charging, however, that the Clintons – Bill and Hillary both – have some measure of indirect but deep and demonstrable *culpability*. The merciless drive-up shooting of 12-year old Tamir by Officer Timothy Loehmann and Officer Frank Garmback, as well as the City of Cleveland's rationalization, justification and *apologia* for the murder of this harmless child, are both legacies of what Dr. Perry Moriearty, Associate Professor at the University of

---

[51] William J. Clinton, "Remarks at the University of Texas at Austin," October 16, 1995.

Minnesota Law School, calls America's "Super-Predator War" of the 1990s. If President Johnson had his War on Poverty and Presidents Nixon and Reagan had their War on Drugs, President Clinton and his helpmeet the First Lady had their Super-predator War aimed specifically at young (i.e. adolescent) Black males. If you are shocked and appalled at the incidences today of elementary school boys – mainly black boys – put in actual handcuffs at their elementary school by police, then to a great extent I suspect you can thank the Clinton's for that too. A legacy of their Super-predator War. Tamir Rice is responsible for his *own* homicide, the City of Cleveland gives us to understand, because that 12-year old had the nerve to physically – and criminally - *look like a big, scary adult*. His crime was that he *refused to look like the adolescent that he was*. And *that* is a crime punishable by death, if you are a Black male.

But it was not that young Tamir didn't actually look like the adolescent that he was. He did. It was that Officer Loehmann was incapable of *seeing* and *acknowledging* Tamir's youth. And *that*, I most definitely charge, is part of Bill and Hillary's legacy. Officer Loehmann was only "bringing to heel" that stone-cold Super-Predator who was menacing that Cleveland park and the whole of this nation with that horrifyingly dangerous *toy gun*. 1996 Hillary would be so proud of Officer Loehmann.

Hillary Clinton *must not* be given a pass for her 1996 "Super-Predator" remarks. Her apology during this year's campaign should be rejected because it was deceptive and thus disingenuous. Her claim to Jonathan Capehart of the **Washington Post** that she was not talking about the young people but about the drug cartels that victimize the young people – "kids" in her language – is flatly contradicted by her own statement.[52] While on the campaign trail for her husband in

---

[52] Jonathan Capehart, "Hillary Clinton on 'superpredator' remarks: 'I shouldn't have used those words'," **Washington Post** February 25, 2015.

New Hampshire, the First Lady told her audience, justifying President Clinton's draconian and racist 1994 Crime Bill:

> We also have to have an organized effort against gangs, just as in a previous generation we had an organized effort against the mob. We need to take these people on, they are **often connected** to big drug cartels, they are not just **gangs of kids** anymore. They are often **the kinds of kids who are called superpredators**. No conscience. No empathy. We can talk about why they ended up that way but first we have to bring them to heel.

It is thus *not* the cartels that are here described as Super-predators. It is specifically certain *kinds of kids* who are *connected* to the cartels. And these certain kinds of kids must be brought to heel, like the dog brought under the control of his master. There is no question at all what "kinds of kids" the First Lady was talking about.

Hillary Clinton did not invent the term "super-predator." Rather, she learned it and its meaning from the term's actual coiner, right-wing political scientist John J. DiIulio from (at the time) Princeton University. And Professor DiIulio was clear and bold: young black males, even pre-puberty elementary school black boys, have become a demographic crime bomb about to explode on all of America if they are not "brought to heel." In two articles DiIulio laid out the looming threat to America; how this new breed of youth predator is "fatherless, Godless, and jobless" and thus can "kill or maim on impulse without any intelligible motive."[53] These "super crime-prone young males" – mainly *black* – "mean big trouble ahead" for America: "the number of young black criminals (is), " he claimed, "likely to surge, but also the black crime rate, both black-on-black and black-on-white, is increasing, so that as many as half of these (coming) super-predators could be young black males."

---

[53] John J. DiIulio, "The Coming of the Super-Predators," *the Weekly Standard* Nov 27, 1995; idem, "My Black Crime Problem, and Ours," *City Journal* Spring 1996.

DiIulio theorized that "nothing affects crime rates more than the number of young males in the population." So in order to avoid the predicted tsunami of merciless crime on the streets of America, reduce the number of young males in the population. Simple math. Draconian measures were thus enacted in order to do just that: reduce the number of black males walking around. These measures were justified because, as DiIulio claims, "the black kids who inspire the fear seem not merely unrecognizable but *alien*." These are not humans but Godless *aliens* who have invaded the country. And as Dr. Barry Krisberg, criminologist from UC Berkley notes: "When you describe another group as Godless, you can do anything to them."[54] The Clintons understood that well.

Professor John J. DiIulio

We know that this is what the First Lady had in mind when she spoke on behalf of her husband in New Hampshire. Early in 1995 President Clinton hosted a "working White House dinner" on juvenile crime. Of the twelve invitees was DiIulio, who thoroughly schooled his hosts on the Super-Predator threat: "Over gourmet Szechwan wonton and lamb, the meeting dragged on for three-and-a-half hours. President Clinton took copious notes and asked lots of questions," DiIulio recounts. So when the First Lady was stomping in New Hampshire, she did not just invoke an empty term: she invoked a term pregnant with very specific content and meaning, meaning that she learned firsthand from the term's own inventor while dinning with him at the table in her own home.

---

[54] "The Super Predator Scare," (1014) Retro Report documentary presented by *The New York Times* at http://www.nytimes.com/video/us/100000002807771/the-superpredator-scare.html.

DiIulio and colleagues, with the help of the major media, created a national moral panic that targeted young Black boys. But when the White House cosigned this Super-Predator scare, it was official and official policy would soon be created to "bring them to heel."

But there is one big problem: it was a fabricated scare. As Dr. Krisberg points out: "This country went into a moral panic over superpredators. [But] the calculations were wrong. *They made it up.*" He says further:

> It was a myth. And unfortunately it was a myth that some academics jumped on to. The fear of the superpredator led to a tremendous number of laws and policies that we are just not (or: now?) recovering from.[55]

Even DiIulio himself later confessed on *The New York Times* short documentary about the myth: "The super-predator idea was wrong. Once it got out there though, it was out there. There was no reeling it in." Steve Drizin of *The Huffington Post* says the myth of the super-predator was premised on "junk science and inaccurate predictions,"[56] but when so many *brilliant* minds collude to make government policy based on *junk science*, know that it was intentional. The junk science was nothing but the alibi.

And no age was too young to be held up as the personification of evil in this society. To justify the onslaught against the Black youth that was coming, President Clinton exploited the 1994 murder of eleven-year old Robert "Yummy" Sandifer in Chicago. Abandoned and homeless by the time he was only eight years old, "Yummy" – whose name derived from his love of donuts – allegedly killed fourteen year-old Shavon

---

[55] "The Super Predator Scare," (1014) Retro Report documentary presented by *The New York Times* at http://www.nytimes.com/video/us/100000002807771/the-superpredator-scare.html. See further Dr. Barry Krisberg, "Youth Violence Myths and Realities: A Tale of Three Cities." Testimony before the House Subcommittee on Crime, Terrorism, and Homeland Security. Youth Violence: Trends, Myths, and Solutions. February 11, 2009.

[56] Steve Drizin, "The Superpredator Scare Revisited," *The Huffington Post* June 9, 2014.

Dean. His fellow gang members then killed him to quite him, we are told. Yummy then became – literally – the poster boy for the Super-Predator and the coming doom. But as Elaine Brown points out:

> Perhaps the most interesting thing about Yummy's case and the infamy heaped upon him in the press was this: not only had he never been charged with or tried for, or convicted of this murder for which he stood publicly accused, but also, and even more curiously, he was dead...Yummy's tragic death...could not keep him from being held up as a ruthless killer.[57]

And the President seized the opportunity. In his President's Radio Address of September 10, 1994 Clinton spoke at some length on Yummy's story, as presented by the morally paniced media, and used Yummy's case as the justification for his "get tough" policies. President Clinton's Super-Predator War was on.

Through this fabricated Super-Predator War of the Clintons, the segment of the American population which was always shown restraint and shielded from public scorn by law and by custom, the youth, were now the target of "a veritable domestic war," as elaborated by Prof Perry L. Moriearty and William Carson in their very important article, "Cognitive Warfare and Young Black Males in America." But only a segment of this segment was targeted: Black youth. This dark myth of "tinny thugs" or "thugs in basinets" and adolescent super-predators robbed all Black boys of their most obvious characteristic – their youth. Just as Snapple's bumblebee is born fully grown, so too do black babies come out of the womb fully grown, and fully menacing to society.

---

[57] Elaine Brown, *The Condemnation of Little B: New Age Racism in America* (Boston: Beacon Press, 2002).

> At the same time the 'super-predator' war amplified the American public's predisposition to associate adolescents of color, and in particular young black males, with violence and moral depravity, it also led the public to disassociate young black males from the one trait that should not have been up for debate: their youth.[58]

Rather, according to this dark myth and the social psychology and social policies that it shaped, "The most violent, the most *adult-like*, and the most amoral of adolescents were young black males." As a result, during the Clinton '90s nearly every state in the country enacted laws that denied these children their youth by making it much easier to try them as adults.

> The result was the incarceration of literally thousands of youth, the majority of whom were black males. By 1998, African-Americans constituted about 15% of youth under age eighteen, but nearly two-thirds of those transferred to adult court.

In 1988 there were approximately 1600 juvenile offenders in adult jails. Toward the end of the Clinton '90s, specifically 1997, there were more than 9000.

The Clintons literally waged war against our Black children. This is why I call them Black Baby Eaters.

What does this have to do with Tamir Rice in 2014? As Moriearty and Carson explain: "By all accounts, the politics, rhetoric, and imagery endemic to the 'super-predator' war were extreme in its demonization *and adultification* of adolescent offenders." In the American social psychology this social war

> altered the social meaning of 'young, black male' in profound and intractable ways. Because the majority of the people in this country now harbor such stereotypes about criminality, deviance and adultness of young black males, large segments of the public remain willing to

---

[58] Perry L. Moriearty and William Carson, "Cognitive Warfare and Young Black Males in America," *The Journal of Gender, Race & Justice* 15 (2012): 281-313.

enact, administer, and support policies that cause substantial and disproportionate harm to this segment of our youth population...[59]

Policies such as the police execution of a twelve year boy playing with a toy at a park.

Yes, the Clintons are absolutely culpable. The Super-Predator War was *their* war, and it specifically targeted our children and robbed our children in the public mind of their youth and thus of the *protections* that their youth should grant them, just as it grants their white peers. This is why the City of Cleveland can blame Tamir Rice for his own murder: because that young man "looked" like a big, scary adult in the mind of the approaching white officers, his slaughter was justified. The officers did nothing but "bring to heel" a super-predator, just as First Lady Hillary Clinton called good American's to do.

The Clinton's foreign policies are but extensions of their domestic policies. Both domestic and foreign policy show the Clintons to be Super Predators and Black people are their prey.

III. *Global Super Predators*

### RWANDA

Lieutenant-General Roméo Dallaire, Force Commander of the United Nations Assistance Mission for Rwanda (UNAMIR) during the notorious Rwanda Genocide of 1993-1994, recounted his frustration after the U.S. bullied the U.N. Security Council to remove the peacekeepers:

> My force was standing knee-deep in mutilated bodies, surrounded by the guttural moans of dying people, looking into the eyes of children bleeding to death with their wounds burning in the sun and being invaded by maggots and flies. I found myself walking through villages where the only sign of life was a goat, or a chicken, or a songbird, as all

---

[59] Moriearty and Carson, "Cognitive Warfare and Young Black Males in America."

the people were dead, their bodies being eaten by voracious packs of wild dogs.[60]

On April 22, 1993 Bill Clinton stood before an audience at the U.S. Holocaust Museum and declared that the U.S. must never permit such an act of genocide as occurred in Germany to occur again. Almost exactly a year later, on April 7, 1994, one of the twentieth century's gravest crimes against humanity began in the Central African nation of Rwanda. But contrary to his public declaration President Clinton not only remained coldly silent in the face of one the worst genocides of modern history, his administration actively, callously and successfully thwarted all U.N. efforts to intervene. As a result, over the course of 100 days 800,000 mainly Tutsi Rwandans were ethnically cleansed by machete wielding Hutu Rwandans. Samantha Power, in her three-year, 51 page investigation notes:

> As the terror in Rwanda had unfolded, Clinton had shown virtually no interest in stopping the genocide, and his Administration had stood by as the death toll rose into the hundreds of thousands...[The] U.S. government knew enough about the genocide early on to save lives, but passed up countless opportunities to intervene... In reality the United States did much more than fail to send troops. It led a successful effort to remove most of the UN peacekeepers who were already in Rwanda. It aggressively worked to block the subsequent authorization of UN reinforcements. It refused to use its technology to jam radio broadcasts that were a crucial instrument in the coordination and perpetuation of the genocide. And even as, on average, 8,000 Rwandans were being butchered each day, U.S. officials shunned the term "genocide," for fear of being obliged to act.[61]

And *act*, the Clinton Administration simply was not going to do. The administration deliberately downplayed the atrocities being committed on innocent Rwandans, refusing to publically acknowledge that what was occurring was genocide. This was because, per the U.N. Genocide Convention, acknowledging the genocide would bind the U.S. to act. So while *privately* and in official documents senior officials freely referred to the Rwanda

---

[60] Samantha Power, "Bystanders to Genocide," *The Atlantic* September 2001.
[61] Power, "Bystanders to Genocide."

massacres as a genocide being perpetrated by the Hutu government, there was an official policy to never *publicly* utter the "g-word." The Clinton Administration not only adopted this policy of genocide denial, it pressured other U.N. nations to do so also, like Czechoslovakia. Nathan Robinson explains the implications:

> The evidence...proves that the Clinton Administration went far beyond inaction. It also attempted to stop others from acting. But worst of all, it adopted a conscious policy of genocide denial. It knew there was a genocide, but publically fudged the truth so as not to have to stop it. This is actually far, far worse than Holocaust denial; after all, the most harmful time to deny a genocide is while it is occurring, especially if your denial is made deliberately so that nobody will stop the genocide. At the peak of one of the 20th century's worst mass slaughters, Bill Clinton presided over an act of institutionalized genocide denial so as to allow the slaughter to continue.[62]

The only action the Clinton Administration would engage in and permit other U.N. nations to engage in was the evacuation of their own nationals. When US ambassador to Rwanda David Rawson and his wife were evac'd, 300 terrified Rwandans had fled to his residence for refuge. Dawson's closest personal aids, such as his chief steward who served his dinner and washed his dishes, begged Dawson for help. Dawson left every last one of them behind to be slaughtered, including the 35 Rwandan employees of the American embassy. Elsewhere, 2000 Rwandans including 400 children had grouped in a gated school, the Ecole Technique Officielle, under the protection of 90 Belgian soldiers from the peacekeeping mission. Just outside the school gates the murderous government troops squatted, drinking beer and chanting "Pawa, Pawa" ("Hutu Power"). When the Belgian soldiers received the order to leave the Rwandans and help Europeans evacuate, they left out one gate and the Hutu forces entered right in through the other gate. Most of the 2000 were slaughtered. In the three days during which 4000 foreigners were evacuated some 20,000 Rwandans were butchered. This was a

---

[62] Nathan J. Robinson, *Super Predator: Bill Clinton's Use & Abuse of Black America* (W. Somerville, MA.: Current Affairs Press, 2016) 160.

cause for celebration for the Clintons. After it was reported that the American evacuees were safely out, leaving machete-hacked bodies behind their caravan, and that the U.S. embassy was closed (with all of its local employees dead), Bill and Hillary visited the emergency-operations room at the State Department where the evacuation was coordinated and offered the people an enthusiastic congratulations and a "job well done."[63] I can imagine Bill and Hilary high-fiving each other.

As to why the Clintons and his Administration acted so callously, President Clinton's close political advisor Dick Morris later confessed: "The real reason was that Rwanda was black. Bosnia was white."[64] Samantha Power too reports that one US official inked his frustration with the bureaucratic obstructionism in a journal that he kept during the crisis, lamenting:

> [We are] a military that wants to go nowhere to do anything-or let go of their toys so someone else can do it. [We are] A White House cowed by the brass...An [National Security Council] that does peacekeeping by the book-the accounting book, that is. And [we are] an assistance program that prefers whites (Europeans) to blacks.

Why the callousness during the Rwandan Genocide vs. such decisive action in Kosovo to save white lives from genocide? Because for Bill Clinton and his Administration, #BlackLivesDontMatter. But in this the Clintons only reflected the larger White American sentiment. As to why the Congress was unmotivated to intervene, Congressman Pat Schroeder of Colorado said regarding his constituents that they "are terribly concerned about the gorillas...But - it sounds terrible - people just don't know what can be done about the people."[65]

Yes, the fact that gorilla life matters more to white people than Black life did not begin with the killing of Harambe.

---

[63] Power, "Bystanders to Genocide."
[64] Dick Morris and Eileen McGann, *Because He Could* (New York: Harper, 2005) 64.
[65] Power, "Bystanders to Genocide."

One of the worst genocides of modern history simply did not have to happen. It was very preventable. The Clinton Administration had sufficient forewarning of exactly what was brewing; it had the resources to save a great many of the nearly one million lives that were lost; and it had the power to, if not inclined to act itself, delegate authority through the U.N. to other nations to act. But the Clinton Administration was dead set on allowing *no* intervention that would have halted the genocide in Africa's poorest nation. President Clinton's 1998 "apology" to Rwandans was disingenuous political spin. Bill Clinton is, after all, *the* master at political spin, especially where Black life is concerned.

Clinton's foreign policy was only an extension of his domestic policy. Black lives don't matter abroad and Black lives don't matter at home. Black voters are free to vote to return the Clintons to the White House if that is how your conscience compels you. But those Black folk who voted Bill Clinton into the Black Hall of Fame as an honorary "Soul Brother" should be ashamed of themselves, and anyone today trying to spin the Clintons as anything other than the vicious but profoundly savvy Super Predators that they are risk making themselves tacit aiders and abettors. Vote your conscience, but tell the truth.

## HAITI

The Clintons have seen and treated Haiti as their personal cash cow, and the Haitian people have suffered dearly under their *de facto* rule. Journalist Jonathan M. Katz, the only full-time American news correspondent stationed in Haiti during the January 2010 earthquake, describe Bill and Hillary as "The King and Queen of Haiti," noting that "the world's most powerful couple have an abiding interest in this out-of-the-way place."[66] Their interest in Haiti is purely personal economics.

---

[66] Jonathan M. Katz, "The King and Queen of Haiti," *Political Magazine* May 4, 2015.

*President Clinton's Double-cross*

The three military leaders who in 1991 overthrew Haiti's first popular, democratically elected president – Lt. General Raoul Cédras, commander of the army; Brig. General Philippe Biamby, army chief of staff; Lt. Colonel Michel François - were all trained in the U.S. and even were on the payroll of U.S. intelligence agencies.[67] It can thus be argued that the overthrow of Haiti's democratic government was a U.S. operation. It comes as no surprise then that President George Bush One cruelly intercepted the Haitians fleeing the terror of the new military junta and used the Coast Guard to forcefully return them to the new politically inspired dangers of Haiti, denying them the right to even seek political asylum. Bill Clinton, while campaigning for president in 1992, condemned the Bush Administration for a "cruel policy of

---

[67] Gilbert A. Lewthwaite, "Trio holds fast in Haiti," *The Baltimore Sun* August 7, 1994; Brian Concannon, Jr. Esq., "Lave Men, Siye Atè: Taking Human Rights Seriously," in *Let Haiti Live: Unjust U.S. Policies Towards Its Oldest Neighbor*, ed. Melinda Miles and Eugenia Charles (Coconut Creek, FL: Educa Vision Inc., 2004) 83: "The *de facto* regime's top military leaders all received training in the U.S., and the U.S. continued to train Haitian army personnel after the 1991 coup, at least into 1993. Many of the coup leaders were on protect the CIA payroll for years. One CIA analyst, in a widely circulated report in 1992, praised the junta's leader, General Raoul Cedras...The U.S. also worked to the *de facto* military leadership from justice...The U.S. [later] made the exiles of many *de facto* leaders possible. The two top generals, Raoul Cedras and Philippe Biamby, were flown to refuge in Panama, aboard U.S. planes. The American Embassy even rented three of Cedras' luxurious villas for expatriate housing. Most of the remaining members of the high command were allowed to settle in the U.S."; Tim Weiner, "Key Haiti Leaders Said to Have Been in the CIA's Pay," *The New York Times* November 1, 1993: "Key members of the military regime controlling Haiti and blocking the return of President Jean-Bertrand Aristide were paid by the CIA for information from the mid-1980s at least until the 1991 coup that forced Aristide from power, according to U.S. officials.

As part of its normal intelligence-gathering operations, the CIA cultivated, recruited and paid generals and politicians for information about everything from cocaine smuggling to political ferment in Haiti, they said. Without naming names, a government official familiar with the payments said that "several of the principal players in the present situation were compensated by the U.S. government." It was not clear when the payments ended or how much money they involved, although they were described as modest."

returning Haitian refugees to a brutal dictatorship without an asylum hearing." Clinton said:

> If I were President, I would-in the absence of clear and compelling evidence that they weren't political refugees-give them temporary asylum until we restored the elected Government of Haiti.[68]

However, immediately upon assuming office (less than a week after his inauguration) President Clinton betrayed the Haitians just as he betrayed the hope of Black American's that he would fix the crack cocaine sentencing disparity. *The New York Times* January 15, 1993 said:

> Saying that he feared a mass exodus of Haitians unless he acted, President-elect Bill Clinton announced today that he would at least temporarily abandon a campaign pledge and would continue the Bush Administration's policy of forcibly returning Haitians who try to emigrate to the United States...Mr. Clinton had promised to give Haitians refuge and make it easier for them to apply for political asylum until democracy is restored in their country...That promise prompted Haitians to build nearly 1,000 boats that could accommodate as many as 150,000 people, many of whom are poised to set sail in stormy seas in the hopes of arriving on American shores at the moment of Mr. Clinton's inauguration Wednesday. But in a bluntly worded taped radio message broadcast this morning directly to Haiti and Haitian communities in the United States, Mr. Clinton said that Haitians who fled by boat would be intercepted and returned to the island.[69]

President-elect Clinton said in the broadcast:

> The practice of returning those who flee Haiti by boat will continue, for the time being, after I become President. Those who leave Haiti by boat for the United States will be intercepted and returned to Haiti by the U.S. Coast Guard. Leaving by boat is not the route to freedom.

This is the signature "Clinton Double-Cross." That's their way. We see it again and again. The Clintons signature strategy of dealing with Black people, our interests and demands, have been

---

[68] Elaine Sciolino, "Clinton Says U.S. Will Continue Ban on Haitian Exodus," *The New York Times* January 15, 1993.
[69] Elaine Sciolino, "Clinton Says U.S. Will Continue Ban on Haitian Exodus," *The New York Times* January 15, 1993.

and continues to be the double-cross. The Clintons' involvement in Haiti is a shining example.

*President Clinton's Active Support of Black-on-Black Terrorism*

President Clinton continued Bush's policy of returning fleeing Haitians back to Haiti where they faced the terror of the anti-Aristide death squads that reportedly raped, tortured and murdered supporters of the populist, democratically elected president. These death squads were established, financed and supported by U.S. intelligence. Michel François, Chief of National Police (1991-1994) under General Cédras, terrorized the Haitian people, killing 4000 according to some reports. He was on the CIA payroll according to award winning journalist of ***The Nation***, Allan Nairn. Nairn won a George Polk Award for his reporting on Haiti and the CIA, where he broke the story of the direct links between U.S. intelligence agencies and Haitian paramilitary death squads.[70] With Aristide in exile, the morale and the will of his populist movement back home was broken by the U.S. government, specifically the Clinton Administration, through terror. When President Clinton gave his national "Haiti Address" from the Oval Office on September 15, 1995 announcing that he ordered U.S. military intervention in Haiti to stop the reign of terror from the paramilitary deaths squads under the command of General Cédras, what the American people were unaware of was that "many of the officials whom Clinton was claiming to be fighting were actually his employees."[71] While Clinton invaded Haiti in 1994 under the pretense of re-installing President Aristide and the democratically elected government, he was covertly supporting the violent, right-wing opposition. A wonderful example of this Clinton double-talk – or double-cross – in the *USS Harlan County* Affair of October 7, 1993. The *USS Harlan County*

---

[70] Allan Nairn, "Our Man in FRAPH: Behind Haiti's Paramilitaries," ***The Nation*** October 24, 1994, pp. 458-461; idem, "Haiti Under the Gun: How U.S. Intelligence has been exercising crowd control," ***The Nation*** January 8/15, 1996, pp. 11-15; idem, "Haiti: Different Coup, Same Paramilitary," ***Democracy Now!*** February 26, 2004.

[71] Allan Nairn, "Haiti: Different Coup, Same Paramilitary," ***Democracy Now!*** February 26, 2004.

was a Naval ship carrying 200 American and Canadian military personnel sent to Haiti to assist in the re-installation of President Aristide and the transition back to democracy. The ship was prevented from docking in Port-au-Prince by a violent, machete-wielding mob led by Emmanuel "Toto" Constant, founder of the most notorious paramilitary death squad, the Front for the Advancement and Progress of Haiti (FRAPH). This first step of Clinton's democratic mission was thus a failure. Except, it was not. It was a complete success. Toto Constant was on the payroll of both the Defense Intelligence Agency and the Central Intelligence Agency.[72] His group FRAPH, which was responsible for hundreds if not thousands of murders and rapes of Aristide supporters, received covert shipments of U.S. arms at least into 1993.[73] As *The New York Times* reported:

> The leader of one of Haiti's most infamous paramilitary groups was a paid informer of the Central Intelligence Agency for two years and was receiving money from the United States while his associates committed political murders and other acts of repression, Government officials said today. Emmanuel (Toto) Constant, the head of the organization known as Fraph, was on the C.I.A.'s payroll in October 1993, when his group organized a violent demonstration that prevented the docking of the Navy ship Harlan County, the officials said...It was not clear why the payments to Mr. Constant continued after his group had played the leading role in temporarily derailing the Clinton Administration's policy toward Haiti.[74]

But it in fact *is* clear why these payments continued. While the Clinton Administration was publically supportive of the democratic presidency of Aristide and the wishes of the Haitian people – he called the invasion Operation Uphold Democracy - it covertly supported the opposition and worked to literally *crush* the populist wishes of the people.

---

[72] Allan Nairn, "Haiti: Different Coup, Same Paramilitary," **Democracy Now!** February 26, 2004; "Our Man in FRAPH: Behind Haiti's Paramilitaries," *The Nation* October 24, 1994, pp. 458-461.
[73] Allan Nairn, "Haiti Under the Gun: How U.S. Intelligence has been exercising crowd control," *The Nation* January 8/15, 1996, pp. 11-15.
[74] Stephen Engelberg, "A Haitian Leader of Paramilitaries was Paid by C.I.A.," *The New York Times* October 8, 1994.

What was Clinton's strategic interest in supporting the right-wing terrorist opposition? Toto Constant himself informs us that the U.S. defense attaché in Haiti, Colonel Patrick Collins, instructed him to oppose the populist majority in order to "balance the Aristide movement," to counter and quail the populism in particular and to put Aristide in a weakened position when he is returned to power.[75] By supporting FRAPH, the U.S. increased its bargaining power in negotiations with President Aristide. The Clinton Administration was pressuring Aristide to reject the original populist plan of wealth redistribution – 20% of the Haitian households accounted for 64% of the country's total income - and to accept the IMF/World Bank austerity and privatization program that will benefit the country's elite and foreign investors but ruin the masses economically. The Clinton Administration purposely fomented violent discord in the country by supporting the terrorist opposition in order to ensure that President Aristide was compliant once he got back in office.[76] He was.

*Destroying the Economy and Starving the People*

The economic aspects of Clinton's Haiti policy have literally starved the people. Rice accounted for 23% of the people's caloric intake and almost all of the rice was grown locally. 70% of the Haitian people were farmers and rice farmers were an important part of the Haitian economy. Prior to the Clinton Administration's interventions Haiti was growing economically. In the 1970's only 19% of the food was imported. The country was self-sufficient and maybe on the road to becoming the "Taiwan of the Caribbean." Bill Clinton's economic policy destroyed that possibility. The IMF/World Bank "restructuring" program that the administration imposed on President Aristide required the lowering of import tariffs from 50% to 3%. Clinton then gave hundreds of millions of dollars in farm subsidies to American rice

---

[75] Allan Nairn, "Our Man in FRAPH: Behind Haiti's Paramilitaries," *The Nation* October 24, 1994, pp. 458-461.
[76] Nathan J. Robinson, *Super Predator: Bill Clinton's Use & Abuse of Black America* (W. Somervillw, MA, 2016) 195.

farmers, primarily his hometown pals– Producers Rice Mill and Riceland, two Arkansas-based rice producers. This policy allowed Clinton's Arkansas pals to flood Haiti with cheap rise, driving the local farmers out of business and into the slums of Port-au-Prince. After the destruction of the local rice market, the American rice producers raised the price on their rice, double. This sparked "rice riots." Jesse Jackson thus rightly told Ali Velshi: "Our agricultural policy…allowed the Riceland Rice company to drop rice on Haiti, drive Haiti farmers out of business, and then raise the price of rice and have rice riots."[77] Haiti went from growing practically all of its rice to today, importing 80% of it. The Clinton/IMF/World Bank policy of dropping tariffs is known locally in Creol as *plan lanmo* "death plan." Even Bill Clinton would later admit that his policy was a "devil's bargain," that increased Haiti's poverty.[78] A Devil's bargain indeed.

*Haiti as the Clintons' Cash Cow*

The disastrous economic fleecing of Haiti continued under Secretary Hillary Clinton. When she assumed her positon in 2009 Secretary Clinton claimed Haiti as a priority pet project, if you will.[79] And in case there was any confusion regarding what the State Department's Haitian policy will really be about, not long after Hillary was confirmed as Secretary of State U.N. Secretary-General Ban Ki-moon deputized Bill Clinton as special envoy to Haiti. As U.N. envoy Bill Clinton was to spearhead development after the Haitian hunger crises – a crises which his own "devil's bargain" caused. When he returned to Haiti as U.N. envoy the Haitian press joked that he must be returning to lead a new

---

[77] Jim Dexter, "Fact Check: Do U.S. Food Policies Contribute to Haiti's Poverty?" *CNN* January 27, 2010; Maura R. O'Conner, "Subsidizing Starvation: How American tax dollars are keeping Arkansas rice growers fat on the farm and starving millions of Haitians," *Foreign Policy* January 11, 2013.
[78] Maura R. O'Conner, "Subsidizing Starvation: How American tax dollars are keeping Arkansas rice growers fat on the farm and starving millions of Haitians," *Foreign Policy* January 11, 2013.
[79] Robinson, *Super Predator*, 199.

colonial regime and they dubbed him *Le Gouvernuer*.[80] I'm sure they were not really joking.

Haiti is a money tree for the Clintons. When Bill attended the February 2015 dedication of Port-au-Prince's new luxury Marriott hotel, the former President affirmed that his work in Haiti represented "one of the great joys of my life." I'm sure it is. As Jonathan Katz points out: "The Clintons have also had a hand in nearly *all* the new luxury hotel projects that have sprung up around the Haitian capital."[81] And these hotel's signal another fact about the Clintons' true interest in Haiti: "Many of the most notable investments the Clintons helped launch, such as the new Marriott in the capital, have primarily benefited wealthy foreigners and the island's ruling elite, who needed little help to begin with."[82] Or to put it another way: "While striking a populist pose, in practice [the Clintons] are attracted to power in Haiti."[83]

Proof of the Clintons' total indifference to the poor Haitian masses and their singular concern for the moneyed elite, often foreign, is not hard to find. One of Secretary Clinton's first order of business was the suppression of the Haitian minimum wage. A 2009 Haitian law rose the minimum wage from 24 cents per hour to 61 cents per hour. The business elite like Hanes and Levi were furious. They were only willing to agree to a 7 cents raise per hour, even though Hanes' CEO Richard Noll could have paid the raise for his 3,200 t-shirt makers with just 1/6 of his $10 million salary and bonuses. Instead, they appealed to the U.S. State Department, which pressured Haitian president René Préval to block the increase, which he did.[84]

But the Haitian people have no reason to be as poor as they are. Even before the devastating earthquake of January 12, 2010 the Clinton Foundation was able to secure commitments of

---

[80] Jonathan M. Katz, "The King and Queen of Haiti," *Political Magazine* May 4, 2015.
[81] Jonathan M. Katz, "The King and Queen of Haiti," *Political Magazine* May 4, 2015.
[82] Jonathan M. Katz, "The King and Queen of Haiti," *Political Magazine* May 4, 2015.
[83] Jonathan M. Katz, "The King and Queen of Haiti," *Political Magazine* May 4, 2015.
[84] Robinson, *Super Predator*, 200.

$130 million from foreign leaders "for Haiti." But Haiti has not yet benefitted from that. $16.3 billion were pledged for Haiti recovery after the earthquake. Most of it is totally unaccounted for today. As Oliver Laurent of *Time Magazine* and Belgium photographer who photographed Haiti for ten years, Grael Turine, pointed out:

> Given the costs of recovery from such a shattering catastrophe, it might seem logical that an impoverished country such as Haiti would still feel the effects a half-decade later, if it weren't for the unprecedented help the Republic received in its aftermath. "When you look at the history of humanitarian relief, there's never been a situation when such a small country has been the target of such a massive influx of money and assistance in such a short span of time," says Turine. "On paper, with that much money in a territory the size of Haiti, we should have witnessed miracles; there should have been results."[85]

As U.N. special envoy it was Bill Clinton who was tapped to lead the recovery effort in Haiti. He co-chaired with Haitian Prime Minister Jean-Max Bellerive the Interim Haiti Recovery Commission (IHRC), charged with rebuilding Haiti and directing the spending.[86] With the Clintons in control of the rebuilding effort in Haiti, we are not surprised to discover that the Clinton Foundation controlled $36 million dollars of Haiti money in 2010; The Clinton-Bush Haiti Fund controlled $55 million; and the Clinton Global Initiative Haiti Action Network $500 million. But we are hard pressed to see the good that *any* of that money went toward in Haiti, other than a few unfinished, half-backed or small scale pilot projects. The 2013 Government Accountability Office investigated the matter and found that most of the money for the recovery was not being dispersed.[87] As a result, "Haitians find themselves in a social and economic situation that is *worse* than before the earthquake," says Grael Turine. And as Katz notes also:

> Five years after the hemisphere's deadliest single natural disaster, when both Clintons assumed leading roles in the rebuilding efforts, little progress has been made on many core problems in Haiti, and the

---

[85] Oliver Laurent, "Haiti Earthquake: Five Years After," *Time* January 12, 2015.
[86] [86] Jonathan M. Katz, "The King and Queen of Haiti," *Political Magazine* May 4, 2015; Robinson, *Super Predator*, 201-204.
[87] Robinson, *Super Predator*, 203.

government that Hillary Clinton helped put in power during that January 2011 trip-and that both Clintons have backed strongly since-has proven itself unworthy of that trust...[F]ar from transforming this poorest of countries, many of the Clintons' grandest plans and promises remain little more than small pilot projects—a new set of basketball hoops and a model elementary school here, a functioning factory there—that have done little to alter radically the trajectory of the country...Many of the most notable investments the Clintons helped launch, such as the new Marriott in the capital, have primarily benefited wealthy foreigners and island's ruling elite, who needed little help to begin with.[88]

In Haiti $16.3 billion gets you little more than a basketball court if the Clintons are in control of that money. As Nathan Robinson of *Current Affairs* states: "A large amount of the money raised by Bill Clinton after the earthquake, and pledged by the U.S. under Hillary Clinton, simply disappeared without a trace, its whereabouts unknown."[89]

---

[88] Jonathan M. Katz, "The King and Queen of Haiti," *Political Magazine* May 4, 2015.
[89] Robinson, *Super Predator*, 207.

Part Two

# The Global Project

## Feminizing the Black God

# 4     The Global Strategy: The Samburu and The Zulu as Examples

I.     *The Global Strategy*

One of the reasons most people fail to grasp and take seriously the depth of the problem of this assault on the Black male is because we assume it to be an isolated historical American phenomenon restricted to antebellum America. It is not. The American assault on the Black man – his manhood and his masculinity – from slavery till today was and is part of a Global Project, and only by understanding that Global Project and its methods repeated all over the world can we fully appreciate what is going on here in America and appreciate what the Black man in America is dealing with. The white man feminized the Black man everywhere he went and gained dominion. Where ever the white man sets his boot, *his* is the only manhood that is tolerable to him. So all where he conquers on the earth he must neutralize the masculinity and manhood of the local men. It is part of his strategy of domination. And his methods are the same everywhere.

II.     *Killing and Feminizing the Black God*

Plate 2 is a picture taken in 2001 at the installation of Virgilio Dante as Catholic Bishop of Maralal, a town in Kenya in 2001. Bishop Dante is surrounded by Samburu women. The Samburu are a Nilotic-speaking people of northern Kenya. The foreground of the picture is filled with young Samburu children. There is an important group missing from this picture: the men. Samburu society is divided into age-sets or generational groupings, if you will. The two important male age-sets are the Elders and the *Murran*. The Murran is the age-set of the young, unmarried warriors. The Elders, the paramount authority among the Samburu, are the most powerful male element of Samburu society. So the two major male age-sets are absent here from the Bishop's installation. This white man has Samburu women and children at his service. The Samburu women sewed the beads on his vestment.[90] This picture perfectly illustrates the words of the Honorable Brother Minister Farrakhan.

> It was the slavemaster's idea in conquering the black man to conquer the ideals and the ideas and the ideology and the philosophy and the nature of the black man so that you would have no power as a man with your own woman. When the power of the man is broken over his own woman, then an alien force becomes her master and her teacher. And he puts his seed in her physically, then he puts his ideas in her spiritually; so she rears children not for the black man, but children for the conqueror of the black man.[91]

This was part of a global strategy. During Algeria's colonial period the French attempted to use the female population to continue colonial rule. Frantz Fanon describes the strategy of the colonial administration devised to destroy Algerian society by encouraging Algerian women to revolt against the indigenous patriarchal hierarchy. By pitting women against Algerian men, the French sought to dilute the Algerian capacity for resistance. Fanon reports:

> the woman...was given the historic mission of shaking up the Algerian man. Converting the woman, winning her over to foreign values, wrenching her free from his status, was at the same time achieving a real power over the men and attaining a practical, effective means of destructing Algerian culture.[92]

So here in this photo we see the white man standing majestic in a sea of deferential Black women and their children at hand. Where is the Black man? You see one elder standing up. The only one.

---

[90] Paul Spencer, "The Transfiguration of Samburu Religion," in idem, *Youth and Experiences of Ageing among Maa: Models of Society Evoked by the Maasai, Samburu, and Chamus of Kenya* (Berlin : Walter De Gruyter, 2014) 111ff.

[91] The Honorable Brother Minister Farrakhan, "Heaven Lies at the Foot of Mother," May 13, 1984.

[92] Frantz Fanon, *A Dying Colonialism*, tr. Haakon Chevalier (New York: Grove Press, 1967) 39.

## Killing God
### Exceptional Moments in the Colonial Missionary Encounter
#### by Bilinda Straight

*This paper pivots around an exceptional moment of colonial missionary encounter—the attempted "murder" in the 1930s of an incarnation of Samburu Divinity (pastoralists, northern Kenya). Examining this event through a comparative focus on other strange cases of "divinicide," I elucidate certain key moments of intense metaphysical struggle that typically become effaced, forgotten, or flattened in the process of colonial witness. Focus on the ontological micropolitics of exceptional moments of the colonial encounter such as these affords us the opportunity to illuminate crucial, often elusive, even substantially forgotten dimensions of the unequal process by which shared cultural imaginaries are forged.*

Professor Belinda Straight is a cultural anthropologist and feminist scholar at Western Michigan University. She did field work among the Samburu people. In 2008 she wrote a significant article: "Killing God: Exceptional Moments in the Colonial Missionary Encounter." She documents the early missionary practice in Africa of *divinicide*: acts of metaphysical violence against the local gods in order to prepare the way to conversion to Christianity.

> divinicide has been an enduring historically and culturally crosscutting Christian missionary *tactic* that 'smooths' the way for conversion by creating a metaphysical condition of *terra nullius* ("nobody's land").[93]

Straight cites a very important example, an incident that occurred at the beginning of the Samburu encounter with white colonial Christiandom. It's the story of Charles Scudder, the Anglican missionary who arrived with his wife in Kenya in 1934. Scudder was a gun-toting cowboy, remembered for driving wildly across the open African savanah. His missionizing Christianity was very muscular and masculine; that entitled, exclusivist, white male masculinity. One day Scudder noticed some Samburu women going to a sacred cave on a religious mountain to make offerings to their God, the Black God Nkai. The God of the

---

[93] Belinda Straight, "Killing God: Exceptional Moments in the Colonial Missionary Encounter," *Current Anthropology* 49 (2008): 837-860 (850).

precolonial Samburu was the Black God. What is the Black God? He is the Creator of the Heavens and the Earth, the Lord of all Creation, who is a Man and is Black. The Black God is the true God.[94] This was the God of the Samburu before the white man came among them.[95] Seeing the women venerate the Black God Nkai, Scudder got jealous: He was jealous as a Christian missionary toward a deity competing with his deity Jesus Christ and as an entitled white man he was jealous that these Black women were venerating a male other than him and his god. As David Henosian and Daniel Walther point out in the German colonial context, the colonial officers had a need to be recognized by the subject peoples as *Herr*, a title that means both "Master" and "God," and they deployed violence to ensure such recognition.

> for the Europeans, the stability of colonial society depended on being recognized as master ("Herr") by the natives...Significantly, the word "Herr," which means both master and is a term for the Christian God,

---

[94] Wesley Muhammad, "As the image of God: Adam and the Original Black Man," *The Final Call* 32 (January 8, 2013) 24, 32; idem, "The God of Israel is a man, a Black man," *The Final Call* 32 (January 29, 2013) 24; idem, *Religion of the Black God: Indic Sacred Science and the Black God* (Atlanta: A-Team Publishing, 2013) idem, *Egyptian Sacred Science and Islam: A Reappraisal* (Atlanta: A-Team Publishing, 2012); idem, "Who is the Original Man," *The Final Call* 32 (December 25, 2012) 24; idem, *Take Another Look: The Qur'an, the Sunna and the Islam of the Honorable Elijah Muhammad* (Atlanta: A-Team Publishing, 2011); idem, *Who Is God? The Debates* (Atlanta: A-Team Publishing, 2009); True Islam, *The Book of God: An Encyclopedia of Proof that the Black Man in God* (Atlanta: A-Team Publishing, 2007); idem, *The Truth of God: the Bible, the Qur'an and the Secret of the Black God* (Atlanta: A-Team Publishing, 2007).

[95] Nkai/Ngai/EnKai is the God of the Samburu, Kikuyu, Akamba of Kenya and the Masaai of Tanzania. He has as a fiery, inner aspect of his nature (*Enkai Nanyokie*) while His outward appearance is black (*Enkai Narok*). His wife is Olapa, goddess of the moon. See Wesley Muhammad, *The Book of God*, Volume II: *Allah and the Sacred Science of the Black God in African Traditional Religions* (Atlanta: A-Team Publishing, forthcoming); the *Encyclopedia of African Religion* s.v. Ngai by Ama Mazama, 447-448; Hans Stoks, "A Perception of Reality within an East-Nilotic People: point of departure for a philosophy of perception," in *I, We and Body: Writings in Philosophy of Difference*, vol. 3 (Amsterdam: Verlag B.R. Grüner, 1989) 79-92.

implies both the political and spiritual superiority of the (white) Germans.[96]

Thus we understand Scudder's action and motivation. A Black male God who commands the religious loyalty of the local women in environments under his control is totally unacceptable. So he tricked the Samburu women into taking him to the Cave of Nkai and when he confirmed from them that they believe Nkai actually resided in that cave with his wives and children and that he communicated with them from that cave, the Christian cowboy pulled out his shotgun and blasted into the cave. He intended to kill the Black God, either physically or in the minds of those women and all of the Samburu. He succeeded, sort of. The religious observations carried at that sacred cave ceased till this very day. No more did Nkai ever communicate with his people there.

Symbolically and literally killing the Black God (by killing the Black bull) was one of the white man's earliest and most enduring blood sports. But just killing the Black God was never sufficient. Part of the "metaphysical violence" against the local gods aimed at facilitating the path of the hypermasculine Christian god is the *feminization* of the local gods. Under European colonialism and missionary Christianity, the *only* legitimate male in the country was to be the white man and his god, Jesus. All other males – divine and human – had to be feminized. Thus, as Paul Spencer describes, in 1960 Nkai was still very much a male God among the Samburu.[97] By the time Prof. Bilinda Straight did her field work among the Samburu in 2002, however, the Black God Nkai had been made into a *white woman* (among some of them)![98] Get this point: making God other than a man is one of the enemy's key steps in feminizing the Black man. By feminizing our God our masculinity is sure to follow.

---

[96] Kenosian, "Colonial Body Politic," 185; Walther, "Sex, Race and Empire," 52;
[97] Spencer, "Transfiguration of Samburu Religion."
[98] Bilinda Straight, ***Miracles and Extraordinary Experience in Northern Kenya*** (Philadelphia: University of Pennsylvania, 2007) 38-39.

III.   *Neutralizing the Renowned Zulu Masculinity*

In January of 1879 the crack Zulu soldiers of southern Africa decimated the British army at Iskandlwana and Nyezane, humiliating Queen Victoria and handing the British Empire its worst defeat since the Crimean War (1854-1856). In six hours the British army lost 1300 of its 1700 men sent to the battle – 60 British and 300 African auxiliary troops were all that was left standing. Thus began the Anglo-Zulu War. The British would regroup and come back, ultimately destroying the Zulu army on July 4, 1879 and ending the War, making Zululand a British colony in 1887. The British never forgot that humiliating defeat, like the French to this day never forgot nor forgave Haiti for that marvelous and humiliating defeat of Napoleon and the French army. Colour Sergent J.W. Burnett of the 99th Regiment of the British forces wrote about the Zulu to a friend after Nyezane: "I never thought [Africans] would make such a stand. They came on with utter disregard for danger…our 'school' used to laugh about these [Africans], but I assure you that fighting with them is truly earnest work, and not child's play."[99] Sergent E. Jervis of the 90th Regiment confessed too: "I confess that I do not think that a braver lot of men than our enemies in point of disregard for life, and for their bravery under fire, could be found anywhere."[100]

### A Peculiar Masculinity

The Zulu people of South Africa today are a great people. The Zulu of pre-colonial southern African were a *mighty* people. The mighty greatness of the historic Zulu was no doubt at least partly anchored in the peculiar brand of *masculinity* that anchored Zulu society. The colonial educational officer C.T. Binns lived among the Zulu for 59 years, after which he wrote the book ***The Warrior People***. He was a racist and a white supremacist, yet he intensely admired the Zulus, saying:

---

[99] Frank Emery, ***The Red Soldier – The Zulu War 1879*** (London, 1977) 185-186.
[100] Emery, ***The Red Soldier***, 172-173.

> Throughout his life, the Zulu of *the olden times* was subjected to a remarkable system of unremitting discipline, but it was a discipline that 'Made him honest, brave and wise, respectful toward king and neighbor...He was a cunning and daring opponent, a keen logician and consummate diplomatist, not a mongrel but a man of repute, not a debased savage but an intelligent being. He was, in short, a man of right with an undeniably just and overwhelmingly strong claim to be dealt with as such', even by his conquers and every other Whiteman living in Africa (emphasis added).[101]

This Zulu masculinity made the Zulu kingdom the chief threat to the advancement of White Supremacy in Africa, as James Gump writes: "A defensible self-governing white dominion could only exist if black resistance was eliminated. The Zulu kingdom represented the principle African obstacle."[102] Pre-colonial Zulu manhood was not just about martial prowess but had a moral conscience and put a premium on integrity. As Egodi Uchendu remarks:

> the preferred masculinity, by Zulu standards, combined martial prowess with honesty; high morality, as shown in the absence of pre-marital penetrative sexual interactions with a female subject[103]...; loyalty; aggressiveness; a sense of responsibility; courage; self-reliance; athleticism; alertness; endurance; and absence of emotions.[104]

An illustrative sign of this peculiar Zulu masculinity is the practice of sick-fighting that was (!) so crucial to the socialization of Zulu boys. The stick-fight evoked challenges of future manhood and the glories of bygone battles. But it was not simply a martial recreation. It specifically promoted the traditional, pre-colonial form of Zulu masculinity. Stick-fighting was a martial art that expressed the grammar of honorable restraint. It adhered to

---

[101] J. Stuart, *Boyhood Among the Zulu* [pamphlet], cited in C.T. Binns, *The Warrior People* (London: Robert Hale, 1975) 183.
[102] James Grump, "The Subjugation of the Zulus and Sioux: A Comparative Study," *Western Historical Quarterly* 19 (1988): 31 [art.=21-36].
[103] "Penetrative sexual encounters...before marriage were unmasculine acts. It was inappropriate behavior to prove one's masculinity through sexual conquest": Egodi Uchendu, "Introduction: Are African Males Men? Sketching African Masculinities," in *Masculinities in Contemporary Africa*, ed. Egodi Uchendu (Dakar: CODESRIA, 2008) 8 [art.=1-17].
[104] Uchendu, "Are African Males Men?" 8.

rules of competition that privileged rhetoric, honor, defense (rather than aggression), physical restraint, and the subordination of personal ego to the communal good. It imbued Zulu masculinity with an ethos of self-control, discipline (*inkuliso*) and respect (*inhlonipho*).[105] A small boy carries his stick and grows up with it. It "served as a signifier of generational deference and homestead security." As Benedict Carton and Robert Morrell write:

> a boy who received his original stick knew he held more than a weapon or switch. His stick epitomizes a customary obligation to shield his lineage resources from any harm, especially the cattle his patriarch sacrificed when propitiating the ancestors (*amadlozi*).[106]

---

[105] Benedict Carton and Robert Morrell, "Zulu Masculinities, Warrior Culture, and Stick Fighting: Reassessing Male Violence and Virtue in South Africa," *Journal of Southern African Studies* 38 (2012): 31-53.

[106] Carton and Morrell, "Zulu Masculinities, Warrior Culture, and Stick Fighting," 34.

## THE BLACK GOD AND SOUTHERN CRADLE PATRIARCHY

The Zulu masculinity and manhood that every white man living in Africa had to respect and which made the Zulu the principle obstacle to white dominion in Africa was a manhood anchored in the truth of the Black God, *uNkulunkulu*. The pre-colonial Zulu like the pre-colonial Samburu knew and reverenced the Black God: the God who is a divine Black Man (*umuntu*), male (*indoda*).[107] The amaZulu (ama= "people") of South Africa are a Bantu ethic group, their language (*isiZulu*) is from the Nguni branch of the Bantu family which includes also the amaSwazi, amaXhosa and amaNdebele. A case has been made that the religion and customs of the Zulu in its pre-colonial form preserves basic elements of the primordial religious culture, not only of Africa, but of all of humanity.[108] I believe there is some truth in this.

---

[107] See Wesley Muhammad, *The Book of God*, **Volume II:** *Allah and the Sacred Science of the Black God in African Traditional Religions* (Atlanta: A-Team Publishing, forthcoming); *Encyclopedia of African Religions* 452-453 s.v. Nkulunkulu by Molefi Kete Asante and 744-745 s.v. Zulu by Afe Adogame; Ana Maria Monteiro-Ferreira, "Reevaluating Zulu Religion: An Afrocentric Analysis," *Journal of Black Studies* 35 (2005): 347-363; K.A.J. "Acculturation and the Zulu Concept of God," *Missionalia* 1 (1973): 142-146; H. Callaway, *The Religious System of the Amazulu* (Springvale, Natal, 1868-1884 [reprint: Cape Town, 1970]);Wm. H.I. Bleek, *Zulu Legends* (Pretoria: J.L. van Schaik, Ltd., 1952).

[108] This was the position of the Prussian philologist and comparative religion scholar Wilhem H.I. Bleek (1827-1875), arguably the "founder of southern African linguistics" and a major influence on African linguistics in general, as well as of philology, ethnography and philosophy worldwide. Bleek is more well-known for salvaging at the last minute the literature of the San Busman of the north-central Cape of Southern Africa. He was probably the first Western scholar notice the symbolic importance of San rock art. Bleek's various researches led him to conclude – contrary to his Victorian contemporaries who saw the Zulu religion as a degenerate form - that the Zulus were the primitive ancestors of all humanity and that Zulu religion reserves on fossilized form the primordial religion of Africa and indeed the world. See W.H.I. Bleek, "Research into the Relations Between the Hottentots and Kafirs," *Cape Monthly Magazine* 1 (1857): 199-208, 289-296; David Chidester, *Savage Systems: Colonialism and Comparative Religion in Southern Africa* (Charlottesville and London: University Press of Virginia, 1996) 141-152. On Bleek's place and contributions see further: Robert Thornton, "The Foundation of African Studies: Wilhelm Bleek's African Linguistics and the First Ethnographers of Southern Africa";

Like the Nguni cultures in general, the pre-colonial Zulu were a patriarchal culture: "Zulu society was highly hierarchal and men enjoyed positions of power from the home into the wider society. Maleness was superior..."[109] In the home, "the position of the paterfamilias (= male head of a family or household) in the Zulu family was perfectly clear. His word was law, his will supreme, his person sacrosanct."[110] His person was sacrosanct because he was literally God in the home: he was "the *uNkulunkulu* (God) of his own house."[111] This was *Southern* Cradle Patriarchy rather than the Northern Cradle Patriarchy of Europe which Cheikh Anta Diop discussed.[112] While the latter (Northern Cradle or European patriarchy) was characterized by the almost total devaluing and disempowering of women *as* women, in the former (Southern Cradle of African patriarchy) the leaders of the home and of the society were paramountly men but women also held public positions and wielded authority in the society in their own right.[113] European patriarchy was characterized by misogyny, while African patriarchy was characterized by mother-

---

Hermann Wittenberg, "Wilhelm Bleek and the Khoisan Imagination: a study of censorship, genocide and colonial science," *Journal of Southern African Studies* 38 (2012): 667-679; D. Lewis-Williams, *Believing and Seeing: Symbolic Meanings in Southern San Rock Art* (London, 1981); Andrew Bank, "Anthropology, Race and Evolution: Rethinking the Legacy of *Wilhelm Bleek.*" Paper presented to the History Seminar at the University of Natal, 1998.
[109] Uchendu, "Are African Males Men?" 8.
[110] Quoted in Norma Masuku, "Perceived Oppression of Women in Zulu Folklore: A Feminist Critique," doctoral dissertation, University of South Africa, 2005: 64.
[111] H. Callaway, *The Religious System of the Amazulu* (Springvale, Natal, 1868-1884 [reprint: Cape Town, 1970]) 106.
[112] Cheikh Anta Diop, *the Cultural Unity of Black Africa: The Domains of Matriarchy & of Patriarchy in Classical Antiquity* (London: Karnak House, 1989 [1963]).
[113] See e.g. Sean Hanretta, "Women, Marginality and the Zulu State: Women's Institutions of power in the Early Nineteenth Century," *Journal of African History* 39 (1998): 389-415; Jennifer Weir, "Chiefly women and women's leaders in pre-colonial southern Africa," in Nomboniso Gasa (ed.), *Women in South African History: They Remove Boulders and Cross Rivers* (Cape Town: HSRC Press, 2006): 3-20.

centeredness and the acknowledgment of and the incorporation of the divine feminine.[114]

Within the patriarchal culture of the pre-colonial amaZulu, gender duties, roles and spaces were rigidly separated.

> In nothing perhaps are they...stricter than in the different duties and occupations they assign to both sexes...According to the traditions of the Zulus, and other tribes in Natal and the Zulu country, this division of labour has, together with their other institutions, their manners and customs, its origin in Unkulunkulu, the Creator of man and everything else. The Inhlamvu or Chapters in which the sacred literature of the Zulus consists (sic), say on the subject: 'Unkulunkulu said: - The women must dig (or plant); the men shall build the huts, they shall cut down the trees, to clear the ground for planting corn. He said: - the men shall provide the pickaxes (hoes), put a handle in and give [them] to the women that they may dig...He said: - the women must cook the food: they must cook for the men.[115]

The traditional Zulu community was the *umuzi* or homestead, which was a cluster of nuclear families whose huts were built around a cattle kraal. The head of each homestead was the male owner of the kraal, called *umnumzana* or head of household. The most important economic activities of the Zulu, cattle rearing and agriculture, were divided by sex: cattle husbandry was an exclusively male preoccupation and crop cultivation an exclusively female one.[116] The social hierarchy was bound to this social economy: "The homestead economy [was] the center of male dominance," as Lindan Hadebe affirms.[117] Within

---

[114] See the full document for a fuller discussion of Southern Cradle Patriarchy.
[115] W.H.I. Bleek, "Researches into the Relations Between the Hottentots and Kafirs [Part I]," *Cape Monthly Magazine* 1 (1857): 205-206 [art.=199-208]; [Part II] 289-296.
[116] Masuku, "Perceived Oppression of Women," 62: "Within the Zulu traditional societies, the most important economic activities are cattle rearing and agriculture. These are not carried out haphazardly but with a clearly demarcated division of labor based upon sex. On the whole, the rougher the tasks requiring strength are done by men, while the women does the work that requires more continuous attention." Masuku, "Perceived Oppression of Women," 62.
[117] Lindan Hadebe, "Zulu Masculinity – Culture, Faith and the Constitution," in *Men and Masculinities in South Africa*, **Volume 2: *Understanding Masculinity in South Africa- Essays and Prescriptions*** (South Africa: PACSA and Sonke Gender Justice Network, 2013) 9.

the *umuzi* or homestead men and women sat separately (as is typical, for example, in Muhammad's Mosque of the Nation of Islam). The head of the house, like the head of the homestead, was the father and husband, the *ubaba walayikkaya* "the father of the house." The wife, irrespective of age, was considered a *girl*. As Norma Masuku points out: "Historically, the Zulu culture has stressed the status of a woman in marriage as being that of a minor..."[118] This was not a cultural peculiarity of the amaZulu. It characterized Southern Bantu and is found as well in Nilotic culture of East Africa. Ingrid Fandrych reports regarding the Lesotho:

> Traditionally, a woman becomes a member of her husband's family once she gets married. Legally and socially, a married woman is regarded as her husband's 'child'.[119]

She elaborates:

> Until recently, married women in Lesotho were legal minors, which meant that they could not purchase cars or property, obtain loans or even apply for a telephone line without their husbands consent. Legally, this situation changed with the Legal Capacity of Married Persons Equality Act in 2007.[120]

Regarding the Maasai of Tanzania (East Africa) Dorothy L. Hodgson writes in her article, "Women as Children: Culture, Political Economy, and Gender Inequality Among Kisongo Maasai":

> The association of women with children is expressed by Maasai in both their language and in their code of respectful conduct...For husbands then and now, the sometimes significant age differences between husbands and wives could be a salient factor in calling their wives children. Husbands are usually at least ten to fifteen years older then (*sic*)

---

[118] Masuku, "Perceived Oppression of Women," 184.
[119] Ingrid Fandrych, "Between tradition and the requirements of modern life: Hlonipha in Southern Bantu societies, with special reference to Lesotho," *Journal of Language and Culture* 3 (2012): 67-73 (70).
[120] Fandrych, "Hlonipha in Southern Bantu societies," 70 n. 7.

their senior wives, and sometimes thirty to forty years older than their most junior wives.[121]

The language and code of respectful conduct mentioned by Hodgson is, in the language of the Zulu and other Southern Bantu languages, called *hlonipha*. Meaning "respect," *hlonipha* is a complex social and linguistic behavioral codex that requires deferential conduct toward superiors: the wife demonstrates *hlonipha* and deferential behavior towards her husband and in-laws, boys and men demonstrate it toward elders, and all demonstrate it toward the homestead head and, later, the king.

*Hlonipha* has two basic components, behavioral (*ukuhlonipha*) and linguistic (*isihlonipha*). These both involve "respect through avoidance."[122] The wife shows respect to her husband – and shows herself a "dignified, respectable and 'proper' Zulu women" – through posture, a dress code, and by avoiding any direct physical contact with male-in-laws (no incidental touching). She avoids being alone in the same room with senior male in-laws, avoids walking in front of male in-laws, etc. When a Maasai woman encounters any male her age or older, she greets him in the way respectful Maasai juniors greet adults: she quietly waits to be verbally greeted and then she silently bows her head.[123] Regarding dress code,

> Practically all married women are expected to have their bodies fully covered at all times when they go public. Hence they all wear long *imibhaco* (3/4) and long dresses that drop as far as their ankles. There arms are under cover and their heads are also covered with head scarves...The major reason for showing no body parts is to *hlonipha* male relatives-in-law.[124]

---

[121] Dorothy L. Hodgson, "Women as Children: Culture, Political Economy, and Gender Inequality Among Kisongo Maasai," *Nomadic Peoples* NS 3 (1999): 115-129 (117, 118)

[122] On *hlonipha* see O.F. Raum, *The social function of avoidance and taboos among the Zulu* (Berlin: Mouton de Gruyter, 1973); Robert K. Herbert, "Hlonipha and the Ambiguous Woman," *Anthropos* 85 (1990): 437-455; Knobel Sakhiwo Bengela, "Isihlonipho Among the amaZhosa," doctoral dissertation, University of South Africa, 2001;

[123] Hodgson, "Women as Children," 118.

[124] Bengela, "Isihlonipho Among the amaZhosa," 39.

In terms of the linguist *hlonipha*, the married woman avoids uttering the name of her male in-laws. Instead she addresses them indirectly. According to Robert K. Herbert's study,

> What seems to be crucial to an understanding of this process (of avoiding the name of male in-laws) is the 'attention calling' function of personal names, i.e. the fact that the uttering of someone's personal name directs their attention to the speaker.[125]

In other words, this avoidance ensures that male attention is not on the new wife. A "respectful" Maasai woman speaks in a soft voice when responding or talking to men her age or older, especially their husbands.[126] This "respect through avoidance" is ultimately anchored in the *reverence* that a wife shows to her husband. As John Henerson Soga reported: "The word *ukuhlonipha* – to respect, *to reverence*, to be bashful.[127]" This agrees with the Honorable Elijah Muhammad: "A mother by nature loves and admires her son because by nature she was made to honor and *worship* man."[128]

### THE CHURCH'S ASSAULT ON ZULU GENDER CULTURE

Western commentators, especially feminists, are highly critical of pre-colonial Zulu culture. They interpret the practice and the spirit of *hlonipha* as "disempowering" to women.[129] On the other hand, traditional Zulu women unimpressed by Western encroachments on the culture reject this interpretation.

> Many Zulu women we interviewed...virulently rejected the assertion that the practice of *hlonipha* could disadvantage them or place them in an inferior or vulnerable position. Various female interverees claimed that *hloniph*, both its linguistic and its social component, expresses more

---

[125] Herbert, "Hlonipha and the Ambiguous Woman," 467.
[126] Hodgson, "Women as Children," 119.
[127] John Henderson Soga, *The AmaXhosa Life and Customs* (Alice: Lovedale Press, 1931) 208.
[128] The Honorable Elijah Muhammad, *The Divine Sayings of The Honorable Elijah Muhammad, Messenger of Allah*. Volumes 1,2 & 3 (Secretarious Publications, 2002) I: 6.
[129] Stephanie Rudwick and Magico Shange, "Hlonipha and the Rural Zulu Woman," *Agenda* 82 (2009): 66-75.

appropriately their respect for people, particularly in relation to the family of their husbands.[130]

Traditional Zulu women today still see *hlonipha* as "essential Zuluness" and insist that the discrepancy is not between *hlonipha* and principles of equality; rather it's a discrepancy between Zuluness and "white culture."[131] This respect through avoidance and social deference, *hlonipha*, was fundamental to traditional Zulu life and what was considered proper behavior within the community. Nevertheless, it did not survive the Western onslaught, except in some rural pockets. In fact, the colonial enterprise – it's political, military and religious sectors – specifically targeted the traditional Zulu gender ethos as a means to neutralize the Zulu masculinity that anchored it. The Church spearheaded the social disruption.[132] As Hadebe observes:

> Another influence on Zulu masculinity was the missionary enterprise. Missionaries introduced a form of faith which was different from the Zulu religion. They set new standards which would change many basic behaviour and structural patterns. Firstly, the roles played by men and women in the Church were different from and so changed the traditional separation of roles between genders…The influence of Christianity indicates that the effects of modifications in roles played by men and women were constructed in opposition to the traditional separation of roles between genders.[133]

As Amanda Porterfild argues, the pretext of this assault on traditional Zulu culture was an alleged concern for the "elevation" of the woman, the exact same ploy used by the French in Algeria, as we saw. What resulted in fact was no elevation but the "missionary involvement in the *deterioration* of women's roles in Zulu culture."[134] She writes

---

[130] Rudwick and Shange, "Hlonipha and the Rural Zulu Woman," 70.
[131] Rudwick and Shange, "Hlonipha and the Rural Zulu Woman," 72.
[132] Amanda Porterfield, "The Impact of Early New England Missionaries on Women's Roles in Zulu Culture," **Church History** 66 (1997): 67-80.
[133] Hadebe, "Zulu Masculinity," 9, 31.
[134] Porterfield, "Impact of Early New England Missionaries," 68.

the missionary desire to liberate African women from the patriarchal oppression imposed by Zulu religion obscured the importance of women in Zulu society and their limited but traditionally sanctioned opportunities for protection, wealth, and status. Missionaries efforts...threatened not only the structure of the family and gender relations but also the customary means by which women obtained influence in a patriarchal society. Indeed, at several points in time, British missionaries found that African women led the resistance against them... *Both groups respected patriarchal authority and invested it with religious meaning*, and both abhorred female promiscuity. But this common ground was obscured because *each culture conceptualized these fundamentals in very different ways*...While Zulu culture was firmly patriarchal, powerful women were not unknown. Shaka's mother played a central role in his ascent to power, and in Zulu mythology, Uzembeni was a 'great woman' who 'devoured the men of the country where she lived...In addition to this ambivalent image of female power in Zulu folklore, women with spiritual powers were an important part of everyday life. Indeed, the great majority of Zulu diviners were women...(emphasis added).[135]

Colonial religion deliberately reversed gender roles. In traditional society the man was the religious leader of the whole family. He pleaded with the ancestral deities on behalf of all of the people in the home. He sacrificed for them and performed the religious duties. In the missionary Church, however, the woman assumed the leading role in religious life. "This is because the women have, on the whole, been more receptive of Christianity than men...they are responsible for the conversion of men into the Christian faith."[136] Again, the strategy of domination always targeted the woman. This targeting of the Zulu woman by the Church in order to "liberate" her from her traditional culture had pernicious effects.

Traditional Zulu culture imposed a standard of morality and sexual purity on men and women that insured women's respectability, provided a certain degree of safety, and established the basis for children's well-being. Sexual propriety and discipline were so obvious in traditional society that even missionaries acknowledged it.[137]

---

[135] Porterfield, "Impact of Early New England Missionaries," 68.
[136] A. Velakazi, *Zulu Transformations: A Study of the Dynamics of Social Change* (Pietermaritzburg: University of Natal Press, 1962) 137.
[137] Porterfield, "The Impact of Early New England Missionaries," 73.

The Christian missionaries acknowledged this virtuousness of the traditional Zulu man and woman, and targeted it.

> While the Zulu had once been renowned for their universal restraint from casual or unsanctioned sex, by the early twentieth century sexual promiscuity became a problem that concerned missionaries and African Christians as well as traditionalists. Premarital pregnancies rose sharply with the decline of sex-based initiation groups that instructed young people in the rituals of proper sexual activity, and with the breakdown of patriarchal authority and supervision as mining and other forms of industry drew men away from their homes.[138]

What's more, the church *banned the fighting-stick,* so important to the socialization of the Zulu boy into traditional Zulu masculinity and manhood.[139]

## KILLING THE BLACK GOD (AGAIN)

And this was facilitated by a gradual change in the concept of God. The peculiar Zulu masculinity and paradigm of manhood that was such a thorn in the side of White Supremacy in Africa sprung from the fount of the Zulu knowledge of God, the Black God. The whites of South Africa did everything they could to obliterate this Zulu manhood, including covertly transforming under Christian tutelage the Black Man (Male) God of the earth, uNkulunkulu, into a white sky-god, and even into a woman.[140] As M.R. Masubelele documents:

> with the translation of the Bible, the concept of the Supreme Being that was originally known by the Zulu people was changed and cast into a

---

[138] Porterfield, "Impact of Early New England Missionaries."
[139] Hadebe, "Zulu Masculinity," 32.
[140] Wesley Muhammad, *The Book of God,* **Volume II:** *Allah and the Sacred Science of the Black God in African Traditional Religions* (Atlanta: A-Team Publishing, forthcoming); Graeme Lang, "Correaltions Versus Case Studies: The Case of the Zulu in Swanson's *The Birth of the Gods," Journal for the Scientific Study of Religion* 28 (1989): 273-282 (277 n.3); Jennifer Weir, "Whose uNkulunkulu?" *Africa* 75 (2005): 203-219; Irving Hexham, *Texts on Zulu Religion: Traditional Zulu Ideas About God* (Lewiston, NY: Edwin Mellen, 1987); idem, "Lord of the Sky-King of the Earth: Zulu traditional religion and belief in the sky god," *Sciences religieuses/Studies in Religion* 10 (1981): 273-285; A. Berglund, *Zulu Thought-Patterns and Symbolism* (Bloomington and Indianapolis: Indiana University Press, 1976).

Christian mould...Although at present the Zulu people use the word *uNkulunkulu* for the Supreme Being to refer to the Christian God, this was not the case when the people were introduced to Christianity. Traditionally, the Zulu people spoke of *uNkulunkulu* to refer to the Supreme Being whom they regarded as the original ancestor of all people, the one who created all things and instituted the present order of society. He was not worshipped 'for he was said to have died so long ago that no one knows his praises, and as he left no progeny, no one can worship him'...The Christian concept of *uNkulunkulu* has now effectively displaced the traditional concept so that no clear account can be obtained of the patter and his attributes[141]...The Christian term refers to a different concept than the one referred to in Zulu traditional religion because the attributes of the Supreme Being in both types of religious practices differ.[142]

See also Olof Pettersson:

> The ideas of uNkulunkulu or uMvelinqangi among the Zulu has been heavily influenced by Christian thoughts...In olden times the Zulu believed according to the myths that uNkulunkulu came from the interior of the earth or from the Uthlanga, the reed-grove. This idea does not seem to exist in the myths and sayings according to the modern Zulu traditions. The Christian influences have resulted in uNkulunlulu being now placed in heaven. His connection with the inner part of the earth or with Uthlanga has no place in the Zulu idea of God in our times.[143]

And what do post-colonial Zulu say of this sky-god? "Zulu informants are emphatic that everything in the sky is white. The Lord-of-the-Sky himself is regarded as being white, some informants saying 'perhaps he is white like water (i.e. transparent)."[144] Once the connection is broken between the Black God uNkulunkulu and the male head of the home, it became easy

---

[141] On the contrary. See Wesley Muhammad, *The Book of God,* **Volume II:** *Allah and the Sacred Science of the Black God in African Traditional Religions* (Atlanta: A-Team Publishing, forthcoming).

[142] M.R. Masubelele, "Missionary Interventions in Zulu Religious Practices: The Term for the Supreme Being," *Acta Theologica Supplementum* 12 (2009)76.

[143] Olof Pettersson, "Foreign Influences on the Idea of God in African Religions," in *SYNCRETISM: based on papers read at the symposium on cultural contact, meeting of religions, syncretism held at Åbo on the 8.-10. of September, 1966,* ed. Sven S. Hartman (Stockholm : Almqvist & Wiksell, 1969) 41-65 (48).

[144] Belgrund, *Zulu Thought-patterns,* 51-52.

to reverse the balance of power in the home. And that is exactly what happened.

## THE ECONOMIC UPROOTING OF TRADITIONAL ZULU MANHOOD

The reversal of gender roles was further facilitated by the colonial economic policies that targeted (for destruction) the traditional homestead economy which served as the base of the traditional gender hierarchy. The homestead economy was replaced by a capitalist economy. As a result of the free market men now had to sell their cattle for cash to purchase goods from colonists and migrate to the cities for work.[145] The diamond and gold mines were the backbone of the South African economy and it developed on the back of the migrant labor system. Early 20th century colonial seizure of land, the introduction of government taxes, and the hunger for labor in the mines pulled African men into the colonial labor market far away from home, which proved to be culturally devastating.

> The democratic system in South Africa has heralded an era that is having an impact on African society. Men have seen their power dwindle and there has been a reversal of roles. The men who used to be the head of the family and responsible for taking care of his family are in most cases forced to assume the role of dependent.[146]

> *Colonial capitalism* introduced the need to find new ways to obtain the resources needed for the homestead, especially wage labour to earn money. *This resulted in the evolution of a new Zulu masculine identity* (emphasis added)...Different policies promoting gender equality, along with the high rate of unemployment generally, have disrupted man's position as the sole 'provider' and hence their domination in the house hold. Many men now face role changes, trapped between old and new style roles, with households beginning to be headed by women (emphasis added).[147]

---

[145] J. H. Shope, " 'Lobola is here to stay': rural black women and the contradictory meaning of lobolo in post-apartheid South Africa," in *Agenda Empowering Women for Gender Equality* (Durban: Agenda Feminist Media Company, 2006) 64-72; Lindani Hadene, "Zulu Masculinity: Culture, Faith and the Constitution in the South African Context," MA thesis, University of KwaZulu-Natal, 2010.
[146] Masuku, "Perceived Oppression of Women," 186.
[147] Hadebe, "Zulu Masculinity," 9, 11.

The evolution of a new Zulu masculinity? The colonial policy of requiring men to leave their rural homes and travel to the city to do wage-labor was part of the process of feminizing the Zulu man. They would often be required to do domestic work for colonial officers which were considered feminine tasks in the rural homes and which they would never normally do. This had the effect of emasculating the Zulu wage-earner. They were further 'infantilized' by paternalistic employers who spoke to them as "My boys," thus "conveying the emasculating forms of proprietary fondness."[148] The migrant laborers' masculinity started to reflect the Western cultural norms. In traditional Zulu society being an *amagwala* or effeminate is a humiliation. This had a negative impact on home life to which they returned. The women, left behind in the village to fend for themselves, lost respect for and deference to their husband's authority. The men in their home lost *amandla*, power, and *anginawo amandla*, "I don't have power," became their constant lament.[149] Western democracy and capitalism was the near death of the traditional Zulu ethos of manhood and masculinity, and thus the near total disruption of traditional society.

The imposition of Christianity cemented the disempowerment of the Zulu and Southern Bantu male and the overturning of the Zulu/Bantu gender norms in South Africa. As Knobel Sakhiwo Bengela laments in his doctoral study of *hlonipha* among the amaXhosa:

> Because South Africa in general and the Eastern Cape in particular could not escape the vicious assault on their living heritages by (...) Christian influences plus the domination of their indigenous cultures by the western culture, most of the Black customary practices have been abandoned and some are facing extinction...the large majority of modern women of today no longer stick to tradition and custom. Their attire is largely determined by what the modern fashion offers: short dresses and skirts, lack of head gear; imitation of European style of dressing....These modifications...illustrate a massive affectation and transition of *hlonipha*

---

[148] Carton and Morrell, "Zulu Masculinities, Warrior Culture, and Stick Fighting,"49.
[149] Mark Hunter, "Fathers without amandla: Zulu-speaking men and fatherhood," in ***Men and Fatherhood in South Africa***, ed. R. Morrell and L. Richter (Cape Town: HSRC Press, 2006) 99-117.

traditional practices...(With) the arrival of western civilization, Christianity, industrialization and democracy in Southern Africa the culture of the amaXhosa which had for centuries remained rich, intact and stable, now began to vanish gradually at the mercy of the vanquishing white culture...That...accounts for the disappearance of...the *hlonipha* language, *hlonipha* ethics and other cultural traits in most parts of the Eastern Cape.[150]

The targeting of the practice and the ethic of *hlonipha* by the Western religious culture was in accord with the objective of the disempowering of the Zulu male. The colonial and post-colonial transformations – industrialization, urbanization, political upheaval, and racism – dislocated and emasculated – also feminized - the Zulu male, smothering in the process traditional Zulu manhood and masculinity. White Supremacy also reshaped the masculinity of the Shona in Zimbabwe in the precise same way. The masculinities of the newly urban Shona were constructed through the assimilation of colonial definitions. For example these urban wage-earners took to wearing *mabhogadhi* (tight jeans). Yes, putting Black men in skinny-jeans is an age-old colonial tactic. The traditional Shona looked upon these tight jeans as representing a "satanic masculinity," and they were right. In towns, Shona men became the "boys" of the colonizers. In fact, the very name "Shona" is a colonial construct that says it all. Chenjerai Shire writes:

> Men who once constructed their identities through a rich vocabulary of totemic connectedness were renamed using a term signifying an area for colonial government: the 'Shona'...The definition and meaning of this term are embedded in colonial power relations...I suggest that it derives from the name 'Shona,' the feminine version of the Gaelic man's name 'Sean' (...). 'Shona' men, within this setting, internalized a masculinity designed to place them in emasculated, subordinated relations with the colonial power.[151]

The white man's strategy of global domination does not change its tactics.

---

[150] Bengela, "Isihlonipho Among the amaZhosa," 141, 143, 168.
[151] Chenjerai Shire, "Men don't go to the moon: Language, space, and masculinities in Zimbabwe," in ***Dislocating masculinity: Comparative ethnologies***, ed. Andrea Cornwall and Nancy Lindisfarne (London and New York: Routledge, 2003 [1994]) 146-157.

# 5    European Expansion and the Homosexual Enterprise

### I.    *Imperial Sodomy*

Ronald Hyam is right when he says "sexual dynamics crucially underpinned the whole operation of British Empire and Victorian expansion."[152] But we are not talking, as he claims, about opportunistic sexual liaisons between colonizer and the colonized. We are talking about strategic sexual violence as political praxis.[153] Speaking of German expansion Daniel Walther points out:

> the body became the site to demonstrate the 'superiority' of the white over the black...Not surprisingly then, the instances of rape were frequent in the colonies. [154]

Hyam is right also about a "sexual imperative [that] formed part of the imperial exercise," but it was not just *heterosex* that "underpinned the whole operation" of European expansion. "Homosexuals, pure, heroic and martial, were the spearhead of this childish dream which constituted French colonization," notes Jean-Edern Hallier.[155] "Homophila represents a common trait of all of the great colonials, whether British or French, and the connecting thread which makes sense of their destiny," writes Cristian Gury.[156] Sarah Suleri speaks of the "predominantly homoerotic cast assumed by the narrative of colonialism."[157]

---

[152] Ronald Hyam, *Empire and Sexuality: The British Experience* (Manchester, 1990) 1.
[153] David Kenosian, "The Colonial Body Politic: Desire and Violence in the Works of Gustav Frenssen and Hans Grimm," *Monatshefte* 89 (1997): 182-195.
[154] Daniel J. Walther, "Sex, Race and Empire: White Male Sexuality and the 'Other' in German Colonies, 1894-1914," *German Studies Review* 33 (2010): 52 [art.=45-71].
[155] Christian Gury, *Lyautey-Charlus* (Paris, 1998) 111.
[156] Gury, *Lyautey-Charlus*, 62.
[157] Sarah Suleri, *The Rhetoric of English India* (Chicago, 1992) 16.

It is Prof. Robert Aldrich of the University of Sydney who has most thoroughly documented "the empire as a homosexual playground" in his mammoth *Colonialism and Homosexuality* (2003). He documents the "connections between homosexuality and imperialism from the late 1800's - the era of 'new imperialism' - until the period of decolonization."

> Colonial lands, which in the late nineteenth and early twentieth century included most of Africa, South and Southeast Asia, and the islands of the Pacific and Indian Oceans and the Caribbean, provided a haven for Europeans whose sexual inclinations did not fit neatly into the constraints of European society. Certain colonies became known as sites of homosexual licence (*sic*).[158]

Homosexual men fleeing Britain, France, Germany and the Netherlands found warm welcome in the colonies. Homosexuality was particularly endemic among the various militaries.[159] But European men of all professions - explorers, merchants, writers, etc. - engaged in the colonial enterprise as homosexuals. The French slang *faire passer son brevet colonial*, which literally meant "to give someone an examination for a colonial diploma," came to mean "to initiate him to sodomy."[160] Homosexual encounters were widespread in the colonies, and not just among those on the margins of empire. The empire builders themselves are representative of this imperial homosexual push.

> some of the leading figures in the imperial pantheon - British imperial heroes did not come much greater than [Henry Morton] Stanley and [Cecil] Rhodes, [General Charles George] Gordon and [Lord] Kitchner, and Lawrence of Arabia. [Marshall Hubert] Lyautey was the quintessential French imperialist and [Sir Wilfred] Thesiger, arguably, is the most famous surviving explorer. [Alexander von] Humboldt was the leading German explorer of the early 1800's; [Nikolay] Przhevalsky, the premier Russian explorer of his time.[161]

---

[158] Robert Aldrich, *Colonialism and Homosexuality* (London and New York: Routledge, 2003).
[159] Aldrich, *Colonialism and Homosexuality*, Chapter 2.
[160] Aldrich, *Colonialism and Homosexuality*, 1.
[161] Aldrich, *Colonialism and Homosexuality*, 99.

Likewise, Orientalist novelists, poets, journalists, travel writers, sociologists and ethnographers from various European nations travelled to the Arabic Orient or Near East in pursuit of sex with local males, preferably boys.[162] Men of color were the imperialist's fetish: "Europeans fantasised (*sic*) about brown skin."[163] But imperial homosexuality was not just about physical gratification but political and social control. It represented the "collusion of phallocratic and colonial interests," in the words of Joseph Boone.[164] Homosexual sex was "part of the violence perpetrated throughout the colonial world," remarks Aldrich.

Colonial post card showing European soldier sodomizing an African soldier. From Robert Aldrich, *Colonialism and Homosexuality* (2003)

---

[162] Joseph A. Boone, "Vacation Cruises: Or, the Homoerotics of Orientalism," *PMLA* 110 (1995): 69-107.
[163] Aldrich, *Colonialism and Homosexuality*, 406.
[164] Joseph A. Boone, "Vacation Cruises: Or, the Homoerotics of Orientalism," *PMLA* 110 (1995): 90 [art.=69-107].

"Many if not most of the sexual encounters between European men and African and Arab men involved domination and violence," confirms Heike Schmidt.[165] It was General Lamoricière, one of the conquerors of Algeria, who was quoted as matter-of-factly stating: "There [in Africa] we were all [pederasts]." The French military feasted on African boys in Algeria, as the American imperialists feast on the Black boys here.

So the fact that the European Expansion was a "homosexual enterprise" is well documented. Homoeroticism motivated or at least seized colonialists from the top down. But how does one square this fact with another indisputable fact: colonial expansion had a very "manly" and even hypermasculine ethos?[166] Indeed, homosexuality was actually legally *prohibited* in many of the colonies among European men, even while a bonafide "homosexual culture" flourished there (e.g. Australia). Also, heterosexual masculinity was considered and treated as the sole prerogative of European men. Among the Germans

> maleness was also supposed to entail heterosexuality, at least for whites. To act otherwise, especially with a non-European, was viewed by colonial officials as a danger to the entire colonial endeavor...In a sense one could perhaps argue that homosexuality was a crime not only against the state but also against whiteness and, by association, Germanness, at least in the colonial setting.[167]

Yet, we learn that

> At the turn of the century same-sex desire was prevalent in upper-class culture in the (German) metropole. Homosexuality was also common among the German emperor's closest confidants and political allies...[168]

---

[165] Heike Schmidt, "Colonial Intimacy: The Rechenberg Scandal and Homosexuality in German East Africa," *Journal of the History of Sexuality* 17 (2008): 28 [art.=25-59].

[166] Aldrich, *Colonialism and Homosexuality*, 10; P. Levine, "Venereal Disease, Prostitution, and the Politics of Empires: The Case of British India," *Journal of the History of Sexuality* 4 (1994): 596.

[167] Daniel J. Walther, "Racializing Sex: Same-Sex Relations, German Colonial Authority, and Deutschtum," *Journal of the History of Sexuality* 17 (2008): 13, 23-24 [art.=11-24].

[168] Schmidt, "Colonial Intimacy," 28.

How do we account for this apparent contradiction? Quite easily, it turns out. In order to maintain the ideal of white heterosexual masculinity in the face white homoeroticism toward the colonial subjects, the whole colonized world – i.e. the indigenous men of the colonies - was *feminized*. "Colonial thinkers perceived colonial cultures as feminine, thus justifying their conquest of them," observes Carol Christ.[169] Joseph Noon notes further:

> a paradigmatic example of the mechanisms of orientalism: the masculinized, penetrating West possesses for its own purposes the East's fecundity, gendered as female...the figure of the effeminate Asiatic...represents one 'face' of the orientalist homoerotic fantasy.[170]

Mrinaline Sinha, in her important work *Colonial Masculinity: The "Manly Englishmen" and the "Effeminate Bengali" in Late Nineteenth Century* (1995) shows how the construction of "masculine" and "feminine" were central to the colonial political discourse between the two elites of 19th century Britain and India, the colonizing British and the colonized Bengalis. Stereotyping the Bengali men as effeminate and the British men as manly helped secure the fragile British identity and justified continued British presence in India.[171] Similarly, the Europeans continually presented the Omyènè men of Gabon, Africa as effeminate.[172] This dichotomy between manly European men and feminized native men was strongly preserved: "In the politics of empire, there was no room for even a hint of the effeminacy assumed to exist among subject men," writes P. Levine.[173]

---

[169] Carol Christ, "Whose history are we writing? Reading feminist texts with a hermeneutic of suspicion," *Journal of Feminist Studies in Religion* 20 (2004): 59-82.
[170] Boone, "Vacation Cruises," 92.
[171] Mrinaline Sinha, *Colonial Masculinity: The "Manly Englishmen" and the "Effeminate Bengali" in Late Nineteenth Century* (Manchester, UK: Manchester University Press, 1995).
[172] Jeremy Rich, "Torture, Homosexuality, and Masculinities in French Central Africa: The Faucher-d'Alexis Affair of 1884," *Historical Reflections* 36 (2010): 12 [art.=7-23].
[173] Levine, "Venereal Disease," 596.

This is the context of the colonial description "virgin territory": the European male conquers the 'virgin' (and female) land (and culture), a conquest that parallels male sexual conquest of a woman.[174] "Thus, the actual conquest of non-Western territory was simultaneously the metaphorical penetration of the virgin, i.e. the establishment of male domination over the woman."[175] The colonized cultures were thus "the woman." They were either feminized or infantilized or both: "white man's civilizing mission...saw the non-European peoples of the world as innocent children or defenseless women needing the protection of European 'adults',"[176] specifically adult *men*.

The "metaphorical penetration of the virgin" is an important aspect of this colonial propaganda that bridged the gap between the colonial manly ethos and the simultaneous colonial homoeroticism toward and fetish for dark meat: the man is the *penetrator*, the women (=feminized native cultures) is the *penetrated*. In the homosexual encounter the European colonials were normally the "dominant" *sodomizer* and the native male was the "weak" *sodomized*, and by a rather bizarre twist of logic this allowed the European to preserve his masculinity and heterosexuality.[177] Thus, it is sodomized natives that are the homosexuals, not the European sodomizers,[178] according to this imperial propaganda. In German East Africa, "African men initiated most of the cases of same-sex rapes tried...; they brought charges against European men for sexual violation."[179] These Africans charged that such rapes were an assault on their masculinity. The Kiswahili word *kuainishwa* was used to denote

---

[174] Anne MacClintock, *Imperial Leather: Race, Gender and Sexuality in the Colonial Context* (New York: Routledge, 1995) 30.
[175] Daniel J. Walther, "Sex, Race and Empire: White Male Sexuality and the 'Other' in Germany's Colonies, 1894-1914," *Journal of Feminist Studies in Religion* 20 (2004): 49 [art.=54-82].
[176] Walther, "Racializing Sex," 21.
[177] Walther, "Racializing Sex," 20; Mwalimu K. Bomani Baruti, *Homosexuality and the Effeminization of Afrikan Males* (Atlanta: Akoben House, 2003) 49-50.
[178] That homosexuality "was a condition of the colonial subject was one of the familiar claims underwriting the project of colonial difference in India," notes Anjali Arondekar, "Without Trace: Sexuality and the Colonial Archive," *Journal of the History of Sexuality* 14 (2005): 19 [art.=10-27].
[179] Schmidt, "Colonial Intimacy," 32.

the passive, effeminate role of the slave "Chosen," i.e. penetrated by his master. This made the "chosen" one a *mke-si-mume*, "woman-not-man."[180]

The establishment of the colonies in the Americas and the Caribbean were part of this Homosexual Enterprise, and the plight of the African male enslaved in the America's was not only similar to that in the other European possessions, but far worse, as we shall see.

II.     *America's Delectable Negro*

Richard Suggs, in his revolting book ***Mummies, Cannibals and Vampires: The History of Corpse Medicine from the Renaissance to the Victorians*** (2011), documents a two-century-plus phenomenon in Europe of cannibalism and vampirism that involved the crown and the church, as well as the common citizen.

> For well over 200 years in early modern Europe, the rich and the poor, the educated and the illiterate, all participated in cannibalism on a more or less routine basis. Drugs were made of Egyptian mummies and from the dried bodies of those drowned on North African desert sandstorms. Later in the era the corpses of hanged criminals offered a new and less exotic source of human flesh. Human blood was swallowed: sometimes fresh and hot, direct from a donor's body; sometimes dried, powdered, or distilled with alchemical precision…[A] shadowy network of suppliers, sea captains, grave robbers, executioners and anatomists oversaw the acquisition of bodies, blood, bones, and fat…[181]

This very organized system supplied the royal likes of cannibals Charles II, Frances I, Christian IV of Demark and William III. It was overwhelmingly a Christian enterprise:

> these educated Christian man-eaters…were the real cannibals of the early modern world. They read and wrote in Latin, dressed in silk, debated theology, painted many of the greatest Western artworks, threw up some

---

[180] Schmidt, "Colonial Intimacy," 56.
[181] Richard Suggs, *Mummies, Cannibals and Vampires: The History of Corpse Medicine from the Renaissance to the Victorians* (London and New York: Routledge, 2011) 1, 203.

of Christandom's most astonishing palaces and cathedrals and churches.[182]

The theological logic of these European Christian man-eaters is important. Many believed it was possible to consume the powers of the dead man's soul.[183] At least part of the motive behind medicinal cannibalism seems to have been the attempt to consume the strength or spiritual force of those they devoured. Many believed that there was a 'spiritual fire' in the corpse that the lucky cannibal could harvest. This was a "distinctive vampirism of the soul."[184] Many Christians believed that all people have a preordained life span and if anyone is cut down prematurely, the remainder of the life-span is in the corpse and can be harvested out. This is why the so-called *Paracelsian corpse* was so favored. This was the corpse of a young, otherwise healthy man who died a particularly violent premature death, preferably by hanging. *Hanging* (=lynching). His corpse was assumed to be animated with life forces that could be extracted. Some Christians connected these forces in the blood with the spirit of God that can be harvested.[185]

### RITUAL CANNIBALISM AND HOMOSEXUALITY INSTITUTIONALIZED IN AMERICAN SLAVERY

This European and Christian practice of human flesh-eating and soul-harvesting – as well as his sexual fetish for brown flesh - travelled to the colonies in the Western Hemisphere with them and produced the U.S. institution of slavery as a "culture of homoeroticism and consumption," as documented most forcefully by the late Vincent Woodard in his ***The Delectable Negro: Human Consumption and Homoeroticism within U.S. Slave Culture*** (2014). Woodard argues that the 19th century was "a moment in which black masculinity, racial identity, homoeroticism, and a

---

[182] Suggs, *Mummies, Cannibals and Vampires*, 203.
[183] Suggs, *Mummies, Cannibals and Vampires*, 173.
[184] Suggs, *Mummies, Cannibals and Vampires*, 180.
[185] Suggs, *Mummies, Cannibals and Vampires*, 181-188.

distinctive American appetite for black male flesh and soul congealed."[186]

> this culture of consumption took the form of whites literally flaying and smoking African American flesh and overt references in slave narratives to masters literally and metaphorically consuming the slaves.[187]

Through sustained contact and observation of Europeans the Gambians and Sierra Leoneans of West Africa correctly ascertained the esoteric purpose of the Slave Trade: a trade in African bodies to be ritually sacrificed to the Christian god and consumed and in African souls to be harvested and spiritually ingested by the Europeans.[188]

This consumptive culture of slavery had a homoerotic – rather, homosexual – component to it. Woodard documents "how thoroughly homoerotic and homosexual desire shaped the master/slave relation and informed white male codes of honor."[189] Thomas Foster too documents that "The sexual exploitation of enslaved black men took place within a cultural context that fixated on black male bodies with both desire and horror."[190] This American slave culture was so homoerotic that a number of scholars maintain that the image of flesh exposed by whippings carried a homosexual charge.[191] The fabricated Orientalist and colonial myth of "Negro effeminacy" which we discussed earlier shaped this European homoeroticism.[192]

It is important to emphasize that slave masters derived more than sexual pleasure from the rape of black men: they derived social empowerment, masculine self-identity and even self-deification: "white men experienced a sense of deific power."[193] The African's exploited body and harvested soul fed the American process, which was simply a localization of a global

---

[186] Vincent Woodard, *The Delectable Negro: Human Consumption and Homoeroticism within U.S. Slave Culture* (New York and London: New York University Press, 2014) 24.
[187] Woodard, *Delectable Negro*, 12.
[188] Woodard, *Delectable Negro*, 49.
[189] Woodard, *Delectable Negro*, 64.
[190] Thomas A. Foster, "The Sexual Abuse of Black Men Under Slavery," *Journal of the History of Sexuality* 20 (2011): 445-464; Baruti, *Homosexuality and the Effeminization of Afrikan Males*, 194-195.
[191] Foster, "The Sexual Abuse," 450.
[192] Woodard, *Delectable Negro*, 14-15, 37.
[193] Woodard, *Delectable Negro*, 47.

project of white male deification.[194] The slave master was the American *Herr*. In fact, white masculinity itself was ennobled and reified by the consumption, degradation and domination of the Black male.[195]

It must be pointed out that the institution of slavery deliberately and systematic attempted to obliterate gender distinctions among the enslaved Africans. As Aliyyah I. Abdur-Rahman speaks on this process of "ungendering" that rendered the slaves "neuter-bound":

> While racial slavery allowed for the full exploitation of black bodies in slavery in whatever gendered capacity, it simultaneously – and paradoxically – disallowed distinctions of gender among black people. Enslaved black men were feminized by virtue of their subjugation as slaves, the regularity with which they were castrated, and the denial of patriarchal and citizenship rights. Enslaved black women were masculinized by virtue of their back-breaking labor on par with black men and their being denied male protection and provision...The slave body was rendered "neuter" in that in spite of the slave's anatomical referent, as a non-person, the slave did not register gender legibly, according to established paradigms of masculinity or femininity.[196]

Slaveholders were obsessed with emasculating the Black male, as this gave the slaveholder some type of "psycho-sexual superiority complex," in the words of Keri Leigh Merritt. One particularly oppressive method of emasculation was forcing boys, young men and even grown men to wear the same "dresses" that the girls and women wore. As Merritt describes:

> Perhaps one of the slave owners' more innovatively cruel strategies concerned the ways they sought to completely emasculate enslaved boys and men-by denying them the right to wear pants. By forcing young African American boys and men to wear dress-like shirts, the owners of flesh attempted to feminize and humiliate enslaved males on a daily basis. According to scores of interviews with the formerly enslaved,

---

[194] Woodard, *Delectable Negro*, 51.
[195] Woodard, *Delectable Negro*, 74, 84.
[196] Aliyyah I. Abdur-Rahman, "'The Strangest Freaks of Despotism': Queer Sexuality in Antebellum African American Slave Narratives," *African American Review* 40 (2006): 223-237.

denying black boys and young men the right to wear pants was a relatively widespread practice throughout the Deep South.[197]

This was a one-piece garment resembling a nightgown that was tied around the waist with a string. Young boys and girls wore the same garment, obscuring gender difference at a young age. As the boys grew, slave owners would deny them pants even into adulthood. The impact on the psychology of the enslaved male is incalculable. As for the impact on the psychology of the salve owner, "By feminizing African American males, slave owners likely reassured themselves that they were the most masculine men on the plantation, which could be demonstrated, of course, by the rape and sexual abuse of women and girls."[198]

## JIM CROW LYNCHINGS AND SACRIFICE TO THE CHRISTIAN GOD

That the terror unleashed on the Black man and women's body and soul in America had a distinctly *religious* or sacred countenance is further demonstrated by the lynchings of Black men during the Jim Crow era. Orlando Patterson documents that, in the post-Emancipation South where the Southern white male's ego, his sense of manhood, his sense of godhood and codes of honor were all deeply wounded by the Confederate loss during the Civil War and the emancipation of their slaves, the reign of violent terror that was unleashed on the Black community and the Black male in particular were in many cases ritual blood sacrifices to the white Southerner's god.[199] The lynchings in the American South often took place on the Lord's Day, and the sanctified lynch mod was frequently presided over by clergymen. Professor Pater Ehrenhaus of Pacific Luthern University together with Professor A. Susan Owen of the University of Puget Sound have likewise argued that the lynchings were a ritualistic reenactment of the blood sacrifice of Christ - his Passion (also a Black man who,[200] in the Gospels, the white man sadistically lynched).

---

[197] Keri Leigh Merritt, "Men without Pants: Masculinity and the Enslaved," *African American Intellectual Historical Society* September 11, 2016.
[198] Keri Leig Merritt, "Men without Pants."
[199] Orlando Patterson, "Rituals of Blood: Sacrificial Murders in the Postbellum South," *The Journal of Blacks in Higher Education* 23 (Spring 1999): 123-127; idem, "Feast of Blood: 'Race,' Religion and Human Sacrifice in the Postbellum South," in idem, *Rituals of Blood*, 171-232.
[200] See Wesley Muhammad, "Color struck: America's White Jesus is a global export and false product," *The Final Call* 32 (January 1, 2013) 3, 8.

The explanation for such sadism and bloodletting is not found in a retreat from Christian doctrine, but in its embrace. Public ritual lynching was a performative affirmation of fundamentalist Christian faith in a white supremacist national community...[E]ven the most brutal and barbaric features of the sacrificial lynching-slow, drawn out torture and mutilation; burning and incineration; the collection of body fragments[201] and the purchase and circulation of photographs as sacred relics-were constitutive acts of the perpetrators' Christian faith. In the post-Reconstruction era of Jim Crow, the ritual performance of mass mob, sacrificial lynching functioned for the dominant white Christian community as acts of devotion and defense, as blood sacrifices to a God whose covenant with the white Christian community had been violated by the intrusion of blackness into the sacred spaces of the covenant...Within this Evangelical worldview, sacrificial lynching reaffirmed a sacred covenant among the members of the white Christian community and between that community and their god...[T]he ritual sacrifice of black citizens was a performance of Christian faith... complex performances that reproduce pre-emancipation race relations in a social order sanctified by sacred covenant.[202]

The lynching also produced a *Paracelsian corpse* whose vital energy could be harvested, like the Good Christians did in the old country. These American Good Christians could also identify the flames that consumed the black body of their sacrificial victim during burnings with the fire of God at the Burning Bush and with the fire that conveyed the burnt offerings to Jehovah. And this sacrificial ritual was cannibalistic. The roasted body of the sacrificial Black victim was frequently described as "barbeque," which term denoted not a southern flavored sauce but a southern method of meat preparation – slow cooked over an open fire. The sacred centrality and importance of the cannibalistic consumption of Black male flesh is no better illustrated than with the Christian Eucharist, where white folks ritualistically consume the flesh and blood of the Black Jesus whom they murdered.

---

[201] On which see also Harvey Young, "The Black Body as Souvenir in American Lynching," *Theatre Journal* 57 (2005): 639-657.
[202] Peter Ehrenhaus and A. Susan Owen, "Race Lynching and Christian Evangelicalism: Performances of Faith," *Text and Performance Quarterly* 24 (2004): 276-301.

The body of George Meadows, lynched near the Pratt Mines in Alabama's Jefferson County on January 15, 1889. A *Paracelsian corpse*.

The sadistic burning of William Brown, Omaha 1919. Brown was a sacrificial victim, a burnt offering to the Christian god of the white mob. The flames charring and consuming Brown's body considered by some to be the flames of Jehova at the Burning Bush.

## CASTRATION AS A TRANSFER OF POWER

Of the 2,462 Black victims during the Lynching Era, the five decades between the end of Reconstruction and the beginning of the Great Depression (1889-1930), 3 percent were female. The victims of lynching were thus overwhelmingly (97 percent) Black males. And these lynchings had a sexualized undercurrent. As Michael Awkward said in *Negotiating Difference* (1995): "The black phallus...was the focus indeed, very often, the site of much of lynching's ritualistic concern and energy." The white man has always had to balance feelings of envy and disgust toward the Black male, an emotional quandary that fueled the distinctly American phenomenon of ritual castration. As noted in Wilkinson and Taylor (1977), the white man "sees in the Negro the essence of his own sexuality, that is, those qualities that he wishes for but fears he does not possess...[a]nd that is why he must castrate him."[203] Part of the underlying logic of the ritual of castration therefore is a "sexualized transfer of power":

> through the castration rite, white men hope to acquire the grotesque powers they have assigned to the Negro phallus which they symbolically extol by the act of destroying it.[204]

But there is another underlying dynamic to the American ritual obsession with the black phallus. William Pinar appropriately asks: "How does one avoid hypothesizing a *sexual* motive in choosing muscular young black men to castrate (emphasis added)?" Pinar correctly points out the "homoerotic character" of the "queer violence" which is the ritual lynching of Black men.[205] And the ultimate aim of this queer violence is clear. As Marques Richeson points:

---

[203] Doris Y. Wilkinson and Ronald L. Taylor (edd), *The Black Male in America: Perspectives on His Status in Contemporary Society* (Rowman and Littlefield Publishers, 1977) 141, *apub* Marques P. Richeson, "Sex, Drugs, and...Race-To-Castrate: A Block Box Warning of Chemical Castration's Potential Racial Side Effects," *Harvard Black Letter Law Journal* 25 (2009): 107 [art.=95-131].

[204] Calvin Hernton in Iwan Bloch, *Sexual Life of Our Time in its Relations to Modern Civilization* (London: Heinemann, 1908) 115.

[205] William F. Pinar, "Strange Fruit," *Counterpoints* 163 (2001): 52 [art.=47-115].

In America, castration emerged as a white supremacist tool designed to invite the demasculinization, dehumanization, and invisibilization[206] of black men...Castration on American soil ultimately represented a flank of a strategic attack upon black masculinity...Once castrated, the victimized black male body could be presented for public display as subordinate and feminized. Mutilating the icon of black male prowess and virility, castration reduced the black male from *hyper*masculine to *hypo*masculine, thereby negating black masculinity and affirming white male hegemony (emphasis added).[207]

*Excursus: Modern Example*

Proof that neither the European's nature, his global objectives, his methods, nor his fetishes have in any way changed since slavery is in the facts that have come out of the Abu Ghraib prison in Iraq, where America holds its War on Terror detainees. Listen to Prof. Mary Ann Tetreault of Trinity University, in her article, "The Sexual Politics of Abu Gharib: Hegemony, Spectacle, and the Global War on Terror," (2006):

> News of abusive treatment, torture, and murder of detainees by U.S. military and intelligence personnel at Abu Ghraib prison in Iraq shocked

---

[206] Invisibilization: the process by which society's cloud of stereotypes renders individual black men invisible behind the haze of the black male collective.
[207] Richeson, "Sex, Drugs, and...Race-To-Castrate," 97, 102, 108.

the world. Bursting into public view in May 2004...the stories were accompanied by sensational photographs of naked prisoners, some engaged in simulated sexual acts...With few exceptions, the subjects of these photos...are living persons in the thrall of powerful and sadistic captors...They document the crimes as well as the impunity with which they were committed...These photos-some depicting corpses and brutal interrogation practices-are like stills from (pornographic) snuff films, statements of the utter worthlessness of the prisoners and the life-and-death power over them exercised by their captors...[The] politics of Abu Gharib [is] a tradition of orientalism that fetishizes and feminizes the sexuality of subject peoples as part of a strategy of domination. The photographs record rituals of violence affirming power relations between occupier and occupied...Sexuality, coded according to complex cultural norms of feminine subjection to masculine power, infufes the language and acts of members of dominant groups against those they seek to subjugate. The pornography of Abu Ghraib constitutes a field report on the production and reproduction of U.S. global dominance...In Abu Ghraib photos, Arab male captives are feminized by showing them in settings that emphasize both their sexuality and their helplessness. Perhaps the best example is the photograph of Private Lynndie England holding a leash while the other end is wrapped around the neck of a naked Arab prisoner...The Abu Ghraib images and documents describe violations of the captives' bodily integrity, masculine self-image, and religious rules about cleanliness...Their manhood is disparaged in many ways. Indeed, they are feminized - unmanned...being forced to wear women's panties on their heads; and being physically violated, beaten and sodomized, and subjected to women's intrusions on their bodily privacy...[The] spectacle of Abu Ghraib is an outward sign of the hidden rituals that, since 9/11, distinguish Americans from others.[208]

I will only disagree with Prof Tetreault in this: these sadistic hidden rituals of the American strategy of domination that is outwardly evidenced by the Abu Ghraid documents neither began with 9/11 nor distinguishes the American white man. It has always been the strategy of the White Man all over the world to forcefully feminize the men in the populations they dominate.

III.   *The Lady of the Races*

Robert E. Park (d. 1944), one of America's most influential sociologists, studied race-relations with Book T. Washington at

---

[208] Mary Ann Tetreault, "The Sexual Politics of Abu Gharib: Hegemony, Spectacle, and the Global War on Terror," *National Women's Studies Association Journal* 18 (2006): 33-50.

Tuskegee Institute for several years (1907-1914). From there he went to the University of Chicago where is became the father of the School of Sociology. During a seminar on "The Negro in the Old South," Park claimed:

> The Negro is the lady of the races; delicately proportioned, small boned, devoted to the arts of music and dance, with exquisite manners, the utmost in politeness, *she* cannot bear to hurt anyone's feelings (emphasis added).[209]

He claimed further:

> [The Negro] has always been interested rather in expression than in action; interested in life itself rather than in its reconstruction or reformation. The Negro is, by natural disposition, neither an intellectual nor an idealist, like the Jew; nor a brooding introspective, like the East Indian; nor a pioneer and frontiersman, like the Anglo Saxon. He is primarily an artist, loving life for its own sake. His métier is an expression rather than action. He is, so to speak, the lady among the races.[210]

Park coauthored with Ernest W. Burgess the first American textbook on sociology geared toward research, *Introduction to the Science of Sociology* (1921). He exerted an enormous influence on the development of a scientific theory of race relations. At his time he may have been responsible for more studies on race and ethnicity than any other American sociological theorist.[211] His "Negro as the Lady of the Races" theory therefore made a deep impact, giving pseudo-scientific support for the earlier propaganda employed by the European colonists and American slave masters to justify their fetish for black male flesh.

Another example of this pseudo-scientific support is the Minnesota Multiphasic Personality Inventory (MMPI), the most widely used and researched standardized psychometric test of adult personality. This psychological instrument asks the subject the applicability to himself of over 500 simple statements. In the

---

[209] James E. Tule, *E. Franklin Frazier and Black Bourgeoisie* (Colombia and London: University of Missouri, 2002) 57.
[210] Christopher Douglas, *A Genealogy of Multiculturalism* (Ithica and London: Cornell University Press, 2009): 119-124.
[211] Vernon Franklin White, "An analysis of the Race Relations Theory of Robert E. Park," master's thesis, Atlanta University, 1948.

1960's two Black male populations were tested and compared to white males: Alabama prisoners and Wisconsin working-class veterans with tuberculosis.[212] Reinforcing the "Lady of the Races" theory of Robert Park the researchers suggested that "Black males score higher than white males on a measure of femininity."[213]

> The results suggest that in contrast to whites, Negroes tend to show less concern over conventional social mores; demonstrate a greater emotional vigor and buoyancy; are more prone to act on their ideas and impulses; manifest more of what are considered to be bizarre or unusual thoughts and behavior; and, exhibit a more feminine pattern of interests.[214]

Harvard professor Thomas Pettigrew assumed these findings to indicate "the effeminate aspects of the 'Negro' role many of these men must play in adult life."[215] But the results are based on very shallow and ambiguous indicators, statements such as "I would like to be a singer" or "I think I feel more intensely than most people do." Robert Staples is surely correct that this evidence of the Black male's effeminacy is "feeble": "The only thing this demonstrates is that white standards cannot always be used in evaluating black behavior."[216] Indeed, the MMPI results, like Robert Park's racial theorizing, are only postbellum articulations of antebellum racist and homoerotic propaganda.

IV.   *The "Man" and His "Boy": Why Saggin is Faggin*

What is behind the custom of white males referring to Black males of all ages as "boy"? What are the implications of the sons of former slaves (Black males) referring to the sons of their former slave masters (white males) as "The Man"? And what do

---

[212] Jack E. Hokanson and George Calden, "Negro-White Differences on the MMPI," *Journal of Chemical Psychology* (1960): 32-33; Thomas F. Pettigrew, *A Profile of the Negro American* (Princeton, NJ: D. Van Nostrand Company, INC, 1964) 19.
[213] Pettigrew, *A Profile of the Negro American*, 19.
[214] Hokanson and Calden, "Negro-White Differences on the MMPI," 32-33.
[215] Pettigrew, *A Profile of the Negro American*, 20.
[216] Robert Staples, "The Myth of the Impotent Black Male," *The Black Scholar* 2 (1971): 5 [art.=2-9].

the answers of these two questions have to do with the "Saggin" phenomenon of American Black male youth?

As we saw, the establishment of the American colonies was part of an imperial homosexual enterprise and the colonialists – from all of the European colonial nations - had a distinct fetish for black and brown flesh, but especially *young* black and brown flesh. As Robert Aldrich documents in **Colonialism and Homosexuality** (2003), "Desire of adult men for younger partners has been widespread in Europe and overseas, with antecedents reaching back into antiquity."[217] These ancient precedents are most important for our discussion.

Ancient Greek culture was characerised not just by homosexulity but also by pederasty (*paiderasty* < *pais* "boy" + *erastes* "lover"). As Gayle Zive explains in her "A Brief History of Western Homosexuality":

> The Ancient Greeks regarded homosexuality as a normal part of life, but only within certain parameters. The relationship was supposed to be between a "beardless" youth and an older man. The elder was supposed to be the 'active' partner; it was shameful for him to be the 'passive'

---

[217] Aldrich, *Colonialism and Homosexuality*, 10.

partner...It was considered disgusting to continue sexual relations with a slave who was old enough to have facial hair.[218]

Roman homosexuality differed from Greek only in that pederasty with freeborn Roman boys was forbidden. Slaves of both genders and all ages were sexually violated.[219] Greek pederasty was not exclusively about sexuality either. It was also about the reinforcing of social hierarchy. In both ancient Greece and Rome the homosexual relationship was a relationship of power dominance which reinforced the parameters of social power relationships. Mwalimu Baruti, in his *Homosexuality and the Effeminization of Afrikan Males*, best brings out the implications of these relevant facts for our discussion:

> we find in both Greece and Rome the predominant presence of power specific roles within homosexual relationships. And these power specific roles are in conformity with the Western *asilic*[220] drive to separate individuals into dominators and dominatees based on differences in power...now referred to as the 'active' and 'passive' homsexual roles.[221]

In Greece this pederasty was for "educational" purposes. The boy was taught, among other things, his rightful place in the social order vis-à-vis men (=The Man) via a rite of passage that involved the ritual sodomization of the boy by the man. Baruti describes this "education" as a "Pedagogy of Submission." Its purpose was to control the ego and the ambition of society's male youth, thus protecting the power and position of the "Man" of society from any threat from the "Boy" of society. Michael Bradley of course told us that the white man, his people, has a Chronos

---

[218] See also Paul Veyne, "Homosexuality in Ancient Rome," in *Western Sexuality: Practice and Precept in Past Present Times*, ed. Philip Ariés and André Béjen (New York: Basil Blackwell, 1985) 29-30.

[219] See Craig Williams, *Roman Homosexuality. Second Edition* (Oxford and New York: Oxford University Press, 2010).

[220] According to Baruti *asili* refers to the germinal principle of the *being* of a culture, its essence and template that carries within it the archetypal model for cultural development. Baruti, *Homosexuality and the Effeminization of Afrikan Males*, 602 n. 1.

[221] Baruti, *Homosexuality and the Effeminization of Afrikan Males*, 49-50.

Complex[222]: like the Greek deity Chronos the white man seeks to kill his father and consume his own children because he fears his sons will eventually depose him from his throne or social status. White males thus see their own sons as the chief threat to their position. In Greece this threat was thwarted by ritual sodomization of Greek boys by Greek men, teaching the boys their proper place. The distinction between "the Man" and "the boy" thus had profound social significance, both in Ancient Greece and in modern America. And because the "boy" was the passive partner, he was feminized.[223] As Baruti explains:

> The adult male forced [the boy] to bend forward, spread his buttocks cheeks and, then be forcefully sodomized. The adult male used his penis as a weapon. With the boy in a fully compromised position, it became a very effective instrument for teaching him humility and obedience to men. Boys were in no position mentally or physically, to negotiate their sexual exploitation.[224]

In ancient Crete, Cretan pederasty also involved the ritual kidnapping (*harpagmos*) of a noble boy by an adult man of the aristocratic class. This element of *abduction* is important. As we demonstrated above, this practice was instituted in the American colonies. The kidnapped African male slaves – by social definition perpetual "boys" - were both ritually castrated and ritually sodomized in order to reinforce their place in society vis-à-vis "the Man," i.e the slave master who was the *active sodomizer*. As the passive victim, the enslaved African male can only be the "boy."

That the designation "boy" has sexual, pederastic meaning in the context of European colonialism is further demonstrated by a 400-page manual of sexual practices in the colonies published in 1893: ***L'Art d'aimer aux colonies*** by Dr. Jacobus (a *nom de plume*). Dr. Jacobus describes two sexual servants employed during the early days of the French conquest: 1.) the *nay*, which was a porter

---

[222] Michael Bradley, ***The Iceman Inheritance: Prehistoric Sources of Western Man's Racism, Sexism and Aggression*** (Toronto: Dorset Publishing Inc., 1978) 20-21.

[223] Veyne, "Homosexuality in Ancient Rome," 29-30: "To be active was to be male, whatever the sex of the compliant partner. To take one's pleasure was virile, to accept it servile…Woman was passive by definition…"

[224] Baruti, ***Homosexuality and the Effeminization of Afrikan Males***, 54.

or errand boy and 2.) the *boy*, the male youth employed as household servant. The *nay* and the *boy* were both local male youth who rendered sexual services to European men.[225] In America, the *boy* was the enslaved and emasculated African male. The Black male in white society is the perpetual *boy* because he is the perpetual pederastic desire of the white male, *pederastic* because this society will never allow the Black male anything other than a *subordinate masculinity*, like that of a boy in the presence of a man . And when white males insist on calling Black men "boy," it *does* have a sexual – a pederastic, homosexual – underlying significance. So too does the designation of white people as "the Man" by Black males. We should never in life use that language, not even in jess.

What does this have to do with saggin? Baruti noted regarding the ancient Greek ritual of sodomization: "boys gave access to their anuses in exchange for men's philosophical lessons...teaching boys to properly submit to men through the trauma of sexual violence."[226] It was the "boy" who publically exposed his anus, and such exposure signified he is a sodomitee, or is about to be. In the above colonial postcard showing a European soldier sodomizing an African soldier – *boying* him - the European's pants are all the way down to his ankles, while the sodomized African has his pants down to his knees. We could say he is saggin.

Don't be the "Boy" for "The Man". Don't sagg. Saggin truly *iz* faggin.

### V. Conclusion

The white man by nature is a sadistic, cannibalistic homosexual for whom homosexuality is a necessary part of his sense of manhood and masculinity, and he has an insatiable appetite for African flesh, Black male flesh in particular. The American institution of slavery was not just a capitalist economic enterprise in which the white man – Jew and Gentile – bartered

---

[225] Aldrich, ***Colonialism and Homosexuality***, 14-19.
[226] Baruti, ***Homosexuality and the Effeminization of Afrikan Males***, 55.

and exploited black bodies for commercial gain. It was that. But there was also an esoteric purpose for the trade in African flesh. The American institution of slavery was a cultic enterprise to harvest African Souls. Not only was the Black man and woman sacrificed to the slave masters' Christian God, but the white male ritualistically enacted and legitimated his own self-deification on and through the African male. The Black male's subjugation and domination was the process through which the white male experienced his own godhood and his own manhood, then and now. And in this process the white man sexually conquered as many Black men as he could - physically, chemically, culturally, and socially - and literally ate the flesh of the Black male, believing that by so doing, he is consuming some of his soul and his power.

But this is not just an American phenomenon. Everywhere the white man has gone on this earth and conquered, his manhood and masculinity is the only manhood and masculinity that is recognized and is legalized, even while his masculinity is built upon a sadistic homosexuality. Every single place where he succeeded in dominating, the architecture of that dominance was built on the mandate and the strategy to feminize the local male population. He always must be the *only* man in town, and thus did everything he could to stomp out all signs of manhood in the Black man. In America, he used his science to make the lie of the feminine Black man stick, and then he used his science to make the lie – true. At least in some cases.

Plates 1-8

Plate 1. Bill Clinton at the Stone Mountain Correction Institute. With Democratic Leadership Council leader Sam Nunn, Georgia Governor Zell Miller and Georgia Congressman Ben Lewis.

Plate 2. The installation of Virgilio Dante as Catholic Bishop of Maralal, Kenya.

Plate 3. Painting by Heinrich Harder (1858-1935) showing an Aurochs bull fighting off a Eurasian wolf pack

Plate 4. Forensic reconstruction of the tauroctony (bull-killing) in the fourth century cave sanctuary of Jajce (Bosnia). The white god Mithras is slaying the Black Bull (God).

102

Plate 5. The Mathematics of the Black God

Amun-Ra: The Sapphiric God

■■

Osiris, The Black (Body of) God

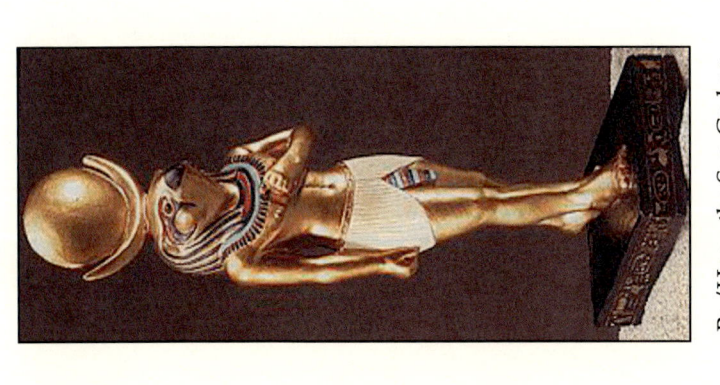

✚

Ra/Heru, the Sun God or Luminous Anthropos

Plates 6 and 7. Indo-Aryan deity Yama, the Black God/First Man. He is depicted both black and blue, as is the Egyptian deity Amun.

Plate 8. The Honorable Elijah Muhammad with Blue and Gold FOI Uniform and the Blue and Gold God Amun

104

PART THREE

# The Esoteric Agenda

## KILLING THE BLACK GOD

# 6    The Black God, the Black Bull, And the Black Man

> *He (God) came out of total darkness and He was dark. He proved that He came out of darkness, because His own color corresponds with the conditions of what is now the Heavens and the Earth, that was nothing then but total darkness. A totally dark man came out of total darkness.* The Honorable Elijah Muhammad

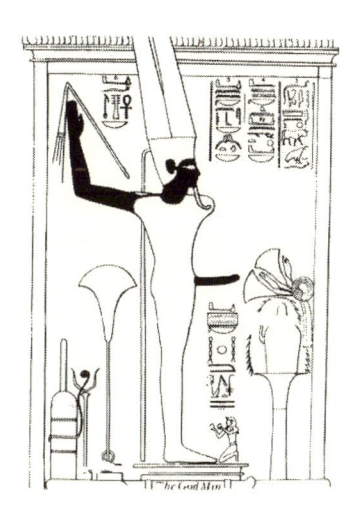

I.    *Who is the Black God?*

The Honorable Elijah Muhammad says in *Message to the Black Man of America*:

> For thousands of years, the people who did not have the knowledge of the person, or reality, of God worshiped their own ideas of God. He has been made like many things other than what He really is.[227]

Compare this with the observation by James L. Kugel, former Starr Professor of Hebrew Literature at Harvard University and currently Director of the Institute for the History of the Jewish Bible and Professor of Bible at Bar-Ilan University in Israel:

---

[227] Elijah Muhammad, *Message to the Black Man in America* (Chicago: Muhammad's Temple No. 2, 1965) 1.

> The God of the world's great religions – all-powerful, all-knowing, invisible, and omnipresent – has been a staple of Western thought for some time. *Yet...this God is not the same as the God of most of the Bible,* the God who appeared to Abraham, Moses, and other biblical heroes. That God, the 'God of Old,' was actually perceived in a very different way.[228]

Dr. Kugel, a world-renowned biblical scholar, affirms what the Honorable Elijah Muhammad said forty years ago: the world today is worshipping a god that is different from the true God of the Bible, what Kugel calls the 'God of Old.' Who is this 'God of Old,' the God of the Prophets? How was he perceived by ancient Israel and the biblical authors? How is it, why is it, that this God is no longer acknowledged or worshipped by the Jewish and Christian worlds who claim the Bible as the foundation of their faith?

The Honorable Elijah Muhammad teaches that, contrary to popular theological wisdom, God is *not* a formless, immaterial spirit. God is a man. But more than that: God, he declared, is a Black man, indeed, *the Black Man*. Not man as we currently understand man; but Man as he was before the great "Fall of Man." This Man is divine, Supreme in knowledge, wisdom, understanding, holiness and power. Muhammad said:

> The Black Man is the God of the Earth. He is the Creator. I don't care how you have been mistreated, still your Father was a Black Man and He is the One who created this Earth and is now taking it over. This is our Earth.[229]

The scientific study of the History of Religions teaches us that, at one time, the whole ancient world agreed with the Honorable Elijah Muhammad, *including the white world*. This is critical, because, as we shall show, White Supremacy's assault on the Black man is consciously an assault on the Black God.

---

[228] James L. Kugel, ***The God of Old: Inside the Lost World of the Bible*** (New York: The Free Press, 2003) front jacket.
[229] Elijah Muhammad, ***Theology of Time***, Lecture Series printed transcript by Abass Rassoul (Hampton: U.B.U.S., 1992), 125.

II. *The Attribute Animal*

In antiquity various aspects of the gods were represented zoomorphically. That is to say, different animals were used to symbolize distinct characteristics or attributes of a deity,[230] who was otherwise anthropomorphic. The paramount 'attribute animal' of the black creator-god was the black bovine, usually a bull. The bull represented potency, fecundity, and primordial materiality, all essential characteristics of the creator-god.[231] The color of the bull was not arbitrary. As René L. Vos pointed out, "Color reflected the nature of a god" and thus the skin color "constituted the vehicle of the divine nature of a sacred animal."[232] Over against the golden lion or falcon, which symbolized morning/midday sunlight, the black bovine symbolized night and materiality.[233] The black bovine was associated with the black

---

[230] On the 'attribute animal' of ancient Near Eastern religion see Erik Hornung, *Conceptions of God in Ancient Egypt: the One and the Many* (Ithaca: Cornell University Press, 1982)109-25; P. Amiet, *Corpus des cylinders de Ras Shamra-Ougarit II: Sceaux-cylinres en hematite et pierres diverses* (Ras Shamra-Ougarit IX; Paris: Éditions Recherche sur les Civilisations, 1992) 68; "Attribute Animal" in idem, *Art of the Ancient Near East*, trans. J. Shepley and C. Choquet (New York: Abrams, 1980) 440 n. 787.

[231] On the symbolism of the bull see Mircea Eliade, *Patterns in Comparative Religion*, translated by Rosemary Sheed (1958; Lincoln and London: University of Nebraska Press, 1996) 82-93; Karel van der Toorn, Bob Becking and Pieter W. van der Horst (edd.), *Dictionary of Deities and Demons in the Bible*, 2nd Edition (Leiden and Grand Rapids, MI.: Brill and Eerdmans, 1999) s.v. "Calf," by N. Wyatt, 180-182; *ERE* 2:887-889 s.v. Bull, by C.J. Caskell. See also René L. Vos, "Varius Coloribus Apis: Some Remarks of the Colours of Apis and Other Sacred Animals," in Willy Clarysse, Antoon Schoors and Harco Willems (edd.), *Egyptian Religion: The Last Thousand Years*, **Part 1. Studies Dedicated to the Memory of Jan Quaegebeur** (Leuven: Uitgeverij Peeters en Departement Oosterse Studies, 1998) 715, who notes that the bulls of Egypt "materialize upon the earth the creative forces of the hidden demiurge (creator-god)."

[232] "Varius Coloribus Apis," 711.

[233] Asko Parpola, "New correspondences between Harappan and Near Eastern glyptic art," *South Asian Archaeology* 1981, 178 notes: "Indeed, the golden-skinned hairy lion is an archetypal symbol for the golden-rayed sun, the lord of the day…Night…is equally well represented by the bull, whose horns connect it with the crescent of the moon." On the bull and the moon-god in ancient Near Eastern mythology see also Tallay Ornan, "The Bull and its Two Masters: Moon and Storm Deities in Relation to the Bull in Ancient Near Eastern Art," *Israel*

primordial waters from which the creator-god emerged;[234] it thus came to symbolize the black material body that the creator-god will form for himself, the black skin of the bovine signaling the black skin of the deity[235] ; see e.g. the black skin of the Egyptian deity Min, the "creator god *par excellence*," and his attribute animal the black bull (*Mnevis*).[236] In

---

*Exploration Journal* 51 (2001) 1-26; Dominique Collon, "The Near Eastern Moon God," in Diederik J.W. Meijer (ed.), **Natural Phenomena: Their Meaning, Depiction and Description in the Ancient Near East** (North-Holland, Amsterdam, 1992) 19-37. On the falcon as symbol of the sun-god see J. Assmann, *Liturgische Lieder an den Sonnengott. Untersuchungen zur ägyptischen Hymnik I* (MÄS 19; Berlin, 1969) 170-1.

[234] Parpola, "New correspondences," 181 suggests that "the dark buffalo bathing in muddy water was conceived as the personification of the cosmic waters of chaos". In the *Ṛg Veda* the cosmic waters are cows (e.g. 4.3.11; 3.31.3; 4.1.11) and in *Pañcaviṃśa-Brāmana* 21.3.7 the spotted cow Śabalā is addressed: "Thou art the [primeval ocean]." On water and cows in Indic tradition see further Anne Feldhaus, **Water and Womanhood. Religious Meanings of Rivers in Maharashtra** (New York and Oxford: Oxford University Press, 1995) 46-47. On the black bull and the black waters of creation see also Vos, "Varius Coloribus Apis," 715, 718.

[235] Thus the Buchis bull of Armant, whose name means something like "who makes the *ba* dwell within the body." See Dieter Kessler, "Bull Gods," in Donald B. Redford (ed.), **The Ancient Gods Speak: A Guide to Egyptian Religion** (Oxford: Oxford University Press, 2002) 30.

[236] Martin Bernal, **Black Athena: The Afroasiatic Roots of Classical Civilization, Volume II: *The Archaeological and Documentary Evidence*** (New Brunswick, NJ: Rutgers University Press, 2002) 166-177, who notes (170): "There is no doubt that Min's principle animal was a bull. Not only was he called *K3 mwt.f* but also *K3 nfr* (Beautiful Bull) and *K3 nḫt* (Mighty Bull)." G.D. Hornblower, "Min and His Functions," **Man** 46 [1946]: 116 [art.=113-121] had already suggested that Min might have been the original 'bull god' prototype of the numerous sacred bulls of Egypt. 'Attribute Animals' were fauna that symbolically represented particular attributes or characteristics of the anthropomorphic gods. Mnevis is the Greek name of the black bull god of Heliopolis associated with the god Atum whom the Egyptians called *Mr Wr*. But it appears that at an earlier time he was Min's primary Attribute Animal and one of the many Min-to-Atum inheritances. The untranslatable name *Mr Wr* is probably an evolution from *Mn Wr*, since from the earliest times there had been interchange of the biconsonantals *mr, mn, nm*, all of which are associated with cattle (Bernal, **Black Athena**, II: 174). This would make Mnevis's original native name not "The Great *Mr*" but the "Great *Mn* (Min)." Hornblower's ("Min and His Functions," 116) reasoning and conclusion are thus sound: "It would seem that the theological origin of Mnevis had long been lost to memory and that in the early days it was an incarnation, or

Osiris.        Apis Bull

at least intimate symbol, of Min, for in the classical age its name was *Mr Wr*, of which the meaning is not known, but in the Late Period the reading *mnĭ* occurs, which was probably the name current among the people and thus found its way into the Greek records. A simple explanation of *mnĭ* may be that the bull belonged to Min (*mn*). It is interesting to note that it was also giving in the Abydos table of kings and the Turin papyrus as the name of the first king of Egypt, transcribed by the Greeks as Menes, who, it may be noted, was called also Mnevés by Diodorus (I, 94)."

During the New Kingdom, specifically the Eighteenth and Twentieth Dynasties, he was associated with a great white bull, particularly during his *prt Mnw* festival (Gauthier, ***Les fêtes du dieu Min***, 200). But his priesthood included those called 'keepers of the black cow (*iḥt kmt*) of Min" indicating that a black cow was a part of the cult (H.Gauthier, ***Les fêtes du dieu Min*** 2 vols. [Le Caire, 1931; IFAO. Recherches d'Archéologie] 2:55-57; Bernal, ***Black Athena***, II: 176). We have seen that the black bull Mnevis was likely called *Mn Wr* (the Great Min) and originally associated with the god Min in the Predynastic and early Dynastic periods. Ironically, this may account for the later association of Min with the white bull, for whenever the required completely black bull could not be found for the Mnevis cult, a contrasting completely white bull was chosen in its place. We can thus easily see how the original black god (Min)/black bull (Mnevis) association could by dint of circumstance become the black god/white bull association of later times. This happenstance may have been reinforced by Min's later association with the Egyptian long-leaf lettuce (*Lactuca sativa*), which is known as "White Bull." Further, from the Middle Kingdom on the cult of Min is characterized by the religious semantics of other deities, contributing in part to new manifestations of Min (**IDD** s.v. Min by Carsten Knigge Salis and Maria Michela, 1). In this regard, Min's specifically New Kingdom white bull seems to have been influenced by the earlier white bull of Hermonthis (Armant), the Buchis bull of the god Montu, first mentioned in the Thirteenth Dynasty during the reign Nectanebo II. See Pat Remler, ***Egyptian Mythology, A to Z*** Revised Edition (New York: Chelsea House, 2010) 34 s.v. Buchis Bull; Wainwright, "Some Celestial Associations," 158.

Egypt also the Black God Osiris had the black bull (*k' km*) Apis, who personified the waters of the Nile which was regarded as a type of Nu, the dark, primeval watery mass out of which creation sprang.[237] In Sumer the god Enki was called *am-gig-abzu*, 'black bull of the Apsû (primordial waters).'"[238] The hide of the sacrificial bull of ancient Sumer/Akkad, which was required to be 'black as asphalt,' was ritually identified with the skin of the Sumerian/Akkadian creator-deity Anu, who is also Enki.[239] According to the 'Theology of the Black God' that was a central component of the ancient Mystery Schools, the creator-deity emerged from these waters as a so-called 'sun-god,' initially possessing a body of brilliant white or golden light, but later chose to cloak this fiery, *transcendent* body with a more accessible, tolerable (for his creatures) black body, made out of the matter of the primordial waters. It is this aquatic black body that is represented by the black bull.

This Divine Bull, that is to say the bull used to represent the all-powerful male creator-god, was therefore a black bull, in particular the now extinct (sic) *Bos primigenius* or aurochs bull (see Plate 1).[240] Standing two meters to the shoulders and weighing upwards of a ton with a meter-wide spread of horns, the *Bos primigenius* was an immense beast, a contemporary of the other

---

[237] See Émile Chassinat, "La Mise a Mort Rituelle D'Apis," *Recueil de travaux relatifs a la philology et a l'archeologie egyptiennes et assyriennes* 38 [1916] 33-60; E.A. Wallis Budge, *The Egyptian Book of the Dead (The Papyrus of Ani). Egyptian Text Transliterated and Translated* [New York: Dover Publications, Inc. 1967] cxxiii).

[238] See Albright, "Mouth of the Rivers," 167. On the black bull and the black waters of creation see also Vos, "Varius Coloribus Apis," 715, 718.

[239] In one description of the Babylonian *kalū*-ritual the slaying and skinning of the black bull is mythologized as the god Bēl's slaying and flaying of the god Anu, whose characteristic attribute animal was the black bull. See Daum, *Ursemitische Religion*, 204; E. Ebeling, *Tod und Leben nach den Vorstellungen der Babylonier* 2 vols. (Berlin-Leipzig, 1931) 1:29; C. Bezold, *Babylonisch-assyrisches Glossar* (Heidelberg: C. Winter, 1926) 210 s.v. sugugalu; Georgia de Santillana and Hertha von Dechend, *Hamlet's Mill: An essay on myth and the frame of time* (Boston: Gambit, Inc., 1969) 124. On Anu see further Herman Wohlstein, *The Sky-God An-Anu* (Jericho, New York: Paul A. Stroock, 1976). On Anu as Enki see Wesley Muhammad, *Black Arabia and the African Origin of Islam* (Atlanta: A-Team Publishing, 2009) 91-109.

[240] Rice, *Power of the Bull*, 23-24.

megaforms: the mammoth and huge Irish elk. This bull had powerfully developed and coordinated flesh, muscle and bone, making him the paragon of power and nobility. As Michael Rice writes in his study of the ancient and wide-spread bull-cult:

> The essential and distinctive elements in the bull's status in antiquity are the recognition of his nobility as a lordly beast...and his concentrated, highly coordinated power...the bull is the epitome of cheiftaincy, hence of kingship...The bull is always portrayed in all his vigour, potency and beauty.[241]

The beauty of the aurochs bull has much to do with its distinctive dense black coat with a white stripe running down its spine and white curly tuft between its horns. In the ancient bull-cult of the historic religions this black bull-hide is associated with the black primordial waters and signals the black skin of the creator-god who emerged out of those waters and produced therefrom an earthly body.

This association between divine and bovine skin is explicitly articulated, for example, in the Indic[242] scripture *Śatapatha-Brāhmaṇa*[243] with regard to the black *tārpya* garment worn by the king during the Indic royal consecration ceremony called *Rājasūya*. During this ceremony the king ritually impersonated the creator-god and divine king Prajāpati-Varuṇa.[244] The black *tārpya* garment worn by the king represented the body of the royal creator-god (Prajāpati-Varuṇa) whom the king impersonated here.[245] Regarding the *tārpya* garment and by

---

[241] Ibid., 274.
[242] I will use 'Indic' throughout this work to refer to the traditions of ancient India, as opposed to 'Indian,' which is popularly, though erroneously, associated with the indigenous groups of the early Americas.
[243] Brāhmanas are Vedic texts dealing with priestly sacrifices and rituals.
[244] See J. Gonda, "Vedic Gods and the Sacrifice," *Numen* 30 (1983): 1-34; Walter O. Kaelber, "'Tapas,' Birth, and Spiritual Rebirth in the Veda," *History of Religions* 15 (1976): 343-386; Johannes Cornelis Heesternman, *The Ancient Indian Royal Consecration: The rājasūya described according to the Yajus texts and annotated* (The Hague: Mouton & Co., 1957).
[245] See Heesternman, *Ancient Indian Royal Consecration* on the somatic significance of the ritual garments. Specifically, the black antelope skins represent the black skin of the divine king Varuṇa who personifies the primordial waters. On the black skinned Varuṇa see *Śatapatha-Brāhmana* 11.6.1. On

implication its divine counterpart, *Śatapatha-Brāhmaṇa* 3, 1, 2, 13-17 notes:

> it (i.e. the *tārpya* garment) is indeed his (i.e. king's) own skin he thereby puts on himself. Now that skin which belongs to the cow was originally on man. The gods spake, 'Verily, the cow supports everything here (on earth); come, let us put on the cow that skin which is now on man; therewith she will be able to endure rain and cold and heat. Accordingly, having flayed man, they put that skin on the cow, and therewith she now endures rain and cold and heat. For man was indeed flayed; and hence wherever a stalk of grass or some other object cuts him, the blood trickles out. They then put that skin, the (*tārpya*) garment, on him; and for this reason none but man wears a garment, it having been put on him as his skin...Let him, then, not be naked in the presence of a cow. For the cow knows that she wears his skin, and runs away for fear lest he should take the skin from her.[246]

In explaining the relation between the black ritual garment and the black cow skin, it is here recalled that the latter actually was once man's own skin, who lost it to the cow (man was 'flayed'). This black bovine skin apparently once covered man's fleshy skin as an exterior layer, according to this mythical account. In place of this lost exterior layer, man was given the black *tārpya* garment. Now whenever the cow sees a naked man it flees in fear of him trying to retrieve his original 'garment,' the black skin that now protects the cow from inclement weather. It must be kept in mind that the Vedas are the literary work appropriated and edited by the invading Indo-Aryan tribes, and this description of the flaying of man's black skin reflects the actual experience of the indigenous 'black, snub-nosed' Dasyus tribes who were indeed flayed by the

---

Varuṇa and the black sacrificial garments see further Alfred Hillebrandt, **Vedic Mythology**, trans. from the German by Sreeramula Rajeswara Sarma, 2 vols. (Delhi: Motilal Banarsidass Publishers, 1999; reprint) 2: 41, 44-45. On Varuṇa in Indic mythology generally see ibid. 2:1-47; Alain Daniélou, **The Myths and Gods of India** (1964; Rochester, Vermont: Inner Traditions International, 1985) 118-121; F.B.J. Kuiper, **Varuṇ and Vidūṣaka. On the Origin of the Sanskrit Drama** (Amsterdam/Oxford/New York: North-Holland Publishing Company, 1979); Sukumari Bhattacharji, **The Indian Theogony: A Comparative Study of Indian Mythology From the Vedas to the Purāṇas** (Cambridge: Cambridge University Press, 1970) Chapter One.

[246] Trans. J. Eggeling, **The Śatapatha- Brāhmana according to the text of the Mādhyandina school.** I-V. **Sacred Books of the East** (Oxford, 1882-1900) II: 9f.

Aryan hordes. This historical flaying is mythologized in the *Ṛg Veda* (I. 130-8) where the Aryan deity Indra is described as tearing off the black skin of the Asura, the gods of the pre-Aryan black tribes.[247] In this *Rājasūya* or consecration ritual the human king is impersonating the divine king, God, whose skin is represented by the bovin skin. The black garment/bovine skin represents the black skin of the pre-Aryan black gods. Asko Parpola has demonstrated that both the *tārpya* garment and its divine analogue, the 'sky garment' of the gods (i.e. the divine body), are associated with the skin of the mythic 'bull of heaven.'[248]

III.     Birth of the Black Man (God)

*our First Father formed and designed Himself. Think over a Man being able to design His own form and He had never seen another Man before He saw Himself. This is a powerful thing.* The Honorable Elijah Muhammad

Before creating the cosmos, according to ancient African tradition, the black god created himself, or, rather, his body: "O Rē' who gave birth to righteousness, sovereign who created all this, who built his limbs, who modeled his body, who created

---

[247] On the historical conflict between the invading Aryans and the indigenous black tribes of India, and its mythic portrayal in the Vedas as the conflict between the Devas and the Asuras, see Ram Sharan Sharma, **Sūdras in Ancient India. A Social history of the lower order down to circa A.D. 600** (Delhi: Molilal Banarsidass, 1980) Chapt. II; Daniélou, **Myths and Gods of India**, 139-146. On the racial background of the Asuras see also R. Ruggles Gates, "The Asurs and Birhors of Chota Nagpur," in T.N. Madan and Gopāla Śarana (edd.), **Indian Anthropology. Essays in Memory of D.N. Majumdar** (New York: Asia Publishing House, 1962) 163-184.

[248] **The Sky-Garment: A Study of the Harappan religion and its relation to the Mesopotamian and later Indian religion** (SO 57; Helsinki, 1985); idem, "The Harappan 'Priest-King's' Robe and the Vedic Tārpya Garment: Their Interrelation and Symbolism (Astral and Procreative)," **South Asian Archaeology** 1983, vol. 1, 385-403. On the garments of the gods in ancient Near Eastern tradition see A. Leo Oppenheim, "The Golden Garments of the Gods," **Journal of Near Eastern Society of Columbia University** 8 (1949): 172-193; Herbert Sauren, "Die Kleidung Der Götter," **Visible Religion** 2 (1984): 95-117; David Freedman, "Ṣubāt Bāàti: A Robe of Splendor," **JANES** 4 (1972): 91-5. See also Alan Miller, "The Garments of the Gods in Japanese Ritual," **Journal of Ritual Studies** 5 (Summer 1991): 33-55.

himself, who gave birth to himself."[249] According to this mythic tradition there was in the beginning only darkness, material darkness universally described as 'water.'[250] Hidden within this dark primordial water was the deity in a formless, luminous state. This primordial 'water' was characterized by what the Indic texts call *jāmi*, the unproductive state of non-differentiation of its constituent elements. All potential dualities (e.g. light/darkness, spirit/matter, male/female), which are a prerequisite to the generative process, lay undistinguished and negatively homogeneous; the ancient Egyptians called it the "state in which did not yet exist 'two things'." Creation begins with the distinguishing and separation of these elements.[251] How long this primeval, homogeneous mass with its hidden divine luminosity existed is not indicated. At some point, however, God's luminosity concentrated itself within the primordial waters into a single point, producing the first distinguishable particle of

---

[249] From Theb. Tomb 157: translation from J. Zandee, "The Birth-Giving Creator-God in Ancient Egypt," in Alan B. Lloyd (ed.), *Studies in Pharaonic Religion and Society, in Honour of J. Gwyn Griffiths* (London: The Egypt Exploration Society, 1992) 175 [art.=168-185]. See also the hieratic Coffin Text 714: "I (Atum) created my body in my glory; I am he who made myself; I formed myself according to my will and according to my heart." Translation from John D. Currid, in his *Ancient Egypt and the Old Testament* (Grand Rapids, Michigan: Baker Books, 1997), 58.

[250] An ancient Egyptian Coffin Text (Spell 80) mentions "the darkness *(kkyt)* of Nun." See Helmer Ringgren, "Light and Darkness in Ancient Egyptian Religion," in *Liber amicorum. Studies in honour of Professor Dr. C.J. Bleeker. Published on the occasion of his retirement from the chair of the history of religions and the phenomenology of religion at the University of Amsterdam* (SHR 17; Leiden: E.J. Brill, 1969) 143 [art.=140-150]. On the primordial waters in ancient myth see also Tamra Andrews, *Legends of the Earth, Sea, and Sky: An Encyclopedia of Nature Myths* (Santa Barbara, California: ABC-CLIO, 1998) s.v. Primordial Sea, 181-82; Eliade, **Patterns**, Chapter Five; Philip Freund, *Myths of Creation* (New York: Washington Square Press, Inc, 1965) Chapter Four.

[251] Hans-Peter Hasenfratz, "Patterns of Creation in Ancient Egypt," in Henning Graf Reventlow and Yair Hoffman (edd.), *Creation in Jewish and Christian Tradition* (JSOTSup 319; Sheffield: Sheffield Academic Press, 2002) 174 [art.=174-178]; John Irwin, " 'Asokan' Pillars: The Mystery of Foundation and Collapse," in Gilbert Pollet (ed.), *India and the Ancient World: History, Trade and Culture Before A.D. 650* (OLA 25; Leuven: Departement Oriëntalistiek, 1987) 87-93.

luminous matter,[252] the mythical 'golden germ' or fiery a-tom,[253] the quark of modern-day quantum physics.[254] This soon developed into an atom,[255] described mythically as the 'golden egg.'

## THE COSMOGONIC EGG AND THE PRIMORDIAL ATOM

*How came the Black God, Mr. Muhammad? This is the way he was born - in total darkness. There was no light nowhere. And out of the orbit of the universe of darkness there sparkled an Atom of Life. Long before there was a where and a when, He (the Black God) was God. A little small Atom of Life rolling around in darkness...building up itself...just turning in darkness, making its own self...How came the Black God, Mr. Muhammad? He is Self-Created.* The Honorable Elijah Muhammad

Ancient tradition described the primordial atom, in which everything (including God) was originally contained and out of which everything (including God) emerged, as an egg. [256] This

---

[252] Françoise Dunand and Christiane Zivie-Coche, ***Gods and Men in Egypt: 3000 BCE to 395 CE***, translated from the French by David Lorton (Ithaca and London: Cornell University Press, 2002) 51 note: "Matter was already in Nun, waiting to be coagulated to a point where the dry contrasted with the unformed matter."

[253] On the cosmogonic egg in Egyptian tradition see Clifford, ***Creation Accounts***, 106, 112; Clark, ***Myth and Symbol***, 56. On the Sumerian creator-god An/Anu planting the primordial seed see Richard J. Clifford, ***Creation Accounts in the Ancient Near East and the bible*** (CBQMS 26; Washington, DC; Catholic Biblical Association of America, 1994) 26-29 and 39, where the author quotes an ancient Sumerian text entitled *Bird and Fish*, where mention is made of "the life-giving waters that begat the fecund seed."

[254] Marie-Louise Von Franz, ***Creation Myths***, revised edition (Boston and London: Shambhla, 1995) in her discussion of cosmogonic "Germs and Eggs" appropriately describes the mythical germ as "an enormous concentration of energy in...one center,", 232. These descriptions identify the 'golden germ' with the quark (a-tom) of modern physics, the fundamental particle of matter, which is also a "ball" and "center of (fiery) energy." See Lawrence M. Krauss, ***Atom: An Odyssey from the Big Bang to Life on Earth...And Beyond*** (Boston: Little, Brown and Company, 2001); Leon Lederman with Dick Teresi, ***The God Particle: If the Universe is the Answer, What is the Question*** (New York: Dell Publishing, 1993); Isaac Asimov, ***Atom: Journey Across the Subatomic Cosmos*** (New York: Truman Talley Books, 1992).

[255] On the relation of the a-tom (quark) and the atom see sources cited above n. 502.

[256] On the cosmogonic egg see von Franz, ***Creation Myths*** Chapter Eight ("Germs and Eggs"); de Vries, ***Dictionary***, 158-9 s.v. egg; *ER* 5:36-7 s.v. Egg by Venetia

'Cosmogonic' or 'Mundane' Egg symbolized the key to the mystery of Origins. The Egg symbolized *prima material*,[257] that 'primeval* substance in creation,'[258] or 'progenitive germ,'[259] from which the world evolved. As Philip Freund pointed out in 1965, this cosmogonic egg is the same as the 'primordial atom' of modern scientific theories on the origin of the universe.[260] In fact, the primordial atom, first proposed by Abbé Georges Lemaître, physicist at Louvain University, has since been called by scientists "Lemaître's Egg" in recognition of its relation to the cosmogonic egg of the ancients. Isaac Asimov, for example, in his *Atom: Journey Across the Subatomic Cosmos*, describes the beginning of the universe from a scientist's perspective in a way that radically approaches the beginning as described by these ancient religious texts:

> there was a time when the matter and energy of the Universe were literally squashed together into one exceeding dense mass. (The Belgian astronomer Abbé Georges Henri Lemaitre) called it the cosmic egg...If we consider the situation before the cosmic egg was formed, we might

---

Newall; idem, *An Egg at Easter: A Folklore Study* (Bloomington: Indiana University Press, 1971) Chapter One; Eliade, *Patterns*, 413-416; Anna-Britta Hellbom, "The Creation Egg," *Ethnos* 1 (1963): 63-105; Robert Wildhaber, "Zum Symbolgehalt und zur Ikonographie des Eies,' *Deutsches Jahrbuch für Volkskunde* 6 (1960): 7ff; H.J. Sheppard, "Egg Symbolism in Alchemy," *Ambix* 6 (August, 1958): 140-148; Freund, *Myths of Creation*, Chapter Five; Martti Haavio, *Väinämöinen: Eternal Sage* (Helsinki, 1952) 45-63; Franz Lukas, "Das Ei als kosmogonische Vorstellung," *Zeitschrift des Vereins für Volkskunde* (Berlin, 1894) 227-243; James Gardner, *The Faiths of the World: A Dictionary of All Religions and Religious Sects, their Doctrines Rites, Ceremonies and Customs*, 2 vols. (Edinburgh: A. Fullarton & Co., 1860) 1:797-8 s.v. Egg (Mundane). In Indic tradition see further F.B.J. Kuiper, "Cosmogony and Conception: A Query," *HR* 10 (1970): 100-104 [art.=91-138]; Gonda, "Background"; H. Lommel, "Der Welt-ei-Mythos im Rig-Veda," *Mélanges Bally* (Geneva, 1939) 214-20. On the cosmic egg as *prima materia* see also C.G. Jung, *Psychology and Alchemy* (2nd ed.; Princeton: Princeton University Press, 1968) 202. On the golden cosmogonic egg and the primordial atom see Freund, *Myths of Creation*, Chapter 15; True Islam, *The Book of God: An Encyclopedia of Proof that the Black Man is God* (Atlanta: All in All Publishing, 1999) 148-151.

[257] Jung, *Psychology and Alchemy*, 202.
[258] Hillbom, "Creation Egg," 64.
[259] Freund, *Myths of Creation*, 49.
[260] Ibid., 180.

visualize a vast illimitable sea of nothingness...The nothingness contains energy...The Pre-Universe...had energy, and although all of its properties were otherwise those of a vacuum, it is called a false vacuum. Out of this false vacuum, a tiny point of matter appears where the energy, by blind forces of random changes, just happens to have concentrated itself sufficiently for the purpose. In fact, we might imagine the illimitable false vacuum to be a frothing, bubbling mass, producing bits of matter here and there as the ocean waves produce foam.[261]

## THE PRIMORDIAL ATOM AND THE BIRTH OF GOD

*The Atom out of which Man was created came from space. It was out in space where He originated. An Atom of Life was in the darkness of the space and He came out of that Atom...What came out of space was a Human Being.* The Honorable Elijah Muhammad

According to these ancient texts this 'egg' or atom (also depicted as a lotus plant) began rotating and moving 'on the waters,' which movement originated time.[262] Within this atom the creator-deity now resided and, eventually, from this atom he emerged as a luminous *anthropos* (man),[263] the so-called sun-god

---

[261] Asimov, *Atom*, 304-310 On the congruence between modern quantum physics and ancient Eastern thought see the still insightful Fritjof Capra, *The Tao of Physics* (3rd ed.; Boston: Shambhala, 1991).

[262] On the birth of time in Egyptian cosmogonic tradition see Dunand and Zivie-Coche, *Gods and Men in Egypt*, 64-70.

[263] As von Franz remarks: "the motif of the human form of the first creative being, an anthropos figure...is another very widespread archetypal motif in creation myths." *Creation Myths*, 34. See also Dunand and Zivie-Coche, *Gods and Men in Egypt*, 48: "This (creator-)god was autogenous...He modeled his own body, and we must say that this was almost always anthropomorphically". In African Near Eastern and Indic tradition, cosmogony (birth of the cosmos), theogony (birth and evolution of God/gods) and anthropogony (creation of man) are all revealed to be the same evolutionary process described from different perspectives. Thus, in Egyptian and Indic wisdom embryogony, i.e. the development of the human embryo in the womb, recapitulates and therefore gives insight into the theo-cosmogonic process. See David Leeming and Margaret Leeming, *A Dictionary of Creation Myths* New York and Oxford: Oxford University Press, 1994) 31-33 s.v. Birth as Creation Metaphor; Jan Assmann, *Egyptian Solar Religion in the New Kingdom. Re, Amun and the Crisis of Polytheism*, translated from the German by Anthony Alcock (London and New York: Kegan Paul International, 1995) 175; Ragnhild Bjerre Finnestad, *Image of the World and Symbol of the Creator. On the Cosmological and Iconological Values of the Temple of Edfu* (SOR 10; Wiesbaden: Otto Harrassowitz, 1985); F.B.J. Kuiper, "Cosmogony and Conception: A Query," *HR* 10 (1970): 91-183

such as Atum-Rē' of Egypt.[264] When the creator-god first emerged, the ancient sources tell us, he lacked the black-body. Indeed, he was light that separated from and emerged out of the darkness.[265] His body, we are told, was originally a body of light described variously as white gold, yellow gold or red gold.[266] The brilliance of this body surpassed that of the sun, which the creator-deity (sun-god) created only as a sign and a 'vicar.'[267]

---

[=*Ancient Indian Cosmogony*, 90-137]; Mircea Eliade, "Cosmogonic Myth and 'Sacred History'," **Religious Studies** 2 (1967): 171-83; Manly P. Hall, ***Man: Grand symbol of the Mysteries. Thoughts in occult anatomy*** Los Angeles: The Philosophical Research society, 1972).

[264] "there was in the beginning neither heaven nor earth, and nothing existed except a boundless primeval mass of water which was shrouded in darkness and which contained within itself the germs or beginnings, male and female, of everything which was to be in the future world. The divine primeval spirit which formed an essential part of the primeval matter felt within itself the desire to begin the work of creation, and its word woke to life the world, the form and shape of which it had already depicted to itself. The first act of creation began with the formation of an egg out of the primeval water, from which broke forth Rā, the immediate cause of all life upon earth." Quoted from Budge, ***Egyptian Book of the Dead***, xcviii. See also Zandee, "The Birth-Giving Creator-God," 182: "Atum is 'complete' as an androgynous god. He unites within himself masculinity and femininity. He possesses all conditions to bring forth the all out of him. He was a Monad and made himself millions of creatures which he contained potentially in himself. He was the one who came into being of himself (ḫpr ds.f), who was the creator of his own existence, the *causa sui*." In a New Kingdom royal inscription Atum is described as he "who generates himself within the egg." See Assmann, ***Egyptian Solar Religion***, 112. Another image used by the Egyptians to depict the primordial atom out of which the creator-god emerged is the primordial mound (*benben*) that raised out of the primordial waters at the beginning of creation (see Clifford, ***Creation Accounts***, 105-6). This mound was the "first solid matter" brought from the bottom of the waters and it was identified with Atum himself (Traunecker, ***Gods of Egypt***, 77; Irwin, "'Asokan' Pillars," 92. On the Primordial Mound see further idem, "The Sacred Anthill and the Cult of the Primordial Mound," **HR** 21 [1982]: 339-360; idem, "The Mystery of the (Future) Buddha's First Words," ***Annali Instituto Orientale di Napoli*** 41 [1981]: 623-664). It is no coincidence that this primordial atom is identified with and personifies Atum, the god born from that atom.

[265] See Ringgren, "Light and Darkness," 141-42

[266] The Egyptian sun-god is "the brilliant one (h'y)," "white light (wḥḥ ḥddwt)." See Ringgren, "Light and Darkness," 145. Rē' is "gold of the gods," "white gold" with a body "cast ...from gold." See Assmann, ***Egyptian Solar Religion***, 27, 94, 95.

[267] See Budge, ***Egyptian Book of the Dead***, xcvi.

He (God) created Himself and was Light of Himself." "He emitted light from the live atom of Self."[268] "When the first man created Himself, He was the light of the circle. Then He willed the Sun into being. It was six trillion years between the making of the Sun and the creation of man."[269] "When first life germ created in darkness it brought itself into being and became a light of himself and from himself he produced a sphere and mattered it into matter. How could man be a self-light? We need that which gives off a light and the lightning bug is in their own light. The God did that to give you a sign. Jehovah made Moses' skin to shine. Electric is in the light and the light is part of us and we created that sun but the sun did not create us. We are self-created. Since you can't find the end of light, you can't find the end of God. If you can't understand the source of light you can't understand the source of God."[270] ""The Light of God is the light of the Hereafter which will guide the people like the light of the sun."[271]

This brilliantly luminous body proved lethal to his future creation. His creatures were perishing at the sight of it and his cosmos was being scorched.[272] The creator-deity decided to cloak his luminosity in a bodily 'veil,' which he made from the primordial waters out of which he emerged. That primordial matter, black and aqueous, became the substance of his new body, which he wore over the luminous form like a garment, concealing its brilliance.[273] The act of cloaking the divinely luminous form in

---

[268] The Honorable Elijah Muhammad, *Our Savior Has Arrived*, 46.
[269] *The Divine Sayings of the Honorable Elijah Muhammad, Messenger of Allah* (Secretarius Publications, 2002) 17.
[270] The Honorable Elijah Muhammad, "The Position of Men and Women," *Muhammad Speaks Newspaper*
[271] Muhammad, *Divine Sayings*, I:7.
[272] See for example the tales in the *Mahābhārat* (O'flaherty, *Hindu Myths*, 38-43) of Prajāpati-Brahmā's scorching the primordial creation with his 'fiery energy' and in the *Mārkaṇḍeya Prurāṇa* (Ibid., 66-70) of the sun-god Vivasvat whose form radiated excessive heat, scorching the three worlds. On Egyptian parallels see below. On the lethality of seeing the god's luminous body in Egyptian tradition see also Meeks, "Divine Bodies," 58.
[273] In Egypt, Rēʿ transforms (ḫpr) his luminous body into a black body symbolized by the gods Atum and Osiris, both of whom had black bulls as their attribute animal; on Atum's black bull Mnevis see George Hart, *The Routledge Dictionary of Egyptian Gods and Goddesses* [2nd edition; London and New York: Routledge, 2005] 95 s.v. Mnevis; Ions, *Egyptian Mythology*, 40). On Rēʿ darkening and transforming into Atum see See Ringgren, "Light and Darkness," 150; Karl W.Luckert, *Egyptian Light and Hebrew Fire. Theological and Philosophical Roots of Christendom in Evolutionary Perspective* (Albany: State University of

a black body was considered a divine sacrifice[274] - a sacrifice that resulted in the first human being (Allah The Original Man) and which permitted the creation of the (more densely) material world.[275] The First Man, in other words, was the Black God.

Some of this brilliance shown through the hair-pores of the new black body,[276] and the interaction of the white light with the

---

New York Press, 1991) 73. Most often, Rē''s black body is identified with the black god Osiris, who represents the black primordial waters of Nun; see Chassinat, "Mise a Mort Rituelle." On black Osiris as the netherworld body of Rē' see Hasenfratz, "Patterns of Creation," 176; Jan Assmann, *The Search for God in Ancient Egypt*, translated from the German by David Lorton (Ithaca and New York: Cornell University Press, 2001) 41; idem, *Death and Salvation in Ancient Egypt*, translated from the German by David Lorton (Ithaca and London: Cornell University Press, 2005) 188; Clark, *Myth and Symbol*, 158; Martin Lev and Carol Ring, "Journey of the Night Sun," *Parabola* 8 (1983): 14-18; Albert Churchward, *Signs & Symbols of Primordial Man: The Evolution of Religious Doctrines from the Eschatology of the Ancient Egyptians* (Brooklyn: A&B Publishers Group, 1994, reprint ) 63-66, 274-6, 322.

[274] According to the cosmogonic account of Berosses, priest of Bēl-Marduk of Babylon, published in Greek ca. 250 BC, after cleaving the villainous primordial water (Grk. *Omorka*; Baby. *Tiamat*) and creating the cosmos, Bēl-Marduk's luminosity was unbearable for living creatures who were therefore perishing. Bēl-Marduk thus ordered a god to cut off his (i.e. Bēl-Marduk's) head (self-sacrifice); his blood was mixed with earth to form men and animals that could survive. See K.K.A. Venkatachari, "Babylonian, Assyrian and Other Accounts," in Dange, *Myths of Creation*, 36-37. See also Brian K. Smith, "Sacrifice and Being: Prajapati's Cosmic Emission and Its Consequences," *Religion* 32 (1985): 71-87; Gonda, "Vedic Gods and the Sacrifice"; idem, "The Popular Prajapati," *HR* 22 (1982): 129-149; Joshi, "Prajāpati in Vedic Mythology and Ritual."

[275] This sacrificial 'incarnation,' if you will, is often represented metaphorically as the creator-god (re-)uniting with his wife/daughter, the celestial ocean (primordial matter) depicted as the primordial cow. When Rē' as Bull begets with the Divine Cow, i.e. Nut-Nun, the material world with its planets and humans are produced. Thus, "we are all cattle" (see G.S. Bedagkar, "Egyptian, Hebrew and Greek Accounts," in Dange, *Myths of Creation*, 33).

[276] See above and also *Mahābhārata* 5.129.11 which mentions "rays of light, like the sun's, [shining] from [Kṛṣṇa's] very pores." Translated James W. Lane, *Visions of God: Narratives of Theophany in the Mahābhārata* (Vienna 1989) 134. Now Kṛṣṇa, whose name means 'black' (A.L. Basham, *The Wonder that was India* [London: Sidgwick and Jackson, 1954] 305) is in many ways the paradigmatic blue-black god. As David R. Kinsley, *The Sword and the Flute: Kali and Krishna, Dark Visions of the Terrible and the Sublime in Hindu Mythology* (Berkeley: University of California Press, 1975) noted, Kṛṣṇa with his blue-black complexion is the "quintessence of divine beauty": "His appearance is

black body produced a dark-blue iridescence or glow. The result was the sapphiric body of the creator-deity (see Plate 5).[277]

## THE BLUE GOD (LORD OF SAPPHIRE)

In his *Praeparatio Evangelica* (III, 115a, 7) the fourth century church historian Eusebius of Caesarea quoted from Porphyry's (ca. 233-309) lost work, *Concerning Images*, a note on an Egyptian view of the Creator: "The Demiurge (creator-god), whom the Egyptians call Cneph, is of human form, but with a skin of dark

---

redeeming in itself...Over and over again we read of his luminous dark complexion, large dark eyes, black curly hair. For devotees of Kṛṣṇa the image of their blue lord is the quintessence of divine beauty. The *Brahma-vaivarta-purāa*...describes Kṛṣṇa as emanating a blinding light...But Kṛṣṇa's devotees see within that dazzling light to an even more dazzling and redeeming image of their darling...(the) lovely image of Kṛṣṇa located in the center of this light. He is blue like a new cloud." The "dazzling light" is the light emanating through the hair-pores from the dangerously luminous form within the black body (his 'Universal Form', *viśvarūpadarśana*; see *Bhagavadgītā* 11; Lane, **Visions of God**, 135-141). The description "luminous dark complexion" nicely captures the divine paradox.

[277] In ancient Egyptian tradition see e.g. the famous story of the Withdrawal of Rē' to Heaven. After incinerating most humans with his fiery fury personified as his daughter, the ferocious lioness Sekhmet (who, incidentally, got out of hand), Rē' re-entered the primordial water (he mounted the back of Nut-Nun personified as the primordial cow). He thus concealed his luminous body within Nut-Nun. He is now "(he) who conceals his image in the body of Nut," "who conceals his image in his heaven." (P. Leiden I 344 v50.I. 4 and viii.7 in J. Zandee, **Der Amunshymnus des Papyrus Lkeiden I 344**, 3 vols. [Leiden, 1992]. See also Assmann, **Egyptian Solar Religion**, 70-72]. By concealing his luminous body within the body of Nut, Rē' becomes the sapphire-bodied Amun-Re, described as "beautiful youth of purest lapis lazuli (*ḥwn-nfr n-ḥsbd-m3'*) whose "body is heaven" (*ḥt. K nwt*)." See above n. 31. In the Leiden Papyrus stored at the museum in Leiden (see Adolf Erman, "Der Leidener Amons-hymnus," *Sitzungsberichte der Preussischen Akademie der Wissenschaften* 11 [1923]: 66ff) Rē''s dangerously luminous body is described as his 'secret form' hidden within Amun (70-73). On the myth of Rē''s Withdrawal see Robert A. Armour, **Gods and Myths of Ancient Egypt** (2nd edition; Cairo and New York: American University in Cairo Press, 2001) 87-89; Clark, **Myth and Symbol**, 181-186; Stephen Quirke, **The Cult of Ra: Sun-Worship in Ancient Egypt** (New York: Thames & Hudson, 2001) 35-6; Rudolf Anthes, "Mythology in ancient Egypt," in Samuel Noah Kramer (ed.), **Mythologies of the Ancient World** (Garden City, New York: Anchor Books, 1961) 17-22. On Amun's sapphiric body see above.

blue, holding a girdle and a scepter, and crowned with a royal wing on his head."[278] The leading gods of the ancient Near East were not just black, but blue-black. This dark 'blueness' of the divine body had profound significance. It was not just any blue, but sapphire blue.[279]

In biblical tradition and in ancient and medieval texts generally the term 'sapphire' denoted the semiprecious stone lapis lazuli.[280] Considered the "ultimate Divine substance," sapphire/lapis lazuli possessed great mythological significance in the ancient African Near East.[281] In its natural state lapis lazuli is dark blue with fine golden speckles[282] recalling the "sky bedecked with stars"[283]; thus the visible heaven is often said to be sapphiric.[284] This sapphiric heaven, called the 'sky- garment' of

---

[278] Trans. E.H. Grifford, 1903.

[279] The dark blue skin of the anthropomorphic deities of Egypt was *jrtyw* or *ḥsbd* (lapis lazuli), which is a blue-black: See Caroline Ransom Williams, *The Decoration of the Tomb of Per-Nēb* (New York: The Metropolitan Museum of Art, 1932) 52f; J.R. Harris, *Lexicographical Studies in Ancient Egyptian Minerals* (Berlin: Akademie-Verlag, 1961) 226.

[280] Michel Pastoureau, *Blue: The History of a Color* (Princeton: Princeton University Press, 2001) 7, 21f; *The Interpreter's dictionary of the Bible: an illustrated encyclopedia identifying and explaining all proper names and significant terms and subjects in the Holy Scriptures, including the Apocrypha, with attention to archaeological discoveries and researches into life and faith of ancient times* 5 vols. (George Arthur Buttrick et al [edd.]; New York: Abingdon Press, 1962-76) s.v. "Sapphire," by W.E. Stapes; *Dictionary of the Bible*, ed. James Hastings (New York: MacMillian Publishing Company, 1988) 497, s.v. "Jewels and Precious Stones," by J. Patrick and G.R. Berry.

[281] F. Daumas, "Lapis-lazuli et Régénération," in Sydney Aufrère, *L'Univers minéral dans la pensée Égyptienne*, 2 vols. (Le Caire: Institut Français d'Archéologie Orientale du Caire, 1991) 2:463-488; John Irwin, "The Lāṭ Bhairo at Benares (Vārāṇasī): Another Pre-Aśokan Monument?" *ZDMG* 133 (1983): 327-43 [art.=320-352].

[282] On Lapis Lazuli see Lissie von Rosen, *Lapis Lazuli in Geological Contexts and in Ancient Written Sources* (Partille: Paul Åströms förlag, 1988); idem, *Lapis Lazuli in Archaeological Contexts* (Jonsered: Paul Åströms förlag, 1990); Rutherford J. Gettens, "Lapis Lazuli and Ultramarine in Ancient Times," *Alumni de la Fondation universitaire* 19 (1950): 342 357.

[283] See Irwin, "Lāā Bhairo," 332.

[284] Exod. 24:10; Ez. 1:26 (LXX); William Brownlee notes "This dome (of heaven) was thought of as sapphire in color, and as crystalline and transparent." *Ezekiel 1-19* (Waco, TX: Word Books, 1986), 13. Nut, the ancient Egyptian sky goddess, "glistens like lapis lazuli." See Assmann, *Liturgische Lieder*, 314ff. text III 4. The

the gods,[285] was associated with the divine body,[286] 'garment' being an ancient and widespread metaphor for body.[287] Thus, the leading deities of the ancient African Near East had sapphiric-blue bodies. This is particularly the case with deities associated with

---

association of the heavens with precious stones is found in Babylonian cosmologies as well, which may have influenced biblical cosmology. According to W.G. Lambert, the Babylonians associated their three heavens (upper/middle/lower) with stones, the lower deriving its blue from the jasper stone ("The Cosmology of Sumer and Babylon," in Carmen Blacker and Michael Loewe (edd.), *Ancient Cosmologies* [London: George Allen & Unwin Ltd, 1975] 58). In rabbinic literature, the firmament is often made of crystal, whench the heavens derive their light (See Louis Ginzberg, *The Legends of the Jews* [7 vols; Baltimore: John Hopkins University Press, 1911, 1939], vol. 1, 13).

[285] See especially Parpola, *Sky-Garment*; idem, "Harappan 'Priest-King's' Robe"; Oppenheim, "Golden Garments." This designation arises from the golden star-like ornaments or appliqué work sewn into the garment recalling the star-spangled night sky.

[286] Amun-Re is "beautiful youth of purest lapis lazuli (*ḥwn-nfr n-ḥsbd-m3'*) whose "body is heaven" (*ḥt. K nwt*). See J. Assmann, *Sonnenhymnen in thebanischen Gräbern* (Mainz: a.R., 1983) 5, #6:5; 124, # 43:14; A.I. Sadek, *Popular Religion in Egypt During the New Kingdom* (Hildsheim, 1987) 14. See also Grey Hubert Skipwith, " 'The Lord of Heaven.' (The Fire of God; the Mountain Summit; The Divine Chariot; and the Vision of Ezekiel.)," *JQR* 19 (1906-7): 693-4 and illustrations in Othmar Keel, *The Symbolism of the Biblical World. Ancient Near Eastern Iconography and the Book of Psalms* (London: SPCK, 1978) 33-4. In Manichaean tradition, the Mother of Life spread out the heaven with the skin of the Sons of Darkness according to the testimony of Theodore bar Khonai, *Liber Scholiorum* XI, trns. H. Pognon in *Inscriptions Mandaïtes des coupes de Khouabir*, II (Paris: Welter, 1899) 188. In the *Greater Bundahišn*, 189, 8 the cosmic body is said to have "skin like the sky." See also the anthropomorphic body of Zurvan, called *Spihr*, which is associated with both the blue firmament and a blue garment: see R.C. Zaehner, *Zurvan, A Zoroastrian Dilemma* (Oxford, 1955; rep. 1972), 11f, 122. The stars covering the garment signified rays of celestial light emanating from the hair-pores of the divine skin (see below). Thus, in some depictions of this 'sky-garment,' the garment itself is missing and the stars are painted on the very skin of the anthropos. See e.g. the golden statue found in Susa and published by R. de Mecquenem, *Offrandes de fondation du temple de Chouchinak*, (Paris, 1905) vol. II, Pl. XXIV 1a. See also Oppenheim, "Golden Garments," 182 Fig. 2.

[287] Geo Widengren, *The Great Vohu Manah and the Apostle of God: Studies in Iranian and Manichaean Religion* (Uppsala: A.-B. Lundequistska Bokhandeln, 1945) 50-55, 76-83; J.M. Rist, "A Common Metaphor," in idem, *Plotinus: The Road to Reality* (London: Cambridge University Press, 1967) 188-198; Dennis Ronald MacDonald, *There is no Male and Female: The Fate of a Dominical Saying in Paul and Gnosticism* (Philadelphia: Fortress Press, 1987), 23-25.

fecundity or creation.[288] In Egypt, "The traditional colour of (the) gods' limbs (was) the dark blue lapis lazuli."[289] The ancient cult statue, which was considered the earthly body of the deity,[290] was ideally made of a wooden core platted with red gold or silver, overlaid with sapphires,[291] all of which signified substances from

---

[288] John Baines, *Fecundity Figures: Egyptian Personification and the Iconology of a Genre* (Wiltschire: Aris & Phillips and Chicago: Bolchazy-Carducci, 1985) 139-142.

[289] Lise Manniche, "The Body Colours of Gods and Man in Inland Jewellery and Related Objects from the Tomb of Tutankhamun," *Acta Orientalia* 43 (1982): 5-12 (10). On the color of the god's skin as indicative of its status and role, with the sapphiric-bodied deity as 'king of the gods' see Robins, "Color Symbolism," in Redford *Ancient Gods Speak*, 58-9; Monika Dolińsks, "Red and Blue Figures of Amun," *Varia aegyptiaca* 6 (1990): 5-6 [art.=3-7]. On the association of a deities skin color and character see also John Baines, "Color Terminology and Color Classification: Ancient Egyptian Color Terminology and Polychromy," *American Anthropologists* 87 (1985): 284 [art.=282-97]

[290] On the ancient African Near Eastern cult of divine images see Neal H. Walls (ed.) *Cult Image and Divine Representation in the Ancient Near East* (American Schools of Oriental Research Books Series 10; Boston: American Schools of Oriental Research, 2005); Zainab Bahrani, *The Graven Image: Representation in Babylonia and Assyria* (Philadelphia: University of Pennsylvania Press, 2003); Michael B. Dick (ed.), *Born in Heaven, Made on Earth: The Making of the Cult Image in the Ancient Near East* (Winona Lake, Indiana: Eisenbrauns, 1999); idem, "The Relationship between the Cult Image and the Deity in Mesopotamia," in Jiří Prosecký (ed.), *Intellectual Life of the ancient Near East: Papers Presented at the 43rd Rencontre assyriologique international, Prague, July 1-5, 1996* (Prague: Oriental Institute, 1998) 11-16; T. Jacobsen, "The Graven Image," in P.D. Miller Jr., P.D. Hanson and S.D. McBride (edd.), *Ancient Israelite Religion: Essays in Honor of Frank Moore Cross* (Philadelphia: Fortress Press, 1987) 15-32, esp. 16-20;

[291] When King Nabu-apla-iddina of Babylon (ca. 887-855 BC) restored the image (*ṣalmu*) of the god Shamash, it was made of "red gold and clear lapis lazuli": L.W. King, *Babylonian Boundary-Stones and Memorial-Tablets in the British Museum: With Atlas of Plates* (London: British Museum, 1912) 120-127, #36 IV 20. Lugal-zagesi, *ensi* (governor) of Ummah, during his sack of Lagash (ca. 2340 B.C.E.) is said to have plundered the temple of the goddess Amageštin and robed her "of her precious metal and lapis lazuli, and threw her in the well." H. Steible, *Die altsumerischen Bau- und Weihinschriften* (Freiburger Altorientalische Studien 5; Wiesbaden: F. Steiner, 1982): Ukgagina 16:6:11-7:6. The reference is likely to the goddesses cult statute. See Michael B. Dick, "The Mesopotamian Cult Statute: A Sacramental Encounter with Divinity," in Walls, *Cult Image*, 49. See also the lament of Ninšubur on the occasion of Inanna's 'Descent to the Netherworld" (II. 43-46):

the body of the deity: "his (i.e. Rē''s) bones are silver, his flesh is gold, his hair genuine lapis-lazuli."[292] But the hair too was a metaphor for rays of light emanating from the hair-pores covering the body[293] and lapis lazuli was considered 'solidified celestial light'.[294] The deity's whole body was therefore depicted blue.[295]

---

O Father Enlil, let no one in the Netherworld kill your child!
Let no one smelt your fine silver along with crude ore! (on the translation of this line see A.R. George, "Observations on a Passage of 'Inanna's Descent'," *JCS* 37 [1985]: 109-13)
Let no one cleave your fine lapis lazuli along with the lapidary's stones!
Let no one cut up your boxwood along with the carpenter's timber!
Let no one in the Netherworld kill the young woman Inanna!

Inanna's statue is thus made of boxwood (*taškarinnu*), plated with silver and overlaid with lapis lazuli. Cf. the *eršemma* of Ningirgilu (*CT* 15 23). On the above passage as a reference to Inanna's cult statue see also Giorgio Buccellati, "The Descent of Inanna as a Ritual Journey to Kutha?" *Syro-Mesopotamian Studies* 3 (1982): 3-7. On Egyptian cult statues and lapis-lazuli see Daumas, "Lapis-lazuli et Régénération," 465-67. On the materials used for the construction of divine images see Victor Hurowitz, "What Goes In Is What Comes Out – Materials for Creating Cult Statues" in G. Beckman and T.J. Lewish (edd.), *Text and Artifact – Proceedings of the Colloquium of the Center for Judaic Studies, University of Pennsylvania, April 27-29, 1998*, Brown Judaic Series, 2006 (in press).
[292] Gay Robins, "Cult Statues in Ancient Egypt," in Walls, *Cult Image*, 6; idem, "Color Symbolism," 60; Claude Traunecker, *The Gods of Egypt*, translated from the French by David Lorton (Ithaca and London: Cornell University Press, 2001) 44; Dmitri Meeks, "Divine Bodies," in Dimitri Meeks and Christine Favard-Meeks, *Daily Life of the Egyptian Gods*, translated by G.M. Goshgarian (Ithaca and London: Cornell University Press, 1996) 57; Hornung, *Conceptions of God*, 134.
[293] Ad de Vries, *Dictionary of Symbols and Imagery* (Amsterdam and London: North-Holland Publishing Company, 1974) 39 s.v. Beard; Marten Stol, "The Moon as Seen by the Babylonians," in Diederik J.W. Meijer (ed.), *Natural Phenomena: Their Meaning, Depiction and Description in the Ancient Near East* (North-Holland, Amsterdam, 1992) 255.
[294] On lapis lazuli as "solidified celestial light" see Robins, "Color Symbolism," 60. On rays of light emanating from the divine hair pores see for example *Śatapatha-Brāhmaṇa* 10, 4, 4, 1-2: "When Prajāpati was creating living beings, Death, that evil, overpowered him. He practiced austerities for a thousand years, striving to leave evil behind him. 2. Whilst he was practicing austerities, lights went upwards from those hair-pits of his; and those lights are those stars; as many stars as there are, so many hair-pits there are." Translation by Eggeling. See also below. On ancient Near Eastern parallels see Parpola, *Sky-Garment*, 74.

Mediating between the gold flesh and lapis lazuli 'hair' of the creator deity is the divine black skin signified by the bull hide. The black bull, Ad de Vries informs us, "mediated between fire (gold) and water (lapis lazuli), heaven and earth" (inserts original).[296] The light of the 'golden flesh' passing through the hair-pores of the divine black skin therefore produced a sapphiric 'surrounding splendor.'[297]

This blue-black body of the deity was the most arcane secret of the ancient mysteries. In Egypt it was the mystery of the unity of Rēʿ and his black body Osiris.[298] As one text from a New Kingdom royal tomb associated with the mystery rites reveals: "It is a great mystery, it is Rēʿ and Osiris. He who reveals it will die a sudden death."[299] According to the *Book of Gates* this is the "Mystery of the Great God."[300] In Vedic India, "the central theme of what can be denoted by no other term than Aryan

---

[295] Thus the blue bodied deity Amun. See Traunecker, *Gods of Egypt*, 44; Wainwright, "Some Aspects of Amūn"; Dolińsks, "Red and Blue Figures of Amun."

[296] *Dictionary of Symbols and Imagery*, 69 s.v. Bull. As the 'bull of heaven' the bovine has sapphiric associations as well. See e.g. the statuette from Uruk, Jemdet Nasr period (c. 3200-2900 BC) with trefoil inlays of lapis lazuli: H. Schmökel, *Ur, Assur und Babylon: Drei Jahrtausende im Zweistromland* (Stuttgart, 1955), plate 8, top. In the *Epic of Gilgamesh* (Old Babylonian Version, Tablet IV 170-3) the Bull of heaven has horns of lapis lazuli. Nanna-Sin, moon-god of Sumer and Babylon, is the 'frisky calf of heaven' and the 'lapis lazuli bull.' See Ornan, "The Bull and its Two Masters," 3; Stol, "The Moon," 255. On Nanna-Sin see further *DDD*, s.v. Sîn 782-3 by M. Stol. See also the sapphiric bearded bull in Jeremy Black and Anthony Green, *Gods, Demons and Symbols of Ancient Mesopotamia: An Illustrated Dictionary* (London: British Museum Press, 1992) 44 s.v. bison.

[297] See e.g. A. Massy, *Le Papyrus de Leiden I $_{347}$* (Ghent, 1885) 2 where an Egyptian deity is described as "robed in brilliance and wrapped in turquoise." See further Meeks, "Divine Bodies," 57.

[298] According to Jan Assmann "the most secret Arcanum known to the mysteries of the solar journey" is "the nocturnal union of Re and Osiris." Assmann, *Egyptian Solar Religion*, 28; Idem, *Death and Salvation in Ancient Egypt*, trans. from the German by David Lorton (Ithaca and London: Cornell University Press, 2005) 186. On Osiris as the black body of Rē# see above.

[299] Assmann, *Search for God*, 79.

[300] Quoted in Assmann, *Death and Salvation*, 189.

mysticism"[301] is the secret of Agni (fire) hidden in water (Varuṇa), *viz.* the mystery of the luminous Prajāpati-Brahmā (creator-god) hidden within the black and aqueous body.[302] The Akkadian 'bull-ritual' likewise associated the pelt of the black bull with the "mystery of Anu, Enlil, Ea(Enki) and of Ninmah," i.e. the black gods of Sumer/Akkad.[303]

IV.   *The Great Ancestor and His Sons*

The Self-Created Black God – the first human and the first Black man – is understood to be the biological Ancestor of humanity and Black men in particular are looked at as his blood descendants. The Black God of the Zulu people of pre-colonial South Africa, uNkulunkulu, is described as *Ukoko wetu*, "Our Ancestor." This makes all of us (African people) his blood relation. Thus, Zulu children would sometimes run and shout together, "We are uNkulunkulu."[304] But the male descendents of the God, as his nearest blood relation, are the uNkulunkulu of their own household: "uNkulunkulu is the stalk (of maize =*uhlanga*) and each seed in its turn becomes the head of a family, and each is the uNkulunkulu of his own house."[305] M.J. McVeigh is therefore not off base when he says of the Akan of West Africa: "God is not the wholly other but the 'Great Ancestor', 'the trunk of the tree from which man is a branch', so that Akan religion is in a sense 'the worship of the race'…"[306] J.B. Danquah is even more descriptive, also speaking of the Akan but his observations have more general application as it relates to African spirituality:

> The Great Ancestor is the great father, and all men of the blood of that ancestor are of Him, and are of one blood with all other men created of

---

[301] F.B.J. Kuiper, "The Bliss of Aša," *Indo-Iranian Journal* 8 (1964): 124 [art.=96-129;= *Ancient Indian Cosmogony*, Chapter Four].
[302] Kuiper, "Bliss of Aša"; idem, "Remarks on 'The Avestan Hymn to Mithra'," *Indo-Iranian Journal* 5 (1961): 36-60; idem, "The Heavenly Bucket," in idem, *Ancient Indian Cosmogony*, Chapter 6.
[303] Wohlstein, *Sky-God An-Anu*, 118, 122.
[304] Quoted in Edwin W. Smith, "The Idea of God Among South African Tribes," in idem, *African Ideas of God: A Symposium* (London: Edinburgh House Press, 1950) 103.
[305] Smith, "The Idea of God Among South African Tribes," 106.
[306] M.J. McVeigh, *God in Africa. Conceptions of God in African Traditional Religion and Christianity* (Cape Cod: Claude Stark, 1974) 28.

His blood and breadth. Life, human life, is one continuous blood, from the originating blood of the Great Source of that blood. The continuance of that blood in the continuance of the community is the greatest single factor of existence...[The Great Ancestor] his blood continues to flow in the offspring. He had...created them his enduring family.[307]

In the contemporary world, then, the Black man – especially the male – is the proxy for the Self-Created Black God. As His blood descendent the contemporary Black male is His representative, His deputy, even His *incarnation*.

This point is very important for our discussion of the assault on the Black male in America. As we will demonstrate in the next chapters, European peoples recognized (and recognize today) contemporary Black peoples as the blood relation and proxy of the Self-Created Black God. And by going to war with the Black peoples they encountered, Indo-European peoples were consciously going to war with God.

---

[307] J.B. Danquah, *The Akan Doctrine of God: A Fragment of Gold Coast Ethics and Religion* Second Edition (London: Frank Cass & Co. ltd., 1968) 28, 168.

# 7    White Supremacy and the Black Gods

I. *War of the Gods*

At the end of the famous epic of early Irish literature entitled *Táin Bó Cúalnge*, "The Cattle-Raid of Cooley," we learn of two powerful bulls that warred with each other, a dark brown or black bull named Donn Cúalnge ("Dark[308] [Bull] of Cooley") and a white bull named Findbennach Aí ("The White horned of Aí"). According to one of the tale's prologues[309] these bulls were actually (originally) two humans, each serving a different king. They both were skilled in wielding the power of magic and a rivalry thus developed between them. This rivalry led to their becoming enemies and to a duel of their powers. They used their powers to metamorph into bulls and their brutal battle we read about in *Táin*.

Findbennach Aí and Donn Cúalnge engaged in mortal battle

In the beginning we are not surprised to discover that the white bull's presence in his city sort of feminized the other bulls there: "Because of Findbennach no male animal between the four fords dared utter a sound louder than the lowing of a cow."[310] But then the Donn came to town. On this day when the bulls caught

---

[308] In modern Gaelic Donn is "brown," but earlier it was "dark (covering also black)," probably having an Indo-European etymology *dhus-no* "dark in color." See John Shaw, "A Gaelic Eschatological Folktale, Celtic Cosmology and Dumézil's 'Three Realms'," *The Journal of Indo-European Studies* 35 (2007): 256 [art.=249-273]; Bruce Lincoln, "The Lord of the Dead," *History of Religions* 20 (1981): 229 [art.=224-241].
[309] Entitled *De Chophur in da Muccida*, "The Quarrel of the Two Pig-Keepers."
[310] Bruce Lincoln, *Priests, Warriors, and Cattle: A Study in the Ecology of Religion* (Berkley: University of California Press, 1980) 87.

sight of each other they pawed the ground, their eyes blazing like balls of fire and their nostrils swelled like a smith's bellows in a forge. They rushed each other and collided, each gorging and piercing the other seeking to slaughter and to slay. This went on all day and all night, the men of Ireland able to do nothing but listen to the uproar from the safety of their homes. When they came out of their homes the next morning they saw "the Donn Cúailnge coming past Crúachu from the west with the Findbennach Aí a mangled mess on his antlers and horns."[311] After this long drawn battle, the victorious Black Bull tossed Findbennach's disparate remains around the island which, when they touched the ground, formed various parts of the Ireland landscape.

This is an Irish "epicized" variant of an ancient Indo-European myth of a cosmic war between two gods who personified two peoples. The black bull Donn is both a pre-Christian Irish deity and a conceptual descendent of an important Proto-Indo-European Black God (*Yama*).[312] This epic tale is also rooted in an ancient and widespread Indo-European "myth of black and white conflict," a mytheme documented by Armen Petrosyan and Eric Berne which characterized by a black deity and his white adversary.[313] But this "mytheme" of cosmic war actually recounts a part of Indo-European early *history* that was deemed so important to them that this history was sacralized as myth and ritual. The history I am speaking of is the history of a ancient, long, protracted race war between Indo-European tribes and certain groups of Black indigenes, a war in which most of the battles the Indo-Europeans lost badly (like Findbennach Aí). In fact, "Donn" is no doubt etymologically related also to "Dānu" (<

---

[311] Lincoln, *Priests, Warriors, and Cattle*, 89.
[312] Shaw, "A Gaelic Eschatological Folktale," 254, 256; Lincoln, *Priests, Warriors, and Cattle*, 92 n. 175; idem, "Lord of the Dead," 229.
[313] Armen Petrosyan, "Armenia and Ireland: Myths of Prehistory," in *Ireland and Armenia: Studies in Language, History and Narrative*, ed. Maxim Fomin, Alvard Jivanyan and Séamus Mac Mathúna (Washington D.C.: Institute for the Study of Man, 2012) 126 [art.=113-131]; idem, *The Indo-European and Ancient Near Eastern Sources of the Armenian Epic* (Washington D.C.: Institute for the Study of Man, 2012); Eric Berne, "The Mythology of Dark and Fair: Psychiatric Use of Folklore," *The Journal of American Folklore* 72 (1959): 1-13.

IE *deh₂nu- [*dānu-]), the name of a family from the Asuras,³¹⁴ the Black Gods with whom the early Indo-Aryans battled in route to India. The oldest documented Indo-European religious text – and the religion behind it – had as its chief tenet reflection on and celebration of this five centuries long war and the ultimate Indo-Aryan victory.³¹⁵

II.     *Indo-Aryan War Religion*

Composed probably between 1500 BCE to 1200 BCE the Sanskrit *Ṛig veda* is the oldest extant textual document in an Indo-European language and it is also the oldest extensive document of Indo-European religion.³¹⁶ That means that this textual tradition is window to our earliest look at Indo-European (specifically Indo-Aryan) religious preoccupations. And as Malati Shendge documents, the Ṛig veda is sacred text to "The religion created by Aryans out of the wars waged against Asuras".³¹⁷ The Indo-Aryan steppe peoples who advanced in the Indo-Gangetic plain in the second millennium BCE and eventually conquered the Indus Valley peoples may have originated in the south-eastern region of the Ural Mountains in western Russia.³¹⁸ This advance from western Russia to India was greatly opposed along the way by indigenous peoples whom they encountered during their trek. Their many attempts to settle down in the Indus Valley led to long

---

[314] See Armen Petrosyan, "The Indo-European *H₂ner(t)-s and the Dānu Tribe," *The Journal of Indo-European Studies* 35 (2007): 297-310.
[315] See below.
[316] On the textual history of the Ṛig veda see Michael Witzel, "Vedas and Upaniṣads," in *The Blackwell Companion to Hinduism* ed. Gavin Flood (Blackwell Publishing, 2003): 68-98; idem, "The Development of the Vedic Canon and its Schools: The Social and Political Milieu," in *Inside the Texts, Beyond the Texts: New Approaches to the Study of the Vedas*, ed. Michael Witzel (Cambridge, 1997): 257-345. See also Rein Fernhout, *Canonical Texts, Bearers of Absolute Authority: Bible, Koran, Veda, Tipiṭaka. A Phenomenological Study* (Amsterdam and Atlanta, GA: Rodopi, 1994).
[317] Malati J. Shendge, *The Civilized Demons: The Harappans in Ṛgveda*(New Delhi: Abhinav Publications, 1977) 378.
[318] See e.g. David W. Anthony, *The Horse, the Wheel and Language. How Bronze-Age Riders From the Eurasian Steppes Shaped the Modern World* (Princeton: Princeton University Press, 2007) 397-405.

drawn conflicts with the Black inhabitants.[319] A great many battles were fought and the Aryans lost most of them to their technologically and civilizationally superior opponents, who are called in the Ṛig veda variously *Dasyu, Dāsa,* and *Asura* (i.e. followers of the god *Asura*).[320]

The Aryans contrasted their white/fair complexion (*svitnya*) with the black skin (*kṛṣṇā tvac*) of their enemies, the native Indians, and the latter's gods, whom the Ṛig veda identified as *Ahuras/Asuras*.[321] The Indo-Aryans identified themselves and their deities as *Devas.*

---

[319] On the ethnic background of the ancient Indus Valley populations according to the skeletal remains see discussions by Dr. B.K. Chatterjee and Sri G.D. Kumar, *Comparative Study and Racial Analysis of the Human-remains of Indus Valley Civilization with Particular Reference to Harappa* (Calcutta: W. Newman & Co., n.d.); G.D. Kumar, "The Ethnic Components of the Builders of the Indus Valley Civilization and the Advent of the Aryans," *Journal of Indo-European Studies* 1 (1973): 66-80; Pratap C. Dutta, "Biological Anthropology of Bronze Age Harappans: New Perspectives," in John R. Lukas (ed.), *The People of South Asia: The Biological Anthropology of India, Pakistan, and Nepal* (New York and London: Plenum Press, 1984) 59-75; Kenneth A.R. Kennedy, "Biological Anthropology of Human Skeletons From Harappa 1928 to 1988," *The Eastern Anthropologist* 45 (1992): 55-85. Cf. Kenneth A.R. Kennedy, "Have Aryans been identified in the prehistoric skeletal record from South Asia? Biological anthropology and concepts of ancient races," in George Erdosy (ed.), *The Indo-Aryans of Ancient South Asia: Language, Material Cultural and Ethnicity* (Berlin and New York: Walter de Gruyter, 1995) 32-66. The linguistic evidence strongly suggests that the Indus Valley residents were largely Dravidian and some Austro-Asiatic (Munda speakers). See Asko Parpola, *Deciphering the Indus Script* (Cambridge: University Press, 1994); Walter A. Fairservis, *The Harappan Civilization and its Writing. A Model for the Decipherment of the Indus Script* (Leiden: E.J. Brill, 1992); Iravatham Mahadevan, "Dravidian Parallels in Proto-Indian Script," *Journal of Tamil Studies* 2 (1970): 157-276. See also Gilbert Slater, *The Dravidian Element in Indian Culture* (London: Asian Education Services, 1924).

[320] On these designations for the native peoples encountered by the Aryans see Wash Edward Hale, *Ásura- In Early Vedic Religion* (Delhi: Motilal Banarsidass, 1999 [1986]).

[321] Bisht, "Harrapans and the Ṛgveda," 394: "On entering the Indus plains, (the Aryans) destroyed... the prosperous cities of the non-Āryans who were described by their tribal/ethnic/community names such as *Dāsa, Dasyu* and *Paṇī* and, sometimes, as *Asura*, as the followers of the god *Asura*. They are repeatedly described as adversaries and enemies...and repeatedly looked down upon as *kṛṣṇayonis* (of black race or breed [cf. II.20.7]), and of *kṛṣṇa tvachas* (black skin [cf.

> the non-Āryans ...were described (in the Ṛig veda) by their tribal/ethnic/community names such as *Dāsa, Dasyu* and *Paṇī* and, sometimes, as *Asura*, as the followers of the god *Asura*. They are repeatedly described as adversaries and enemies...and repeatedly looked down upon as *kṛṣṇayonis* (of black race or breed [cf. II.20.7]), and of *kṛṣṇa tvachas* (black skin [cf. I.130.8; IX.41.1]), *kṛṣṇas* (blacks [cf. IV.16.13; VIII.62.18]), *anāses* (flat-nosed [cf. V.29.10]).[322]

We have to qualify "looked down upon" though. As Shendge notes: "On the one hand, the asuras inspired admiration in the devas (Aryans) but on the other, they were hated for exactly those qualities which inspired admiration."[323] These native Blacks encountered by the northern steppes people were the latter's cultural and civilizational *superiors*.[324] The *Ṛig veda* describes them as rich (*dhanīn*, I.33.4) and strong (*śārdhata*, VI.23.2) "regaling in opulence and residing in forts".[325] Their country was covered with a network of prosperous cities with strong centralized and well-established governments, it appears.[326]

The earlier portions of the Ṛig veda attests to violent conflict between the incoming Aryans and the Dāsa/Dasyus/Asura (e.g. II.12.4). It is apparent that, with their fortified settlements (*pur*) on the outskirts of the major cities, the Black indigenes initially had the upper-hand, despite the horse-drawn chariots and metal weapons of the Aryans.[327] The latter thus took loss after loss for generations: "the Brāhmaṇas (texts) are very clear that as long as the Aryas fought on the battle-field, they were constantly defeated by the opponents"[328]; "The Aryans found in these people foes with whom they could not match in

---

I.130.8; IX.41.1]), *kṛṣṇas* (blacks [cf. IV.16.13; VIII.62.18]), *anāses* (flat-nosed [cf. V.29.10])."

[322] Bisht, "Harrapans and the Ṛgveda," 394.
[323] Shendge, **Civilized Demons, 49.**
[324] Shendge, **Civilized Demons**, 144.
[325] Bisht, "Harrapans and the Ṛgveda," 594.
[326] J. F. Hewitt, "Notes on the Early History of Northern India, Part II," *JRAS of Great Britain and Ireland* 21 (1889): 188 [art.=187-359].
[327] Shendge, **Civilized Demons**, 10: "The Aryans found in these people foes with whom they could not match in might."
[328] Malati J. Shendge, *The Aryas: Facts Without Fantasy and Fiction* (New Delhi: Abhinaw Publications, 1996) 31.

might."[329] These circumstances prevailed for approximately 500 years, from ca. 1850 BCE till probably ca. 1300 BCE.

The pendulum seems to have finally swung in favor of the Aryans due to the emergence among them of a particularly effective and cunning war-leader called in the texts *Indra*, both a human military leader and a god (deva).[330] Aided by the treachery employed by a fellow Aryan (Hari), Indra was able to subdue the Asuras. He would thus be lionized in Sanskrit literature for his brutality toward his black enemies. He is praised as *asura-hān*, "Asura killer" and *dasyu-han*, "slayer of the Dasyu" whose "black skin Indra hated" (*Rig Veda* 9.73.5). They Aryans further boast: "After slaying the Dasyus and the Simyus...let him (Indra) with his *white friends* (*sákhibhih śvitnyébhih*) win land, let him win the sun water..." (*Rig Veda* 1.100.18); "Indra elevated the Aryan color/race, he struck down the Dāsa color/race" (Śāṅkhāyana-Śrautasūtra 8.25.1). Indra hated the black skin (*Rig veda* IX.73.5) and punished it (*Rig veda* I.130.8). In IV.16.3 Indra is praised for, among other things, slaying fifty thousand Blacks (*kṛṣṇa*s) and demolishing their cities (IV.16.13). He "took the manliness from the Dasyu (*Rig veda* X.48.2)," a possible reference to castration. This unmanning of the Black Gods by the White God is of particular importance to our discussion, and we will return to it below. Sharma notes further:

> The Āryan deity Soma is described as killing people of black skin, who apparently were Dasyus...The god (Indra) is also described as tearing off the black skin of the Asura...The above-mentioned references...leave little doubt that the Āryan followers of Indra, Agni, and Soma had to fight against the black people of India...The struggle against the Dasyus was attended with much bloodshed...[331]

There are two points of upmost importance to our discussion here:

---

[329] Shendge, *Civilized Demons*, 10.
[330] See R.N. Dandekar, "Vedic Mythology," in *Inside the Texts, Beyond the Texts. New Approaches to the Study of the Vedas*, ed. Michael Witzel (Cambridge, 1997) 37-48; idem., "Vṛtrahā Indra," *Annals of the Bhandarkar Oriental Research Institute* 31 (1950): 1-55.
[331] Sharma, *Śūdras in Ancient India*, 14-15, 16.

1.] This protracted Aryan-Asura war and especially the final Aryan victory was at the heart of the religion of the Vedic Aryans, and thus this race war was *the* preoccupation of the earliest Indo-European religious book available to us today. Many of the earliest hymns in the Ṛig veda were composed to celebrate the Aryan victory over their Black enemies. Shendge describes:

> The Aryan found in these people (Asuras) foes with whom they could not match in might. The struggle was so alive in memory of the Aryans that from *Ṛgveda* onwards their poets were never tired of singing about it and priests never stopped recounting it symbolically during the rites...Right from the earliest stratum of [*Ṛgveda*] the indications of the conflict between the devas and the asuras are found in abundance. It does not end in the Ṛgveda but continues into the Brāhmaṇas, in the Śrauta literature, in the Mahābhārata and a reference to it is found even in the chronicles of Alexander's historian. The initial stages of the conflict as reflected in the Ṛgveda and their religious transformation into Brahmanic ritual show its all-pervading and excruciating character. Though the events took place in the past, yet they seemed to have been fresh in the minds of the poets at the time of the narration. Even in the days of the Brāhmaṇas, the victory of the devas and the defeat of the asuras was fresh enough to be enacted through the rituals and remote enough to be the basis of the belief in the magical efficacy."[332]

The half of millennium of losses to their Black adversaries was no doubt traumatizing to the Indo-European psyche, which is why a thousand or so years later the Celtic epic *Táin Bó Cúalnge* recounts the victory of the Black Bull over the White Bull in gory detail. This equally explains the fascination with black hunters/black warriors in Indo-European lore.[333]

2.] This protracted war was celebrated in myth and ritual as a *war of gods*, of Asuras and Devas/Daevas (the *devāsura* conflict). Both terms refer to divine beings or deities with their moral value depending on which Indo-Aryan religion is called to witness: In the Iranian *Avesta* the Ahura/Asura are the good deities and the

---

[332] Shendge, *Civilized Demons*, 10, 49.
[333] Armen Petrosyan, "Armenian Traditional Black Youths: the Earliest Sources," *The Journal of Indo-European Studies* 39 (2011): 342-354; P. Vidal-Naquet, *The Black Hunter* (Baltimore, 1986).

Devas are the demons, while in the rival Indic Vedas the opposite evaluation prevails.[334] In other words, they are *both* classes of deities or gods, but whether they are considered good gods or condemnable gods depends on which side of the war you are viewing from. The Asura are designated such because they derive from their God, Asura, the supreme god and creator in their pantheon. Also relevant here is the Asura Bull. Their chief deity was figured as the Primordial Bull who was creator of all, described as *viśvarūpa*, "the Omni Form," because he possesses within his being the forms of all creation.[335] Thus, when Sharma reminds us that "The god (Indra) is also described as tearing off the black skin of the Asura,"[336] this will have deep significance when we discuss the Mithraic Mysteries below.

In summary, the oldest texts witnessing to the oldest religious ideas, ideals and sacred preoccupations of Indo-European peoples shows them to be overwhelmingly preoccupied with the 500-year war they (Indo-Aryans) engaged in with the Asura Gods, the Black indigenes of the Indus Valley and India. Indeed, they *created their religion* around this conflict and their ultimate victory.[337] Vedic religion – among the oldest documentable Indo-European religion - is the religion of the ritual celebration of the military victory over and civilizational subjugation of black gods by white gods.

---

[334] On the Asura – Daeva/Deva dichotomy see e.g. Michael York, "Toward a Proto-Indo-European vocabulary of the sacred," **WORD** 44 (AUGUST, 1993): 235-254; N. D. Kazanas, "Indo-European Deities and the Ṛgveda," *The Journal of Indo-European Studies* 29 (2001): 1-38; Subhash Kak, "Vedic Elements in the Ancient Iranian Religion of Zarathustra," *The Adyar Library Bulletin* 67 (2003): 47-63; Hale, *Āsura- In Early Vedic Religion*; Shendge, *Civilized Demons*, 11-30; Grace Sturtevant Hopkins, "Indo-European *Deiwos and Related Words," *Language* 8 (1932): 5-83

[335] On the Asura Bull see Malati J. Shendge, "The Authorship of the Rgveda," *Annals of the Bhandarkar Oriental Research Institute* 81 (2000): 169-178; idem, *Civilized Demons*, 184-205; Doris Srinivasan, "The Religious Significance of Divine Multiple Body Parts in the Atharva Veda," *Numen* 25 (1978): 193-225; idem, "The Religious Significance of Multiple Bodily Parts to Denote the Divine: Findings From the Rig Veda," *Asiatische Studien* 29 (1975): 137-179; Sadashiv Ambadas Dange, "The Bull and the Fiery Fluid from the Ṛgveda," *Journal of the Oriental Institute* 17 (1968): 209-229; Kasten Rönnow, " Viśvarūpa," *Bulletin of the School of Oriental Studies, University of London* 6 (1931): 469-480

[336] Sharma, *Śūdras in Ancient India*, 15.

[337] Shendge, *Civilized Demons*, 283, 378.

# 8     Killing Their Own Black God

I.     *The Proto-Indo-European Black God*

It must be pointed out also that the Black God whose subjugation and even murder is celebrated in Vedic religion is *not* only the "other guy's" god, but the very Creator God recognized by Indo-European peoples themselves. Asura is called in the Ṛig veda [I.131.1] *dyaurasuro,* "Dyaus the Asura who bowed down (to Indra)," signifying the complete defeat of the Asuras. The god Asura is here called *Dyaus,* the Proto-Indo-European name of God the Sky Father (*Dyaus Pitā*). This archaic Indo-European Bull God (*Dyaus*) is said to be Indra's father whom Indra grabs down from heaven and kills! This theme is extremely important as we will encounter it again: the black gods are actually the "father(s)" of the white gods, and so the killing of the black gods is nothing short of patricide.

Michael Witzel's ***The Origins of the World's Mythologies*** is a Herculean synthesis of data from multiple fields.[338] He reconstructs what he calls "Laurasian Mythology," a single mythological system that encompasses and underlies the many various mythic systems of Eurasia and the Americas. This Laurasian system is indigenous basically in the northern (*boreal*) hemisphere and is distinguished from the mythological complex characteristic of the southern (*austral*) hemisphere (Africa, Australia, the Melanesians of New Guinea) which he calls Gondwana. According to Witzel at the root of this very widespread Laurasian mythic system is a particular storyline, an archaic "historical novel" he calls it, that tells a particular story stretching from the creation to the end of the world. This story underlies all of the *boreal* religions or the religions of the peoples of the northern hemisphere. Employing the comparative tools and methods Witzel is confident that he has reconstructed this "story"

---

[338] Michael Witzel, ***The Origins of the World's Mythologies*** (Oxford: Oxford University Press, 2012).

or at least key components of it. This is important for our discussion because one of the subsets of this putative Laurasian mythic complex is the Indo-European religious/mythic complex. Bruce Lincoln too has gone far in reconstructing the basic or Proto-Indo-European myth.[339] Together these sources establish that the "Theology of the Black God"[340] is at the center of the religion of the very first Indo-Europeans.

The Indo-European basic myth begins with a primordial aquatic darkness.[341] This darkness seems to have been personified as a great Primordial Bull.[342] This is of course consistent with the (non-Indo-European) Indic (=Indus Valley), Egyptian and Sumerian traditions, as we saw earlier. A black bull personified the primordial dark waters. In contrast to the black bull, the fire of the sun was personified in the lion and also the horse.[343] The white fiery horse and the black aquatic bull are thus characteristic Indo-European polarities.[344]

---

[339] See e.g. Bruce Lincoln, "The Indo-European Myth of Creation," *History of Religions* 15 (1975): 121-145; idem, "The Myth of the 'Bovine's Lament'," *Journal of Indo-European Studies* 3 (1975): 337-362; idem, "The Indo-European Cattle-Raiding Myth," *History of Religions* 16 (1976): 42-65; idem, *Priests, Warriors, and Cattle*; idem, "Of Meat and Society, Sacrifice and Creation, Butchers and Philosophy," *L'Uomo* 9 (1985): 9-29; idem, *Myth, Cosmos, and Society: Indo-European Themes of Creation and Destruction* (Cambridge: Harvard University Press, 1986); idem, "Once Again the Bovine's Lament," in *Religion, fiction and history. Essays in memory of Ioan Petru Culianu* (Bucures: Nemira, 2001) 83-98. See further Ranko Matasović, *A Reader in Comparative Indo-European Religion* (Zagreb, 2010).
[340] See True Islam, *The Truth of God*, 126-154.
[341] Witzel, *Origins*, 105-116.
[342] Witzel, *Origins*, 120-121. Srinivasan ("Multiple Body Parts...Rig Veda," 147) notes regarding the Vedic tradition: "The Asura Bull thus symbolizes the raw material out of which the world is shaped."
[343] Asko Parpola, "New correspondences between Harappan and Near Eastern glyptic art," *South Asian Archaeology* 1981, 178 notes: "Indeed, the golden-skinned hairy lion is an archetypal symbol for the golden-rayed sun, the lord of the day…Night…is equally well represented by the bull, whose horns connect it with the crescent of the moon." He suggests also who suggests that "the dark buffalo bathing in muddy water was conceived as the personification of the cosmic waters of chaos".
[344] On the fiery horse of Hindu tradition see Wendy Doniger O'Flaherty, "The Submarine Mare in the Mythology of Śiva," *Journal of the Royal Asiatic Society* 1 (1971): 9-27. On horse mythology in Iranian tradition see Prods Oktor Skjaervø,

According to the Indo-European story, from this material darkness will emerge a Primordial Giant Man[345] who is also the Creator. In Lincoln's reconstruction, the Indo-European Creation begins, not with one giant man but with two men – the twins *Manu- "man" and *Yəmo- "twin" – and a bull. But it can be shown that all three of these are aspects of that single Primordial Giant who is the Creator God. *Yəmo-, who becomes the Vedic Yama and the Iranian Yima, has a solar nature.[346] He is "bright Yima" [Yašt 19:31] and called hvaredaresa, the "sun-like-one."[347] But *Yəmo "sacrifices" his own luminous body: he willingly "dies." This only means that he surrendered and subjected his luminous, fiery body to an earthly, black "enclosure." In Proto-Indo-European tradition death is personified as a goddess named *Kolyo "the coverer" whose domain is underground.[348] And Indo-Aryan gender classification is perfectly articulated in the Phalavi Indian Bundahišn [39.10]: "These four things are said to be male and female respectively: Sky, metal, wind, and fire come into being as male and never otherwise. Water, earth, plants, and fish come into being as female."[349] The implications of this are brought out in the myth: in the Indo- variant of this P-IE myth, the luminous, anthropomorphic creator-deity Prajāpati-Brahmā (=

---

"The Horse in Indo-Iranian Mythology," *Journal of the American Oriental Society* 128 (2008): 295-302.
[345] Witzel, *Origins*, 117-118.
[346] Shaul Shaked, "First Man, First King: Notes on Semitic-Iranian syncretism and Iranian mythological transformations," *Gilgul. Essays on transformation, revolution and permanence in the history of religions dedicated to R.J.Zwi Werblowsky*, ed. S. Shaked, D. Shulman, G.G. Stroumsa (Leiden: Brill 1987) 238-256: "Yima the Luminous...is a conspicuous solar figure (244)."
[347] Albert J. Carnory, "Iranian Views of Origins in Connection with Similar Babylonian Beliefs," *Journal of the American Oriental Society* 36 (1916): 317 [art.=300-320]. Yima's characteristic shinning "kingly glory," $x^v arənah$ derives from Proto-Indo-European *swel-n-o-s "solar essence": Lincoln, *Priests, Warriors, and Cattle*, 79.
[348] Bruce Lincoln, "Mithra(s) as Sun and Savior," *La soteriologia Dei cultic orientali nell'impero romano*, ed. Ugo Bianchi and Maarten J. Vermaseren (Leiden: Brill, 1982): 507-508 [art.=505-526].
[349] See discussion in Bruce Lincoln, "Embryological Speculation and Gender Politics in a Pahlavi Text," *History and Religions* 27 (1988): 355-365, esp. 363-364.

Puruṣa = Yama[350]) is said to have wrapped himself in the primordial water which was symbolically personified as his daughter/wife Vāk/Virāj.[351] This only means that he created a body from this material and then "entered" it/her. He then became *haritah śyāvah*, dark brown like night (*śyāvah*, Ṛg Veda 6.48.6.) with a ting of yellow; a yellow glow, *haritah*. Recall Donn Cúalnge the Dark Brown/Black Bull of our Celtic tale above.[352] The yellow glow here is similar to the blue glow elsewhere: they both describe the visual effect of the divine light interacting with the divine black body as it passes through the hair pores. Prajāpati-Brahmā's "enclosing" his luminous body within a body made from the black primordial water has a number of implications:

1.] His own being is "twined," *Yəmo*, the one Primordial Man. He combines within his person the two polarities, fire and water.[353] As Helmut Humbach explains:

> Yima was a twin in himself insofar as he was the prototype of mankind in which both good and evil are inseparable. In Yima, the twin, the two antagonistic primeval spirits started the fight against each other...[354]

In Indo-Aryan tradition the conjunction of the polarities is symbolized by the submarine mare, the horse (= fire) submerged in the ocean yet spitting fire. As Wendy Doniger O'Flaherty

---

[350] On Yama lying behind the Vedic Puruṣa and Prajāpati see Lincoln, "Myth of Creation," 133. On Puruṣa as Prajāpati see J. Gonda, **Prajāpati's relations with Brahman, Bṛhaspati and Brahmā** (Amsterdam: North-Holland Publishing Company, 1989) 61-64; J. R. Joshi, "Prajāpati in Vedic Mythology and Ritual," **Annals of the Bhandarkar Oriental Research Institute** 53 (1972): 114 [art.=101-124].

[351] See G.H. Godbole, "Later Vedic and Brahmanical Accounts," in Dange, **Myths of Creation**, 13). On Vāk as primordial matter see Nagar, **Image of Brāhma**, viii; Joshi, "Prajāpati," 113.

[352] See *Taittirīya Brāhmaṇa* 2.3.5.1; *Śatapatha-Brāhmaṇa* 6.2.2.2. On Vāk and the primordial waters see ibid., 6.1.1.9; *Pañcaaveṃśa-Brāhmaṇa* 20.14.2; *Ṛg Veda* 10.125.3; *Jaiminīya-Brāhmaṇa* 2.252 (Vāk as primordial cow); Bosch, **Golden Germ**, 52-53.

[353] Shaked, "First Man, First King," 240.

[354] Helmut Humbach, "Yama/Yima/Jamšēd, King of Paradise of the Iranians," **Jerusalem Study of Arabic and Islam** 26 (2002): 70 [art.=68-77].

explains: "The image of fire in water is the ultimate resolution of opposition; held in suspended union, each retains its full power and nothing is lost to compromise, but there is complete balance."[355] By uniting his fiery "glory" with aquatic matter, the Primordial Man was able to produce the material world (***idaṃ sarvam***) including progeny (something excluded by his prior somatic condition, a body of fiery light too irradiant for material creation). The first "progeny" produced is Manu, the first earthly, mortal human.[356]

2.] *\*Yəmo*, the first Man God of Proto-Indo-European religion, is a Black God. Not a hideous, terrifying blackness but a beautiful blackness.[357] When the goddess Sāvitrī saw him she described "a person in a yellow robe and a turban, a handsome man resplendent like the sun, smoothly black and red-eyed (*Mbh* 3.281.7ff.)." He is elsewhere described as "dark as a mount of collyrium" yet his "body shines as the luster of lightning. [His body] is as long as three yojanas (four and five miles)."[358] Laurens P. van den Bosh makes the point that Yama's black skin may connect his body with the material earth and his yellow robe may refer (symbolically) to his luminosity(shining through the pores of his black body).[359] As U.N. Dhal points out, the God's pre-incarnated form (*nirākāra*) is luminously white (or yellow) while his material incarnate form (*sakāra*) is black.[360] When the two bodies interact, a brown with a ting of yellow glow or a blue glow is produced. Thus, Yama is depicted both as black skinned and as

---

[355] O'Flaherty, "Submarine Mare," 9.
[356] *Śatapatha-Brāhmaṇa* 6.6.1.19; 9.4.1.12; J. Gonda, "All, Universe and Totality in the Śatapatha-Brāhmaṇa," ***Journal of the Oriental Institute*** 32 (1982): 1-17; Joshi, "Prajāpati in Vedic Mythology and Ritual."
[357] "Originally there seems to have been nothing terrifying about Yamá, as most scholars have agreed, and his realm is presented in the Vedas as primarily characterized by feasting, light, beauty, and happiness." Lincoln, "Lord of Death," 227.
[358] Laurens P. van Bosch, "Yama-The God on the Black Buffalo," in ***Commemorative Figures*** [Leiden: E.J. Brill, 1982] 32, 39 [art.=21-64].
[359] van Bosch, "Yama-The God on the Black Buffalo," 32.
[360] U.N. Dhal, "The Colour Concept of a Deity," ***Vishveshvarand Indological Journal*** 21 (1983): 232 [art.=228-232].

blue skinned. And he too is associated with a black bull (buffalo) (Plates 6 and 7).

So in Lincoln's reconstruction of the basic Indo-European creation myth his twins are really nothing more than the polarities conjoined within the single Primordial Giant, creator of the world, who is also a very *black* creator god. By the same token, the bull that accompanied the twins in this reconstruction (both Witzel's and Lincoln's) is likewise *not* a being distinct from the Primordial Giant, at least not on the secondary stage. Rather, it represents both the primeval cosmic waters and the God's black body that was made from those waters. Lincoln confirms this when he writes, speaking on the cosmic man *Puruṣa* who is a late priestly reflex of Yama:

> the word *púruṣa-* must be understood as a compound that combines a word for "man" (Skt. *pú-*, as in *pú-mān* and *pú-tra-*) and a word for 'bull' (Skr. *irṣa-* → *-ruṣa-* by metathesis). Thus behind the figure of Purṣu, the primordial being, lies an older notion of two primordial beings, a man and a bull together.[361]

Thus the very name or title of this Primordial Giant suggests that the bull is a part of his own person, not a separate entity. We are therefore to see the bull as a reference to the black, material body of the God conjoined to his luminous person.

Thus, the central figures of the ancient creation tale of the Indo-Europeans is actually a single figure: A Black Man God who is the Creator of the world, symbolized by a black bull or buffalo. This is *their* God; at least he is the god whom they acknowledge as the Creator of the world. Yet, the Indo-Europeans went to war with this God *and his progeny* and made a religion out of this war that they waged with the Black Gods. This religion is the oldest one that we can document among Indo-Europeans. In other words, these ancient whites recognized the Black God as God (Creator) and they created a religion out of their waging of war against their own God (father) and killing his black descendants.

---

[361] Lincoln, ***Priests, Warriors, and Cattle***, 75.

Plates 9-19

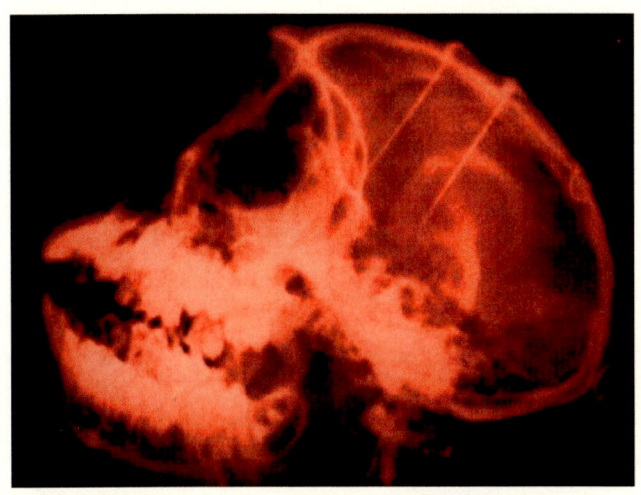

Plate 9 (Above): Scientists such as José Delgado, whose research was funded by military institutions, did brain surgery on laboratory monkeys that made them tame and docile. Plate 10 (Below): The U.S. government funded a program to do that same brain surgery on Black males such as those who riot for social justice or even protest for social justice. The below picture appeared in an important article that sounded the alarm about that program. The article appeared in *Ebony Magazine* in 1973. The picture depicts a Black male undergoing the proposed "psychosurgery" aimed at taming Black men.

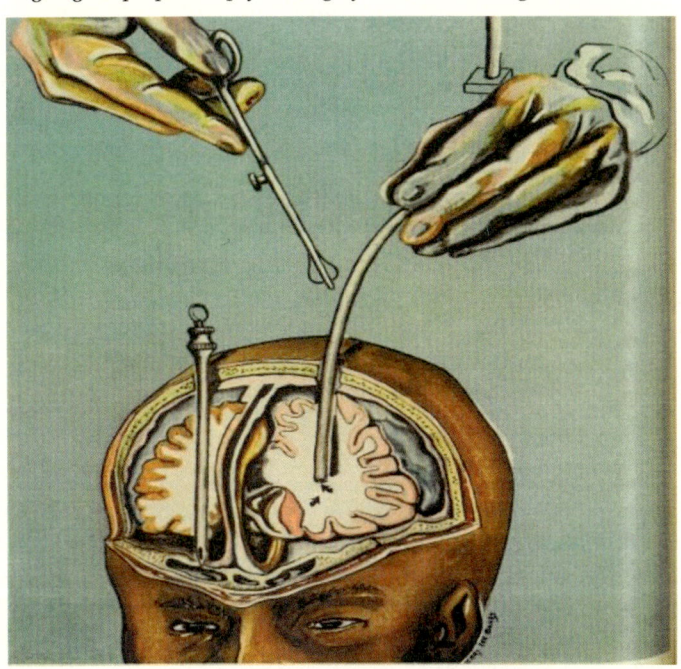

Plate 11. (A) The Hindu creator god Brahma; (B) The Hebrew Tetragrammaton as the fiery, anthropomorphic Glory of Yahweh/Jehovah; (C) The Ancient Egyptian "Sun-God" Heru

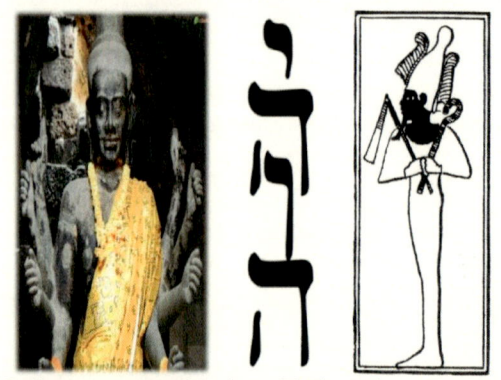

Plate 12. (A) The Hindu preserver god Vishnu; (B) The Hebrew Tetragrammaton as Adam Qadmon, the black body of Yahweh/Jehovah; (C) The Egyptian Osiris, the black body of the Sun God Ra.

Plate 13. (A) Vishnu as the Blue God; (B) The Jewish High Priest of the Temple of Solomon in his blue robe (*me'îl*) symbolizing the earthly body of Yahweh/Jehovah; (C) Egyptian Saphiric God Amen-Ra.

146

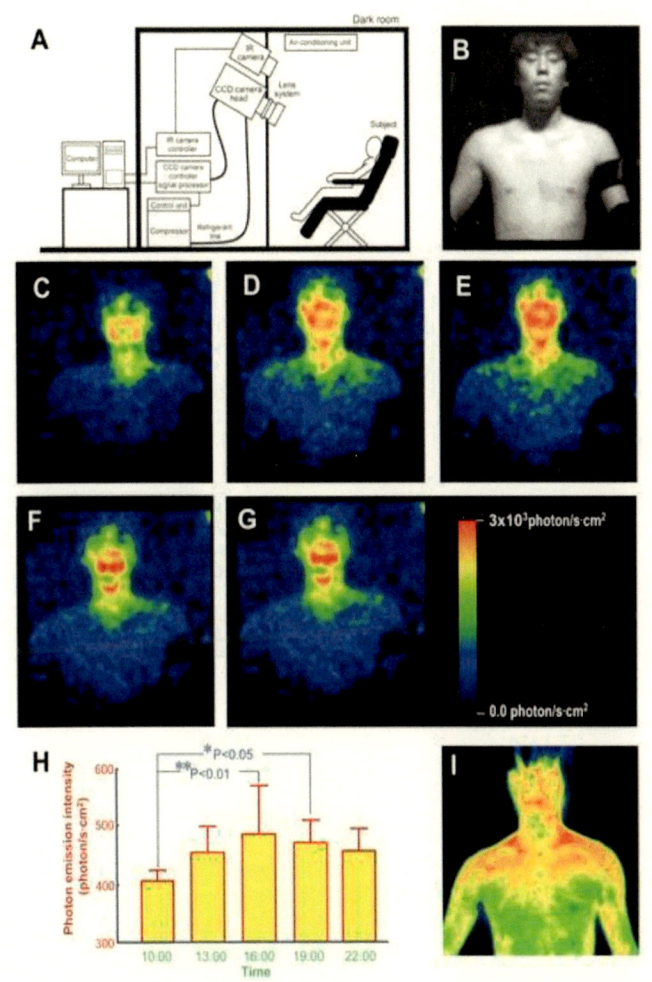

Plate 14. "Figure 1. A. Schematic illustration of experimental setup. B–F. Images of ultraweak photon emission from human body. B. Image of the subject under light illumination. C. Image at 10:10. D. Image at 13:10. E. Image at 16:10. F. Image at 19:10. G. Image at 22:10 with a calibration bar which indicates the estimated radiation intensity expressed by photon number per unit of time per unit of skin surface. H. Daily rhythm of photon emission from face and body from 5 volunteers. Significant difference from the photon emission at 10:00 AM (n = 15, Mean6SD; **P,0.01, *P,0.05). I. A typical thermographic image of the subject from Fig. 1B–G." From Masaki Kobayashi1, Daisuke Kikuchi, Hitoshi Okamura, "Imaging of Ultraweak Spontaneous Photon Emission from Human Body Displaying Diurnal Rhythm," *PLoS One* 4 (2009): 1-4.

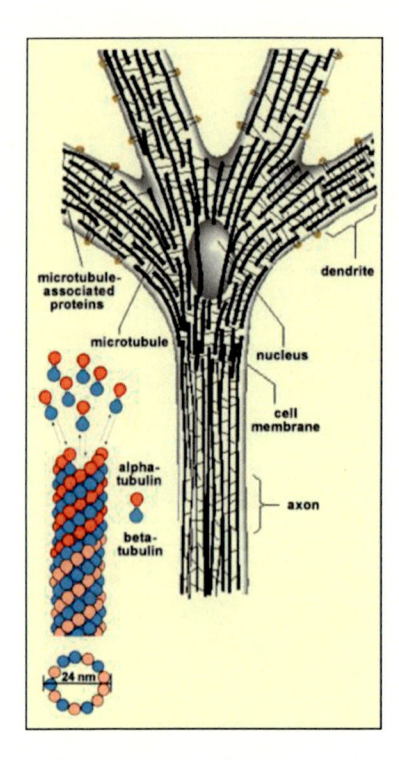

Plate 15. Brain cell with microtubules and tubulins (red and blue)

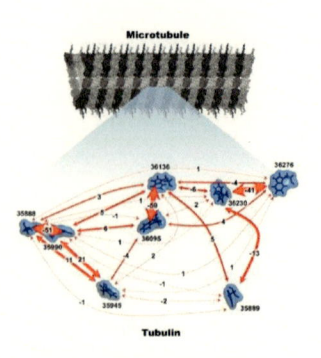

Plate 16. Top: A microtubule, polymer of 'tubulin' proteins inside neurons. Bottom: Tubulin with 8 tryptophan chromophores (blue). Red lines and numbers between tryptophans indicate dipole coupling strengths in cm$^1$ (image courtesy of: Travis J.A. Craddock)

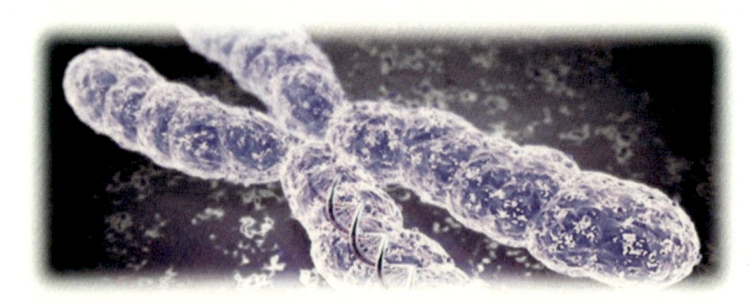

Plate 17. Luminous chromosome

Plate 18. The Honorable Minister Louis Farrakhan on The Breakfast Club, May 24, 2016.

Plate 19. St. Louis Rams running back Todd Gurley put on a pink tutu in his debut Jolly Rancher commercial.

PART FOUR

# Taming The Black Bull

## WAR WITH THE BLACK MALE MIND

# 9   Operation Ferdinand: Creating Docile Black Males

I.  *The New Rebellions and their Aftermath*

The seeming success of the Civil Rights Movement – the Civil Rights Act of 1964 and the Voting Rights Act of 1965 – had already greatly perturbed those elements of American society committed to the old racial hierarchy. The non-violent activism, agitation and social disobedience that were the tools of civil rebellion provoked the ire of the "law and order" establishment. A governmental backlash was already in development when a game changer occurred. After the arrest of Black motorist Marquette Fryre in August of 1965, the Watts section of South Central Los Angeles erupted into six days (August 11-17) of violence and confrontation with the police resulting in 34 dead, 1,032 injured, 3,952 arrested, 600 businesses destroyed and a total damage of $40 million. The Watts Riot or Watts Rebellion was considered at that time the worst race riot in American history. But before the wounds of Watts could heal, in July of 1967 Detroit blew up after a police raid on a local bar: five days of one the most destructive riots in the history of the United States. The Detroit Rebellion resulted in 43 dead, 1,189 injured, more than 7,200 arrested and 2,000 buildings destroyed. But these were just a prelude. After the assassination of Dr. Martin Luther King on April 4, 1968 over 100 American cities saw riots or some form of rebellion during what has been dubbed the "Holy Week Uprising." Some of the biggest rebellions were in Baltimore, Washington D.C., Chicago and Kansas City.

These uprisings shook the nation. The causes were studied and recommendations were made that could prevent future explosions. After the Watts Rebellion the McCone Commission established by California Governor Pat Brown identified the root of the riot as high unemployment, poor schools, and the inferior living conditions of Black people. The 101-page report (*Violence in the City-An End or a Beginning? A Report by the Governor's Commission on the Los Angeles Riots, 1965*) made specific recommendations to eradicate the social causes of the violence, such as more job-training, increased low-income housing, and emergency literary programs, etc. Most of these were not acted upon.[362] Likewise, after the Detroit Rebellion President Johnson established the National Advisory Commission on Civil Disorders, also known as the Kerner Commission, to investigate the causes in Detroit. The final 426-page *Kerner Report* released on February 29, 1968 concluded that the riots resulted from Black frustration at the lack of economic opportunity and called for the creation of new jobs, new housing construction and the end of de facto segregation that created the ghetto environment. Again, these sober assessments and recommendations were ignored. Instead, the U.S. government gave ear to a very *different* analysis of the riots and invested large sums of money to pursue and implement a *different* set of recommendations.

## II. Mind Murder: Creating Black Zombies

*In Philadelphia a black man dies of an overdose of heroin, and a reporter notices peculiar scars on his head. A portion of his brain has been burned out in an experimental attempt to cure addiction. The neurosurgeon is located by the reporter and admits that his monkey experiments were inconclusive before trying his operation on human addicts.* Peter Roger Breggin, "The Second Wave" (1975)

*Dr. Frederick Goodwin, director of the National Institute of Mental Health...made comparisons between inner-city youths and violent, oversexed monkeys in the wild.* **Los Angeles Times** October 14, 1993

In September of 1967, after the Watts and Detroit Rebellions, three Harvard professors published a letter in the ***Journal of the Medical Association*** entitled "Role of Brain Disease in Riots and Urban Violence."[363] Frank Ervin was a psychiatrist

---

[362] Darrell Dawsey, "25 Years After the Watts Riots: McCone Commission's Recommendations Have Gone Unheaded," *Los Angeles Times* July 8, 1990.
[363] Frank Ervin, Vernon Mark and William Sweet, "Role of Brain Disease in Riots and Urban Violence," *Journal of the Medical Association* 201 (September 11, 1967): 895.

while Vernon Mark and William Sweet were neurosurgeons, Mark the head of the department of neurosurgery at Boston City Hospital and Sweet the Director of Neurosurgery at the prestigious Massachusetts General. According to these Harvard professors, the Black rioters were not in fact motivated by frustrations born from unlivable socioeconomic conditions. Rather, the Black males in the middle of the rebellions actually suffered from a brain disease that made them prone to senseless violence. The trio suggested that in addition to the violent urban rioters, social protestors too suffered from a brain dysfunction.[364] The solution: suppress the Black rioters and social protestors as well as their leaders through psychosurgery.[365] As John Horgan remarks: "In their book, *Violence and the Brain*, Ervin and Mark suggest that brain stimulation or psychosurgery might quell the violent tendencies of blacks rioting in inner cities."[366]

Psychosurgery, a form of cerebral destruction, is any surgery to the brain which mutilates or destroys brain tissue in order to control emotion or behavior without treating any known disease. It's a pacifying operation that blunts emotions and subdues behavior.[367] Opponent of the procedure Dr. Peter Breggin, known as "the Conscience of the Mental Health Industry," notes: "its primary and overriding clinical effect is subsequent production of mental dysfunction."[368] Psychosurgery techniques produce docility, making tractable and tame individuals considered intractable and aggressive.

---

[364] Vernon Marks and Frank Ervin, "Is There a Need to Evaluate the Individuals Producing Human Violence," *Psychiatric Opinion* 32 (1968): 5; D. Bird, "More stress urged on causes of civil disorder," *The New York Times* August 14, 1968.

[365] Vernon Mark and Frank Erwin, *Violence and the Brain* (New York: Harper & Row, 1970).

[366] John Horgan, "The Forgotten Brain Chip: The work of Jose Delgado, a pioneering star in brain-stimulation research four decades ago, goes largely unacknowledged today. What happened?" *Scientific American* (October 2005): 71 [art.=66-73].

[367] Peter Roger Breggin, M.D., "Psychosurgery for the Control of Violence: A Critical Review," in *Neural Bases of Violence and Aggression*, ed. W. Fields and W. Sweet (St. Louis. MO: Warren H. Green, Inc., 1975) 350-378.

[368] Peter R. Breggin, "Psychosurgery as Brain-disabling Therapy," in *Divergent Views in Psychiatry*, ed. M. Dongier and E. Wittbower (Hagerstown, MD: Harper and Row, 1981): 302 [art.=302-326].

In his 1973 article in *Ebony Magazine* aptly entitled: "New Threat to Blacks: Brain Surgery to Control Behavior," B.J. Mason sounded the alarm:

> Targets are supposed to be depressed women, hyperactive children, drug addicts, alcoholics, epileptics, neurotics, psychotics, convicts. Targets are often black...[I]t appears that all one has to do to qualify for such an operation is to rub society the wrong way.[369]

Black people as particularly appropriate "patients" (=victims) of this cerebrally destructive procedure go back to the earliest champion of psychosurgery in America, the eminent (and now notorious) neurologist Dr. Walter J. Freeman who, in the 1940's and 1950's, performed or participated in 3,500 lobotomies, the earlier version of psychosurgery.[370]

In a lobotomy the doctor severs neural connections between the brain's prefrontal area and the rest of the brain by damaging brain tissue. Freeman was an advocate of the use by psychiatrists untrained in surgery of the "house of horrors"-like *ice-pick method* of the procedure: hammering an ice-pick-like tool through the patients/victims eye sockets.[371] In his 1950 book co-authored with his junior partner neurosurgeon Dr. James Watts, Freeman identified the ideal patient for his procedure as older, female and Black.[372] He describes a particularly offensive case: an especially aggressive "negress of gigantic proportions" named Oretha who for years was confined to a strong room at St. Elizabeth's Hospital in

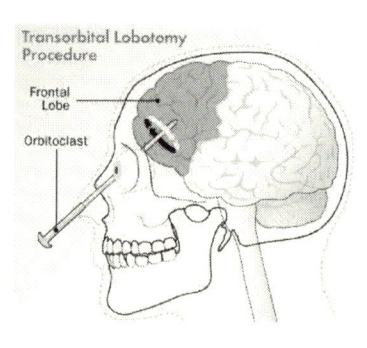

---

[369] B.J. Mason: "New Threat to Blacks: Brain Surgery to Control Behavior," *Ebony* February 1973, 62-74 (63).
[370] On the history of lobotomies and on Dr. Freeman in particular see Miquel A. Faria, Jr., "Violence, mental illness, and the brain – A brief history of psychosurgery: Part 1 – From trephination to lobotomy," *Surgical Neurology International* 4 (2013): 1-23.
[371] Michael M. Philips, "The Lobotomy Files. Part II: How one doctor steered the VA toward a lobotomy program," *Wall Street Journal* December 11, 2013.
[372] Walter Freeman and James Watts, *Psychosurgery* (Charles C. Thomas, 1950).

Washington D.C. She was "300 lbs of ferocious humanity," we are told, and Freeman was determined to make her docile by lobotomizing her. It took five attendants to drag Oretha to the operating room. Once the procedure was complete, however, the "fierce animals become tame." Freeman reported:

> from the day after the operation...we could playfully grab Oretha by the throat, twist her arm, tickle her in the ribs and slap her behind without eliciting anything more than a hoarse chuckle.[373]

This physical and sexual abuse of a surgically incapacitated Black woman is deeply disturbing. Freeman describes these patients as "deadened"; his victims experienced a "loss of self."[374] We have here the early production of human zombies. Freeman conceded that, though lobotomized persons – the brain dead – "may not become leaders in their professions, they *serve* adequately and comfortably."[375] Through psychosurgery, then, zombies that adequately serve society's rulers can be produced: Black zombies.

On the other hand during the 1970's Dr. O.J. Andy, director of neurosurgery at the University of Mississippi, preferred Black children ages 5-12. He "diagnosed" them as aggressive and hyperactive and then surgically intervened by "slic[ing] the child's scalp open, drills holes through his skull and plants a few electrodes in his brain."[376] Electrodes heat the brain and cause coagulation - melting of brain tissue. Andy's procedure mashed the brains of young children turning some of them into vegetables. Most of these children were housed in a segregated Black institution for the developmentally disabled.[377] Andy selected the older children because they had "run afoul of the law," and his was thus a "law and order" use of cerebral destruction of young Black people. Andy said that those Black

---

[373] Freeman and Watts, *Psychosurgery*, 406-407. See further Breggin, "Psychosurgery for the control of violence," 354-356.
[374] Peter Roger Breggin, "The Second Wave," *Mental Health* 57 (1973): 11 [art.=10-13].
[375] See Breggin, "Psychosurgery as Brain-disabling Therapy," 309.
[376] Mason, "New Threat to Blacks," 63.
[377] Peter R. Breggin, M.D. and Ginger Ross Breggin, *The War Against Children of Color: Psychiatry Targets Inner City Youth* (Monroe, Maine: Common Courage Press, 1998) 115-116.

participants of the Watts and Detroit Rebellions could have possessed the "pathological brains" which his brain melting procedures could fix.[378]

The Harvard trio were thus not alone or original in their proposal to target Black people with the brain-disabling procedure of psychosurgery. Sweet made a pitch for brain control of those involved in urban disorder by implanting electrodes in their brain. You may think that these ideas are so outrageous they could never be seriously entertained and could only have a reality in a science fiction or horror movie, but you would be wrong. These terrifying ideas caught fire with President Nixon's government. Elliot Richardson, Director of the Department of Health, Education and Welfare and a longtime advocate of psychosurgery, had been "the (Nixon) administration official most actively supporting Mark, Erwin and Sweet".[379] Richardson showed the trio how to bypass the procedures for normal scientific funding and go directly to Congress to obtain special "personally tailored funds." In addition, Bert Brown, director of the National Institutes of Mental Health (NIMH), went before the Senate Appropriations Committee and argued their case. They were successful. Both the House and the Senate passed special appropriations in 1970 directing the NIMH to award a $500,000 per year grant to Sweet beginning in 1971. The grant came with instructions to Sweet and colleagues to identify *and control* the persons prone to the violence under discussion. Also, the Justice Department's Law Enforcement Assistance Administration (LEAA) got in on the action, investing another $108, 930 in the Harvard trio's brain research and earmarked another $1 million. The LEAA specifically instructed the grantees to "improve, develop and test the usefulness" of electrodes and brain surgery for their law and order purposes.[380] As Mason pointed out at the time: "Judging from [the] language of the directive, the Justice

---

[378] Mason, "New Threat to Blacks," 68.
[379] "Richardson's Expertise: Secy of Lobotomies," *Berkely Barb* 17 (June 29-July 5 1973).
[380] Mason, "New Threat to Blacks," 63; Breggin and Breggin, *War Against Children of Color*, 113; Peter R. Breggin, M.D., "Psychosurgery for Political Purposes," *Duquesne Law Review* 13 (1975): 841-862.

Department is interested in devising an early warning system for riot control."[381]

The U.S. government just invested 1.5 million 1970s' dollars in a "study" to "fix" through techniques of cerebral destruction the brains of a select population. As Harvard professor of psychiatry Dr. Alvine Poussaint remarked after these allocations: "you can bet this study will be more directed at black males *to make them more docile* (emphasis added)."[382] By examining the work and words of two profoundly important fellow collaborators of the Harvard trio, we can confirm Poussaint's suspicion.

## DR. ERNST RODIN'S CASTRATED BLACK BULLS OF THE INNER-CITY

In 1972, as a result of the Detroit Rebellion of 1967, the State of Michigan planed a experimental program aimed at the control of violence, which included psychosurgery *and chemical castration*. This program was to be run out of the Lafayette Clinic of Wayne State University and headed by chief neurosurgeon Dr. Ernst Rodin. Rodin was a collaborator of the Harvard trio; he visited their project site and assessed their psychosurgery patients.[383] Rodin was not satisfied with the Harvard trio's results. He thus proposed his own psychosurgery experiment and got funding from the state to carry it out. The program Rodin and the State of Michigan planned was chilling. In a 1972 speech Rodin spoke on the implications of the riots that had racked his city and he proposed as the solution not only psychosurgery but also chemical castration of the urban males, which he compared to aggressive bulls who should be turned into docile oxen through castration. He said:

> Tolerance and encouragement of free thought is *probably* excellent for the high IQ bracket, but not advisable for the lower one, and one is reminded of the Roman saying: "Quod licet Jovi non licet bovi" (What is allowed for

---

[381] Mason, "New Threat to Blacks," 62.
[382] Mason, "New Threat to Blacks," 63.
[383] Breggin, "Psychosurgery for Political Purposes," 847.

Jupiter is not allowed for the ox). The problem is that the ox may not recognize himself as an ox and demand Jupiter's prerogatives. [384]

In other words, the urban bulls agitate for better living conditions and for rights because they don't recognize their place in the hierarchal order. But much violence could be avoided, Rodin claimed, by castrating the "dumb young males":

> Farmers have known for ages immemorial that you can't do a blasted thing with a bull except fight or kill and eat him; the castrated ox [however] will pull his plow...It is also well known that human eunuchs, although at times quite scheming entrepreneurs, are not given to physical violence. Our scientific age tends to disregard this wisdom of the past...[385]

"The castrated ox will pull his plow": another call for incapacitated Black males to *serve* the beneficiaries of this society. They want a return to slavery. This early proposal of the chemical castration of inner-city Black males is particularly important, as we will confront it again much later in this discussion. This admittedly "cold-blooded" research of Rodin which was funded by the State of Michigan to the tune of a quarter million dollars was a controlled study comparing the effects of the Harvard trio's suggested psychosurgery to Rodin's proposed chemical castration as the solution to the problem of urban violence and civil disorder.[386] In fact, Rodin argued that *both* procedures were necessary in order to turn the targeted Black male into the "hopefully more placid dullard." However, in 1972 before the project could officially take off a Michigan Legal Services lawyer Gabe Kaimowitz intervened in court on behalf of two dozen state psychiatric inmates scheduled for enrolment in the project. A three judge panel was convened and determined that psychosurgery was destructive and should not be performed on

---

[384] Ernst Rodin, "A Neurological Appraisal of Some Episodic Behavioral Disturbances with Special Emphasis on Aggressive Outbursts," quoted in Peter R. Breggin, M.D., "Psychosurgery for Political Purposes," **Duquesne Law Review** 13 (1975): 853 [art.=841-862].
[385] See Breggin, "Psychosurgery for Political Purposes," 853.
[386] Breggin, "Psychosurgery for Political Purposes," 854.

an involuntary basis. The project was killed.[387] Only temporarily though.

## DR. JOSÉ M.R. DELGADO'S REMOTE CONTROLLED BLACK BULLS

Young inner-city males as aggressive black bulls to be scientifically tamed was a consistent theme in the work of this circle of psychosurgeons. The seriousness with which this analogy was taken is demonstrated most clearly in the work of Yale physiology professor Dr. José Manuel Rodriqez Delgado who worked closely with the Harvard trio.[388] In fact, he looms larger than anyone in this earlier governmental effort to scientifically control the Black male mind, for it was he who "pioneered that most unnerving of technologies, the brain chip-an electronic device that can manipulate the mind by receiving signals from and transmitting them to neurons."[389] Also important are Delgado's connections to the intelligence community. His research was primarily funded by military institutions such as the Office of Naval Research and the Air Force AeroMedical Research Laboratory and when he returned to Spain the Spanish

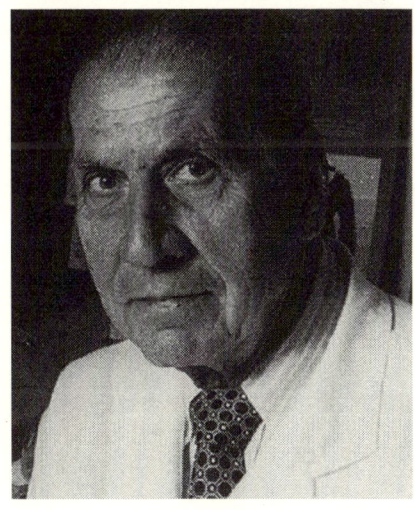

---

[387] Breggin, "Psychosurgery for Political Purposes," 852; Breggin and Breggin, *War Against Children of Color*, 116.
[388] On this work together see Miquel A. Faria, "Violence, mental illness, and the brain – A brief history of psychosurgery: Part 3 – From deep brain stimulation to amygdalotomy for violent behavior, seizures, and pathological aggression in humans," *Surgical Neurology International* 4 (2013): 1-22; Breggin, "Psychosurgery for Political Purposes," 847-848;
[389] John Horgan, "The Forgotten Brain Chip: The work of Jose Delgado, a pioneering star in brain-stimulation research four decades ago, goes largely unacknowledged today. What happened?" *Scientific American* (October 2005): 66-73.

monthly magazine *Tiempo* interviewed him in 2000 and reported that he had ties with the Spanish secret police.[390]

Born in Ronda, Spain in 1915, Delgado accepted a position in Yale's physiology department in 1950. It is there where he did his work, so much of which is truly the stuff of the Twilight Zone. Delgado can be considered the first American master of brain control. He implanted radio-equipped electrode arrays, called "stimoceivers," in cats, monkeys, chimpanzees, gibbons, bulls, and humans, "and showed that he could control subjects' minds and bodies with the push of a button."[391] With electrodes inserted into the brain Delgado in fact was able to "play" monkeys and cats and bulls and humans "like little electronic toys" that yawn, hide, fight, play, mate, and go to sleep on command.[392]

By far Delgado's most famous act of mind and behavior control was his sensational bull experiment. The experiment was conducted in September 1963 at a fighting bull-breeding ranch in Cordoba, Spain. Delgado inserted his brain chip or stimoceiver into the brains of several fighting bulls and stood in a bullring with one bull at a time. Delgado had only a handheld transmitter and when the bull charged the scientist he pressed the appropriate button, forcing the bull to skid to a halt only a few feet away from him.[393] John Osmundsen of *The New York Times* thought this "was probably the most spectacular demonstration ever performed of the deliberate modification of animal behavior

---

[390] Magnus Bartas, Fredrik Ekman and Jose Delgado, "Psychocivilization and its discontents: An interview with José Delgado," *Cabinet* 2 (Spring 2001); Horgan, "Forgotten Brain Chip," 70.
[391] Horgan, "Forgotten Brain Chip," 68.
[392] Jose Delgado, *Physical Control of the Brain: Toward a Psychocivilized Society* (New York: Harper Colophon, 1969): Magnus Bartas, Fredrik Ekman and Jose Delgado, "Psychocivilization and its discontents: An interview with José Delgado," *Cabinet* 2 (Spring 2001).
[393] Horgan, "Forgotten Brain Chip," 70.

José Delgado performing his famous Bull experiment in Spain

through external control of the brain."[394] According to Delgado he was "trying to find out what makes brave bulls brave." This takes on added significance when we consider Delgado's confession that his primary interest in these experiments is their *social* applicability.

> I do believe that an understanding of *the biological basis of social and antisocial behavior* and of mental activities which for the first time in history can now be explored in a conscious brain, may be of decisive importance in the search for intelligent solutions to some of our present anxieties, frustrations *and conflicts* (emphasis added).[395]

Delgado no doubt has the urban rioters in mind and the "bravery of the bulls" is apparently a source of such antisocial behavior and it must be understood and "fixed." We will hear this again later.

In this regard an observation by John Horgan on Delgado's bull experiment has some significance: "articles hailed Delgado's transformation of an aggressive bull into a real-life version of Ferdinand the bull, the gentle hero of a popular children's story."[396] The children's story written in 1936 by Munro Leafe

---

[394] John Osmundsen, "'Matador' with a Radio Stops Wired Bull," *The New York Times* May 17, 1965, pp. 1, 20.
[395] John Osmundsen, "'Matador' with a Radio," 1.
[396] Horgan, "Forgotten Brain Chip," 70.

163

is about Ferdinand, the gentile and kind natured bull who is yet the largest and strongest bull among his peers and is capable of ferocity when stung by a bee. Ferdinand is completely uninterested though in fighting and would rather sit under a tree all day and smell flowers rather than fight, even when forced into the bullfighting ring and suffers multiple provocations by the matador. Ferdinand is precisely the docile ox that Dr. Ernst Rodin sought to turn the "aggressive bulls" of the inner-city into. In fact, Ferdinand is a lot like the Negro that Robert Park described as "the Lady of the Races": "with...the utmost in politeness, *she* cannot bear to hurt anyone's feelings"; "The Negro...is primary an artist, loving life for its own sake. His métier is an expression rather than action. He is, so to speak, the lady among the races."[397]

Delgado actually accomplished this with a live bull. But as we saw, Delgado's real interest was not bovines but human social conflict. These five doctors – Vernon Mark, Frank Ervin, William Sweet, Ernst Rodin and José Delgado – worked with each other or "joined together to impose their idea,"[398] and their idea was the systematic use of psychosurgery – the physical mutilation of the brain of Black males – in order to "tame" them and make them docile, non-aggressive dullards, like Ferdinand. I therefore call their agenda "Operation Ferdinand." It had the official support and funding of the Nixon Administration. Delgado had even bigger sights. He advocated for a $1 billion NASA-like program toward research and development of the physical control of the brain as the solution to political violence.

## Delgado's experiments and the Black matriarchy

In terms of the social applicability of his experiments, Delgado was also much interested in inverting social hierarchy - not the White over Black social hierarchy of course but the male over female hierarchy. In one experiment Delgado implanted a stimoceiver in the brain of a macaque alpha male (which he named Ali) and installed a lever in the cage which, when pressed, sent electrical signals to the brain chip that pacified the alpha

---

[397] See above.
[398] Breggin, "Psychosurgery for Political Purposes," 849.

male. The female macaque (named Elsa) learned to pull the lever and control the dominant male.[399] Delgado reports:

> The old dream of an individual overpowering the strength of a dictator by remote control has been fulfilled, at least in our monkey colonies, by a combination of neurosurgery and electronics, demonstrating the possibility of intraspecies instrumental manipulation of hierarchical organization...a monkey named Ali, who was the powerful and ill-tempered chief of a colony, often expressed his hostility symbolically by biting his hand or by threatening other members of the group. Radio stimulation in Ali's caudate nucleus blocked his usual aggressiveness so effectively that the animal could be caught inside the cage without danger or difficulty. During stimulation he might walk a few steps, but he never attempted to attack another animal. Then a lever was attached to the cage wall, and if it was pressed, it automatically triggered a five seconds' radio stimulation of Ali. From time to time some of the submissive monkeys touched the lever, which was located close to the feeding tray, triggering the stimulation of Ali. A female monkey named Elsa soon discovered that Ali's aggressiveness could be inhibited by pressing the lever, and when Ali threatened her, it was repeatedly observed that Elsa responded by lever pressing. Her attitude of looking straight at the boss was highly significant because a submissive monkey would not dare to do so, for fear of immediate retaliation. The total number of Ali's aggressive acts diminished on the days when the lever was available, and although Elsa did not become the dominant animal, she was responsible for blocking many attacks against herself and for maintaining a peaceful coexistence within the whole colony.[400]

The female macaque pulling the lever (left) and the alpha male (right) cowering at the wall as a result.

The alpha male (right) showing aggression toward the female macaque.

---

[399] Horgan, "Forgotten Brain Chip," 69, 71.
[400] Delgado, *Physical Control of the Brain*, 164-166.

His name was Ali.

In another experiment Delgado succeeded in dismantling the usual power structure within a group of gibbon apes. He implanted electrobes into the brains of several male apes and gave one female gibbon from a lower social position within the group a control box connected to the brain implants in the males. Pressing the button electrically stimulated the implants and pacified the males. She learned to use the box and "to turn the alpha male on and off at will."[401] Delgado's interest here was in the *human* social implications of all of this: how to remotely control human social interactions and upset established social hierarchies.[402] Indeed, he lamented: "How do you replicate the lab situation in society?"[403] In as much as the focused interest of "Operation Ferdinand" and it operatives was the inner-city Black community, we are justified in connecting in our minds these experiments with the calculated creation of the Black Matriarchy during the Nixon Administration that we looked at earlier - the same Nixon Administration that funded "Operation Ferdinand."

III.    *Shutting It All Down (But Not Really)*

Peter Breggin, M.D. is a psychiatrist with an immaculate academic background. He is a graduate of Harvard with honors who trained at Massachusetts Mental Health Center and SUNY. He went on to become a consultant with the National Institute of Mental Health and has held academic appointments at the Washington School of Psychiatry, Johns Hopkins University and George Mason University. As a medical and psychiatric expert Dr. Breggin has been qualified to testify in court approximately 85 times since 1987. He has been dubbed "the Conscience of Mental Health," due to his indefatigable fight against the abuses of the

---

[401] Bartas, Ekman, and Delgado, "Psychociviliation and its discontents."
[402] Horgan, "Forgotten Brain Chip," 69, 71.
[403] Bartas, Ekman, and Delgado, "Psychociviliation and its discontents."

psychiatric industry,[404] including the psychosurgery plot. He explains:

> In the wake of the black urban uprisings of the late 1960s, America became preoccupied with the threatening figure of the young black male as well as the overall danger of rebellion and social chaos. Led by NIMH and the Justice Department, the federal government began to develop an overall program for biomedical control of violence...It...was inspired by fear of violence in the inner-city and aimed at control of young black males.[405]

Breggin and the organization that he founded, The International Center for the Study of Psychiatry and Psychology, led the fight against this particularly evil plan, saying: "It seemed fitting that two white parents should blow the whistle on what looked like a mainstream assault on black children."[406] And blow the whistle they did. Their crusade helped to generate tremendous public awareness and controversy. This campaign proved successful, at least ostensibly. Due to a great extant to his efforts campaigning against the psychosurgery project, the government changed its "official" positon on "Operation Ferdinand" in 1974.

*"...Peter Breggin is the conscience of psychiatry."*
—Bertram Karon, Professor of Psychology Michigan State University

---

[404] *The Conscience of Psychiatry: The Reform Work of Peter R. Breggin, MD*, ed. The International Center for the Study of Psychiatry and Psychology (Ithaca, NY: Lake Edge Book, 2009).
[405] Peter R. Breggin and Ginger Ross Breggen, "a biomedical program for urban violence control in the US: the dangers of psychiatric social control," *Change: An International Journal of Psychology and Psychotherapy* 11 (March 1993): 64 [art.=59-71].
[406] Breggin and Breggin, *War Against Children of Color*, 3.

Vernon Mark and Frank Ervin lost their federal funding for psychosurgery. LEAA ended its $108,000 grant to Ervin and rejected the one million dollar grant that was pending. A guideline signed on June 19, 1974 by LEAA stipulated that any future grant applications involving psychosurgery would be denied and it forbade states to use any LEAA block grants on psychosurgery.[407] This was a spectacular rise and a meteoric fall, all within five years. The controversy forced Delgado back to Spain in 1973-1974.

But "Operation Ferdinand" was in no way shelved. Its methods just changed. Amid the "ethical controversies...researchers drifted to other fields, notably psychopharmacology,"[408] i.e. the use of drugs to mentally incapacity the target population. "Operation Ferdinand" survived. But the means of transforming the aggressive black bulls into docile and dullard oxen is no longer psychosurgery but what would come to be called sociopharmachology.

But there is a remarkable twist to this story: though these government funded scientists through the 1960s and early 1970s were seeking a tamed, non-aggressive Black male, their new sociopharmacological research and covert operations of the late 1970s and 1980s led actually to the production through drug interventions and environmental manipulations of a *hyper-aggressive* Black male: the urban "thug" or John DiIulio/Hillary Clinton's callous "super predator." But this artificially produced hyper-aggressive Black male still "served" this society's rulers/beneficiaries just as Dr. Andy and Dr. Rodin envisioned, in fact even better than the hoped-for "Ferdinand" did. This is because the scientists who created the urban thug had already mastered the control of the urban thug's hyper-aggression.

---

[407] Breggin and Breggin, *War Against Children of Color*, 113; Robert Wright, "The Biology of Violence," *The New Yorker* March 13, 1995, 68-77
[408] Horgan, "Forgotten Brain Chip,"72-73.

# 10 Weaponizing Science Against Black Boys

I. *Super Predator: The XYY Study*

In 1965 British geneticist Patricia Jacobs and colleagues published the results of a chromosome analysis carried out among psychopathic inmates in the State Hospital Carstairs in Scotland.[409] Of the 197 criminals whose blood was tested seven had a unique genetic condition. Instead of the normal male chromosome signature XY (vs. the female XX), these men were XYY, i.e. they possessed an extra Y chromosome. Other studies of chromosome composition of inmates in mental-penal institutions in the 1960s suggested that about 2% of this population was XYY. Jacobs et al. assumed a direct connection between this genetic signature and the imprisonment of these XYY males and therefore claimed that XYY males have "dangerous, violent and criminal propensities." A number of high profile crimes seemed to support these claims. In 1961 Robert Tait of Melbourne, Australia battered a 77 year old woman in her home. Afterwards, he dressed in her underwear and "subjected her body to certain bizarre sexual indignities."[410] While locked up in Pentridge Prison in Melbourne in 1967 a chromosomal survey of the inmates disclosed that Tait was an XYY male. Likewise, Lawrence Edward Hannell in Melbourne murdered an elderly lady with no apparent motive in 1967 and Ernst Dieter Beck in Bielifeld, Germany murdered three women in 1968. They too (the men) were XYY males.

Thus was born the myth of the genetic "super predator," a male characterized by abnormal aggression and sexual pathology. The extra Y chromosome was claimed at that time to turn normal males (XY) into hyper-aggressive, hyper-sexual monsters. By 1968 a typical XYY profile was already worked out: "extremely tall

---

[409] P.A. Jacobs et al, "Aggressive behaviour, mental sub-normality and the XYY male," *Nature* 208:5017 (1965): 1351-1351.
[410] Richard G. Fox, "The XYY Offender: A Modern Myth?" *The Journal of Criminal Law, Criminology and Police Science* 62 (1971): 59 [art.=59-73].

stature, long limbs with strikingly long arm span, facial acne, mild mental illness (including psychosis) and aggression, antisocial behaviour involving a long history of arrests, frequently beginning at an early age."[411]

But these claims proved erroneous. "It was ultimately found that XYY males were not violence-prone, but some may suffer from lower than average intelligence, which is known to be associated with increased rates of criminal conviction and incarceration."[412] The lower intelligence made them easier catches by the police and thus their relatively high presence in penal institutions. But XYY males in prison tended to be *less* violent than control groups.[413] XYY males it turns out are fairly prevalent in society – 1 in every 1000 births – and most exhibit no signs of a predilection toward criminality or aggression. Studies show no obvious difference in testosterone levels.[414] As Laura Re and Jutta Birkhoff summarize:

> In the last 50 years, many studies have focused on XYY trisomy. However, none of them have been able to determine an immediate and unequivocal correlation between 47,XYY genotype and certain physical, neurological or psychological characteristics. The only unchanging correlation emerging from much of the aforementioned literature seems to be the high stature, while other physical abnormalities do not seem clearly related with an extra Y.
>
> Certainly more interesting is the supposed influence of XYY syndrome on psychological development and behavior. What emerges from the research is a frequent intellectual deficit, delays in speech and language, poor writing skills, learning disabilities, and social emotional problems...Despite several studies, a direct relationship between the XYY genetic character and deviant behavior has been never statistically proved...More recent research on this correlation has, however, repeatedly highlighted that the frequency of violent behavior in 47,XYY males and 46,XY subjects would be the same if we consider subjects with the same intellectual deficit and socio-economic conditions.[415]

---

[411] Fox, "The XYY Offender," 62.
[412] Breggin and Breggin, *War Against Children of Color*, 63.
[413] Fox, "The XYY Offender," 64.
[414] Laura Re and Jutta M. Birkhoff, "The 47,XYY syndrome, 50 years of certainties and doubts: A systematic review," *Aggression and Violent Behavior* 22 (2015): 11 [art.=9-17].
[415] Re and Birkhoff, "The 47,XYY syndrome, 50 years of certainties and doubts," 13-14.

At the time though this myth of the XYY super predator caught immediate fire not only with the general public who took solace in the illusion that the "criminal" is an "other" genetically distinct from themselves, but also with the medical and governmental communities, with unfortunate consequences.[416] As Richard Fox pointed out in 1971:

> Because XYY offenders constitute a brand new classification of offender type, one might have thought that here was an opportunity for medical and social scientists to come together to examine the phenomenon free of the mythology which tends to attach to classifications which have been in vogue for much longer periods. It might also be thought that sound decisions could be made in relation to the disposition of XYY individuals on the basis of those research findings. Unhappily, it is obvious that in the five years following the first major research publications a mythology has built up around the XYY male which extends to the definition of the syndrome, the nature of the offences committed, and the offender's rehabilitative potential. Very little of this is warranted by the information in hand. Yet this mythology is not only beginning to shape the limits of further research, it is also seriously presented as the basis of recommendations for far reaching legislative and administrative action within the criminal justice system.[417]

## THE WHITE SUPER PREDATORS

In 1966 in Chicago, Illinois Richard Franklin Speck methodically raped, stabbed and strangled eight nurses. He perfectly fit the profile of the XYY Super Predator: he was over 6 feet, was semi-literate (IQ around 85), face deeply pitted with acne, and he had a history of violence. Because he fit the profile so perfectly it was

---

[416] Dr. John Beckwith and Dr. Jonathan King, "The XYY Syndrome: a dangerous myth," *New Scientist* 64:923 November 14, 1974: 474-476 (474): "there is no evidence that having an extra Y chromosome causes criminal or antisocial behaviour in affected individuals. Yet the idea that XYY males are doomed to a career of anti-social behaviour has so taken hold in the medical and government communities that programs are underway to 'remedy' the situation."
[417] Fox, "The XYY Offender," 72.

widely reported in the press that Speck was a XYY male. In fact, he was deemed the *archetypical* XYY "supermale."[418] However, he was not XYY, only a normal XY male. But there is a final aspect of the typical XYY profile that helped sale the erroneous claim that Speck was such a one: he was an over six feet tall, acne-faced, violent and sexually depraved *white* male. "It also seems evident that researchers have established a presumptive relationship between an extra Y and X chromosomes and mental retardation or subnormal intelligence *in white males*," explains David Skeen.[419] Ernest B. Hook's study indicates that XYY males are 3x's more prevalent among whites than Blacks.

> while for whites in the United States and elsewhere there was evidence for a definite association between these genotypes and a tendency to be found in certain types of security settings (i.e. mental-penal institutions), the prevalence rates of these disorders among blacks in these settings was lower than whites.[420]

So the typical XYY Super Predator would be a type of *white male*. The media as well as the medical and government communities will actively change this profile of the XYY male. The protagonist in this Super Predator Myth would be deliberately changed from 6 feet tall white men to little black boys, even babies.

### FROM TALL WHITE TO YOUNG BLACK SUPER PREDATORS

The National Institute of Mental Health – the same governmental agency that was so heavily invested in the targeting of Black boys for psychosurgery through the so-called Violence Initiative - funded two projects that would knowingly, deceptively change the XYY Super Predator profile from tall white man to young Black boy: one project based at Harvard University

---

[418] Mary A. Telfer, "Are some criminals born that way?" **Think** 34 (1968): 24-8.
[419] David Skeen, "The Genetically Defective Offender," **William Mitchell Law Review** 9 (1983): 227 [art.=217-265].
[420] Ernest B. Hook, "Racial Difference in the Prevalence Rates of Males with Sex Chromosome Abnormalities (XXY, XYY) in Security Settings in the United States," *American Journal of Human Genetics* 26 (1974): 504 [art.=504-511].

in Boston and the other at Johns Hopkins University in Baltimore. They were funded by the NIMH's Center for Studies of Crime and Delinquency. These projects went further than just redefine the XYY Super Predator in the medial and popular imagination, however. The projects used this new myth of the Young Black Super Predator to facilitate the medical *killing* and the *chemical feminization* of Black boys.

## THE BOSTON (HARVARD) PROJECT

In April 1970 two Harvard professors, child psychiatrist Dr. Stanley Walzer and medical geneticist Dr. Park Gerald, initiated a very damaging chromosome screening study of all infant boys born at the Boston Lying-In Hospital. The hospital was located in the Roxbury District, "the heart of Black culture in Boston." The Justice Department and the NIMH Center for the Study of Crime and Delinquency granted the study more than $465,000 over eight years.[421] Walzer and Gerald tested the blood of all male infants – mainly Black – within one or two days of birth for the XYY "syndrome." This had the very damaging effect of stigmatizing Black boys as the primary carries of the mythical XYY "Super Predator" trait.[422] Already by 1970 geneticists considered the XYY theory "scientific rubbish."[423] Yet, the "study" proceeded nonetheless.

Dr. Stanley Walzer

---

[421] Richard Roblin, "The Boston XYY Case," *The Hastings Center Report* 5 (1975): 5-8; Philip Weiss, "Ending the Test for Extra Chromosomes," *The Harvard Crimson* September 15, 1975.
[422] Washington, *Medical Apartheid*, 279-283. As Dr. Jonathan King, one of the opponents to the study, said: "And what is the message of this study? That even though you seem fine, it's in your genes, kid, and one of these days it may come over you...In the XYY study children and their parents were really being harmed": Bauer et al, "The XYY Controversy," 18, 21.

The NIMH also already knew that "XYY, the supposed marker for violence, is a 'white' marker, not a 'black' one, in that it is found more commonly in white men than in blacks."[424] In the early 1970s the National Institutes of Health did a blood sample XYY study of 475 mainly black boys, ages 13-17, who appeared before Juvenile Courts of the District of Colombia and Prince George's County, Maryland. Added to this group were six boys referred by psychiatrists and probation officers due to their unusual size and behavior. None of the 475 boys tested positive for the XYY signature, and only one of the six referred boys was XYY: a 17-year old Caucasian boy.[425] Yet, the search for the mythical XYY Super Predator is now officially moved from tall white men in prison to black baby boys born in hospitals.

Harriet Washington notes:

> It seems strange that accomplished scientists at several major universities would embrace science that was so deeply flawed...a darker logic lurks behind the studies' selection of black males.[426]

A darker logic and a darker *purpose* lurks behind these studies, and we have a strong indication of what it is. Dr. Jonathan Beckwith, molecular biologist from Harvard who led the campaign that ultimately shut down this Boston study, makes a startling revelation:

> Another impact of XYY research is its effect on decisions after amniocentesis (i.e. amniotic fluid test used in prenatal diagnosis of chromosomal abnormalities and fetal infection); this impact is frightening because of its eugenic implication. *XYYs are being aborted after they are discovered by amniocentesis.* Jon King was at a birth defect symposium where *genetic screeners implied that they would suggest or encourage abortion*

---

[423] J. Katz, **Experimentation with Human Beings** (New York: Russel Sage Foundation, 1972) 345.
[424] Washington, **Medical Apartheid**, 282.
[425] W.E. Dodson, M.S. al-Aish, and D.F. Alexander, "Cytogenetic Survey of XYY Males in Two Juvenile Court Populations, with a Case Report," *Journal of Medical Genetics* 9 (1972): 287-288.
[426] Washington, **Medical Apartheid**, 281.

*for XYY fetuses. Distortion of the research results in decisions based on faulty information.*[427]

Yes, you have read correctly: hospital nurses are using the *myth* of the frightening XYY male and *distortion of test results* to encourage mothers to *abort* these babies![428] Dr. Bentley Glass, former president of the American Association for the Advancement of Science, in 1971 openly looked forward to the day when amniocentesis and abortion will "rid us of...sex deviants such as the XYY type."[429] And the "XYY" label has just been artificially tagged on black boys. Walzer, head of the Boston study, informs us that when mothers call him after an amniocentesis and asks if they should abort their XYY child – which may in actuality be a normal XY boy – he calls the mothers into his office and bombards (our term) them with the disproved XYY Super Predator misinformation and then sends them on their way "to make their own decisions."[430] It is thus no surprise at all that, as Beckwith and King report, there are actual cases of mothers opting for abortion of their allegedly XYY son after an amniocentesis.[431] Bentley Glass didn't have to wait long at all. This XYY screening of Black boys was being conducted in New York, New Haven and Denver also.[432]

In other words: the dark agenda of the Harvard-supported and government-funded XYY screening of Black male infants in Boston (and New York, New Haven and Denver) was both the tagging and social stigmatizing of Black males as genetic Super Predators *and* the encouragement and facilitation of the *abortion* of Black male babies under the false pretext that, if they come to term, they will be a "menace to society" as violent, sexual psychopath – the XYY Super Predator.

---

[427] Diane Bauer et al, "The XYY Controversy Researching Violence and Genetics," *The Hastings Center Report* 10 (1980): 1-31 (22).
[428] On mothers opting to abort their child after they were told he was an XYY, see Beckwith and King, "The XYY Syndrome," 475.
[429] Bentley Glass, "Science: Endless Horizons or Golden Age?" *Science* 171:3966 (8 January 1971): 23-29.
[430] Bauer et al, "The XYY Controversy," 10.
[431] Beckwith and King, "The XYY Syndrome," 475.
[432] Washington, *Medical Apartheid*, 281.

In November 1974 the Boston study was terminated thanks to the efforts of Science For The People group led by Dr. Jonathan Beckwith of Harvard and Dr. Jonathan King of M.I.T.[433]

## THE MARYLAND (JOHNS HOPKINS) PROJECT

The same governmental institution that funded the Boston project, the NIMH, also funded a similar endeavor in Maryland. Dr. Digamber Borgaonkar, under the aegis of Johns Hopkins University, was awarded a three year, $300,000 grant to screen adolescent boys in the Maryland juvenile justice system for XYY. Borgaonkar and Johns Hopkins were ostensibly seeking to establish the prevalence and determine the violence of the XYY male. In the three years covered by the grant Borgaonkar planned to screen all juveniles in the State of Maryland. But he and the NIMH knew that by screening Black boys they were swimming in the wrong pool. They had an agenda for the Black boys though.

Borgaonkar selected 6,000 boys, 85% of them Black and most were housed in Maryland state institutions for abandoned and delinquent children. He also selected 500 affluent mostly white boys. As controls Borgaonkar chose 7,500 Black boys enrolled in free-child care programs at Johns Hopkins. Maryland juvenile court probation officers were sent to coerce resisting mothers to sign the permission slip enrolling their sons in the project. Blood was drawn from the boys to screen for the extra Y chromosome. Without the parents' knowledge and permission the blood was sent for examination to the Division of Medical Genetics at Johns Hopkins University.[434]

While the Boston/Harvard project covertly targeted Black boys in the womb for termination via abortion, what was the covert objective of the Maryland/Johns Hopkins project with Black adolescent boys? Jonathan Beckwith and Jonathan King report: "in one institution in Maryland, XYY inmates were treated with female sex hormones to restore 'normal' behavior."[435] There

---

[433] Jonathan R. Beckwith, *Making Genes, Making Waves* (Cambridge and London: Harvard University Press, 2002) 116ff.
[434] Washington, *Medical Apartheid*, 279-283.
[435] Beckwith and King, "The XYY Syndrome," 474.

it is: the darker purpose was the chemical feminization of the Black boys. The XYY "studies" of the 1970s which were based on a disproven myth therefore had three covert but recognizable objectives:

1. Change the profile of the mythological XYY Super Predator in the public consciousness from white man to Black boy, thereby stigmatizing Black boys throughout the country. This is the genesis of the pernicious "Black Youth as Super Predator" lie championed by Hillary Clinton which made it easy to criminalize Black children in a way that white children would never be allowed. This criminalization then allowed the mass incarceration of hundreds of thousands of young Black males, many of them juveniles.
2. "Kill the Male": Looking at the Boston project, we see that these XYY studies could serve as a cover under which the coerced abortion of Black male babies can occur. Doctors and nurses give Black parents distorted results of an amniocentesis and then frighten them with false information about a "XYY syndrome" and encourage abortion of the boy child.
3. Feminize Black Boys: Looking at the Maryland project, we learn that these XYY "studies" can serve as an excuse to chemically feminize Black boys under the authority of the State. As we shall see, pumping boys with female hormones does not "normalize" behavior; it feminizes the body. Thus, we have both objectives of White Supremacy carried out under the false pretension of the XYY Syndrome: Kill the Black Man (God) and Feminize the Black Man (God).

### SCIENTIFICALLY DEMONIZING BLACK BOYS

But there also seems to be another aspect to the "dark logic" undergirding these studies. Laura Re and Jutta Birkhoff note: "Boys of this genotype seemed to become a modern version of the *reo nato* (born criminal) of Cesare Lombroso (1876)."[436] Lombroso (1835-1909) popularized scientific racism in Italy. He introduced a theory of atavism, according to which men who are criminals were born that way and have certain physical characteristics. African and Asian peoples are the primitive "born criminals" and African and Asian blood and physiognomy predisposes one to criminality. Thus, criminal tendencies in whites are proof of a "residual blackness."

Lombroso's atavisim and *reo nato* theory is a form of a broader thought model called *inner causality*. This thought model is historically rooted in the medieval theory of demonology: the belief that men who engage in criminal behavior are possessed or driven by internal entities, forces, demons, id-impulses, etc. This is the belief that drove the Inquisition of the Middle Ages. But enlightenment did not banish the belief: "The demonic myth has not dissolved in the light of experience but remains a lively fiction; it has taken on many forms and guises, among them the phrenology of Gall and Spurzheim, the evolutionary atavism of Lombroso, and the genetic theories of Goddard and Dugdale."[437]

According to Theodore Sarbin and Jeffrey Miller, modern criminology has its demonism theories also. The site of internal causes is either the organ of intelligence (thus "mental illness") or the chromosomes (evil genes). The XYY Super Predator myth is a subset of the latter theory. The XYY theory is thus "a form of scientific demonism," Sarbin and Miller inform us.[438] The XYY set are the biological site of evil – there are demons in the genes - and the source of behavioral evil. This totally unscientific belief is rooted in "the model of internal causality – the model that provided the political and cognitive background for causal demons in medieval times and for causal chromosomal patterns (i.e. XYY) in modern times."[439]

This means that the XYY "studies" that were based on the disproven myth of the XYY criminal type not only helped to

---

[436] Re and Birkhoff, "The 47,XYY syndrome, 50 years of certainties and doubts,"9.
[437] Theodore R. Sarbin and Jeffrey E. Miller, "Demonism Revisited: The XYY Chromosomal Anomaly," *Issues in Criminology* 5 (1970): 196 [art.=195-207]
[438] Sarbin and Miller, "Demonism Revisited," 201.
[439] Sarbin and Miller, "Demonism Revisited," 205.

*stigmatize* Black boys as natural Super Predators; it not only helped to *neutralize* Black boys through deception and coerced abortions; and it not only helped to *feminize* Black boys by providing a false pretense for chemical feminization through estrogen treatments. On Sarbin and Miller's reading, the XYY "studies" also scientifically *demonize* Black boys in American society.

# 11 The Pharmacological Solution: Keeping the Black Male Subordinate

I.  *Dominance Hierarchy Studies*

The controversy over psychosurgery forced Frank Ervin out of Massachusetts General and from Boston. He landed at the University of California in Los Angeles (UCLA), 1972-1978, where he continued his violence research and even his psychosurgery research. He collaborated with a group of UCLA scientists who in the 1970's and early 80's conducted research on the mechanics of and the biological (biochemical) role in social dominance hierarchy.[440] They studied the interrelationships between dominant male groups and subordinate male groups; what distinguishes dominant males from subordinate males, behaviorally and biochemically and how dominant male groups thwart challenges from subordinate males to maintain their dominance.

---

[440] Lois Timnick and *The Los Angeles Times*, "Students Take to the Wild in Search of Man's Closest Relatives," *The Washington Post* April 22, 1979; M.J. Raleigh, J.W. Flannery and F.R. Ervin, "Sex differences in social behavior among captive juvenile vervet monkeys (*Cercopithecus aethiops sabaeus*)," **Behav. Neural Biol.** 26 (1979): 455-465; L. Fairbanks, M.T. McGuire, and N. Page, "Social roles in captive vervet monkeys (*Cercopithecus aethiops sabaeus*)," **Behav. Processes** 3 (1978): 335-352; M.J. Raleigh et al, "Serotonergic Influences on the Social Behavior of Vervet Monkeys (*Cercopithecus aethiops sabaeus*)," **Experimental Neurology** 68 (1980): 322-334; Michael T. McGuire, "Social Dominance Relationships in Male Vervet Monkeys: A Possible Model for the Study of Dominance Relationships in Human Political Systems," *International Political Science Review* 3 (1982): 11-32; M.T. McGuire, M.J. Raleigh and C. Johnson, "Social dominance in adult male vervet monkeys: Behavior-biochemical relationships," **Biology and social life** 22 (1983): 311-328; Michael J. Raleigh et al, "Social and Environmental Influences on Blood Serotonin Concentrations in Monkeys," **Arch Gen Psychiatry** 41 (1984): 405-410; Michael J. Raleigh, Michael T. McGuire et al, "Serotonergic mechanisms promote dominance acquisition in adult male vervet monkeys," **Brain Research** 559 (1991): 181-190.

By studying colonies of African Green Monkey (Vervet Monkey or *Cercopithecus aethiops sabaeus*) and applying their observations to the human social setting, Michael Raleigh, Michael McGuire and their team at UCLA postulated that a society's dominant male (DM) group (e.g. white males) and subordinate male (SM) groups (e.g. Black males) will engage in competitive relationships over resources and each will display a wide array of competitive behaviors in order to gain an advantage to either maintain dominance in society (the DM group) or acquire dominance in society (the SM group). For example, the UCLA scientists postulated that increases in the number of subordinate males threaten the status of dominant males. Besides physically reducing and/or restricting the number of actual subordinate males, a defensive strategy available to dominant males is to permit the subordinate males to freely engage in otherwise restricted (illegal) behaviors. This frequently engaged in "deviant" behavior will distract subordinate males from engaging in confrontations with dominant males.[441] In other words, America's dominant white males gain an advantage by permitting subordinate Black males to engage freely in illegal behavior in the isolated ghettos of America, for this keeps the Black SM from challenging the white DM.

These African Green Monkey studies were undertaken not just with human society in mind,[442] but with an eye to the biosocial control of Black American males in particular. Beginning in 1975 the "Operation Ferdinand" operative and psychosurgery enthusiast Frank Ervin teamed up with his UCLA colleagues Michael Raleigh and J.W. Flannery and undertook a study at the Behavioral Science Foundations laboratory at Estridge, St. Kitts that will have ghastly implications for Black life in the 1980's and 90s, and beyond.[443] The lab where these studies took place was housed in the slave quarters of a former sugar plantation. Most

---

[441] McGuire, "Social Dominance Relationships," 28.
[442] McGuire, "Social Dominance Relationships," 28-29: "All of the non-human primate studies discussed above were undertaken with the view that they may be applicable to studies of humans."
[443] Lois Timnick and *The Los Angeles Times*, "Students Take to the Wild in Search of Man's Closest Relatives," *The Washington Post* April 22, 1979.

fitting and not an accident. Ervin et al. seem to have had four research interests:

1. Assessing the impact of environmental change on the biochemistry of normal monkeys/(man). For example the scientists created an "experimental 'depression'" in some juveniles by separating them from loved ones and then measuring any changes in brain chemicals.
2. Studying the social consequences of scientifically produced brain damage. The researches damaged the brain of some normal monkeys through psychosurgery – removing tiny pieces of tissue from a part of the frontal cortex thought to be associated with emotion and mood – and then returned the brain damaged monkey back with the troop and studied the behavioral changes in the monkey and how the troop responded to him and he to them.
3. Assessing the effects of brain-altering drugs on the monkeys, "making them 'crazy' or violent, for example," and then trying to reverse the damage.
4. Manipulating the levels of a particular brain chemical, serotonin, and noting the behavioral consequences.

Ervin and colleagues observed that the brain damaged males were less aggressive and spent more time alone – like Ferdinand the Bull – and if they did engage in any one-on-one fighting they typically lost, limiting their access to resources: females, food and shelter. They observed that social role and status impacted the consequences of specific brain damage. In other words, damage to the brain of a DM would produce behavioral consequences distinct from the behavioral consequences caused by the same damage to the brain of a SM.

These efforts to effect behavioral change through the purposeful damaging of the male brain through the combined methods of psychosurgery, brain-altering drugs and social/environmental manipulation will soon have dire consequences for Black America. With the demise of the reputation of psychosurgery in the mid-1970s, the use of brain altering drugs and social/environmental manipulation along with a disguised form of psychosurgery will be the selected methods of "Operation Ferdinand" in the 1980s and 1990s. Fellow "Operation Ferdinand" operative José Delgado himself noted in 1973:

> There are two ways to control behavior: one is through the environment; the second (...) is through the brain. And in the brain we have mainly three types of controls: (1) mechanical, through surgery, (2) electrical, through brain stimulation, and (3) chemical, by placing drugs inside the brain...[444]

Option 1, the mechanical method (psychosurgery) had just been outlawed. However, it will have an afterlife in disguised form. Option 3 – the pharmacological manipulation of the brain and control of behavior through drugs – will be the focus of research (and covert operations) through the 1980s and 1990s. UCLA will play a key role in the Black carnage produced by this forced shift from (undisguised) psychosurgery to what would come to be called sociopharmacology, a marriage of social/environmental manipulation and the use of brain-altering drugs for the purpose of behavioral control. Sociopharmacology will be the matrix out of which arose the catastrophic culture of urban violence, the urban Crack Epidemic, as well as the Black Autism Epidemic.

II.   *Sociopharmacology: The Scientific Roots of Urban Carnage*

Michael McGuire and his UCLA colleagues – who worked with Frank Ervin - elaborated this new research paradigm.[445]

---

[444] Henry K. Beecher et al, "Physical Manipulation of the Brain," *The Hastings Center Report* 3 (1973): 2 [art.=1-22].
[445] M.T. McGuire and M.J. Raleigh, "Biosocialpharmachology," *McLean Hospital Journal* 2 (1980): 73-84; M.T. McGuire, M.J. Raleigh et al, "Biosociopharmacology: I," in *Sociopharmamachology: Drugs in social context* ed. C. Chein (Dordrecht: Reidel, 1982); Michael T. McGuire, Michael J. Raleigh and Gary L. Brammer, "Sociopharmacology," *Annual Review of Pharmacology* 22 (1982): 643-61.

Sociopharmacolgy (society + pharmacology), previously called *biosociopharmacology* (biology + society + pharmacology), investigates the interrelationships between biology (biochemical and physiological), social and physical environment, and social status. It assesses the effects of various pharmaceutical agents (drugs) on different biochemical/genetic profiles and on the social behavior of individuals of different social statuses. Sociopharmacology has as its most important investigative question the social consequences of drug induced behavioral changes. In this regard their research indicated that individuals of different social statuses will have different behavioral responses to the equivalent doses of the same drug. This means for example that dominant male group members have behavioral responses to a chemical agent different from that of subordinate male group members, and vice versa.[446] The researchers also learned that these social statuses themselves have some correlation with distinct biochemical profiles that are not permanent but environmentally informed and thus malleable and manipulatable. This means that a certain biochemical profile is associated with dominance and another biochemical profile is associated with subordination. But these biochemical profiles can be manipulated and altered – by drugs for example – thereby altering status, making DMs subordinate and making SMs dominant.

The bridge between biochemical profile and status (dominance or subordination) is behavior. The researches learned that there are a set of behaviors that facilitate dominance and a set of behaviors that are associated with subordination or non-dominance and they learned that a particular biochemical – serotonin – modulates these behaviors. Thus, a certain level of serotonin makes possible certain dominance-related behaviors which facilitate dominance acquisition or maintenance while an inadequate level of serotonin facilitates *counter*-dominance behaviors, the result of which is often subordination. Serotonin, they discovered, is the biochemical key to social hierarchy. It will also be their magic bullet for the biosocial control of Black America, the Black male in particular.

---

[446] McGuire, Raleigh and Brammer, "Sociopharmacology," 644.

III. *Serotonin: The Biochemical Key and the Magic Bullet*

There are two forms of this important biochemical: brain serotonin produced in the raphe nuclei of the brainstem and the hypothalamus (central) and whole blood serotonin produced mainly in the gut and the pineal gland (peripheral). Because serotonin (also known as 5-hydroxytryptamine or 5-HT) does not cross the blood-brain barrier, the two forms function separately. Their biogenesis is related but distinct as well. Serotonin's dietary amino acid precursor, tryptophan, comes in two forms: tryptophan hydroxylase 1 (TPH-1), which metabolizes into whole blood serotonin, and tryptophan hydroxylase 2 (TPH-2), which is neuronal specific - it metabolizes into brain serotonin. Brain serotonin acts as a neurotransmitter carrying messages between cells. It is involved in a host of physiological processes. In the central nervous system serotonin acts as a neuromodulator that is implicated in the regulation of sleep pattern, mood, appetite control, body temperature, pain sensitivity, arousal, sexual activity and aggression. What the UCLA scientists discovered was that serotonin was the "Rosetta Stone" for decoding the mysteries of aggression, violence and also social hierarchy, among other things.[447] They found that high levels of serotonin was distinctly related to male social dominance and low levels of serotonin was associated with low social status or subordination. As *The New York Times* announced in 1983 regarding the UCLA investigations:

> Studies of monkeys and college students suggest that social status is reflected in the chemistry of the brain. Scientists say that studies show that the dominant males in colonies of vervet monkeys had twice as much circulating serotonin in their blood as any other males...The findings imply that the ability to convert food substances (with tryptophan) efficiently into serotonin helps an animal achieve dominance.[448]

---

[447] Ronald Kotulak, "New Drugs Break Spell of Violence," *Chicago Tribune* December 15, 1993;

[448] Harold M. Schmeck, Jr., "Domination is Linked to Chemical in the Brain," *The New York Times* September 27, 1983; n.a. "Rise in brain chemical found a factor in dominant behavior," *Chicago Tribune* October 2, 1983.

Douglas Madison of the University of Iowa did follow-up studies in 1985 that suggested to him that power seekers are biochemically different from everyone else and that serotonin was tied to "a syndrome of human behaviors and orientations characteristic of a drive for power."[449] High serotonin thus inspires the drive for power, he suggested. "[S]erotonergic mechanisms robustly influence the acquisition of male dominance"[450] because elevated brain and body serotonin produces certain moods (quiescent, tranquil, deliberate, self-controlled) and promotes certain behaviors (prosocial) that facilitate the dominance of certain males (serotonin synthesis is 52% higher in men than in women[451]).

Dominant and non-dominant/subordinate males differ in select biochemical measures and these correlate with behavioral differences. A perfect example of the difference between dominant and non-dominant/subordinate behavior is illustrated by a maze experiment conducted by the UCLA researchers. Dominant and non-dominant animals were separately placed in a large maze and observed. The behavioral differences were conspicuous. Subordinate animals were highly excitable entering the maze and traversed it rapidly, seldom stopping their movement. This hyperactivity indicated a lack of caution, deliberation and deliberateness. In contrast, dominant male animals approached the maze calmly and cautiously, initially exploring it slowly and then only minimally engaging in high risk exploration of the maze throughout the remainder of the text. Premeditation on the part of the dominant male animals was obvious, while it was conspicuously absent in the non-dominant animal.[452] These different dominant and subordinate male behaviors are influenced by biochemistry. How so?

---

[449] Douglas Madison, "A Biochemical Property Relating to Power Seeking in Humans," *The American Political Science Review* 79 (1985): 448-457; idem, "Power Seekers are Different: Further Biochemical Evidence," *American Political Science Review* 80 (1986): 261-270.

[450] Raleigh et al, "Serotonergic mechanisms," 182.

[451] S. Nishizawa et al, "Differences between males and females in rates of serotonin synthesis in human brain," *Proceedings of the National Academy of Sciences USA* 94 (1997): 5308-5313.

[452] McGuire, Raleigh and Johnson, "Social dominance," 321-322.

Serotonin is our brain's key modulator of several physiological processes, including our primitive drives and emotions. It is the brain's chemical *breaks*, our impulse inhibitor (it puts a lid on our impulsive behavior). High serotonin is required to rein in our basic drives – appetite, sex, aggression, etc. – and keep them from racing out of control. When serotonin is low, "all the basic drives that it regulates can burst out of control," because low serotonin results in loss of impulse control.[453]

If serotonin is the brain's chemical breaks, noradrenalin is the chemical *accelerator*. When the brain perceives a threat, noradrenalin gets turned on and prepares the mind to deal with the impending crisis and prepares the body for fight or flight.[454] Together, serotonin and noradrenalin play a key role in determining how a person will respond to different situations such as emergencies. For example, most "healthy" people in a "healthy" environment are born with a balance of these two hormones which allows them to react to events in reasonable, moderate ways.[455] Serotonin studies have indicated however that a threatening environment triggers an imbalance in these

---

[453] Ronald Kotulak, "Tracking Down The Monster Within Us," *Chicago Tribune* December 12, 1993.

[454] Ronald Kotulak, "How Brain's Chemistry Unleashes Violence," *Chicago Tribune* December 13, 1993).

[455] As Dr. Ned Kalin, chief of psychiatry at the University of Wisconsin affirms: "an enriched environment can change the chemistry of the brain for the better." Dr. William Greenough, neuroscientist from the University of Illinois at Champaign-Urbana, demonstrated this clearly. He exposed rats to an enriched environment full of toys, food, exercise devices, and playmates. An autopsy of these rats found that they each had a "super brain" that showed 25% more connections between brain cells than those of rats raised in standard, drab lab cages. Tests showed that enriched rats were more intelligent than depressed ones. Dr. Craig Ramey of the University of Alabama proved the same thing with humans. He exposed a group of impoverished inner city children staring as young as six weeks to an enriched environment: learning, good nutrition, toys, and playmates. He used a similar, unenriched group as a control. Dr. Ramey tested the IQ of the youth at 12 years old, "The enriched youngsters had significantly higher IQs than the control group." He says further: "PET scans, which measure brain activity, showed that the brains of the children exposed to stimulating environments were perking along at a more efficient rate than those of the control group." See Ronald Kotulak, "Reshaping Brain For a Better Future," *Chicago Tribune* April 15, 1993.

chemicals.[456] A threatening environment induces *low serotonin* as a self-preserving adaptation: low serotonin allows an individual to become more impulsive and aggressive in order to deal with the threat. This is an example of an "environmentally induced brain change."[457]

Another environmental factor that induces brain change is chronic stress, especially the stress caused by what's called low socioeconomic status (SES). Studies have demonstrated that such stress can deplete serotonin and is associated with low serotonin reactivity.[458] Thus socioeconomically poor, depressed and violent (threatening) environments – i.e. the purposefully created urban ghetto – triggers low serotonin and high noradrenalin, and all of the resultant consequences: highly impulsive, easily excitable, aggressive males; random, emotion-driven violence; anti-social behavior; and perpetual subordinate social status. Remember, in the 1975-1979 St. Kitts experiment discussed above Ervin and his UCLA colleagues manipulated the environment to induce experimental depression in juvenile monkeys. As Ronald Kotulak of the *Chicago Tribune* notes: "The environment plays on the brain like a computer keyboard,"[459] and these scientists have mastered the manipulation of the environment to produce desired results. Ervin's UCLA colleagues will admit in 1983: "Alterations in selected social and environmental conditions result in *predictable* biochemical parameters (emphasis added)."[460]

The deliberate manipulation of this biochemistry – indirectly by altering environment and directly through brain

---

[456] A threatening, deprived environment produced the opposite results of the enriched environment: "abuse, poverty, neglect or sensory deprivation can reset the brains chemistry": "Using sophisticated imaging devices that can peer inside the brain, scientists have observed how a threatening environment influences the brain production of [the] two key chemicals implicated in violence and aggression – serotonin and noradrenalin." Ronals Kotulak, "Why Some Kids Turn Violent," *Chicago Tribune* December 14, 1993.

[457] Kotulak, "Tracking Down The Monster Within Us."

[458] Molly J. Crockett, "The Neurochemistry of Fairness: Clarifying the Link Between Serotonin and Prosocial Behavior," *Annals of the New York Academy of Science* 1167 (2009): 83 [art.=76-86]; Kotulak, "Reshaping Brain For a Better Future."

[459] Kotulak, "Reshaping Brain For a Better Future."

[460] McGuire, Raleigh and Johnson, "Social dominance," 311.

interventions - was the goal and the breakthrough of American scientists, and UCLA was Ground Zero. Serotonin and noradrenalin are the two "brain buttons" that scientists discovered they can push and thereby determine a person's future, [461] "two potent brain chemicals that researchers have successfully manipulated to make animals more violent or less violent," in the words of Kotulak.[462] "[A]ggression can be controlled by manipulating brain levels of serotonin."[463] By "twisting the architecture of the brain" scientists can "push noradrenalin production into overdrive and serotonin into low gear,"[464] thereby making an individual or group hyper-impulsive, hyper-aggressive and violent: "the raging monster was being forced into the open where scientists could begin to understand and tame it."[465] Tame it, or tame *him* – the Black male. That's the goal. It is important to point out here that all violence is *not* the same. Not all aggression is associated with low serotonin; only impulsive, emotion-driven, reactionary aggression which is socially maladaptive and characteristic of low social status is. This is to be distinguished from proactive, premeditative, deliberate, predatory aggression characteristic of dominant males. Impulsive aggression is often severe, unrestrained, dysfunctional, and frequently results in the wounding or death of the aggressor.[466] This is the aggression artificially produced by evil scientists who have mastered the manipulation of these chemical buttons of the brain.

In terms of dominance hierarchy, low serotonin among subordinate males favors dominant males, because in the interest of self-preservation low serotonin discourages the conspicuous

---

[461] Kotulak, "Reshaping Brain For a Better Future."
[462] Kotulak, "Tracking Down The Monster Within Us."
[463] Kotulak, "How Brain Chemistry Unleashes Violence."
[464] Ronald Kotulak, "How Brain Chemistry Unleashes Violence," **Chicago Tribune** December 13, 1993.
[465] Kotulak, "How Brain Chemistry Unleashes Violence."
[466] Menahem Krakowski, "Violence and Serotonin: Influence of Impulse Control, Affect Regulation, and Social Functioning," **Journal of Neuropsychiatry and Clinical Neurosciences** 15 (2003): 294-305; Molly J. Crockett, "The Neurochemistry of Fairness: Clarifying the Link Between Serotonin and Prosocial Behavior," *Annals of the New York Academy of Science* 1167 (2009): 76-86.

challenging of dominant males who are, by virtue of their high-status, in a position to punish such insolence.[467] So the aggression, the raging monster, is unleashed instead against fellow subordinate males only: "Even as low (serotonin) keeps him from challenging dominant males, he may behave recklessly toward those closer to him on the social ladder," explains Robert Wright.[468] It is therefore to DMs advantage to keep the serotonin levels low among SMs, for "raising brain serotonin function...promotes acquisition of dominance in males,"[469] while on the other hand by inducing serotonergic dysfunction the chances of dominance acquisition are curtailed for SMs. Increasing serotonin decreases anti-social quarrelsome behavior and increases dominance in humans: decreasing serotonin increases antisocial behavior and decreases dominance.[470]

This is how scientists looking to produce a non-aggressive, docile Black male ended up producing a hyper-aggressive "super predator." Because high serotonin is accompanied by the drive for power and dominance acquisition and low serotonin perpetuates low social status, it was in the interests of these American scientists to induce serotonergic dysfunction in Black males. Low serotonin also ensured that the resultant aggressiveness and violence was a problem *only* for fellow subordinate Black males, *not* dominant white males. So the 1980's saw a number of covert operations aimed at causing serotonergic dysfunction among inner-city Black males, including the Crack cocaine epidemic, the Autism epidemic and the homosexuality epidemic among Black people. As sociopharmacology stipulated, the main methods involved the weaponized use of drugs.

---

[467] Robert Wright, "The Biology of Violence," *The New Yorker* March 13, 1995, 74-75 [art.=68-77].
[468] Wright, "Biology of Violence," 75.
[469] D.S. Moskowitz at al, "The Effect of Tryptophan on Social Interaction in Everyday Life: A Placebo-Controlled Study," *Neuropsychopharmacolgy* 25 (2001): 278 [art.=277-289].
[470] Moskowitz at al, "Effect of Tryptophan on Social Interaction," 287.

IV.    The Pharmacological Assault on the Black Male Mind

*American medicine has not spared black children its very worst abuses in the name of scientific research.* Harriet A. Washington, **Medical Apartheid** (2006)

In 1993 Dr. Ned Kalim of the University of Wisconsin made an ominous prediction:

> We're going to be able to identify these (brain-impaired) children (i.e. uncontrolled Black children) within the first five years of life and make interventions to change their brains right then. Just as an enriched environment can change the chemistry of the brain for the better, exposure to the right drug *at the right time* may reset the development of the brain in a positive way.[471]

These evil scientists are targeting the brains of Black babies with their laboratory drugs. They want to "intervene" early to change the chemistry of the Black (male) brain. The changes will be "better" and "positive," but not for the Black babies or the Black community. Rather these changes will be better for dominant white males. The emphasis on intervening *at the right time* with their brain-altering drugs should be kept in mind when we discuss the autism operation and the CDC's insistence that the MMR vaccine be administered to children at a specific time much earlier than all of the good, unbiased science says it should be. Ominous then is Ronald Kotulak's comment regarding Dr. Kalim's prediction: "Children someday may be *immunized* against stunted brains," which must be read as: Our brain-altering/damaging drugs are and will be administered to Black male children through immunizations.

Kotulak reported in 1993 that "drugs are being developed that...quiet the raging brains of the most violent patients,"[472] i.e. drugs that targeted serotonin and noradrenalin.[473] But the UCLA researchers had already successfully targeted serotonergic

---

[471] Kotulak, "Reshaping Brain For a Better Future."
[472] Kotulak, "New Drugs Break Spell of Violence."
[473] Crockett, "Neurochemistry of Fairness," 83: "In laboratory studies, 5-HT has been manipulated artificially using both pharmacological and dietary treatments."

function pharmacologically back in the late 1970s and early 1980s. They altered and manipulated the serotonin neurotransmission of their research monkeys through chronic drug treatment. They increased serotonin in their monkeys which resulted in dominance and they depleted serotonin which resulted in the loss of dominance. The researchers used what they called a "battery-of-drugs" strategy: they assaulted their test subjects' serotonergic system with multiple chemical agents or drugs. Among this battery of drugs investigated under the sociopharmacology program were both marijuana and cocaine: "The effects of cannabis and cocaine have been investigated under a variety of experimental conditions."[474] Two drugs that proved to be particularly effective in depleting serotonin was fenfluramine, an amphetamine derivative, and parachlorophenylalanine or p-chlorophenylalanine (p-CPA), also called fenclonine, which selectively inhibited the enzyme tryptophan (Trp) from synthesizing serotonin. [475]

Fenfluramine assaults the serotonergic mechanism.

> Acutely (=one time), fenfluramine releases serotonin from presynaptic storage vesicles and may act as an indirect agonist. Chronically (=repeated over time) however, fenfluramine disrupts serotonergic storage vesicles, diminishes tryptophan hydroxylase activity, decreases [cerebral spinal fluid] 5-HIAA (the main metabolite of serotonin) and brain serotonergic concentrations and produces effects compatible with decreased serotonergic function.[476]

The acute or initial effect from a single treatment of fenfluramine has created the false impression that the drug *promotes* serotonergic function, even though the chronic, long-term detrimental effects have been known. But we now know that in laboratory animals within a few hours – sometimes after 20 minutes – of a single dose there is a marked reduction in brain serotonin. A single sufficient dose can cause long-lasting

---

[474] McGuire, "Sociopharmacology," 647.
[475] McGuire, Raleigh and Johnson, "Social dominance," 318-320; Raleigh et al, "Serotonergic Influences"; Gary L. Brammer, Michael J. Raleigh et al, "Fenfluramine Effects on Serotonergic Measures in Vervet Monkeys," *Pharmacology Biochemistry & Behavior* 40 (1991): 267-272.
[476] Raleigh, McGuire et al, "Serotonergic mechanisms," 182.

serotonergic dysfunction: depletion of brain and whole body 5-HT, degeneration of 5-HT nerve terminals throughout the forebrain, and loss of 5-HT transporters (SERT).[477]

This serotonergic dysfunction caused by fenfluramine results in a decrease in dominance. The researchers discovered that when dominant males were administered fenfluramine, they became subordinate, aggressive and locomotive.[478] Fenfluramine is thus a drug perfectly suited to be weaponized against subordinate male groups to thwart any chances of dominance acquisition. And this is precisely what is documented that they did.

These monkey studies had their eye to urban Black males. That the primary "interest" (= target) of this serotonin "research" is Black males can be demonstrated easily. In 1993 the University of Illinois Medical School did a study on the West Side of Chicago that examined the blood of Black children for serotonin levels. This study was headed by Dr. Markus J. Kruesi, chief of child and adolescent psychiatry at the university's Institute for Juvenile Research. Dr. Kruesi did a previous study of 29 West Side youth allegedly with Disruptive Behavior Disorder and found that they had low serotonin levels. The new study was designed to discover at what point in childhood serotonin levels plummet and what environmental factors contribute to the plummet.[479] The purpose of this 1993 study was no doubt to assess the results of the sociopharmacology covert operations of the 1980s, including the creation of the violent urban ghetto. Dr. Kruesi said:

> What we are all beginning to conclude is that the bad environments that more and more children are being exposed to are, indeed, creating an epidemic of violence...Environmental events are really causing molecular changes in the brain...(so that) people are more impulsive. It's frightening

---

[477] Garry L. Brammer, Michael J. Raleigh et al, "Fenfluramine Effects on Serotonergic Measures in Vervet Monkeys," *Pharmacology Biochemistry & Behavior* 40 (1991): 267-271; Ibrahim Pirinçci, Ahmet Ateşşahin, Izzet Karahan, "The Effects of Fenfluramine on Blood and Tissue Serotonin (5-Hydroxytrypamine) Levels in Rats," *Turkish Journal of Veterinary and Animal Sciences* 29 (2005): 857-863; B. Clineschmidt et al, "Fenfluramine and Brain serotonin," *Annals of the New York Academy of Sciences* 305 (1978): 222-241.
[478] Raleigh, McGuire et al, "Serotonergic mechanisms," 182.
[479] Kotulak, "Why Some Kids."

to think that we may be doing some very dreadful things to our children.[480]

We should take this as a confession.

Just how dreadful are the things this government is doing to Black children – Black males in particular – is frighteningly illustrated by the fenfluramine studies conducted between 1992 and 1996 by the New York State Psychiatric Institute (NYSPI) and Columbia University Lowenstein Center for the Prevention of Childhood Disruptive Behavior Disorders, all with the blessing, funding and assistance of the federal government. One hundred and twenty six poor "Black and Hispanic" boys ages 6 to 10 in the Manhattan, Bronx and Brooklyn areas were recruited through coercion and deception to participate in this very stressful, very painful, very dangerous and very *illegal* "study" allegedly to test the responsiveness of their serotonergic system to environmental stressors. All of the boys were the innocent younger siblings of juvenile offenders in the New York City probation system. The researchers obtained the names of these boys illegally. In December 1992 Family Court officials reportedly gave confidential probation records for the more than 100 Black juveniles to the researching institutions. Court records of juvenile offenders are sealed by law. As Adil E. Shamo and Carol A. Tauer explain:

> The research protocols...involved flagrant violation of confidentiality regarding the incarcerated sibling, his family, and hence the child subject. Because the offenses leading to incarceration were committed by juveniles, the court records were sealed. The investigators gained access to these sealed records by means that are not disclosed in the research articles; however, press reports indicate that the investigators had the cooperation of the New York City Board of Education and the Department of Probation, reportedly with the approval of Peter Reinharz, the city's chief juvenile prosecutor at the time.[481]

When local newspapers exposed the reprehensible involvement of public officials in this study, the Board of

---

[480] Kotulak, "Why Some Kids."
[481] Adil E. Shamo and Carol A. Tauer, "Ethically Questionable Research with Children: The Fenfluramine Study," *Accountability in Research* 9 (2002): 157 [art.=143-166].

Education through a spokesperson lied about their involvement, but the documents were damning.[482] The researchers used the vulnerability of the incarcerated son as well as the low socioeconomic condition of his family to coerce the parent into surrendering the younger son for this study,[483] which in fact was not a "study" but a covert assault on the healthy serotonergic system of selected Black boys. The poor mothers were promised anywhere from $125 to $260 for surrendering their son, and the boy was given a Toys-R-Us gift certificate.

The description of this study provided by the Colombia University researchers claimed that 44% of the boys were Black and 54% were Hispanic, but this is grossly misleading. "Hispanic" is really only a linguistic description (i.e. those whose first language is Spanish). In fact, the "54% Hispanic" boys were all Black Dominicans.[484] Gail Wassermen, professor of child psychiatry at Colombia and one of the chief researchers in this study affirmed that "it is proper to focus on blacks and other minorities as they are overrepresented in the courts and not well studied."[485] What is worse: white boys were *explicitly excluded from this study*,[486] for reasons that will be painfully clear shortly. As Harriet A. Washington notes: "The boys were all black, and this was by design. The experimental protocol specifies that eligible participants must be 'African American or Hispanic' and specifically excludes whites from participation."[487]

---

[482] Mitchel Cohen, "Is Violence in Your Genes? Psychology, Racism, & the Violence Initiative Project," @ http://www.mitchelcohen.com/?p=2805.

[483] Mark Schoofs, "Half-Truths and Consequences," *Village Voice* Tuesday, May 5, 1998.

[484] Harriet A. Washington, *Medical Apartheid: The Dark History of Medical Experimentation on Black Americans from Colonial Times to the Present* (New York: Anchor Books, 2006) 272.

[485] Gail Wasserman, Grant Application to the Lowenstein Foundation to Establish a Center for the Study and Prevention of Disruptive Behavior Disorders in Children at Columbia University Department of Child Psychiatry. The Lowenstein Foundation granted Wasserman $1.2 million to study the prediction and prevention of juvenile delinquency. See Cohen, "Is Violence in Your Genes?"

[486] Mark Schoofs, "Half-Truths and Consequences," *Village Voice* Tuesday, May 5, 1998: "in the original research plan, white children were explicitly excluded from the study. Only African and Hispanic boys were to be allowed in."

[487] Washington, *Medical Apartheid*, 272.

The reason white youth were explicitly excluded from this study is because the study was nothing short of "technological child abuse."[488] These Black boys – 6 to 10 years young – were forced to fast – no food or water – for 18 straight hours; they were subjected to five continuous hours with an indwelling catheter in their veins and blood drawn multiple times; and for a month prior to their arrival at the test site they were required to abstain from their medications, even those for life-threatening chronic conditions such as asthma. This shows a callousness and indifference on the part of the white researchers to the wellbeing of the young Black subjects. But the *greatest* abuse to these children was subjecting them to a massive dose of the very dangerous drug fenfluramine. This drug was banned by the FDA in 1997 – a year after the completion of this evil study – because it caused potentially fatal heart valve damage in 30% of adults that took it. It also triggers pulmonary hypertension, a life-threatening form of high blood pleasure. 90% of all adults who took a low dose of this drug experienced adverse side effects. In laboratory animals fenfluramine caused brain damage at low dose. Fenfluramine had never been given to children under twelve years old until this study. Why now? As Vera Hassner Sharav, head of Citizens for Responsible Care in Psychiatry, said:

> Since there is no study to show the drug is safe for children, but there is plenty of evidence to show that it is unsafe for adults and it is unsafe for animals, I mean it causes brain damage in animals, you would think that little children would never be exposed to it.[489]

And this is precisely why their own little white children were explicitly excluded from this study and *not* exposed to the drug and why Black boys were explicitly and exclusively targeted in this study. The dose given to the Black boys was massive (10mg/kg) and potentially toxic. A dose less than 1/10 its size (.078 mg/kg) caused adverse side effects in adults and the dose given to the children was eight times higher than that which

---

[488] Breggin and Breggin, *War Against Children of Color*, 182.
[489] Michael O. Allen, "Fenfluramine Study Hurt Boy: Mom Single Dose of Controversial Drug Altered Personality, She Says," *New York Daily News* April 26, 1998.

caused brain damage in monkeys.[490] And all this suffering and risk was for a treatment that had *no therapeutic value to the children*, which means they were conducted in violation of federal guidelines.

> All four studies involved the use of children in research that did not promise any therapeutic benefits to them as individuals, and hence could not be approved under section 46.405 of the federal regulations.[491]

The aim of this study was allegedly to test the effects of environmental stressors on serotonergic function, as was done for example in the West Side, Chicago study discussed above. But we know that this was a ruse. Before the tests were done 126 Black boys were given an initial assessment by a blood sample and serotonin levels were no doubt checked.[492] The 34 that were eventually selected all had *normal* and even *elevated* serotonin levels[493]! The researchers specifically cherry picked the Black boys who, despite being raised in a low socioeconomic environment, had a *good* serotonergic mechanism (and thus these children were not behaviorally problematic); "they took a group of Black and Latino (*sic*) youth with no history of trouble, in whom no expected abnormalities were found, whose serotonin levels were basically normal or slightly higher than expected,"[494] and these researchers *assaulted* the boys' good serotonergic system with a massive dose of a very dangerous, known serotonin antagonist. We pointed out above that a single sufficient dose can cause long-lasting serotonergic dysfunction: depletion of brain and whole body 5-HT, degeneration of 5-HT nerve terminals throughout the forebrain, loss of 5-HT transporters (SERT). And here researchers are giving a *massive* dose of this dangerous serotonin antagonist to 6 – 10 year old Black boys with good serotonin levels. There can

---

[490] Breggin and Breggin, *War Against Children of Color*, 182ff; Cohen, "Is Violence in Your Genes?"
[491] Shamo and Tauer, "Ethically Questionable Research," 147.
[492] Valerie Leiter and Sarah Herman, "Guinea Pig Kids: Myths or Modern Tuskegees?" *Sociological Spectrum: Mid-South Sociological Association* 35 (2015): 35 [art.=26-45].
[493] Washington, *Medical Apartheid*, 276.
[494] Cohen, "Is Violence in Your Genes?"

be no question that this was a deliberate assault on the healthy serotonergic system of these Black boys.

And the results were very predictable and consistent with the lab animal studies. Take for example Isaac, whose mother Charise Johnson of Brooklyn sued the research institutions for misleading her about the study and for "transforming the personality" of her son who was a study victim. Isaac had "gone from being a quiet kid to being aggressive and prone to angry outbursts."[495] As the *New York Daily News* reports:

> Her son (Isaac) was happy-go-lucky, did well in school and never had a behavior problem. But she (Charise) figured she had to cooperate with [the study] because her older son was incarcerated on a robbery conviction. Her son ceased being his happy-go-lucky self soon after the experiment, she said. The boy, now 11, suffers anxiety attacks, has severe headaches, has developed a learning disability and is about to be put in special-education classes.[496]

Mission accomplished.

And little Isaac and his 33 fellow New York victims were not isolated. As Mitchel Cohen informs us:

> Similar experiments have been going on at Queens College and Mt. Sinai School of Medicine in New York, and at facilities throughout the United States, under the rubric of the National Violence Initiative Project, supervised and funded through the National Institutes of Mental Health.[497]

But why? What was the point of taking young Black boys and assaulting their minds with such a dangerous drug as fenfluramine, which just happened to be nationally banned only a year after the studies were completed and the damage to black boys was done? Why? Its quite simple, actually:

---

[495] Al Guart, "Mom: I was duped when son became 'drug guinea pig," *New York Post* May 30, 1999.
[496] Allen, "Fenfluramine Study Hurt Boy."
[497] Cohen, "Is Violence in Your Genes?"

raising brain serotonin function...promotes acquisition of dominance in males.[498]

serotonergic mechanisms robustly influence the acquisition of male dominance.[499]

When dominant males were given fenfluramine they became subordinate.[500]

Sociopharmacology's overall interest was dominance hierarchy: how dominant males and male groups (i.e. white males) can maintain dominance and thwart the threat to their social status from non-dominant or subordinate males or male group (i.e. Black males). This fenfluramine "study" is part of the larger sociopharmacological effort.

And this was *not* a rogue operation. With all of the child abuse, racism and illegality, it was *official*. As Harriet Washington tells us:

> Despite the violation of confidentiality, the undue inducement, the medically risky nontherapeutic research on healthy children that clearly violated federal guidelines, and the racially discriminatory recruitment, the Office for Protection from Research Risks (OPRR) investigation exonerated the research institutions. This sent a clear message that no penalties would be ascribed to dangerous research if it were conducted on black children.[501]

This is how America "mind-fixes" the Black man.

---

[498] Moskowitz et al, "Effect of Tryptophan," 278
[499] Raleigh et al, "Serotonergic mechanisms," 182.
[500] Raleigh et al, "Serotonergic mechanisms," 182-185,
[501] Washington, **Medical Apartheid**, 278.

# 12   Mind Suppression and Behavioral Modification of the Black Male

I.   *Mind Fixing The Black Man*

In 1984 Jon Franklin, science writer of the Baltimore *Evening Sun*, wrote a seven day series entitled "Mind Fixers," for which he later won a Pulitzer.[502] The intent of this series was to herald a scientific breakthrough that he called "molecular psychiatry," *viz.* the "ability to readily create powerful new chemicals capable of literally changing the mind...The objective is nothing less than mind control, the therapeutic kind."[503] He proclaimed: "Ahead lies an era of psychic engineering, and the development of specialized drugs and therapies to heal sick minds."[504] As we have already demonstrated, the textbook "sick mind" is the mind of the Black male who riots, protests or in any way is a threat to the current dominance hierarchy. By "psychic engineering" Franklin meant the "precise alteration of the chemical activity of the brain." The chemistry of thought, he said, "was now understood; being understood, it could be specifically manipulated with drugs."[505]

Dr. Frederick Goodwin

One of the 50 scientists that Franklin spoke to for the series was Dr. Frederick Goodwin, "chief scientist at the National Institute of Mental Health". Goodwin is of great importance to our overall discussion. He indicated to Franklin in 1984 his hope of

---

[502] Jon Franklin, *The Mind Fixers* (*The Evening Sun*), A reprint of articles published July 23-31, 1984.
[503] Franklin, *The Mind Fixers*, 2-3.
[504] Franklin, *The Mind Fixers*, 1.
[505] Franklin, *The Mind Fixers*, 5-6.

"altering behavior biologically" as the potential answer to the "crime and violence" problem and he advocated pharmacological intervention and psychosurgery (!) as part of criminal justice.[506] But Goodwin was not just dreaming. By 1984 he put together a program of biomedical social control of the inner cities, specifically Black males. Dubbed a "violence prevention initiative," this program identified Black children by the age of five whom Goodwin could "predict" will grow up to be menaces to society and target them with "preventive intervention." Goodwin's program will become official government policy. If the Nixon Administration set off the first Violence Initiative targeting Black males for mind-murder, the Bush Administration activated the second one. The point man for the Bush Administration's initiative was Goodwin.

> In the wake of the black urban uprisings of the late 1960s, America became preoccupied with the threatening figure of the young black male as well as the overall danger of rebellion and social chaos. Led by NIMH and the Justice Department, the federal government began to develop an overall program for biomedical control of violence...It...was inspired by fear of violence in the inner-city and aimed at control of young black males.[507]

> the US government is planning a massive program of psychiatric intervention into the inner cities aimed at identifying and treating *young children* with presumed genetic and biochemical predispositions to violence...The violence initiative...plans to identify *100,000 inner city children* whose alleged biochemical and genetic defects will make them violence-prone in their later life. Treatment will consist of behavior modification in selected families...Children between the ages of *two and eighteen* will be targeted, with the main focus *on the younger ones*. Since Goodwin emphasized presumed biochemical imbalance in potentially violent children, the major 'treatment' inevitably will be drugs (emphasis added).[508]

---

[506] Franklin, *The Mind Fixers*, 20.
[507] Peter R. Breggin and Ginger Ross Breggen, "a biomedical program for urban violence control in the US: the dangers of psychiatric social control," *Change: An International Journal of Psychology and Psychotherapy* 11 (March 1993): 64 [art.=59-71].
[508] Breggin and Breggin, *War Against Children of Color*, 59-60. Robert Knight, "The Biology of Violence," *The New Yorker* March 13, 1995, pp. 68-77: "Goodwin

This number "100,000 inner city children" will take on chilling significance later. This targeting of Black babies is overt. According to Goodwin, Black (or "inner city") children as young as two or three – even as young as four months - may be selected for pharmacological intervention on the basis of *irritability* and *uncooperativeness!*[509] Goodwin was put in position to execute his plan. He was made head of the Alcohol, Drug Abuse, and Mental Health Administration (ADAMHA). On February 11, 1992 he spoke before the National Advisory Mental Health Council and revealed his program of biomedical social control of inner city Black males, whom he compared to violent, over-sexed rhesus monkeys of the jungle that are used for primate research in the laboratory.[510]. This is an open confession that experiments on lab monkeys had their eye on Black people the whole time.[511] (The government's manipulation of serotonin levels and function through drugs and diet control have deliberately *made* many inner city males violent and over-sexed). The plan Goodwin laid out before the Council to target Black adolescents for preventive intervention was his agency's "top priority" and "number one initiative," he revealed. He said his program would focus on a select population of 100,000 inner city children as targets. When Goodwin's comments were made public they sparked a controversy, being called racist. The result was that he was removed as head of ADAMHA but "kicked up" as director of the National Institute of Mental Health (NIMH). Fitting.

In a document dated March 9, 1992 entitled "Preventing Youth Violence: Physical and Sexual Assault and Homicide on the Street, and in the Home – A Summary Overview of a 25 Year History" and released via a Freedom of Information Act request,

---

concedes that pharmacological therapy was a likely outcome of the initiative (69)."
[509] Breggin and Breggin, *War Against Children of Color*, 61.
[510] Breggin and Breggin, *War Against Children of Color*, 4-5.
[511] In defense of Goodwin's comments, which most took to be racist, Boyce Rensberger of the *Washington Post* admitted: "Some findings...show there are specific biochemical derangements in the brains of certain kinds of violent people – exactly the same chemical imbalances found in monkeys – and that these can be corrected with drugs. The same drugs work in both species": "Science and Sensitivity," *The Washington Post* March 1, 1992.

Goodwin's NIMH acknowledged their intent, not only to use pharmacological interventions as part of this governmental "violence initiative" aimed at inner city Black males, but they specifically name Depo-Provera as a drug to be used![512] As we discuss at length below, Depo-Provera or medroxyprogesterone is the drug that was used to invert sexuality in lab animals.[513] It is the same drug used by the criminal justice system to chemically castrate convicted males, primarily Black, and which we discovered actually feminizes the male body.[514] And as Breggin and Breggin tell us regarding this released NIMH document: "The government is funding both Prozac and Depo-Provera studies for the control of violence."[515] Actually: for the control of Black males. This is a startling disclosure. As we shall see below, the U.S. government is targeting Black male youth for biomedical control through the use of a known agent of chemical castration and chemical feminization. How will the chemical agent be deployed or administered? We are not told. We can bet though that the drug has been administered covertly and that this has something to do with the phenomenal rise of the Black Sissy in the inner cities.

Goodwin's Violence Initiative was only one facet of a broader, agency-wide youth violence prevention initiative of the U.S. Department of Health and Human Services (DHHS) headed by the Secretary of DHHS Dr. Louis Sullivan, a Black man. This $400 million agency-wide effort was coordinated by the NIMH and the CDC. (The CDC's involvement will take on even greater significance later when we discuss the Autism epidemic.) The aim of this broader effort is clearly revealed in a four-volume report published in November 1992 by the National Research Council (NRC) entitled "Understanding and Preventing Violence."[516] The Report, actually a planning document for the government program, was sponsored by the CDC, the Department of Justice (DOJ) and the National Science Foundation. The NRC's aim was

---

[512] Breggin and Breggin, *War Against Children of Color*, 12.
[513] See below.
[514] See below.
[515] Breggin and Breggin, *War Against Children of Color*, 12 n.
[516] Albert Reiss and Jeffery Roth (edd.), ***Understanding and Preventing Violence*** (Washington D.C.: National Academy Press, 1993).

to look for "biological and behavioral characteristics *of infants* that increases their risk of growing up to commit violent crimes (emphasis added)."[517] The NRC planed controlled experiments with random testing of "pharmaceutical interventions." It claimed that ethnicity and poverty were the major demographic variables predicting violence.[518] Thus, as Breggin points out: "Since the report identifies the inner city as the main arena of violence, the research will focus on minority populations, mostly African Americans."[519] But we can be more specific. Under the heading "Research Priorities," the NRC offers a list of "Key Questions" guiding the research (and thus the whole governmental violence initiative). The very first question listed is: "Do male or black persons have a higher potential for violence than others and, if so, why?"[520] The Black male is thus the focus of this whole, $400 million governmental effort at biomedical social control through pharmaceutical interventions – control of the Black male mind and behavior through drugs.[521] As a justification the Report claimed/emphasized: "Blacks are disproportionately represented in all arrests, and more so in those for violent crimes, than for property crimes."[522]

II.     *Criminalizing Black Boys From the Crib to the Womb*

Arthur Koestler was a Hungarian-British author and journalist who served as Commander of the Order of the British Empire in 1972. He advanced an important theory that will have drastic consequences for Black youth in America. His theory is called juvenilization or paedomorphisis (from *paedo* < Greek *pais*

---

[517] Reiss and Roth, *Understanding and Preventing Violence*, 159; Breggin and Breggin, *War Against Children of Color*, 22.
[518] Fox Butterfield, "Study Cites Role of Biology and Genetic Factors in Violence," *The New York Times* November 13, 1992.
[519] Breggin, "a biomedical program," 62.
[520] Reiss and Roth, *Understanding and Preventing Violence*, 380; Breggin and Breggin, *War Against Children of Color*, 23.
[521] Breggin and Breggin, *War Against Children of Color*, 23: "black males are the real focus of this research effort."
[522] Reiss and Roth, *Understanding and Preventing Violence*, 70-71; Breggin and Breggin, *War Against Children of Color*, 23.

"children" + *morphosis*: the manner in which an organism or any of its parts changes form or undergoes development). Koestler postulated that in biological evolution it's the juvenile stage – adolescents, larval, pre-adults – that is the real starting point for the species. The uninhibited modes of ideation, the sudden bursts of 'adaptive radiation' followed by the creative forward leap resides with juveniles. So in order to change a population, target the juveniles: force a desired adaptation on the youth of a people and you change that people. The government's intention to do just that was revealed by CIA operative Timothy Leary, the Agency's "Priest of LSD," who confessed: "The practical conclusion [of Koestler's theory]: if you want to bring about mutations in a species work with the young. Koestler's teaching about paedomorphosis prepared me to understand the genetic implications of the 1960's youth movement and its rejection of the old culture." The CIA drugged the 1960s' youth movement.

Said better: If you want to bring about mutations in a species *work on* the young. This is precisely why America is so obsessed with targeting Black youth with all of her most draconian covert operations. Her objective is *paedomorphosis*: ontologically changing Black people as a species or a specific population by forcing and directing a predetermined change in and through Black youth. The development of the hurtful "Super Predator" myth was purposely contrived in order to justify targeting Black youth with these paedomorphic measures.

In 1997 a disturbing book was published: ***Ghosts from the Nursery: Tracing the Roots of Violence***, by Robin Karr-Morse and Meredith S. Wiley.[523] The book clearly is a project that grew out of the larger "Super Predator" program of criminalizing and then targeting young Black males, the younger the better (despite the white baby gracing the cover). Karr-Morse and Wiley were not satisfied with targeting adolescents. Their book lays out a doom and gloom case for treating *babies and infants* with the same suspicion. Teenage violence, they claim, begins in the first three years of life and in most "criminal children" (!) signs of imminent felony are present by the age of 4. Ya Allah! These "thugs in

---

[523] Robin Karr-Morse and Meredith S. Wiley, ***Ghosts from the Nursery: Tracing the Roots of Violence*** (New York: The Atlantic Monthly Press, 1997).

bassinets" grow into John DiIulio's Black Super Predators, the chief example being Chicago's Robert Sandifer or Yummy. Karr-More and Wiley cite both of these.[524] They claim:

> It is this group of offenders, children twelve and under with a history of chronic aggression, who are forcing us to look earlier. For the majority of these early offenders, the records are clear: By age four they show consistent patterns of aggression, bullying, tantrums, and coercive interactions with others.[525]

So they make the outrageous suggestion:

> In order to understand the tide of violent behavior in which America is now submerged, we must look before preadolescence, before grade school, before preschool to *the cradle of human formation* in the first thirty-three months of life. These months, including nine months of prenatal development and the first two years after birth (33 months), harbor the seeds of violence for a growing percentage of American children.[526]

Wow. Our babies are thugs in bassinets waiting to sprout into murders, rapists, and general menaces to white American society. To head off this threat the threat must be confronted even *in the womb*. Thus, the myth of the XYY Super Predator used as a cover to encourage the abortion of black male babies in Boston and elsewhere.

This criminalizing of Black youth, infants and even fetuses is profoundly disturbing and has put our children at tremendous risk. All of the canons of this society – scientific canons, legal canons, medical canons, political canons – are all aimed at Black male youth in particular as young as fetuses. This is why Tamar Rice could be gunned down so callously and then be blamed for his own unprovoked murder. The Violence Initiatives preoccupation with Black infants 4 years and under is the context against which we can better comprehend the Autism conspiracy (see below), and the casting of Black babies in the womb as criminals-in-waiting is the context to understand a number of

---

[524] And see Karen Wright, "Thugs in Bassinets," *The New York Times* May 10, 1998.
[525] Karr-Morse and Wiley, **Ghosts from the Nursery**, 7.
[526] Karr-Morse and Wiley, **Ghosts from the Nursery**, 13.

facts such as: 79% of all Planned Parenthood's surgical abortion facilities are within walking distance of Black and Brown neighbors and thus, while only 12% of the American population Blacks account for nearly 30% of all abortions.[527] As we saw from the Boston XYY case, Black mothers are being propagandized with false information and deliberately encouraged to abort their babies, especially boy babies.

## CRIMINALIZING BLACK MALE FEARLESSNESS

According to psychologist Adrian Raine of the University of Southern California a 'pathology' that characterizes America's "problem children" of the inner city is *fearlessness*. "If we lack the fear of getting hurt," Raine says, "it may lead to a predisposition to engage in violence."[528] Fearlessness in inner city youth is thus a mental illness that is to be medicated or even remedied through some form of psychosurgery. Remember, the notorious "Operation Ferdinand" operative José Delgado sought to understand – and control – the bravery of the bulls that he experimented with and which were proxy for inner city Black males.[529] Part of this country's "violence initiative" aimed at the biomedical social control of Black men is therefore the criminalization of and, through *pharmacological* intervention, the "medicating" of fearlessness among Black youth.

---

[527] Micaiah Bilger, "Black Lives Matter: 28% of Abortions Done on Black Babies But Blacks Just 12% of Population," *LifeNews.com* May 11, 2016.
[528] W. Wayt Gibbs, "Seeking the Criminal Element," *Scientific American* March 1995: 105 [art.=100-107].
[529] See above.

PART FIVE

# Creation of The Deadhead

## DRUGS AND SOCIAL CONTROLLING THE BLACK MAN

# 13   Jolly West: The CIA's Pivot From Psychosurgery to Crack Cocaine

### I.   Dr. West and "Operation Ferdinand"

In the 1970s, the [National Institute of Mental Health] supported one of the most covert and evil experiments ever aimed at Blacks and Hispanics. Following the 1960's riots in Watts (...), Louis Jolyon West of UCLA's (...) Neuropsychiatric Institute created the theory (sic) that the events were tied to genetic and racial factors and those prone to such violence were mostly young, black urban males. He proposed a "Violence Initiative" that would see to it that offenders be treated with psychosurgery and chemical castration. West's idea was to test his treatment in two high schools-one Black, the other Hispanic.[530]

On May 23, 1972 Dr. William Sweet testified before Congress on behalf of a continuation of federal support for the psychosurgery work of his "Operation Ferdinand" colleagues Dr. Vernon Mark and Dr. Frank Ervin. Sweet revealed that a much broader program of violence control was in the making including mass screening programs and large treatment centers for "violent individuals," i.e. targeted Black males falsely tagged as "violence prone." These diagnostic centers would also screen for "mythical" XYY males. Sweet disclosed that the pilot program will be in California. He therefore requested funds for the chief architect of the California program, saying:

> The testimony is being presented on behalf of the Neuropsychiatric Institute of the University of California at Los Angeles – under the direction of Louis Jolyon West [and] of the Brain Research Institute of the same University under the direction of Professor John French...[531]

---

[530] *Creating Racism: Psychiatry's Betrayal. Report and recommendations on psychiatry causing racial conflict and genocide* (Citizens Commission on Human Rights, 1995) 15-16.

[531] Hearings on H.R. 15417 Before the Senate Committee on Appropriation, 92nd Congress, 2nd Session, Part 5, at 4946 (Testimony of Dr. W. Sweet).

Dr. "Jolly" West, as his colleagues called him, was, then, "one of the boys," *viz.* the "Operation Ferdinand" boys. Dr. Ernst Rodin was one of West's mentors.[532] The sociopharmacology paradigm grew out of West's Ecological Model from his students at UCLA.[533] West's involvement with what we have called "Operation Ferdinand" makes this operation transparently a CIA-directed or managed operation. West was a profoundly influential operative in CIA mind and behavioral control projects. As Walter Bowart observes:

Dr. Louis Jolyon West

Perhaps the greatest champion of a Zombie America is one of the most respected figures in American Psychiatry today, Dr. Louis Jolyon "Jolly" West. Beginning with Brainwashing work for the Air Force, MKULTRA work with the CIA, West has positioned himself smack in the midst of the Invisible War.[534] West's career appears to be a carefully constituted espionage 'cover,' always in the forefront on [Invisible War] technology.[535]

---

[532] Alexander Cockburn and Jeffrey St. Clair, *White Out: The CIA, Drugs and the Press* (London and New York: Verso, 1999) 80.

[533] Michael T. McGruire, one the chief sociopharmacology researchers at UCLA, described wrote in tribute of his mentor: "Jolly West was one of the most creative and farseeing psychiatrists of the century...": Michael T. McGuire, "Louis Jolyon West and the Ecological Model of Psychiatric Disorders: A Lecture in Medical History - October 6, 2024) in *The Mosaic of Contemporary Psychiatry in Perspective*, ed. Anthony Kales, M.D., Chester M. Pierce, MD., and Milton Greenblatt, M.D. (New York: Springer, 1992) 79-88.

[534] Bowart says: "The only safe way to wage war, the warriors realized, was to wage it silently. Toward the end of World War Two various forms of IW research began, and eventually modern warriors came up with a number of insidious ways to subdue enemy populations without their ever knowing that a war had even begun. Today secret "invisible weapons" pose a more ominous threat to life than even thermonuclear holocaust. These weapons have not
only been developed without the knowledge of their intended victims, they cannot even be detected at the very moment they are murdering or robotizing civilian populations." Walter H. Bowart and Richard Sutton, *The Invisible Third World* (1990), 2.

[535] Walter H. Bowart and Richard Sutton, *The Invisible Third World* (1990), 19.

Between 1952 and 1956 West was the Air Force chief of psychiatry at Lackland Air Force Base in San Antonio, Texas. He had a TOP SECRET clearance with Air Force Intelligence, as he interviewed returning American pilots downed and captured in Korea by Communist Chinese.[536] In this way he studied and became expert in the Chinese methods of brainwashing.[537] He moved to the University of Oklahoma, where he was head of the Department of Psychiatry, Neurology and Behavioral Sciences between 1956 and 1969. While there he acquired a TOP SECRET CIA clearance for the MK-ULTRA work that he did.

II.     *Dr. West and MK-ULTRA*

> *Since World War II, the United States government, led by the Central Intelligence Agency, has searched secretly for ways to control human behavior.*
> John Marks, *The Search for the Manchurian Candidate* (1991)

The CIA's behavioral control program officially began (with bureaucratic structure) on April 20, 1950 and was codenamed Operation BLUEBIRD. The object was to find a drug or combination of drugs that effectively allowed the CIA to control the human behavior of targeted groups deemed "enemy."[538] Agency scientists took an interest in the behavioral sciences – psychology, psychiatry, sociology, and anthropology – as help aids to pharmacology in the manipulation of an enemy. With the refinement of the program by Richard Helms, "the most important sponsor of mind-control research within the CIA," the program became MK-ULTRA on April 13, 1953. Its aim was to gain control over human behavior through "covert use of chemical and biological materials." Over 25 years and at the cost of $25 million dollars, thousands of unsuspecting Americans,

---

[536] See Colin A. Ross, M.D., *The CIA Doctors: Human Rights Violations by American Psychiatrists* (Richardson, TX: Manitou Communications, 2006).
[537] I.E. Farber, Harry F. Harlow and Louis Jolyon West, "Brainwashing, Conditioning, and DDD (Debility, Dependency, and Dread)," *Sociometry* 20 (1957): 271-285.
[538] John Marks, *The Search for the "Manchurian Candidate": The CIA and Mind Control* (New York and London: W.W. Norton & Company, 1991)24.

military and civilian, were heavily dosed with numerous drugs without consent or awareness.

From the outset the CIA's mind/behavioral-control program had an explicit domestic agenda.[539] The Agency and the Army Corps will frequently collaborate. Both conceived of clandestinely assaulting urban areas with select chemical and biological agents. One CIA agent admitted: "We thought about the possibility of putting some [LSD] in a city water supply and having the citizens wander around in a more or less happy state, not terribly interested in defending themselves."[540]

Major General William Creasy, chief officer of the Army Chemical Corps, was awarded a budget by Congress to investigate drugs as *psychochemical weapons* to be used in a *new kind of warfare*: "nonkill" warfare or warfare without death. Rather than burn the enemy dead with bombs, Creasy championed the idea of waging war with incapacitating agents. He proposed testing the effectiveness of potential psychochemical weapons on a domestic civilian population: "I was attempting to put on, with a good cover story, to test to see what would happen in subways, for example, when a cloud was laid down on a city. It was denied on reasons that always seemed a little absurd to me."[541] The plan then was to covertly assault a city with a chemical or biological agent and hide the Army's tracks by way of a fabricated cover story. This is the military and intelligence communities' *modus operandi*. Whatever the reasons Creasy's horrible plan was denied (if it actually was denied, *à la* "cover story"), the CIA will certainly carry out unthinkable – and illegal – covert operations against private citizens and urban communities. As Colin Ross, M.D. reports after reading through 15,000 CIA documents released to him per his Freedom of Information Act request:

> The CIA mind control experiments were interwoven with radiation, chemical and biological weapons experiments conducted on children, comatose patients, pregnant women, the general population and other unwitting groups who had no idea they were subjects in secret

---

[539] Martin A. Lee and Bruce Shlain, *Acid Dreams: The Complete Social History of LSD: The CIA, the Sixties, and Beyond* (New York: Grove Weidenfeld, 1992) 10.
[540] Marks, *Search for the "Manchurian Candidate"*, 62.
[541] Lee and Shlain, *Acids Dreams*, 40.

experiments. *Radiation, bacteria and funguses were released over urban areas.* A large cloud of radiation was released over Spokane during OPERATION GREEN RUN; plutonium was injected into a comatose patient in Boston by Dr. William Sweet, a member of the Harvard brain electrode team; plutonium was placed in the cereal of mentally handicapped children at the Fernald School in New England; 751 pregnant women were injected with plutonium at Vanderbilt University; the bacteria *serratia maracens* was released into the air in San Francisco, resulting in a series of infections and plutonium was injected into an amputee at the University of Rochester. All these experiments were conducted without any informed consent or meaningful follow-up. Hallucinogens, marijuana, amphetamines and other drugs were administered to imprisoned narcotic addicts in Lexington, Kentucky, terminal cancer patients at Georgetown University Hospital, hospitalized sex offenders at Ionia State Hospital in Michigan and johns picked by prostitutes hired by the CIA in San Francisco and New York.[542]

Psychosurgery was also a method of mind and behavior control entertained by some CIA MK-ULTRA agents. According to Lee and Shlain some CIA scientists argued that

> "lobotomy would create a person 'who no longer cared,' who had lost all initiative and drive, whose allegiance to ideal or motivating factors no longer existed, and who would probably have, if not complete amnesia, at least a fuzzy or spotty memory for recent and past events." They also pointed out "that certain lobotomy types of operations were simple, quickly performed and not too dangerous."
>
> Along this line a group of CIA scientists entertained the possibility of using an "icepick" lobotomy to render an individual harmless "from a security point of view." A memo dated February 7, 1952, notes that on numerous occasions after using electroshock to produce anesthesia, an unidentified surgeon in the Washington, DC, area performed an operation that involved destroying brain tissue by piercing the skull just above the eye with a fine surgical icepick. This type of psychosurgery had certain advantages, in that it resulted in "nervous confusional and amnesia effects" without leaving a "tell-tale scar." The CIA also experimented with brain surgery via UHF sound waves and at one point during the early 1950s attempted to create a microwave "amnesia beam" that would destroy memory neurons...
>
> In the early 1950s, at least $100,000 was designated for a proposed research project geared toward developing "neuro-surgical techniques for Agency interest." It is not known whether this research was ever carried out. [543]

---

[542] Ross, M.D. **The CIA Doctors.**
[543] Lee and Shlain, **Acids Dreams**, 8-9.

We thus see that the methods of "Operation Ferdinand" were already in the 1950s among the CIA's considered MK-ULTRA methods. And "Operation Ferdinand's" target population (Black men) was already anticipated by MK-ULTRA as well. Black people seem to have been the CIA's preferred guinea pigs to test potential psychochemical weapons. "Whenever the CIA came across a new drug...that needed testing," Martin Lee and Bruce Shlain inform us, "they frequently sent it over to their chief doctor at Lexington, where an ample supply of captive guinea pigs was readily available."[544] The chief doctor of whom Lee and Shlain speak is Dr. Harris Isabell, Director of Research (1945-1963) for the Addiction Research Center of the U.S. Public Health Service Hospital in Lexington, Kentucky, a Federal drug prison. For a decade he was a CIA-funded doctor and tried out the CIA's unproven drugs on inmates, "nearly all black drug addicts."[545] Isabell relished this job, telling his Agency contact: "I will write you a letter as soon as I can get the stuff into a man or two."[546] And their intentions for these Black inmates were not benign: "Isabell and the CIA were interested in drugging people to gather more data *on the disruptive potential* of mind-altering substances," Lee and Shlain inform us.[547] Nor did the CIA overlook the potential of *un-incarcerated* Black guinea pigs. "For continued experimentation, [Dr. Sidney] Gottlieb (director of MK-ULTRA) now (in 1953) decided to begin widespread testing on the *urban poor*: street people, prostitutes, and other undesirables."[548] The CIA

> chose "the borderline underworld" – prostitutes, drug addicts, and other small-timers who would be powerless to seek any sort of revenge if they ever found out what the CIA had done to them.[549]

> The CIA violated the Nuremberg Code for medical ethics by sponsoring experiments on unwitting subjects...Like the Nazi doctors at Dachau, the

---

[544] Lee and Shlain, *Acids Dreams*, 24.
[545] Marks, *Search for the "Manchurian Candidate"*, 66-69 (68); Lee and Shlain, *Acids Dreams*, 24-25.
[546] Marks, *Search for the "Manchurian Candidate"*, 68.
[547] Lee and Shlain, *Acids Dreams*, 76.
[548] Cockburn and St. Clair, *White Out*, 206.
[549] Marks, *Search for the "Manchurian Candidate"*, 96.

CIA victimized certain groups of people who were unable to resist: prisoners, mental patients, foreigners, the terminally ill, sexual deviants, ethnic minorities.[550]

As it turned out, most of the listed categories (prostitutes, drug addicts, prisoners, ethnic minorities) are simply code for "Black subjects." In 1952 the CIA entered into a partnership with the Army to produce first-strike (i.e. *offensive* rather than defensive) chemical and biological weapons. The joint CIA-Army program was codenamed MK-NAOMI and was a part of MK-ULTRA. In 1955 and 1956 MK-NAOMI targeted two black housing communities with offensive biological weapons. In Carter Village in Miami, Florida and in Carter Village in Chatham County, Georgia – both black housing complexes – swarms of *Aedes aegypti* mosquitos bred by the Army Chemical Corps at Fort Detrick, Maryland laboratories and carrying both yellow fever and dengue fever were unleashed on the black residents.[551] The purpose of this experiment was to test the effectiveness of the mosquitos as disease vectors to be used as first-strike biological weapons against the Soviets. 1,080 Miami residents alone came down with whooping cough, some died. This spike in local disease and death convinced the MK-NAOMI operatives that the infected mosquitos indeed made effective bioweapons.

It is Black people – in institutions and on the streets – that are the *choice* guinea pigs for the chemical and biological concoctions of the CIA and its partners.

> the state experimented on people of color in order to develop a drug of social control. Staring with the end of World War II, various U.S. intelligence agencies searched for a "mind-control" drug that could be used in the Cold War, and they generally conducted their research on African American persons. Although the ultimate targets of such experiments were the Soviets and Communist China, they were also aimed at controlling dissident people of color in the United States. A good

---

[550] Lee and Shlain, *Acids Dreams*, 24.
[551] Washington, *Medical Apartheid*, 359-365.

example is the work of Dr. Louis "Jolly" West...a coworker of CIA chemists researching the utility of LSD as an agent of social control.[552]

Indeed, Jolly West was an MK-ULTRA *soldier*. His involvement was first revealed publically by the **New York Times** in 1977 in an article on the CIA's twenty-five year, $25 million mind-control program.[553] We now know that West was a subcontractor for MK-ULTRA subproject 43 and received a $20,000 CIA grant while department chair at the University of Oklahoma to do such research as "Psychophysiological Studies of Hypnosis and Suggestibility"; in other words, on the "hypnotizability, suggestibility [of subjects], and the role of certain drugs in altering these attitudes."[554] West's drug work for the CIA is of critical importance, not simply for our discussion here but for the quality of Black life as it will develop – actually, disintegrate – in the eighties and nineties. Between 1974 and 1989 West received $5,110,099 in federal grant money channeled through the NIMH, as was Dr. Isabell's CIA-funds channeled through the NIMH.

III. *Dr. West and the U.S. Government Target Young Black Men*

Jolly West was among the very first white academic psychiatrists who infiltrated the Civil Rights movement in order to study it.[555] He planted himself along with colleagues as "participant-observer" among the Sit-Ins of the 1960s for the purpose of studying the "psychodynamic factors in the Negro revolt." These observations led to his formulation of racial conflict

---

[552] Curtis Marez, **Drug Wars: The Political Economy of Narcotics** (Minneapolis: University of Minnesota, 2004): 252.
[553] Nicholas Horrock, "Private Institutions Used in C.I.A. Effort to Control Behavior," **NYTimes** August 2, 1977.
[554] EIR Investigative Team, "Dr. L. Jolyon West: the LSD cult behind the Cult Awareness Network," **Executive Intelligence Review** September 6, 1991, p. 59.
[555] McGuire, "Louis Jolyon West," 81.

theories.[556] And these theories led to his racist and draconian "solutions" to racial conflict: "Operation Ferdinand."

The funding that Dr. Sweet requested from Congress on behalf of Dr. West and his California pilot program was granted. In September 1972 West announced the formation of the UCLA Center for the Prevention of Violence. Frank Ervin left Boston to join West at UCLA and help develop the Center.[557] This was an "Operation Ferdinand" project. The Center would be housed in a former military base in an isolated location in Santa Monica. According to the Center's proposal, the primary focus of this violence "prevention" facility would be young Black males. West stated: "The major correlates of violence are sex (male), age (youthful), ethnicity (black) and urbanity."[558] This facility would thus use a number of truly insidious methods to "alter undesirable behavior" of these Black urban boys.[559] West, Ervin and their collaborators selected two junior high schools to source their Center. According to West's précis dated September 1, 1972: "Two junior high schools have agreed to participate in the program. One of those junior high schools is located in a predominately black ethnic area; the other in a predominately Chicano area."[560]

The stated purpose of the Center was to study the "pharmacology of violence-producing and violence-inhibiting drugs," i.e. which experimental drugs make the boys more or less violent; and to study "hormonal aspects of passivity and aggressiveness in boys," i.e. how to manipulate the hormones of boys to make them either passive or aggressive. And the Center's operators had *horrendous* plans for these Black and Brown

---

[556] Chester M. Pierce and Louis Jolyon West, "Six Years of Sit-Ins: Psychodynamic Causes and Effects," *International Journal of Social Psychiatry* 12 (1966): 29-34; Louis Jolyon West, "On Racial Violence," *Northwest Med.* 64 (1965): 679-82; idem, "The Psychobiology of Racial Violence," *Arch Gen Psychiatry* 16 (1967): 645-651.
[557] Samuel Chavkin, *The Mind Stealers: Psychosurgery and Mind Control* (Boston: Houghton Mifflinn, 1978) 97.
[558] Chavkin, *Mind Stealers*, 96.
[559] "Nike Nonsense: Army Offers Nike Bases to UCLA Violence Center," *Berkeley Barr* March 8-14, 1974, p. 8.
[560] The Hastings Center, "Researching Violence: Science, Politics, & Public Controversy," *The Hastings Center Report* 9 (1979): 1-19.

(Chicano) boys. The boys would be screened for the "XYY syndrome,"[561] thus perpetuating the Black Super Predator myth. And

> The group described by West as most prone to violence was young, black urban males. The purpose of his proposed Violence Center was to use the "treatment model" developed in California prison facilities during the CIA's brainwashing research program of the 1960s and 1970s, to treat "pre-delinquent" children before they became a "problem" to society.[562]

What are these treatments to be used on junior high Black and Brown boys? Lee and Shlain explain: "Treatments discussed by West included *chemical castration, psychosurgery*, and the *testing of experimental drugs* on involuntarily incarcerated individuals (emphasis added)."[563] The drug to be used to chemically castrate these juveniles was cyproterone acetate, a sterilizing chemical developed in East Germany.[564]

West also proposed to implant brain electrodes into some boys and some prisoners at Vacaville State Prison, the site of CIA mind control experiments under MK-SEARCH (which MK-ULTRA became in June 1964). After discharge from the prison the men would be monitored remotely through the brain implant which is connected to radio receivers at a central location. If any of the men or boys entered a restricted area, or if they exhibited *any sexual arousal at all*, a signal would be sent to the brain implant completely *immobilizing him/them*, allowing law enforcement to be dispatched to their location to arrest them.[565]

We have here "Operation Ferdinand" at UCLA. As Samuel Chavkin points out: "The link between the Mark-Ervin book (***Violence and the Brain***) and the proposal for the center as outlined by Dr. West, was obvious."[566] And this program to assault Black and Brown junior high school boys with chemical

---

[561] Chavkin, *Mind Stealers*, 96.
[562] EIR Investigative Team, "Dr. L. Jolyon West," 59.
[563] Lee and Shlain, *Acids Dreams*, 190 n.
[564] Chavkin, *Mind Stealers*, 97; Cockburn and Clair, *White Out*, 80.
[565] Colin A. Ross, M.D., ***Bluebird: Deliberate Creation of Multiple Personality by Psychiatry*** (Richardson, TX: Manitou Communications, 2000) 118-119.
[566] Chavkin, *Mind Stealers*, 106.

castration and mind-murder through psychosurgery and drugs got state and federal support. "The development and acceptance of the idea of pinpointing those who may be potentially assaultive or crime-prone because of genetic, hormonal, or brain abnormality received major impetus during the Nixon administration."[567] In January 1973 during his State of the State address California Governor Ronald Reagan formally announced the state and federal support for West's Center. Reagan's Secretary of Health and Welfare, Dr. Earl Brian, affirmed that "more than one million dollars would be invested in the center in the fiscal year 1973-1974."[568] The federal LEAA would contribute matching funds. So West could boast: "Richard Nixon and Ronald Reagan were each going to put up half the money for us..."[569] *Were* going to, because a local controversy erupted and the program got shut down. One of the chief critics of the Center's proposal was West's employee at UCLA Dr. Isidore Ziferstein, associate clinical professor of psychiatry at the Neuropsychiatric Institute. In an interview in February 1974 Ziferstein explained to Samuel Chavkin what the ultimate, hidden agenda was of West and his colleagues:

> And so our prison population is burgeoning with young and vigorous people. There is a rising radicalism in their midst and there is an uppitiness among the blacks and the Chicano prisoners which prison officials find intolerable.
>
> *To subdue them*, the authorities are using new methods. They're employing the psychiatric armamentarium and a new technological tool set — what has come to be known as psychotechnology. Under the guise of therapeutic behavior modification they're applying anything from Anectine and other aversive *drugs* to *psychosurgery*. The wardens do not differentiate between the pathologically violent prisoners and the political militants. In their view these prisoners are all the same — creatures who should be *tranquilized at all costs*.[570]

Tranquilized at all costs through drugs and psychosurgery: this is the agenda for Black militants who are deemed "uppity" to

---

[567] Samuel Chavkin, *The Mind Stealers*, 90.
[568] Samuel Chavkin, *The Mind Stealers*, 95.
[569] Dr. West quoted in The Hastings Center, "Researching Violence: Science, Politics, & Public Controversy," *The Hastings Center Report* 9 (1979) 1-19 (19).
[570] Chavkin, *Mind Stealers*, 102.

Whites because they are agitating for change. The fact that Richard Nixon and Ronald Reagan both enthusiastically supported this blatant and insidious attack on Black and Brown boys is highly significant: *both* presidents declared a War on Drugs, which we now know was an explicit war on Black men. Both men – Nixon and Reagan – were no doubt quite irritated by this program getting halted by protest. They took their anger out on Black males through their respective War on Drugs (see below).

IV.    *The CIA and Social Control Through Drugs*

"West studied the use of drugs for controlling group behavior and said that drugs can be used 'as adjuncts to interpersonal manipulation or assault'."[571] That is precisely what the CIA had in mind (no pun intended), and this is the point of sociopharmacology: modifying and controlling social behavior through the deployment of drugs to select populations. West laid out the CIA's vision and plan in this regard quite explicitly. In a 1974 article on the possible social uses of hallucinogenic drugs West wrote:

> There are many ways that drugs can influence mood, thought and behavior. The extent to which these effects, actual or potential, are employed to exercise a function defined as *control* relates to the pharmacology of the drug, the social context of its use, and the variability of both subjective and behavioral reaction to it.[572]

West then went on to list ten possible social and political uses of drugs, including:

> A. *Weakening the adversary*. There have been many battles won because soldiers were taken by surprise when drunk. George Washington won such a victory. However, the corruption of whole armies, or whole countries, by drugs is presently being discussed. China, with its history of victimization by British commercial interests through the use of opium, was accused of pushing cheap hashish and heroin to weaken the

---

[571] EIR Investigative Team, "Dr. L. Jolyon West," 59.
[572] Louis Jolyon West, "Hallucinogenic Drugs & Possibilities," *The Hastings Center Studies* 2 (1974): 103-112 ( 103).

American military force in Vietnam. Whether or not this is true, the potentiality exists for using drugs in this way.[573]

Indeed, Britain's "Opium Wars" with China are well known, and the militaristic use of alcohol to subdue an enemy population is well documented. Ward Churchill notes how "alcohol [was] used by Europeans/Euroamericans since colonial times as a sort of 'chemical weapon' to dissipate indigenous societies" and the "deliberate use of alcohol to effect the dissolution of many of North America's indigenous peoples."[574] Is there any wonder why liquor stores are the most prevalent retail stores in the Black community? Jolly West then goes on to discuss the use of drugs as a mechanism of "internal control," i.e. the control of elements of one's own society rather than of an external enemy. He lists these uses as "Adjuncts to Social or Political Policy"

> B. *Internal Control*
> 1. *Through prohibition.* The mechanisms necessary for controlling drugs provide leverage for other types of control. An example would be the selective application of drug laws permitting immediate search, or "no knock" entry, against selected components of the population *such as members of certain minority groups* or political organizations.
> 2. *Through supply.* This method, foreseen by Huxley in **Brave New World** (1932), has the governing element employing drugs selectively to control the population in various ways. While a country that requires maximum effort from its total work force (e.g. China today) must take stern measures to eliminate all drug abuse, a more affluent nation can afford to tolerate large numbers of drug-users in various circumstances. To a large extent the numerous rural and urban communes, which provide great freedom for private drug use, are actually subsidized by the society: through parental remittances, welfare and unemployment payments, and benign neglect by the police. In fact, it may be more convenient and perhaps even more economical to keep the growing numbers of chronic drug-users (especially of the hallucinogens) fairly isolated, and out of the labor market with its millions of unemployed. The communards with their drugs are probably less trouble-and less expensive-to society if they are living apart, than if they were choosing one of the alternative modes of expressing their alienation such as those employed by the New Left.[575]

---

[573] West, "Hallucinogenic Drugs & Possibilities," 105.
[574] Ward Churchill, *A Little Matter of Genocide: Holocaust and Denial in the Americas 1492 to the Present* (San Francisco: City Lights Books, 1997) 247, 405.
[575] West, "Hallucinogenic Drugs & Possibilities," 105.

This frankness is stunning. Here the CIA, through Dr. West, outlines its thinking as it relates to the covert use of drugs as a mechanism of social control. He says again in 1975, in a work coedited with his protégé Ronald Siegel (remember him!):

> The role of drugs in the exercise of political control is also coming under increasing discussion. Control can be through prohibition or supply. The total or even partial prohibition of drugs gives the government considerable leverage for other types of control. An example would be the selective application of drug laws permitting immediate search, or "no knock" entry, against selected components of the population such as members of certain minority groups or political organizations. But a government could also supply drugs to help control a population. This method, foreseen by Aldous Huxley in Brave New World (1932), has the governing element employing drugs selectively to manipulate the governed in various ways.[576]

The government can use drugs to control elements within its population such as *minority groups* by two methods: [1.] By prohibiting a drug and then targeting that group by selectively enforcing drug laws against them. This will result in increased arrests and seizures of property, in addition to simple harassment. This hypothetical policy was made real with the fabricated War on Drugs initiated by President Richard Nixon and then again by President Ronald Reagan, both of whom financially supported West's draconian ideas of targeting Black males for social control. [2.] By supplying drugs to a target community! As an affluent nation America can afford to treat certain elements of its population as "expendables" by supplying drugs to them and letting them freely – with minimal police intervention - partake of these drugs in ghettos isolated from mainstream America. It is better for society if these minority groups are sedated and their feelings of alienation numbed than for them to express them through political agitation, as New Left radicals were doing. This, too, became U.S. policy. While the first method became *official* policy through the War on Drugs, the second method too became *covert* policy, also through the waging of the War on Drugs. In other words, the government targeted a select population (Black

---

[576] R.K. Siegel and L.J. West (edd.), **Hallucinations: Behavior, Experience and Theory** (New York: John Wiley, 1975).

people) with repressive law enforcement through a War on Drugs, *and then* flooded that very community with drugs in order to pharmacologically subdue the members of the group who weren't swept up in the mass incarceration arrests. We will elaborate shortly.

THE CIA AND ALDOUS HUXLEY'S ULTIMATE REVOLUTION

As an illustration of his vision of social control through the supply of drugs West cites Aldous Huxley (1894-1963). This deserves a closer look. Huxley, who came to the U.S. from Britain in 1937, is much, much more than a famous novelist. Rather, he was a high-ranking MK-ULTRA asset and propagandist, "regarded as the single most important conceptual architect of the rock-sex-drugs counterculture launched in the mid-1960s," according to Mark Burdman.[577] He was a cult figure in this CIA-spawned rock-drug culture: the Beatles used his image on the cover of one of their albums (Sgt. Pepper) and the rock band The Doors took their name from the title of Huxley' psychedelic manifesto, ***The Doors of Perception*** (1954). Huxley and West were mutual admirers who worked together on MK-ULTRA research; Huxley even counseled West on hypnosis techniques.[578] He suggested West hypnotize his subjects prior to administering LSD to them, in order to be able to give them "post-hypnotic suggestions aimed at orienting the drug-induced experience in some desired direction."[579] In other words, in order to better direct and manipulate the hypnotized subject.

Huxley hailed from a well-established, prominent family of distinguished intellectuals highly esteemed among the British

---

[577] Mark Burdman, "Aldous Huxley in the 1930's: the formative years of an evil man," *Executive Intelligence Review* 21 (October 14, 1994): 44 [art.=44-46].
[578] EIR Investigative Team, "Dr. L. Jolyon West," 59; Lee and Shlain, *Acids Dreams*, 48; *Letters of Aldous Huxley*, ed. Grover Smith (Lincoln: Chatto and Windus, 1966) 824.
[579] Lee and Shlain, *Acids Dreams*, 48.

aristocracy; a scientific family. His grandfather Thomas Henry Huxley was a prominent evolutionary biologist known as "Darwin's Bulldog" because he helped Charles Darwin establish his evolutionary theory. Aldous's father, Dr. Leonard Huxley, was a venerated scientist and writer and his brother, Sir Julian Huxley, was a distinguished biologist and eugenicist. Julian later served as Secretary General of the United Nations Educational, Social, and Cultural Organization (UNESCO) in 1946.

Equally important are the Huxley family's connections to British secret society and intelligence communities. Granddad Thomas Huxley was a member of "one of the most important forces in the formation and execution of British imperial and foreign policy," Cecil Rhodes' secret society which Carroll Quigly called "the Anglo-American Establishment."[580] Thomas Huxley was a lifelong collaborator with Arnold Toynbee (also a member), who headed the Research Division of British intelligence during World War II and served as Prime Minister Winston Churchill's wartime briefing officer. Thomas mentored the famous novelist and also infamous white supremacist and eugenicist H.G. Wells (Wells studied under Huxley at the Normal School of Science in South Kensington).[581] Wells was head of British foreign intelligence during the First World War. He would go on to tutor Thomas Huxley's grandsons Aldous and Julian.

> Aldous Huxley, along with his brother Julian, was tutored at Oxford University, England in the 1920s by futurist H.G. Wells, head of British foreign intelligence during World War I. Well's writings and those of his protégés the Huxleys and George Orwell...spelled out in fictional form the mind-control that MK-Ultra was later to implement.[582]

---

[580] Carroll Quigley, *The Anglo-American Establishment* (New York: Books in Focus, 1981) 31; idem, *Tragedy and Hope: A History of the World* (London and New York: The Macmillan Company, 1966) 130ff.

[581] See Mike Perry, "C.S. Lewis, H.G. Wells, and the Evolutionary Myth," *Discovery Institute* July 1, 1998. Cf. John S. Partington, "The Death of the Static: H.G. Wells and the Kinetic Utopia," *Utopian Studies* 11 (2000): 96-111; idem, "H.G. Wells's Eugenic Thinking of the 1930s and 1940s," *Utopian Studies* 14 (2003): 74-81.

[582] Michelle Steinberg, "Cultism's roots in MK-Ultra," *Executive Intelligence Review* 5 (December 5-11, 1978) 18-19 [art.=18-20].

This last point is important: the literary fiction of Wells and his students Aldous Huxley and George Orwell (author of the classic ***Nineteen Eighty-Four***) were actually *blueprints* for future covert operations. In this regard Aldous Huxley's ***Brave New World*** (1932), normally described as a dystopian satire, is instructive. This novel describes the scientific methods and tools which a small future elite use to keep the rest of the earth's population in a permanent autistic-like condition and in love with their own servitude. The world's population consists of Alpha-types, Beta-types, Gamma-types, Delta-types, and Epsilon-types. The world-ruling elite minority comes from the highest Alpha class and the world's menial laborers and servants come from the lowest Epsilon class. These latter are kept stunted and stupefied by the State (the elite) by means of brain-chemical altering *vaccines* (remember this!) and "regular doses of chemically induced happiness," i.e. drugs mandated by the State that produced a pharmacological "euphoria" in the people while they labored for the interests of the elite. The State practiced both eugenics *and* dysgenics. It legislated certain matting practices that ensured the propagation of the best genetic traits for the elite (eugenics), but the State also engaged in practices that insured, in the Epsilon class, the propagation of *defective* and *disadvantageous* genetic traits (dysgenics). The elite Alpha class wanted the lower Epsilon class to be genetically and mentally impaired.

> In the Brave New World of my fantasy eugenics and dysgenics were practiced systematically. In one set of bottles biologically superior ova, fertilized by biologically superior sperm, were given the best possible pre-natal treatment and were finally decanted as Betas, Alphas and even Alpha Pluses. In another, much more numerous set of bottles, biologically inferior ova, fertilized by biologically inferior sperm, were subjected to the Bokanovsky Process (ninety-six identical twins out of a single egg) and *treated prenatally with alcohol and other protein poisons*. The creatures finally decanted were almost subhuman; but they were capable of performing unskilled work and, when properly conditioned, detensioned by free and frequent access to the opposite sex, constantly distracted by gratuitous entertainment and reinforced in their good behavior patterns

by daily doses of soma (the mandated drug), could be counted on to give *no trouble to their superiors* (emphasis added)."[583]

The future *dysgenics* program is important here: the "subhuman" servant class is produced by prenatally treating fetuses with alcohol and protein poisons. When grown they are distracted by free access and indulgence in sex and gratuitous entertainment and they are drugged with a chemical (soma) that is "capable of making people happy in situations where they would normally feel miserable," thus insuring that they are no threat to their elite masters.

This future society envisioned in **Brave New World** and saluted by the CIA's own Jolly West was not the product of Huxley's free imagination, but a *blueprint* based on advanced insider knowledge gleaned from his elite governmental, secret society and intelligence associations.[584] Huxley's nonfiction writings and lectures make it clear that his dark sci-fi was a *vehicle* for Huxley to introduce future shock-events to the American public. As Joanne Woiak documents:

> [*Brave New World*] was simultaneously a satire on contemporary culture, a prediction of biological advances, a commentary on the social roles of science and scientists, *and a plan for reforming society...Brave New World* is remarkable for its accurate predictions about science and technology, economics and politics, and arts and leisure. It extrapolates future applications of genetics (IVF and cloning via Bokanovsky's Process), endocrinology (Malthusian belts), behaviorism (hypnopaedia), and pharmacology (soma)...The extreme scenario depicted in the book...has most commonly been read as a cautionary tale about the dehumanizing effects of technology and the growing influence of cultural trends that Huxley abhorred...[but it more closely fits] a blueprint for how to build a relatively desirable society using selective breeding (emphasis added).[585]

---

[583] *Brave New World Revisited* (Harper & Row Publishers, 1958) Chapter 2, first paragraph.
[584] As Lee and Shlain, *Acids Dreams*, 48 acknowledges Huxley "consorted with a number of scientists who were engaged in mind control research for the CIA and the US military."
[585] Joanne Woiak, "Designing a Brave New World: Eugenics, Politics, and Fiction," *The Public Historian* 29 (2007): 105-129.

The point of the remarkable later *realization* of elements of Huxley's futuristic **Brave New World** society must be emphasized. As J.G. Ballard points out:

> Aldous Huxley was uncannily *prophetic*, a more astute guide to the future than any other 20th-century novelist. Even his casual asides have a surprising relevance to our own times...*Brave New World* is around us everywhere (emphasis added).[586]

Not uncannily prophetic; covertly informed. That what Huxley described in **Brave New World** was real to him and not at all purely imaginative is made clear by him in a 1949 letter he wrote to his colleague and former pupil (Aldous tutored him at Eton in 1917) George Orwell.

> May I speak instead of the thing with which the book deals - called the ultimate revolution?
>
> ...the ultimate revolution...aims at total subversion of the individual's psychology and physiology...My own belief is that the ruling oligarchy will find less arduous and wasteful ways of governing and of satisfying its lust for power, and these ways will resemble those which I describe in Brave New world...
> But now psycho-analysis is combined with hypnosis; and hypnosis has been made indefinitely extensible through the use of barbiturates,[587] which induce a hypnoid and suggestible state in even the most recalcitrant subjects.
>
> Within the next generation I believe that the world's rulers will discover that *infant conditioning* and *narco-hypnosis* are more efficient, as instruments of government, than clubs and prisons, and that the lust for power can be just as completely satisfied by suggesting people into loving their servitude as by flogging and kicking them into obedience.

---

[586] J.G. Ballard, "Prophet of our Present," *The Guardian Unlimited* April 13, 2002.
[587] Barbiturates are drugs that act as central nervous system depressants, and can therefore produce a wide spectrum of effects, from mild sedation to total anesthesia.

In other words, I feel that the nightmare of the Nineteen Eighty-Four is destined to modulate into the nightmare of a world having more resemblance to that which I imagined in Brave New World.[588]

Nightmare, but a *necessary* nightmare in Huxley's view.[589] What was particularly emphasized by Huxley was the coming *pharmacological* method of subduing the "Epsilon" class of the population. In *The Doors of Perception* (1954) Huxley prophesied

> Now let us consider another kind of drug—still undiscovered, but probably just around the corner—a drug capable of making people happy in situations where they would normally feel miserable. Such a drug would be a blessing, but a blessing fraught with grave political dangers. By making a harmless chemical euphoric freely available, a dictator could reconcile an entire population to a state of affairs to which self-respecting human beings ought not to be reconciled...

In 1961 the University of California, San Francisco Medical Center sponsored a conference to discuss the societal effects of technology. Aldous Huxley, one of the featured conference speakers, said:

> There will be in the next generation or so a pharmacological method of making people love their servitude and producing dictatorship without tears, so to speak. Producing a kind of painless concentration camp for entire societies, so that people will in fact have their liberties taken away from them but will rather enjoy it, because they will be distracted from any desire to rebel – by propaganda, or brainwashing, or brain-washing enhanced by pharmacological methods. And this seems to be the final revolution.[590]

---

[588] Bob King, "In the future, I'm right: Letter from Aldous Huxley to George Orwell over 1984 novel sheds light on their different ideas," **Daily Mail** March 7, 2012.

[589] Woiak, "Designing a Brave New World." In 1930 Huxley wrote: "Any form of order is better than chaos. Our civilization is menaced with total collapse. Dictatorship and scientific propaganda may provide the only means for saving humanity from miseries of anarchy": **Aldous Huxley, Between the Wars: Essays and Letters**, ed. David Bradshaw (Chicago: Ivan R. Dee, 1994) Back cover.

[590] Cited in Robert Ellis Smith, Deborah Caulfield, David Crook and Michael Gershman, **The Big Brother Book of Lists** (Los Angeles: Price, Stern, Sloan, 1984).

At the University of California Berkley in 1962 Huxley elaborated on this pharmacological method of making the lower classes love their low and servile status. In a lecture aptly entitled "The Ultimate Revolution: Slavery by Consent Through Psychology, Manipulation and Conditioning," he describes:

> If you are going to control any population for any length of time, you must have some measure of consent. It's exceedingly difficult to see how pure terrorism can function indefinitely. It can function for a fairly long time, but I think sooner or later you have to bring in an element of persuasion, an element of getting people to consent to what is happening to them...
>
> It seems to me that the nature of the ultimate revolution with which we are now faced is precisely this: That we are in process of developing a whole series of techniques which will enable the controlling oligarchy who have always existed and presumably will always exist to get people to *love their servitude*...A number of techniques about which I talked seem to be here already. And there seems to be a general movement in the direction of this kind of ultimate revolution, a method of control by which a people can be made to enjoy a state of affairs which by any decent standard they ought not to enjoy...
>
> if you can get people to consent to the state of affairs in which they're living, the state of servitude, the state of *being*, having their differences ironed out, and being made amenable to mass production methods on the social level, if you can do this, then you have, you are likely, to have a much more stable and lasting society. Much more easily controllable society than you would if you were relying wholly on clubs and firing squads and concentration camps.
>
> But I think that insofar as dictators become more and more scientific, more and more concerned with the technically perfect, perfectly running society, they will be more and more interested in the kind of techniques which I imagined and described from existing realities in BNW. So that, it seems to me then, that this ultimate revolution is not really very far away, that we, already a number of techniques for bringing about this kind of control are here, and it remains to be seen when and where and by whom they will first be applied in any large scale...
>
> There is for example, the pharmacological method, this is one of the things I talked about in [Brave New World]. I invented a hypothetical drug called SOMA, which of course could not exist as it stood there because it was simultaneously a stimulant, a narcotic, and a hallucinogen,

which seems unlikely in one substance. But the point is, *if you applied several different substances you could get almost all these results even now*...[591]

Astounding. British oligarchy propagandist and CIA MK-ULTRA asset Aldous Huxley just laid out the plan to use a "battery of drugs" method to intoxicate the lower classes into loving their servitude: "the most powerful instruments of rule in the dictator's armory [is the] systematic drugging of individuals for the benefit of the State..."[592] This policy is "an insurance against personal maladjustment (to their fated condition), social unrest and the spread of subversive ideas."

> That a dictator could, if he so desired, make use of these drugs for political purposes is obvious. He could ensure himself against political unrest by *changing the chemistry of his subjects' brains* and so making them content with their servile condition. He could use tranquillizers to calm the excited, stimulants to arouse enthusiasm in the indifferent, hallucinants to distract the attention of the wretched from their miseries. But how, it may be asked, will the dictator get his subjects to take the pills that will make them think, feel and behave in the ways he finds desirable? In all probability it will be enough merely to make the pills available...
>
> Under a dictatorship pharmacists would be instructed to change their tune with every change of circumstances. In times of national crisis it would be their business to push the sale of stimulants. Between crises, too much alertness and energy on the part of his subjects might prove embarrassing to the tyrant. At such times the masses would be urged to buy tranquillizers (opiates) and vision-producers (hallucinogens). Under the influence of these soothing syrups they could be relied upon to give their master no trouble.[593]

This is a description of the "battery of drugs" method of the later UCLA sociopharmacologists laid out plainly. Under certain social conditions, stimulants will be pushed on the people. During other conditions and to achieve different social ends, opiates like heroin,

---

[591] Aldous Huxley, "The Ultimately Revolution: Slavery by Consent Through Psychology, Manipulation and Conditioning," Berkeley Lecture March 20, 1962.
[592] Aldous Huxley, *Moksha: Writings on Psychedelics and the Visionary Experience (1931-1963)*, ed. Michael Horowitz and Cynthia Palmer (New York: Stonehill publishing Company, 1977) 135.
[593] Huxley, *Moksha*, 135, 138, 139.

cocaine and crack or hallucinogens like weed and LSD will be the psychochemical weapons of choice.

*This* is what Dr. Jolly West and his MK-ULTRA colleagues and superiors envisioned as a means of social control, particularly *of Black people!* This method was deployed using LSD and weed on middle-class, educated white youth in the 1960s and 1970s, deliberately turning the radical and militant anti-war youth movement into the docile, drugged and pacifist "Flower Power" counterculture.[594] The government will deploy heroin, weed and crack to totally devastate Black life and advance their *dysgenics* agenda.

---

[594] David McGowan, *Weird Scenes Inside the Canyon: Laurel Canyon, Covert Ops and the Dark Heart of the Hippie Dream* (Headpress, 2014); Joe Atwill and Jan Irvin, "Manufacturing the Deadhead: A Product of Social Engineering," May 17, 2013 @ http://www.gnosticmedia.com/manufacturing-the-deadhead-a-product-of-social-engineering-by-joe-atwill-and-jan-irvin/; Jan Irvin, "Spies in Academic Clothing: The Untold History of MKULTRA and the Counterculture – And How the Intelligence Community Misleads the 99%," May 13, 2015 @ http://www.gnosticmedia.com/SpiesinAcademicClothing_MKULTRA; Richard J. Miller, "Timothy Leary's liberation, and the CIA's experiments! LSD's amazing, psychedelic history," *Salon.com* December 14, 2013; Steve Silberman, "The Plot to Turn On the World: The Leary/Ginsberg Acid Conspiracy," *PLOS* April 21, 2011; Nick Schou, "Lords of Acid," *OC Weekly* July 7, 2005; Lee and Shlain, *Acid Dreams*; David Black, *Acid: A New Secret History of LSD* (London: Vision Paperbacks, 1998); Todd Brendan Fahey, "The Original Captain Trips – Who Was 'Captain' Al Hubbard?" *High Times* November 1991; W.H. Bowart, "Lords of the Revolution: Timothy Leary and the CIA…The Spy Who Came in From the (Ergot) Mold," @ http://www.whale.to/b/bowart8.html; Walter Barney, "Grandfather of LSD Meets the Acid Children," *San Francisco Sunday Chronicle and Examiner* October 16 ,1977; Mary Jo Warth, "The Story of the Acid profiteers," *The Village Voice* August 22, 1974, pp.5-7; Jeffrey and Michele Steinberg, "MK-ULTRA is Alive…and Out to Destroy Your Mind," *War on Drugs* 1 (June 1980): 4-7.

A demonstrator offers a flower to military police at the Pentagon during an anti-Vietnam protest in Washington on October 21, 1967. The 200 pounds of flowers (daisies) distributed at this event which gave rise to the "Flower Power" movement was provided by (paid for by) Walter Bowart's wife, Peggy Mellon Hitchcock of the Mellon banking family, one of the country's wealthiest families. Peggy's brother, William (Billy) Hitchcock Mellon, bankrolled the LSD-counterculture. The Mellon family in general and Billy in particular had strong intelligence connections. In fact, during his tenure as CIA chief Richard Helms (1966-1973), father of MK-ULTRA, visited Mellon patriarchs in Pittsburg frequently. In other words, it can be shown that the CIA helped give birth to the pacifist Flower Power movement.

CIA assets Jolly West and Aldous Huxley, both MK-ULTRA researchers/operatives, have in explicit and unmistakable language articulated what must be understood as the CIA's own vision – plan even - of using drugs as a means of social control, and the CIA's target domestic enemy has always been Black people, Black males in particular. As we shall see, the government unquestionably operationalized this plan. Through agencies such as the CIA, military intelligence, etc., the U.S. Government unleashed a "battery of drugs" on the Black community, both hallucinogens and opiates, with the intended effect no doubt being to preserve the current Dominance Hierarchy.

# 14   Dope and Weed: Manufacturing The Deadhead

I.   *The CIA, the Mafia and Black America's Heroin Scourge*

*Keep the (drug) traffic in the dark people, the coloreds. They're animals anyway so let them lose their souls.* Don Zaluchi to the Council, Godfather I

Clarence Lusane and Dennis Desmond are right: "[The] scene from The Godfather had its duplicate in real life."[595] As Norman Riley discusses in his important article, "The Crack Boom is Really an Echo": "outside groups have targeted the black community as a dumping ground for drugs,"[596] groups including the Italian Mafia.

> In the 1940's organized crime recognized a potential gold mine in the mass sale and distribution of heroin in America. They also recognized the terrible danger in its use...Faced with on the one hand an enormous potential for profit in heroin, while on the other hand, considering the fact that its appeal to young people and addictive qualities could lead to the physical destruction of their own community's children, the Mafia came up with an extremely effective solution. Sell the drug almost exclusively in the darker-minority neighborhoods...The plan worked like a charm. By the mid-1950's heroin was being sold in large quantities in black neighborhoods. It was in the 1950's that *The New York Times* and other print media declared evidence of a teenage drug epidemic.[597]

> By 1951...due to the Mafia's marketing focus, over 100,000 people were addicted in the United States, many of them Black. Heroin traffic in the Black communities of the East was controlled by New York's big five Mafia families [Bonanno, Gambino, Vito Genovese, Thomas Lucchese, Profaci-Maglioco], in addition to the French-Cuban connection...The decision of the

---

[595] Clarence Lusane and Dennis Desmond, *Pipe Dream Blues: Racism and the War on Drugs* (Boston: South End Press, 1991) 38.
[596] Norman Riley, "The Crack Boom is Really an Echo," *The Crisis* March 1989, pp. 26-29 (26).
[597] Riley, "The Crack Boom is Really an Echo," 27.

organized crime families to sell hard drugs almost exclusively to the Black community created a heroin addiction crises of stunning proportions...Every major city with a substantial Black population suffered a heroin epidemic.[598]

But this Mafia dope flooding Black neighborhoods was actually CIA dope, at least CIA-protected dope. The Mafia was the middle man, as Lee and Shlain note: "heroin that was pumped into America's black and brown ghettos often pass[ed] through the contraband networks controlled by mobsters who moonlighted as CIA hitmen."[599] The U.S. heroin problem was not created by the Italian Mafia. It was created by American intelligence agencies. Alfred W. McCoy documents in his vital and mammoth work, *The Politics of Heroin: CIA Complicity in the Global Drug Trade* (1991) that the U.S. drug problem was nearly extinguished during WWII due to the logistical impossibility of international shipping and smuggling caused by the war. The global drug trade fell into disarray causing a forced withdrawal and the number of American addicts dropped meteorically from 200,000 in 1924 to a tenth of that – 20,000 – in 1944-1945. But American intelligence agencies intervened and revived the drug trade. The Office of Navy Intelligence sprung the Mafia Boss Lucky Luciano from prison in 1946 and "deported" him and 100 other mobsters back to Sicily where they immediately revived the heroin trade, all with the support and protection of the OSS and later CIA. Because of this joint OSS/CIA-Mafia venture, the number of American heroin addicts rose again from 20,000 in 1945 to 60,000 in 1952 to 150,000 in 1965.[600]

---

[598] Lusane and Desmond, *Pipe Dream Blues*, 38-39.
[599] Lee and Shlain, *Acids Dreams*, 12.
[600] Alfred W. McCoy, *The Politics of Heroin: CIA Complicity in the Global Drug Trade* (Brooklyn: Lawrence Hill Books, 1991) 17, 25: "at two critical junctions after World War II, the late 1940s and the late 1970s, when America's heroin supply and addict population seemed to ebb, the CIA's covert action alliances generated a sudden surge of heroin that soon revived the U.S. drug trade...With American demand reduced to its lowest point in fifty years and the international syndicates in disarray, the U.S. government had a unique opportunity to eliminate heroin addiction as a major American social problem. Instead, the government – through the CIA and its wartime predecessor, the OSS – created a situation that made it possible for the Sicilian-American Mafia and the Corsican

Along with the Italian Mafia in Sicily the CIA helped restore and empower the Corsican syndicate in Marseille, France. Marseille became the heroin capital of Europe and the source of the majority of America's heroin supply. The Corsican syndicate produced the heroin, Luciano and the Sicilian Mafia smuggled the heroin (via Cuba) to the New York Five Families, who then distributed it to the Black and Brown communities, all "with the compliance of US government agencies, primarily the CIA."[601] This is the French Connection. Frank Matthews was the first Black drug kingpin of the modern era and the earliest to become independent of the Italian Mafia and work directly with the French Connection. Between 1967 and 1971 he reportedly grossed $100 million. His operation had CIA connections. When Matthews was busted, the nine people who were indicted with him as his distributers and importers had their charges unceremoniously dropped, according to a released 1976 TOP SECRET Justice Department report, because "of their ties to the CIA."[602] Cockburn and St. Clair are therefore on point:

> what cannot now be denied is that US intelligence agencies arranged for the release from prison of the world's preeminent drug lord, allowed him to rebuild his narcotics empire, watched the flow of drugs into the largely black ghettos of New York and Washington, D.C. escalate and then lied about what they had done.[603]

Black America's first drug crisis (heroin) was a CIA-Mafia venture, just as Black America's second drug crisis (crack) was a CIA-Contra venture, both ventures authorized by the White House. And this is how the Nation of Islam and the Mafia first ran

---

underworld to revive the international narcotics traffic." See also idem, "The CIA Connection," *Progressive* July 1991, pp. 20-38.
[601] McCoy, *The Politics of Heroin*, 141. See also Cockburn and St. Clair, ***White Out***, Chapter 5; Jonathan Vankin, ***Conspiracies, Cover-ups and Crimes: From JFK to the CIA Terrorist Connection*** (New York: Dell Publishing, 1992) 187-192.
[602] Cockburn and St. Clair, ***White Out***, 141:"Charges against nine of Matthews' Corsican suppliers were dropped at the insistence of the CIA, according to a 1976 Justice Department report. The Corsican had been moonlighting for the CIA and the Agency argued that prosecuting them would compromise national security interests." See also Lusane and Desmond, ***Pipe Dream Blues***, 41.
[603] Cockburn and St. Clair, ***White Out***, 134.

afoul of each other. The Honorable Elijah Muhammad and the Nation of Islam waged a phenomenally effective *war on drugs* in these same Black communities targeted by the Mafia with their CIA-protected drugs. Elijah Muhammad freed many Black men and women from heroin addiction, and this cut into the Mafia's very lucrative business. As Lusane and Desmond observe:

> The Black nationalist organization, the Nation of Islam (NOI), found many of its recruits in the clutches of heroin addiction and grew from a small religious group into one of the major organized forces in the community of the period...With amazing success, the NOI turned hundreds of addicts into disciplined Muslims and members of the growing nationalist group.[604]

A showdown between the Mafia and the Nation of Islam was inevitable and the CIA had a dog in the fight.

CIA asset Dr. Jolly West said: "a government could also supply drugs to help control a population. This method...has the governing element employing drugs selectively to manipulate the governed in various ways." CIA asset Aldous Huxley said: "a dictator could...make use of these drugs for political purposes...He could ensure himself against political unrest by changing the chemistry of his subjects' brains and so making them content with their servile condition. He could use tranquillizers (i.e. opiates like heroin) to calm the excited, stimulants to arouse enthusiasm in the indifferent, hallucinants to distract the attention of the wretched from their miseries." The CIA-Mafia dumping of heroin into Black communities across this nation therefore unquestionably had a political motive as well as an economic motive.

---

[604] Lusane and Desmond, *Pipe Dream Blues*, 39.

## II. The Pot Plot: Weed and the Happy, Defective Slave

*California is the largest producer of marijuana in the United States and law enforcement agencies believe that Mexican and Asian [Drug Trafficking Organizations] and white criminal groups are responsible for the majority of marijuana cultivation in California.* California Department of Justice 2007-2008 Organized in California Annual Report

Lee and Shlain make an important observation:

> nearly every drug that appeared on the black market during the sixties — marijuana, cocaine, heroin, PCP, amyl mitrate, mushrooms, DMT, barbiturate, laughing gas, speed and many others — had *previously* been scrutinized, tested and in some case *refined* by CIA and army scientists...For a time CIA personnel were completely infatuated with the hallucinogen (emphasis added).[605]

It is not a coincidence that they list marijuana first among the drugs that were processed through CIA labs before they appeared on the streets. Indeed, in their search for a behavior modification agent the OSS and the Federal Bureau of Narcotics (FBN) very early tested cannabis and then they *produced a new, more potent form* of cannabis unknown anywhere in the world to be used as a covert chemical agent. Lee and Shlain tell the story so revealingly, I will quote them at length.

> In the spring of 1942 General William "Wild Bill" Donovan, chief of the Office of Strategic Services (OSS), the CIA's wartime predecessor, assembled a half-dozen prestigious American scientists and asked them to undertake a top-secret research program. Their mission, Donovan explained, was to develop a speech-inducing drug for use in intelligence interrogations. He insisted that the need for such a weapon was so acute as to warrant any and every attempt to find it.
>
> The use of drugs by secret agents had long been a part of cloak-and-dagger folklore, but this would be the first concerted attempt on the part of an American espionage organization to modify human behavior through chemical means...The OSS chief pressed his associates to come up with a substance that could break down the psychological defenses of enemy spies and POWs, thereby causing an uninhibited disclosure of classified information...

---

[605] Lee and Shlain, *Acids Dreams*, xxiv-xxv.

Dr. Windfred Overhulser, superintendent of Saint Elizabeth's Hospital in Washington, DC, was appointed chairman of the research committee. Other members included Dr. Edward Strecker, then president of the American Psychiatric Association, and Harry J. Anslinger, head of the Federal Bureau of Narcotics. The committee surveyed and rejected numerous drugs, including alcohol, barbiturates, and caffeine. Peyote and scopolamine were also tested, but the visions produced by these substances interfered with the interrogation process. Eventually marijuana was chosen as the most likely candidate for a speech-inducing agent.

*OSS scientists created a highly potent extract of cannabis, and through a process known as esterification a clear and viscous liquid was obtained.* The final product had no color, odor, or taste. It would be nearly impossible to detect when administered surreptitiously, which is exactly what the spies intended to do. *"There is no reason to believe that any other nation or group is familiar with the preparation of this particular drug,"* stated a once classified OSS document. Henceforth the OSS referred to the marijuana extract as "TD"—a rather transparent cover for "Truth Drug."

Various ways of administering TD were tried on witting and unwitting subjects...

The effects of TD were described in an OSS report: "TD appears to relax all inhibitions and to *deaden the areas of the brain* which govern an individual's discretion and caution. It accentuates the senses and makes manifest any strong characteristics of the individual. Sexual inhibitions are lowered, and the sense of humor is accentuated to the point where any statement or situation can become extremely funny to the subject. On the other hand, a person's unpleasant characteristics may also be heightened. It may be stated that, generally speaking, the reaction will be one of great loquacity and hilarity.[606]

American intelligence, looking for a chemical agent to covertly control human behavior, created a unique, potent form of liquid cannabis that has no color, smell or taste and thus could be secretly administered to an unsuspecting target or targets. They initially investigated cannabis as a "Truth Serum," but instead of compelling subjects to reveal their deepest secrets it induced "a state of irresponsibility" and "made them relaxed, a little high and distracted". This new form of marijuana – the formula for which no other nation or group on earth possessed – *deadens* areas of the

---

[606] Lee and Shlain, *Acids Dreams*, 4.

brain that govern caution and discretion. As we shall see, the government released this or a variant(s) of this enhanced marijuana on the streets in the 1960s as a means of social control and behavior modification.

## CHEMICALLY INDUCED EUPHORIA

Marijuana (*cannabis sativa*) entered the U.S. from Mexico in the early twentieth century with immigrant farm workers in Texas. From there it spread through the rural south and was brought to the Midwest and Northeast by Black people during the Great Migration during and after World War I.[607] Marijuana is considered a mild hallucinogen[608] but a heavy sedative. A cannabis plant possesses about 500 chemical compounds, about 80-100 of which are cannabinoids. The majority of the cannabinoids are of two kinds: cannabidiol (CBD) which is non-psychoactive,[609] and $\Delta^9$-tetrahydrocannabidinol (THC) which is the psychoactive or "intoxicating" chemical of marijuana. "THC induces a variety of sensory and psychological effects, including mild reverie and euphoria,"[610] which is why marijuana was chosen by the U.S. government as *the* pharmacological agent of choice to produce what Aldous Huxley called a "chemically induced euphoria" among the servant class, i.e. Black people, Black men in particular. There is a precedent for this. As Barney Warf describes, "hegemonic groups have at times actively encouraged cannabis smoking in the interest of promoting docility (for example, in British and Portuguese slave colonies)."[611] The British and Portuguese colonial governments from the 16th to the 19th centuries deliberately promoted marijuana use among the

---

[607] Barney Warf, "High Points: An Historical Geography of Cannabis," *Geographical Review* 104 (2014): 414-438.
[608] A hallucinogen is a psychoactive agent which can cause hallucinations, perceptual anomalies, and other substantive subjective changes in thoughts, emotions and consciousness.
[609] A psychoactive or psychotropic agent causes changes in brain function and results in alterations in perception.
[610] Warf, "High Points," 416.
[611] Warf, "High Points," 418.

subjugated populations "rendering docile large bodies of people so that their governance could be effected unproblematically."[612]

Most of the psychoactive THC is found in the sticky resin that the female cannabis plant produces. A lesser amount is found in the plant leaves and the least amount is found in the plant stalk. As a result, the psychoactive potency of a cannabis preparation varies enormously depending on which part of the plant was used. The most potent is the pure resin: hashish is a resin extract. Its THC concentration is 8-14%. The average American joint before the 1960s had a 2% THC concentration. Britain's "Skunk" has a 2-5 times greater potency than normal marijuana.[613] Marijuana is not addictive like the opiate heroin or physiologically devastating like crack. Marijuana's effects are much more subtle, but much more useful for the ruling elite seeking to keep a population subjugated. Marijuana not only served the interests of the ruling elite by sedating and pacifying the servant class – getting them to "love their servitude" - it is also advanced the elite's dysgenics agenda. Chronic marijuana use has a damaging effect on both brain function and reproduction.

### YOUR BRAIN ON WEED

Karen Steinherz and Thomas Vissing inform us:

> New research on marijuana confirms that it damages cognitive functioning...The principle target of delta-9-THC...is the brain... The plant constituent delta-9-THC has been found to produce many characteristic cognitive deficits in both human and animal subjects. It impairs the brain's functioning, particularly with regard to chronic use.[614]

Peter Cohen, a medical marijuana advocate, informs us as well :

> The consensus of workers in the field is that chronic recreational use of marijuana may be associated with cognitive dysfunction and, indeed, that this significant pathology is related to structural changes in the brain...A

---

[612] Warf, "High Points," 417.
[613] "Is a new MK-Ultra drug plaque afoot?" *Executive Intelligence Review* 24 (1997): 44-48.
[614] Karen Steinherz and Thomas Vissing, "The Medical Effects of Marijuana on the Brain," *21st Century* (Winter 1998): 60 [art.=59-69].

recent study demonstrated that smoking four joints or more per week resulted in a decrement in mental test performance; subjects who had smoked regularly for a decade or more did the worst. The investigators found that long-term marijuana users were impaired 70 percent of the time on a decision-making test, compared to 55 percent for short-term users and 8 percent for nonusers.[615]

Weedheads can function very normally in society. Chronic or long-term use of marijuana effects *higher-level* mental activity, called *executive functions*. Discussing "Marijuana and cognitive function," Nadia Solowij writes:

> It is apparent from many years of research that long-term use of marijuana does not result in *gross cognitive deficits*. However, recent reviewers agree that there is now sufficient evidence that it leads to a more subtle and selective impairment of *higher cognitive functions* (Block, 1996; Hall *et al.*, 1994; Pope *et al.*, 1995; Solowij, 1998) which arises from altered functioning of the frontal lobe, hippocampus and cerebellum (Block *et al.*, in press; Hampson and Deadwyler, 1999; Loeber and Yurgelun-Todd, 1999; Solowij, 1998). The findings from recent methodologically rigorous research provide evidence for impaired learning, organization and integration of complex information in tasks involving various mechanisms of attention, memory processes and executive function. It is not clear to what extent the alterations in brain function and cognitive impairments as detected in laboratory testing might impact upon daily life, although users themselves complain of problems with memory, concentration, loss of motivation, paranoia, depression, dependence and lethargy (Reilly *et al.*, 1998; Solowij, 1998). Schwenk (1998) has argued that there is no clear causal relationship between marijuana use and job performance. The nature of the cognitive deficits as assessed by psychological testing suggests that long-term users would perform reasonably well in routine tasks of everyday life, although they may be more distractible and short-term memory may be compromised. Difficulties are likely to be encountered in performing complex tasks that are novel or that cannot be solved by automatic application of previous knowledge, or with tasks that rely heavily on a memory component or require strategic planning and multi-tasking (emphasis added).[616]

---

[615] Peter J. Cohen, "Medical Marijuana: The Conflict Between Scientific Evidence and Political Ideology," **Utah Law Review** 1 (2009): 58 [art.=35-104].
[616] Nadia Solowij, "Marijuana and cognitive function," in **The Biology of Marijuana: from gene to behavior**, ed. Emmanuel S. Onaivi (London and New York: Taylor and Frances, 2002) 326-350 (342).

Likewise, Roy Lubit and Bruce Russetts examine "The Effects of Drugs on Decision Making," and state:

> One cigarette containing 2% THC...produces feelings of well-being and euphoria, accompanied by relaxation, sleepiness, and laughter, depending on dosage and setting. After smoking several joints or more potent forms of THC, "short term memory is impaired and there is *deterioration in capacity to carry out tasks requiring multiple mental steps"* (Jaffe, 1980: 561). Higher doses may result in "hallucinations, delusions and paranoid feelings. Thinking becomes confused and disorganized; depersonalization and altered time sense are accentuated. Anxiety reaching panic proportions" may occur (Jaffe 1980: 561). In addition, chronic use may result in "acute or subacute onset of confusion, visual and auditory hallucinations, paranoia and occasional aggressivity" (Bassuk and Schoonover, 1977: 299). An *amotivational syndrome* has been described by several authors in which long-term users show *apathy, introversion, passivity, decreased drive and ambition*, social disengagement, impaired communication skills, diminished effectiveness in interpersonal relations, magical thinking and difficulty in concentrating, enduring frustration, carrying out long- term plans, following routines, and mastering new material (Bassuk and Schoonover, 1977: 299; Balis, 1974: 414-422)... Marijuana has been found, in general, to *decrease hostility*...[617]

It is not hard to imagine why a ruling elite, in particular White Supremacy, would want to impair the Black male's ability to perform *executive cognitive functions* while not making him totally dysfunctional mentally: this supports the current Dominance Hierarchy by keeping the Black male functionally and happily servile and *unmotivated*. It must be pointed out here that Jolly West was among the first scientists to introduce and define the *amotivational* syndrome caused by chronic marijuana use.[618] The first medical practitioner in the West to do systematic work with marijuana, French psychiatrist Jacques-joseph Moreau (1804-1884), wrote in his ***Hashish and Mental Alienation*** (1845): "One of the first measurable effects of hashish is the gradual weakening of the power to direct thoughts at will... The action of hashish weakens the will—the mental power that rules ideas and

---

[617] Roy Lubit and Bruce Russetts, "The Effects of Drugs on Decision Making," ***Journal of Conflict Resolution*** 28 (1984): 91-92 [art.=85-92]. See also Ernst A. Rodin, Edward F. Domino, and James P. Porzak, "The Marihuana-Induced Social High," ***Journal of the American Medical Association*** 213 (1970): 1300-1302.
[618] McGuire, "Louis Jolyon Wet," 80.

associates and connects them together." As we have seen above, the modern evidence confirms this. Marijuana as a "pacifier" that quiets hostility is important for the same reasons. Chronic use of marijuana decreases hostility and aggression in response to frustration stimulates or circumstances that would ordinarily stimulate a hostile or aggressive response.[619] In other words, it makes people docile.

## WEED AND REPRODUCTION

In Huxley's futuristic Brave New World the elite ensured the poor genetic quality of the lower Epsilon class (dysgenics) by prenatally treating Epsilon fetuses with protein poisons such as alcohol and other chemicals. We now know that marijuana is such a protein poison.

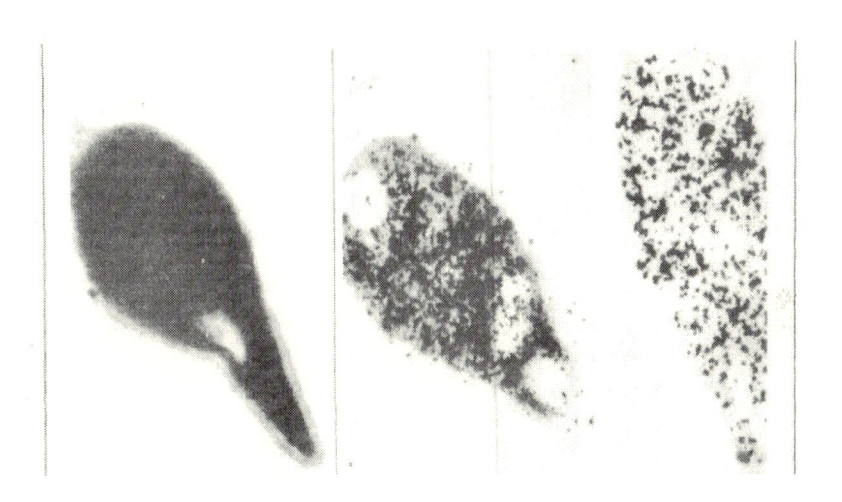

1. Normal sperm head. 2 and 3. Sperm from hashish smoker. Photo from Dr. Gabriel Nahas, "The Biological Effects of Marijuana," (1980)

---

[619] Carl Salzman et al. "Marijuana and Hostility in a Small Group Setting," *American Journal of Psychiatry* 133 (1976): 1029-1033; Rodney Myerscough and Stuart Taylor, "The Effect of Marijuana on Human Physical Aggression," *Journal of Personality and Social Psychology* 49 (1985): 1541-1546.

Dr. Gabriel Nahas and others have documented marijuana's deleterious effect on male sperm. In the above image, the photo to the left is a normal sperm head. The dark staining is evidence of protein and genetic material. The images on the right are sperm head of hashish smokers, showing severe abnormalities in protein and DNA content.[620] Marijuana use reduces the protein and the genetic material in sperm. A 2015 study with 1,215 healthy men showed that regular marijuana use lowered sperm count and affected the quality of sperm.[621] Nahas thus well articulates the *dysgenic value* of marijuana use:

> This evidence indicates the profound changes that marijuana can produce in those cells that are essential for the preservation and transmission of our genetic heritage. There is no question about this abnormality caused by marijuana...[T]here must be something in marijuana smoke or hashish smoke that destroys man's germ cells...[622]

The dysgenic effect of marijuana use is evident on the mother's side as well. According to Dr. Akira Morishima's study chronic administration of THC to sexually developing mice produced an increase in abnormal ova. It is suggested that cannabinoids disrupt the meiotic and the mitotic processes.[623] The effects on the fetus are measurable later in life as well.

---

[620] Gabriel Nahasm "The biological effects of marijuana," **War on Drugs** 1 (1980): 11-13 [art.=8-16]; W. Hembree, G.G. Nahas, P. Zeidenberg, and H.F. Huang, "Changes in human spermatozoa associated with high dose marihuana smoking," **Advances in the Biosciences** 22-23 (1978): 429-39. See further M. Rossato et al., "Human Sperm Express Cannabinoid Receptor Cb1, the Activation of Which Inhibits Motility, Acrosome Reaction, and Mitochondrial Function," **The Journal of Clinical Endocrinology & Metabolism** 90(2):984-991; Jack Harclerode, "Endocrine Effects of Marijuana in the Male: Preclinical Studies," in **Marijuana Effects on the Endocrine and Reproductive Systems**, ed. Monique C. Braude and Jacqueline P. Ludford (Rockville, Maryland: National Institute of Drug Abuse, 1984) 48-64.

[621] Tina Djernis Gundersen et al. "Association Between Use of Marijuana and Male Reproduction Hormones and Semen Quality: A Study Among 1,215 Healthy Young Men," **American Journal of Epidemiology** August 15, 2015, pp. 1-9.

[622] Gabrial Nahasm "The biological effects of marijuana," **War on Drugs** 1 (1980): 12-13 [art.=8-16].

[623] Akira Morishima, "Effects of Cannabis and Natural Cannabinoids on Chromosomes and Ova," in **Marijuana Effects on the Endocrine and**

What about the children of marijuana users? Professor Peter Fried has found in preliminary work that children between 9 and a half years old to 12 years of age suffered from a deficit in what researchers term 'executive function,' a type of cognitive intelligence involving planning for both the present and the future. In this highly controlled study, children of 120 marijuana-smoking mothers were evaluated on a regular basis from birth. These children were found to have problems focusing their attention, and were highly distractable.[624]

If that is not enough, marijuana has been determined to have potential *demasculinizing* effects. According to Lee Ellis and M. Ashley Ames in their discussion of "The Experimental Induction of Sexual Inversions," marijuana is one of the drugs that proved effective as an *antiandrogen*. Androgen is the hormone that controls development and maintenance of male characteristics in men, the opposite of estrogen which controls and maintains feminine characteristics in women. As an *anti*androgen, marijuana can "partially divert or block masculinization of the nervous system during neuro-organization," i.e. during fetal development.[625] Further, in the sociopharmacology (Dominance Hierarchy) studies of UCLA, "The effects of cannabis and cocaine have been investigated under a variety of experimental conditions."[626] This plainly indicates that marijuana is a drug of interest for those studying the methods of ensuring or upsetting current dominance hierarchy patterns.

---

*Reproductive Systems*, ed. Monique C. Braude and Jacqueline P. Ludford (Rockville, Maryland: National Institute of Drug Abuse, 1984) 25-45.
[624] Karen Steinherz and Thomas Vissing, "The Medical Effects of Marijuana on the Brain," 21st Century Science and Technology Magazine (Winter 1997-1998): 67.
[625] Lee Ellis and M. Ashley Ames, "Neurohormonal Functioning and Sexual Orientation: A Theory of Homosexuality-Heterosexuality," *Psychological Bulletin* 101 (1987): 233-258 (241). Also Elaine M. Hull, J. Ken Nishita and Daniel Bitran, "Perinatal Dopamine-Related Drugs Demasculinize Rats," *Science* 224 (June 1, 1984): 1011-1013.
[626] McGuire, "Sociopharmacology," 647.

# THE CIA'S ENHANCED MARIJUANA HITS THE STREETS

> *"Street" marijuana has increased markedly in potency over the past five years. Confiscated materials in 1975 rarely exceeded one percent THC content. By 1979 samples as high as five percent THC content were common. "Hash oil," a marijuana extract unavailable a decade ago, has been found to have a THC content as high as 28 percent, with more typical samples analyzed by University of Mississippi chemists ranging from fifteen to twenty percent THC.* National Institute on Drug Abuse, ***Marijuana Research Findings: 1980*** (1980)

The Sixties were a turbulent decade. There was an explosion of reform movements: civil rights, environmentalism, feminism, gay liberation, and antiwar protests. From the midst of this panoply of revolts an American *counterculture* sprung. But this counterculture did not just spring up organically, on its own. It was partly the product of CIA intervention: the Agency helped launch the psychedelic revolution and counterculture of the 1960s.[627] The protests against American involvement in Vietnam beginning in 1964 and the rise of the New Left irked the U.S. government so much that it waged a covert pharmacological war against its own middle-class, educated, young whites. The selected psychochemical weapon was LSD, a powerful hallucinogen that was first synthesized in a Swiss lab in 1938 and had been the darling of CIA MK-ULTRA research since the 1950s. And as Lee and Shlain document, "the first big surge of street acid hit the college scene in 1965, just when the political situation was heating up."[628] By "hit the college scene," they mean this: MK-ULTRA scientists gave the drug to college professors at Eastern and West Coast universities, who passed it on to their upper classmen students, who passed it on to lower classmen students.

---

[627] On the 1979 ABC News Close-up special "Mission: Mind Control" with correspondent Paul Altmeyer on the CIA's MK-ULTRA program, Timothy Leary, himself an Agency asset, confirmed on camera: "I give the CIA a total credit for sponsoring and initiating the entire consciousness movement counterculture events of the 1960s...the CIA funded and supported and encouraged hundreds of young psychologists to experiment with this drug [LSD]." See above n. 591.
[628] Lee and Shlain, ***Acid Dreams***, 132.

This is the "trickle down" strategy employed by the CIA.[629] The CIA disseminated LSD to deflate the political potency of the youth rebellion.[630] Four million North Americans were turned on to LSD, 70% of them high school or college age.

The politically and socially turbulent Sixties not only saw the CIA's LSD hit the streets: they saw the CIA's enhanced marijuana hit the streets too. Both were released as a means of social control and the depotentiating of rebellious youth, white and Black. Stuart Butler's 1981 analysis of "The Marijuana Epidemic" is revealing. He observes:

> Twenty years ago, marijuana was hardly used in this country. *Only in the late 1960s did the drug become widely used*,[631] and not until the mid-1970s did it become commonplace. The increase in use has been dramatic by any measure...

---

[629] According to a 1969 Bureau of Narcotics and Dangerous Drugs report and Marks, *Search for the "Manchurian Candidate"*, 129 and 130: "It would be an exaggeration to put *all* the blame on-or give *all* of the credit to-the CIA for the spread of LSD. One cannot forget the nature of the times, the Vietnam War, the breakdown in authority, and the wide availability of other drugs (*sic!*), especially marijuana (*sic!*). But the fact remains that LSD was one of the catalysts of the traumatic upheavals of the 1960s. No one could enter the world of psychedelics without first passing, unawares, through doors opened by the Agency. It would become a supreme irony that the CIA's enormous search for weapons among drugs-fueled by the hope that spies could, like Dr. Frankenstein, control life with genius and machines-would wind up helping to create the wandering, uncontrollable minds of the counterculture (emphasis added)." We must read Marks' words here in the light of Lee and Shlain, *Acid Dreams*, xxiv-xxv: "nearly *every drug* that appeared on the black market during the sixties — marijuana, cocaine, heroin, PCP, amyl mitrate, mushrooms, DMT, barbiturate, laughing gas, speed and many others — had previously been scrutinized, tested and in some case refined by CIA and army scientists (emphasis added)."

[630] At the "LSD: A Generation Later" conference at the University of California, Santa Cruz in October 1977 Timothy Leary confessed: "The LSD movement was started by the CIA. I wouldn't be here now without the foresight of the CIA scientists. It was no accident. It was planned and scripted by Central Intelligence, and I'm all in favor of Central Intelligence." Walter Barney, "Grandfather of LSD Meets the Acid Children," *San Francisco Sunday Chemical and Examiner* October 16, 1977; Lee and Shlain, *Acid Dreams*, XX.

[631] Cohen, "Medical Marijuana," 40 n. 17: "it was not until the 1960s, 40 years after marijuana cigarettes had arrived in America, that it was widely used."

> In the 1960s... most of the marijuana smoked in this country was of domestic origin. At that time, most American marijuana had a rather low THC content (0.2 percent to 1 percent), and so a 1 gram joint might contain in the region of 2-10 milligrams of THC. By 1970, however, Mexican marijuana with an average THC of between 1.5 percent and 2 percent, had begun to dominate the market. By the end of the 1970s, Jamaican and Colombian varieties, with concentrations of 3 percent to 4 percent THC began to enter the country in increasing quantities. *In addition, liquid hashish, with a concentration of 30 percent to 90 percent THC, began to appear. At a potency rate of 50 percent THC, an ounce of this oil is sufficient to intoxicate one thousand people...*

That "liquid hashish" that can intoxicate one thousand people by the ounce is no doubt identical with or related to that "clear and viscous liquid" cannabis with enhanced potency that the OSS scientists created through esterification in the 1940s which, they boasted, "no...other nation or group" had any knowledge of how to produce.[632] And as a 1980 National Institute of Drug Abuse Report confirms, "Hash oil [is] a concentrated liquid marijuana extract not available on the street up until a few years ago..."[633] This laboratory marijuana was released to the streets sometime in the late 1960s or early 1970s and has been the standard since then, with new varieties with ever increasing potency continuing to hit the streets till this very day (see "K2").

> The rise in potency of marijuana available in the United States is central to any discussion of the medical impact of the drug. The early, inconclusive studies carried out in this country were based on the low-potency marijuana then being consumed. But now we are dealing with far stronger varieties, and the studies using these strains of marijuana are far from inconclusive...The inescapable conclusion from the scientific evidence now available is that marijuana is a dangerous substance. *The increase in potency in recent years* means that we are dealing with a very different problem than the one faced the 1960s [=before the 1960s - WM].[634]

Just as LSD was targeted at the youth, so too was marijuana. In 1980 the National Institute on Drug Abuse reported:

---

[632] Lee and Shlain, *Acid Dreams*, 4.
[633] *Marijuana Research Findings: 1980*, ed. Robert C. Petersen, Ph.D. (Rockville, Maryland: Department of Health and Human Services, 1980) 12.
[634] Butler, "The Marijuana Epidemic," 3, 23.

By contrast with a decade ago, marijuana use now often begins at a much earlier age and is more likely to be frequent rather than experimental use. The most significant increases noted in the 1977 National Survey of drug use were in marijuana use by 12-to 17-year-olds. Other, more recent sources of data are generally consistent. Among high school seniors, for example, daily use nearly doubled from the Class of 1975 to those of 1978 and 1979 (from 5.8 percent to 10.7 and 10.3 percent for each of these classes). Moreover the percentage of each of these senior classes which began use in the ninth grade or earlier has also nearly doubled (from 16.9 percent of the Class of 1975 to 30.4 percent of the 1979 class).[635]

The tragic implications of this are well spelled out by Steinherz and Vissing:

> In any society where the children and teenagers cannot focus their attention, they might be able to perform boring or low-skilled jobs, such as fast-food service, or running a microchip computer. But their "will," that is, their energies and curiosity to look outside their infantilism, is sapped. These young adults will not have the interest, or the attention span, to develop the economic and cultural well-being of the country in which they are citizens.[636]

Juvenilization or paedomorphisis: directing change in a species by targeting the youth of that species.

### THE GOVERNMENT'S SOMA PILL

In Aldous Huxley's (and Jolly West's) vision, the lower, servile classes would be controlled by the governmental elite through the daily rationing of *soma*, a pill that produces a chemical euphoria. Soma was a drug "capable of making people happy in situations where they would normally feel miserable," in Huxley's words. That is marijuana in the inner city ghetto. After the riots or urban rebellions of the Sixties, the government targeted the inner city with the OSS's enhanced marijuana the same way they targeted their own youth rebels with the CIA's LSD (and marijuana). Weed makes Black life tolerable in the otherwise intolerable conditions of the (scientifically created) urban ghetto, an environment that no human should suffer and most humans

---

[635] *Marijuana Research Findings: 1980*, 1.
[636] Steinherz and Vissing, "Medical Effects," 67.

would revolt against: unless they were chemically made to be happy in their miserable circumstances.

We are thus not surprised to discover that the Carter Administration in 1980-1981 tried to get a "THC pill" created and made available. Top officials from the Food and Drug Administration and the National Institute on Drug Abuse met with representatives of the ten largest pharmaceutical companies in January 1980 for a planning session designed to encourage the creation of a THC capsule.[637] The malicious intent is obvious when we consider that *in that same year* (1980) the National Institute on Drug Abuse released a report confirming the minimal medicinal value of marijuana and its significant health risks.

> A review of marijuana's acute effects on intellectual functioning done for this year's report indicates the data is generally consistent: marijuana intoxication interferes with immediate memory and a wide range of intellectual tasks in a manner that might be expected to impair classroom learning among student users...
>
> While much remains to be learned about the chronic effects of marijuana, there are converging lines of evidence with respect to its pulmonary effects. Both animal and human experiments suggest that marijuana impairs lung function to a greater extent than tobacco cigarettes do. While there is as yet no direct evidence that it can play a causal role in lung cancer, it is known that, like tobacco smoke residuals, the "tar" from marijuana is tumor-producing when applied to the skin of test animals...
>
> Although the evidence is by no means definitive (though, it is today – WM), several kinds of animal and human research have suggested that heavy marijuana use may impair reproductive functioning. Such impairment may include diminished sperm count and motility in males and possible interference with fertility in females. Such preliminary findings may have greater significance for the marginally fertile. Given the many unknowns concerning the effects of marijuana on fetal development, the use of marijuana during pregnancy should continue to be strongly discouraged...
>
> Overall, marijuana, THC and related drugs have shown definite promise in treating the nausea and vomiting which often accompany cancer chemotherapy. While thus far they have not proven to be invariably

---

[637] Nora Hamerman, "Get the dope out of the White House," and Chris Curtis, "White House push THC pills," *War on Drugs* 1 (1980): 2-3, 30.

superior to other medication, they may be enduringly useful with patients for whom other drugs are relatively ineffective.[638]

With this admitted high risk, low reward situation, why would the government push a THC pill on the public? The answer should be obvious by now. This is Huxley's Soma Pill. The pharmaceutical company Eli Lilly produced a synthetic form of THC called Nabilone. Its clinical trials were cancelled after the deaths of several dogs.[639] This is revealing because Eli Lilly produced the CIA's MK-ULTRA LSD unleashed on radical white youth[640] and, as we shall see, Eli Lilly produced the neurotoxic chemical thimerosal which is contributing to the alarming rates of autism in Black boys.[641]

### THE CIA IMPORTS THE STREETS' MARIJUANA

In May of 1988 ex-CIA pilot Michael Tolliver gave sworn testimony before a Senate subcommittee. He declared:

> I was flying weapons from Florida to Honduras on a CIA [op]. On a typical flight we shipped about 28,000 pounds of military supplies – guns, ammunition, things like that.
>
> [Questioner asked]: What kind of cargo did you bring back?
>
> Pot – some 25,000 pounds of it. I mean marijuana. Yeah. Marijuana. We brought the marijuana back to Florida in the same plane.[642]

That much of the weed on the streets is CIA-procured can be surmised. Michael Palmer is reported to be "one of the biggest marijuana smugglers in U.S. history,"[643] having allegedly made billions in the trade. His aviation company, the Miami-based

---

[638] *Marijuana Research Findings: 1980*, 2-3. Also *Marijuana Effects on the Endocrine and Reproductive Systems*.
[639] Curtis, "White House push THC pills," 30.
[640] Lee and Shlain, *Acid Dreams*, 27.
[641] See below Chapter 16.
[642] "CIA and Big Bankers Key Drug Trade Players," *Spotlight* August 8, 1988: 20-40 (31).
[643] Peter Hornbluh, "The paper trail to the top: Crack and the Contras," *The Baltimore Sun* November 17, 1996.

Vortex Air International, was an officially listed CIA asset. The Agency used his planes to fly supplies to Contras in Nicaragua and bring cocaine and marijuana back.[644] Palmer himself, according to the *Los Angeles Times*, was also an undercover drug smuggler for both the DEA and U.S. Customers Service.[645] He had been flying marijuana in from Columbia since 1977. He was protected legally by the CIA during his drug runs.[646] He was also paid hundreds of thousands of dollars by the State Department, while actively smuggling, through the Nicaraguan Humanities Assistance Organization (NHAO). Palmer's CIA-protected smuggled weed ended up in the streets of Miami, Detroit, and other urban areas.

### THE PLOT DEEPENS: GEORGE SOROS

Hungarian-American billionaire speculator George Soros, a Jewish former Nazi-collaborator and current political-economic hit man, apparently is a Rothschild-spawn. It is reported that his start-up money was provided by George Harlweiss, the right-hand man of Baron Edmond de Rothschild.[647] Soros is described as "one of the largest contributors of funding for marijuana legalization efforts around the world."[648] Having given $200 million to fund the "drug reform movement" in America Soros has dominated the pro-legalization side of the debate. He bankrolled medical marijuana ballot initiatives across the country such as Prop 215 in California and Prop 200 in Arizona, as well as the recreational use laws passed in Washington State and Colorado. And Soros efforts are international. His money helped fund Uruguay's effort to become the first country to legalize the

---

[644] Cockburn and Clair, *Whiteout*, 284-286; "Plane in Fatal Crash Linked to Drug Running," *Associated Press* July 28, 1988.
[645] Paul Houston, "Pilot, Heavily Guarded, Testifies at Hearing: Undercover Drug Agent Tells of Helping Contras," *Los Angeles Times* April 07, 1988.
[646] Cockburn and Clair, *Whiteout*, 284-286.
[647] Hector A. Rivas, Jr., "George Soros: Hit-man for The British Oligarchy," in *Your Enemy, George Soros* (Leesburg, VA: Lydon LaRouche PAC, 2008): 2-6.
[648] Alicia Wallace, "This pro-legalization business magnate is Hillary Clinton's biggest billionaire banker," *The Cannabist* September 28, 2016.

commercialization of marijuana.[649] Soros is no benign philanthropist however. He funded nacro-terrorism in South America. As Alexandra Perebikovsky reports:

> Soros threw his weight behind narco-terrorism in Colombia, Peru and Bolivia. His group Human Rights Watch/Americas is a major part of the drug cartel's drug production and terror apparatus, deploying millions of dollars annually for dope propaganda. In Colombia, he became the leading financier in the fight to legalize cocaine and, through Human Rights Watch, attacked government forces deployed against drug cartel guerrillas, who were slaughtering people across the region. On November 8, 1990, the Medellin drug cartel, leading the violent murder and kidnapping operations in Colombia, sent out a letter demanding that the government publish a report by Soros' Americas Watch, which denounced the government's anti-drug actions as violations of human rights. One week later, Juan Mendez, the leader of the Colombian Americas Watch Report, called for "the most total disarmament possible" of the Colombian military in order to allow "free trade" of drugs to resume.[650]

---

[649] Kelly Riddell, "George Soros' real crusade: Legalizing marijuana in the U.S.," *The Washington Times* April 2, 2014; Patrick McGreevy, "Billionaire activists like Sean Parker and George Soros are fueling the campaign to legalize pot," *The Los Angeles Times* November 2, 2016; George Soros, "Why I Support Legal Marijuana," *The Wall Street Journal* October 26, 2010.

[650] Alexandra Perebikovsky, "Does Soros Have a Drug Problem?" in *Your Enemy, George Soros* (Leesburg, VA: Lydon LaRouche PAC, 2008): 7 [art.=6-9].

# 15 "Operation Ferdinand" and the War on Drugs

I. *War on the Black Male*

Both Richard Nixon as President and Ronald Reagan as governor of California supported the many efforts of what we have called "Operation Ferdinand," which sought through various methods to turn young Black males (bulls) into docile, brain dead, and socially *in*active dullards (oxen) that are easily controllable.

> whites viewed black men as animals necessitating domestication – they were untamed "bucks." From this conceptualization, the enslavement of African men arose as a form of chattel slavery. As domesticated bucks, however, whites could tame black men, but only to a certain extent because they always remain a "wolf [held] by the ears."[651]

And if they can't tame him, kill him - even as a child. Dr. Tommy J. Curry, Associate Professor of Philosophy at Texas A&M said it profoundly:

> The Black male [in America] is not born a patriarchal male. He is raced and sexed peculiarly, configured as barbaric and savage, imagined to be a violent animal, not a human being. His mere existence ignites the negrophobia taken to be the agreed upon justification for his death. Black male death lessens their economic competition with, as well as their political radicality against, white society. It is this fear of Black males that allows society to support the imposition of death on these bodies, and consent to the rationalizations the police state offer as their justifications for killing the Black-male beast (the rapist, the criminal, and the deviant-thug). The young Black male's death, the death of Black boys, is merely an extension of this logic—the need to destroy the Black beast cub before it matures into full pathology. The Black boy, that child, is seen as the potential Nigger-beast. This anti-Black dynamic which specifically affects the Black boy has been referred to by Elaine Brown as a new kind of

---

[651] Richeson, "Sex, Drugs, and…Race-to-Castrate," 108.

racism, a racism built upon the anti-Black mythology of America's Black males as the super-predator. This super-predator mythology not only acts to legitimize the violence responsible for the deaths of Black males, but inculcates the rationalization that given what Black males actually are, Black male death is necessary and an indispensable strategy for the safety and security of American society. Overlooking the genocidal disposition of America towards Black males presents an incomplete diagnosis of the impetus behind the levels of violence and sanctions imposed upon Black communities (Black women, Black families) in an effort to control the lives of young Black males.[652]

This is precisely what the War on Drugs was about. There is no question today that the War on Drugs was a Trojan Horse for a war on Black men. Michael Tonry, Sonosky Professor of Law and Public Policy at the University of Minnesota Law School, made these compelling observations in his *Malign Neglect: Race, Crime, and Punishment in America* (1995):

> the rising levels of black incarceration did not just happen; they were the foreseeable effects of deliberate policies...Anyone with knowledge of drug-trafficking patterns and of police arrest policies and incentives could have foreseen that the enemy troops in the War on Drugs would consist largely of young, inner-city minority males. Blacks in particular are arrested and imprisoned for drug crimes in numbers far out of line with their proportions of the general population, of drug users, and of drug traffickers...The War on Drugs foreseeably and unnecessarily blighted the lives of hundreds of thousands of young disadvantaged black Americans and undermined decades of effort to improve the life chances of members of the underclass...War or no war, most people are saddened to learn that for many years 30 to 40 percent of those admitted to prison were black. The War on Drugs was a calculated effort foreordained to increase those percentages and this is what happened.[653]

Between 1976 and 1989 the total number of drug arrests of whites increased by 70%; of Blacks, 450% increase. Between 1986 and 1991 the number of whites incarcerated for drug offenses increased by 50% while that of Blacks increased by 350%. Dr.

---

[652] Tommy J. Curry, "Michael Brown and the Need for a Genre Study of Black Male Death and Dying," paper, pp. 1-6 (2).
[653] Michael Tonry, *Malign Neglect: Race, Crime, and Punishment in America* (New York and Oxford: Oxford University Press, 1995) 4, 82. See also Michael Tonry and Matthew Melewski, "The Malign Effects of Drug and Crime Control Policies on Black Americans," *Crime and Justice* 37 (2008): 1-44.

Kenneth Nunn is thus not being hyperbolic when he exclaims: "As a consequence of the War on Drugs, large numbers of African American males have been virtually erased from African American communities and incarcerated in prison and jails."[654] Michael Tonry and Matthew Melewski argue the Wars on drugs and crime "could not more effectively have kept black Americans 'in their place' had they been designed with that aim in mind."[655] We argue, however, that the War on Drugs under Nixon, Reagan, Bush and Clinton demonstrably *were* designed with that very aim.

## II.   *War on Drugs I: Nixon's Prelude*

*He [Nixon] emphasized that you have to face the fact that the whole problem is really the blacks. The key is to devise a system that recognizes this while not appearing to.* H.R. Haldeman, advisor to Republican candidate Richard Nixon, noted in his diary after Nixon Briefing in 1969.

*It's all about law and order and the damn Negro-Puerto Rican groups out there.* Richard Nixon, after viewing one of his 1968 campaign ads.

President Nixon can probably be credited with launching America's first War on Black Men disguised as the government's War on Drugs. During his 1968 presidential campaign Nixon either innovated or perfected the strategy that both Ronald Reagan and Bill Clinton will later use to great success: dog whistling white supremacy and anti-black racism. Nixon's campaign engaged in "backlash politics"[656]: he appealed to the southern whites disaffected with their historic Democratic party because of the gains of the civil rights movement and the federal government's efforts to end legal segregation. Nixon combated

---

[654] Kenneth B. Nuun, "Race, Crime and the Pool of Surplus Criminality" Or Why the 'War on Drugs' was a 'War on Blacks,'" ***Gender, Race, and Justice*** 6 (2002): 383 [art.=381-445].

[655] Tonry and Melewski, "The Malign Effects," 3. Tonry suggested as well: "Although damaging the lives of countless young blacks was probably not their primary aim, the architects of the War on Drugs no doubt foresaw the result": Tonry, ***Malign Neglect***, 4. We argue of course that such *was* the primary aim of the architects of the War on Drugs, both Nixon's, Reagan's and Bush's.

[656] Josh Zeit, "How Trump is Recycling Nixon's 'Law and Order' Playbook," *PoliticoMagazine* July 18, 2016.

the civil rights successes with his "Law and Order" campaign.[657] That Nixon saw Black people as *the enemy* is well documented from some of his private conversations that would later be revealed (see the two above epigraphs). Indeed, according to Tali Mendelberg's sources "Nixon constantly used the word 'nigger' in private conversation" while his "public rhetoric was remarkably free of explicit racial appeals."[658] As Edmund Carlton writes: "Nixon was able to recodify the social dynamics of white versus black, north versus south, ghetto versus affluence, into a new set of politically correct terms."[659] Nonetheless, Nixon made "the unworthiness of blacks the subtext of his campaign," and won.[660]

In June of 1971 President Nixon launched his War on Drugs. He introduced the framework for his War in 1970 with the Comprehensive Drug Abuse Prevention and Control Act. This was a major move. The drug issue, originally a medical/mental health issue under the authority of the Surgeon General and NIMH, was now a crime issue under the authority of the Justice Department. Nixon's bill had two egregious laws: one permitting "preventive detention" and the other permitting "no-knock" raids of private homes. The preventive detention bill eliminated bail for persons arrested in Washington D.C. and subjected them to indefinite "pre-trial" detention if they were deemed "a danger to the community," thus in effect permitting "the imprisonment of a defendant who has not been convicted, and who is presumed innocent, of the crime with which he stands charged, on the basis of a prediction that he *may*" be a danger.[661]

The second "no-knock" law gave D.C. cops and federal agents conducting drug investigations the authority to smash into homes without first knocking and without announcing themselves. As expected, cops were known to rip down doors of

---

[657] Edmund Carlton, "Richard Nixon's Drug War: Politics Over Pragmatism," B.A. thesis, Harverford College, 2012) 14.
[658] Tali Mendelberg, *The Race Card: Campaign Strategy, Implicit Messages, and the Norm of Equality* (Princeton and Oxford: Princeton University Press, 2001) 97.
[659] Carlton, "Richard Nixon's Drug War," 21.
[660] Anderson, *White Rage*, 105.
[661] Alan M. Dershowitz, "On 'Preventive Detention'," *The New York Review* March 13, 1969.

innocent families, finding no drugs or contraband; just terrorizing citizens. In the words of North Carolina Senator Ervin North (D) who opposed the bill, this gave police "the right to enter the dwelling house of citizens of the District of Colombia in the same way that burglars now enter those dwelling houses." And the racial implications are clear: "Washington D.C. was of course mostly Black. And it would likely be mostly Black people who would feel the brunt of the new policy."[662] These racist, draconian laws, especially the "no-knock" law, of President Nixon should bring to mind the words of CIA asset Dr. Jolly West, whose equally racist and draconian proposal Nixon funded. As we saw, "West studied the use of drugs for controlling group behavior and said that drugs can be used 'as adjuncts to interpersonal manipulation or assault'."[663] West expounded on the value of drug laws to control an enemy population:

> The role of drugs in the exercise of political control is also coming under increasing discussion. Control can be through prohibition or supply. The total or even partial prohibition of drugs gives the government considerable leverage for other types of control. An example would be *the selective application* of drug laws permitting immediate search, or *"no knock" entry*, against selected components of the population *such as members of certain minority groups* or political organizations.[664]

There can be no doubt that Nixon's War on Drugs is the execution of the vision articulated by Jolly West, and there can be little doubt that the vision articulated by West was shared by the CIA: selectively apply drug laws like "no-knock" entry to target select groups, minority groups, as a means of socially *controlling* that minority group.

---

[662] Radley Balko, "Senator Ervin, 'No-Knock' Warrants, and the Fight to Stop Cops From Smashing into Homes the Way Burglars Do," **Huffington Post** July 10, 2013.
[663] EIR Investigative Team, "Dr. L. Jolyon West," 59.
[664] R.K. Siegel and L.J. West (edd.), **Hallucinations: Behavior, Experience and Theory** (New York: John Wiley, 1975).

John Ehrlichman (left) and President Nixon (right).

That this War on Drugs was explicitly a disguised War on Black People has now been confirmed by President Nixon's chief domestic policy advisor John Ehrlichman. Ehrlichman spent 18 months in prison for his central role in the Watergate scandal. In 1994 journalist Dan Braum interviewed Ehrlichman, excerpts of which appeared in last April's cover story of ***Harper's***. Speaking with the bluntness of a man who, after public disgrace and federal prison, had little left to protect, Ehrlichman told Braum:

> You want to know what this was really all about? The Nixon campaign in 1968, and the Nixon White House after that, had *two enemies*: the antiwar left *and black people*. You understand what I'm saying? We knew we couldn't make it illegal to be either against the war or black, but by getting the public to associate the hippies with marijuana *and blacks with heroin*, and then criminalizing both heavily, we could disrupt those communities. We could arrest their leaders, raid their homes, break up their meetings, and vilify them night after night on the evening news. Did we know we were lying about the drugs? Of course we did.[665]

This is astonishing. Associating Black people with heroin in order to wage a war against them is to associate Black people with the very drug that the U.S. government via the CIA-Mafia alliance

---

[665] Dan Braum, "Legalize it all: How to win the war in drugs," ***Harper's*** April 2016.

deliberately flooded our communities with. As Hilary Hanson comments, this confession by Nixon's chief domestic advisor

> pulls back the curtain on the true motivation of the United States war on drugs...the intense racial targeting that's become synonymous with the drug war wasn't an unintended side-effect-it was the whole point.[666]

The whole point, indeed.

### III. *War on Drugs II: Reagan's Crack Conspiracy*

*But for all his bluster, Nixon was a mere prelude to the full fury of the Reagan-Bush-Clinton years, where the War on Drugs became explicitly a war on blacks.* Alexander Cockburn and Jeffrey St. Clair, **White Out: The CIA, Drugs and the Press** (1999)

In October of 1982 President Ronald Reagan officially announced his War on Drugs which, as Professor Michelle Alexander documents, "from the outset had little to do with public concern about drugs and much to do with public concern about race."

> Most people assume the War on Drugs was launched in response to the crisis caused by crack cocaine in inner-city neighborhoods. This view holds that the racial disparities in drug convictions and sentences, as well as the rapid explosion of the prison population, reflect nothing more than the government's zealous-but benign-efforts to address rampant drug crime in poor, minority neighborhoods. This view, while understandable, given the sensational media coverage of crack in the 1980s and 1990s, is simply wrong...[T]here is no truth to the notion that the War on Drugs was launched in response to crack cocaine. President Ronald Reagan officially announced the current drug war in 1982, before crack became an issue in the media or a crisis in poor black neighborhoods. *A few years after the drug war was declared, crack began to spread rapidly in the poor black neighborhoods of Los Angeles and later emerged in cities across the country.* The Reagan administration hired staff to publicize the emergence of crack cocaine in 1985 as part of a strategic effort to build public and legislative support for the war. The media campaign was an extraordinary success. Almost overnight, the media was saturated with images of black 'crack whores,' 'crack dealers,' and 'crack babies'...The media bonanza surrounding the 'new demon drug' helped to catapult the War on Drugs

---

[666] Hilary Hanson, "Nixon Aide Reportedly Admitted Drug War Was Meant To Target Black People," *Huffington Post* March 22, 2016.

from an ambitious federal policy to an actual war...[It is an] odd coincidence that an illegal drug crisis suddenly appeared in the black community *after* – not before – a drug war had been declared. In fact, the War on Drugs began at a time when illegal drug use was on the decline.[667]

Dr. Carol Anderson makes a similar, undeniable observation:

There was just one problem [with the War on Drugs]. There *was* no drug crisis in 1982. Marijuana use was down, heroin and hallucinogenics use had leveled off, even first time cocaine use was bottoming out. But, as Reagan well knew, such a crisis was certainly coming for it had been manufactured and facilitated by his staff in the National Security Council (NSC) along with the Central Intelligence Agency (CIA).[668]

The crack epidemic emerged *after* Reagan declared War on Drugs, *not* before. In other words, the War on Drugs was not the governmental response to the crack outbreak; rather, the crack outbreak was the pre-fabricated governmental response to its own War on Drugs. The crack problem that ran through the inner-city like the Four Horsemen of the Apocalypse was *manufactured* by the U.S. government.

---

[667] Alexander, *The New Jim Crow*, 5, 6.
[668] Anderson, *White Rage*, 124.

# 16 Tailor-made Cocaine: How White Science Made Black Zombies

I.   *The White Lady and the Negro*

Much of the history of cocaine revolved around the relationship between the United States and the Andean republic of Peru in Latin America. Peru can be considered the epicenter of the international cocaine trade. While the white powder (cocaine hydrochloride) is processed today in Columbia and Mexico, the raw materials – the legendary coca plant and cocaine base– comes from Peru. The cocaine alkaloid was first crystalized from the Peruvian coca leaf in 1860. The indigenous people of Peru have chewed the coca plant for thousands of years with virtually no ill-effect or abuse. The plant has medicinal value, as a local anesthetic for example.

> The people of the North and East of this country have used vegetable substances (chamico, ayahuasca, cactus) since very old times for religious ceremonies, healing sessions and magical and divination purposes. During many centuries these uses and rites have not been serious health problems...The flora of Peru is one of the richest and most varied in the world. Since very old times the Indian tribes knew the psychothogenic effects of many plants and Inca healers accompanied the armies giving vegetable extracts for healing wounds and treatment of disease to the soldiers. Coca was chewed by the royal family, the priests, the soldiers and the leaders of the communities (...) on special occasions and for defined purposes...[C]oca is used in social economics and collective rites, in fashions prescribed by social and ethical regulations surrounded by the ceremony formalities and controls exerted by the community. Among the Indians coca is rarely the object of abuse or uncontrolled use, causing damage to heath...In traditional medicine coca is thought to be the cure for many pains and ailments. In this sense coca is one of the outstanding components of the popular native pharmacopeae.[669]

---

[669] R. Raul Jeri, "Guidelines for prevention of drug dependence in Peru," *Revista de la Sanidad de la Fuerzas Policiales* 42 (1981): 38-67 (51, 55).

While the regulated chewing and ritual/ceremonial use of the coca leaf by the native people of Peru produced no abuse or harm over thousands of years, nineteenth century Europeans transformed a plant of God into a tool of Satan. Credit goes to the German chemist Albert Niemann for discovering in 1860 the coca plant's most active alkaloid, which he named *kokain*. This alkaloid when isolated out of the plant is much more powerful and is the cause of the psychoactive and physiological effects of the narcotic cocaine. It was foreigners – Germans, French, Croats – who helped initiate cocaine processing in Peru.[670] While the aboriginal Peruvians chewed the coca plant, Europeans inhaled powder cocaine. To get cocaine hydrochloride from coca requires intensive processing and toxic chemical ingredients. The German firm E. Merck of Darmstadt made its reputation making premium cocaine hydrochloride. Cocaine and all of its subsequent global carnage is thus the result of the fusion of modern Western science and liberal commerce with a dormant national resource of Peru, the coca plant.[671]

The U.S. encouraged Peruvian production of coca. The Navy and U.S. consuls stationed in the Andes worked to ensure coca supply routes during the price crisis of 1884-1887 and the great coca scarcity, and commercial attachés in Lima, Peru's capital city, helped Peruvians upgrade their coca processing and shipping practices.[672] By 1900 the U.S. imported 500-1,000 tonnes of coca leaf annually and there were no proscriptions on its use or cocaine's.

---

[670] Paul Gootenberg, "Secret Ingredients: The Politics of Coca in US-Peruvian Relations, 1915-1965," *Journal of Latin American Studies* 36 (2004): 233-265 (237): "German chemists and agents had brokered the birth of Peru's own cocaine industry."
[671] See Paul Gootenberg, "Between Coca and Cocaine: A Century or More of U.S.-Peruvian Drug Paradoxes, 1860-1980," *Hispanic American Historical Review* 83 (2003): 119-150; Idem,. ed., *Cocaine: Global Histories* (London: Routledge, 1999); Joseph F. Spillane, *Cocaine: From Medical Marvel to Modern Menace in the United states, 1884-1920* (Baltimore: Johns Hopkins University Press, 1999).
[672] Gootenberg, "Between Coca and Cocaine," 122.

## COCAINE, COCA COLA AND THE FEAR OF THE SUPER NEGRO

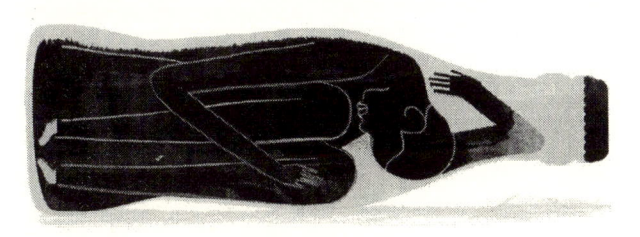

Image from "When Jim Crow Drank Coke," *The New York Times* January 28, 2013

Cocaine was first used medically after its discovery in 1860. In America it was a "miracle drug" of upper-class professionals. But it will trickle down to the middle-class. By 1885 one could get cocaine at the grocery store or salon. The largest manufacturer of cocaine in the U.S. at the time, Parke, Davis & Co. of Detroit and New York, was selling coca and cocaine as medicine in 15 different forms, including coca-leaf cigarettes, cocaine inhalant, cocaine crystals, and cocaine in solution for hypodermic injection. This produced a wave of cocaine addiction mainly among upper- and middle-class whites (who could afford the prescribing doctors and the commoditized forms of cocaine). By 1890 the dangerous effects of inhaling cocaine were being published in medical journals. America's "First Cocaine Epidemic" was born. [673]

But it was not until cocaine and its stimulating effects contributed to post-bellum America's "Negro Problem" did the government and its long time asset, Coca Cola Co., take action. Coca Cola's original 1886 secret formula contained coca plant extract for flavor as well as *cocaine* as a brain stimulant.[674] Middle-class whites gathered around the segregated soda-fountains at Atlanta pharmacies and enjoyed the new cocaine-laced "brain tonic." But in 1899 Coke pioneered its distinctive glass bottle

---

[673] David F. Musto, "America's First Cocaine Epidemic," *The Wilson Quarterly (1976-)* 13 (1989): 59-64; David T. Courtwright, "The First American Cocaine Epidemic," *OAH Magazine of History* 6 (1991): 20-21.

[674] See M. Pendergrast, *For God, Country and Coca-Cola: The Unauthorized History of the World's Most Popular Soft-Drink* (London, 1993).

which moved the drink (and its cocaine) out of the segregated soda fountains and into a nickel's reach of anyone who wanted it, Black or white. Whites became alarmed over what they saw as exploding cocaine use among African American's in the South because of these soft drinks.[675]

> No concern was stressed more than the growing popularity of cocaine among blacks, who could purchase a nickel's worth of the drug and go on a "coke drunk." Editorials in leading medical and pharmaceutical journals pointed to increased cocaine use among blacks as a justification for restrictive legislation.[676]

What whites found so alarming was that the cocaine seemed to have given Black users "super human strength, cunning, and efficiency."[677] This is more than simply "Yellow journalism." Cocaine is medically known as a strong stimulant that, in the short run, can give a user enormous strength and endurance for the moment (as a prelude to the very *damaging* well-known effects of the drug). This is what was observed among some Black male users. In 1910 President William Howard Taft submitted a State Department Report on drugs to Congress claiming cocaine "temporally raises the power of a [Negro] criminal" and in 1914 Dr. Edward Huntington Williams used *The New York Times* to alert whites of this new Negro Menace: sniffing cocaine results in "temporary immunity to shock - a resistance to the 'knock down' effects of fatal wounds". Black men on cocaine can, the claim was, withstand normal .32 caliber bullets so some Southern police departments had to switch to .38 caliber revolvers.[678]

That year Congress debated whether to pass the Harrison Narcotics Tax Act regulating the sale and distribution of drugs. Dr. Hamilton Wright testified that cocaine "made blacks uncontrollable, gave them superhuman powers and caused them

---

[675] Grace Elizabeth Hale, "When Jim Crow Drank Coke," *The New York Times* January 28, 2013.
[676] Courtwright, "The First American Cocaine Epidemic," 21.
[677] Musto, "America's First Cocaine Epidemic," 64.
[678] Edward Huntington Williams, "Negro Cocaine 'Fiends' are a New Southern Menace," *The New York Times* February 8, 1914.

to rebel against white authority." In December of 1914 Congress passed the Act, and "proponents could thank the South's fear of blacks for easing its passage."[679] But by that time Coca Cola, who had made a nickel's worth of cocaine available to the Southern Negro, had already made a decision. "By 1903, [Asa G.] Candler [President of Coca Cola Co.] had bowed to white fears (and a wave of anti-narcotics legislation), removing the cocaine and adding more sugar and caffeine."[680] Not necessarily "bowed" to white fears: Coca Cola culture *shared* those sentiments, no doubt. In 1922 the Jones-Miller Act strictly controlled coca imports and banned all cocaine imports into the country. Thus began America's anti-cocaine era.

Fear of the "Super Negro on Coke" inspired a drug clean-up in America that proves beyond doubt that when the government has the *will* to eradicate the drug problem within its borders, it has the *power* to do.

> cocaine consumption in the U.S. and elsewhere fell dramatically off its 1917 peak during the interwar period, in what one pundit calls "the great drought." To be sure, cocaine found a haven in certain cultural niches: jazz music, horse racing, Hollywood orgies and song, but mainly confined to their realms of folklore. American fiends slowly faded into memory. Cocaine medicinal usage continued to shrink as substitutes like procaine came on line and cocaine research dried up (since it fit poorly with the newly constructed medical or opiate addiction paradigm). And yet notably, almost no organized international network of illicit cocaine emerged after prohibition laws, in contrast to those that coalesced around alcohol, or an even newer ex-miracle drug, heroin. The inescapable conclusion that emerges from a close and critical scrutiny of the era's public health and [Federal Bureau of Narcotics] reports is this: there were fewer and fewer cocaine fiends, and by the 1930s effectively no cocaine was being smuggled from abroad. Confiscations of cocaine were measured in ounces or vials of diverted European medical-grade. No illicit factories came to life and no smuggling sprouted from Andean coca fields… U.S. borders became sealed to cocaine, which withered away early urban cocaine gangs or "combinations," and sent thrill seekers to other drugs…[T]he United States achieved greatest success, however understood, in drying up cocaine use within its borders.[681]

---

[679] Carl L. Hart, "How the Myth of the 'Negro Cocaine Fiend' Helped Shape American Drug Policy," *The Nation* January 29, 2014.
[680] Hale, "When Jim Crow Drank Coke."
[681] Gootenberg, "Between Coca and Cocaine," 130, 136.

This domestic eradication program was so successful that David F. Musto could write: "By the time I was in medical school, during the late 1950s, cocaine was described to medical students as a drug that *used to be* a problem in the United States. It was news to us (emphasis added)."[682] After effectively removing the threat of the "Super Negro on Coke" by sealing this country off (for the most part) to cocaine, the U.S. government replaced cocaine in Black neighborhoods with heroin which subdued and totally destroyed Black life without the initial "power boost" that cocaine provided before it too did its real dirty work. Black America's first true drug crisis was thus produced in the 1950s, as we saw above.

The drying up of America's streets from cocaine does not mean that the government was out of the cocaine business; quite the opposite. America subsequently (1940-1970) got control of Peru's coca plant and thus of the international cocaine trade, for her own commercial, political and social benefit (and that of Coca Cola). After World War II the U.S. emerged as the uncontested power of world drug affairs. America's efforts to control the trade gave rise in 1948-1949 to the first ever international illicit cocaine trade. *Illicit* coca and cocaine really only means the production, movement, sale and/or use of coca and cocaine anywhere in the world that is *not* done by or with the approval of the U.S. government and/or *not* destined for Coca Cola.[683] And the government managed to secure this control with the help of its staunch ally and global operative, Coca Cola Co.

---

[682] Musto, "America's First Cocaine Epidemic," 64.
[683] Gootenberg, "Between Coca and Cocaine"; Paul Gootenberg, "Cocaine's 'Blowback North: A Commodity Chain Pre-History of the Mexican Drug Crisis," *LASA Forum* 42 (2011): 37-42; idem, "The 'Pre-Columbian' Era of Drug Trafficking in the Americas: Cocaine, 1945-1965," *The Americas* 64 (2007): 133-176. Bart Elmore ("What Coke's cocaine problem can tell us about Coca-Cola Capitalism," *Oxford University Press Blog* March 21, 2014) thus notes: "The Federal Bureau of Narcotics (FBN) also played a pivotal role in this trade. Besides helping to pilot a Hawaiian coca farm, the US counternarcotics agency negotiated deals with the Peruvian government to ensure that Coke maintained access to coca supplies. The FBN and its successor agencies did this even while initiating coca eradication programs, tearing up shrubs in certain parts of the Andes in an attempt to cut off cocaine supply channels. By the 1960s, coca was becoming an enemy of the state, but only if it was not destined for Coke."

The *Executive Intelligence Review* January 18, 1977 issue reported:

> Coca-Cola utilizes its vast, worldwide bottling and distribution network as a vehicle for various CIA-type covert operations ranging from bribery of politicians and government officials up through the fostering of terrorism, destabilization operations, and coups d'etat. Chief among Coca-Cola's subversive activities is its probable involvement in a major international drug-running network spanning several continents, including North America.[684]

The 1922 Jones-Miller Act which outlawed imports of coca and cocaine into this country did two other, notable things: it gave Coca Cola a special exemption to its prohibition and it led to the creation of the Federal Bureau of Narcotics (FBN) in 1930, the predecessor of President Richard Nixon's Drug Enforcement Administration (DEA). The FBN under its first commissioner Harry J. Anslinger (retired in 1962) would enter into a compact with Coca Cola that will last for three decades, and then no-doubt transitioned over to the DEA when this agency in 1973 replaced the FBN and its immediate successor the Bureau of Narcotics and Dangerous Drugs. Through this alliance with the U.S. drug agency Coca Cola Co. became not only a staunch government ally, but a vital intelligence asset and covert operative,[685] reportedly involved even today in such operations as funding terrorist groups and political assassinations in Colombia,[686] illegal

---

[684] "Mr. Carter's Coca-Cola Connection," *Executive Intelligence Review* 4 (1977): 22-25.

[685] See especially Paul Gootenberg, "Secret Ingredients: The Politics of Coca in US-Peruvian Relations, 1915-65," *Journal of Latin American Studies* 36 (2004): 233-265; Bartlow J. Elmore, *Citizen Coke: The Making of Coca Cola Capitalism* (New York: W.W. Norton & Co., 2015).

[686] In 2001 a lawsuit was filed in Miami against Coca-Cola and its bottlers accusing them and other corporations operating in Colombia of financing a violent Colombian paramilitary group and, allegedly, terrorist organization: the United Self-Defense Forces of Colombia. Coca-Cola is accused of hiring the assassins who killed 10 labor union leaders. See Juan Forero, "Union Says Coca-Cola in Colombia Uses Thugs," *The New York Times* July 26, 2001; Sibylla Brodzinsky, "Coca-Cola boycott launched after killings at Colombian plants," *the guardian* July 23, 2003; Andriaan Alsema, "Coca Cola facing terrorism support charges in Colombia," *Colombia Reports* August 30, 2016.

intelligence gathering in Communist China,[687] and smuggling $56 million worth of cocaine into France.[688]

It is today a violation of U.S. federal law to import the coca plant or cocaine or to possess or manufacture either – unless you are Coca-Cola or its subsidiary. Coca-Cola is officially exempt from a number of the domestic anti-cocaine laws and the international prohibition regime. The Jones-Miller Act granted Coca Cola and its affiliate lab an exemption that no one else was granted, then or since. This exemption was secret until 1988 when *The New York Times* revealed it.[689] Coca Cola's New Jersey coca processing lab is the Illinois-based Stepan Company. It is the nation's only legal commercial importer of coca leaves, which it obtains mainly from Peru. The lab produces the coca flavoring for Coke after extracting the cocaine from the coca leaves. Bales of coca destined for Stepan labs in Maywood, New Jersey are shipped through New York and New Jersey ports with their own DEA-issued import permits. According to *Naturalnews.com*, approximately 100 metric tons of coca leaves each year are imported to Stepan by special permission from the DEA, enough to make over 300 kilos of cocaine.[690] What happens to the cocaine? Stepan sells it to the St. Louis-based pharmaceutical manufacturer Mallinckrodt, Inc., formerly Mallinckrodt Chemical Works.

Mallinckrodt is a government asset. It developed the chemical process for purifying large quantities of uranium for atomic weapons, and it conducted its uranium operation for the

---

[687] In 2013 China investigated Coca Cola for its employees using GPS technology to illegally obtain classified information that could be used to carry out missile attacks on its military. See Hunter Stuart, "China Investigating Coca-Cola Over Illegal Intelligence Gathering: Report," *The Huffington Post* March 14, 2013.

[688] In August 2016 370 kilos of bagged cocaine, a street value of $56 million, were discovered at a Coca-Cola factory in France. They were shipped to the Coke plant from Costa Rica in a shipment of orange juice concentrate. This was one of the largest such discoveries on French soil. See Christopher Mele, "Bags of Cocaine Worth $56 Million Are Found at Coca-Cola Factory in France," *The New York Times* September 1, 2016; Justin Worland, "$56 Million of Cocaine Found at Coca-Cola Factory in France," *Time* September 1, 2016.

[689] Clifford D. May, "How Coca-Cola Obtains Its Coca," *The New York Times* July 1, 1988.

[690] Mike Adams, "To this day, Coca-Cola still imports coca leaves which are used to manufacture cocaine in the United States," *NaturalNews* July 9, 2011.

Atomic Energy Commission. It was Mallinckrodt's uranium that was used in the atomic bombs that destroyed Hiroshima and Nagasaki in 1945.[691] Mallinckrodt ceased its uranium operation for the government in 1966 and pharmaceuticals became its main business – for the government. Given that such company executives as August Homyer had previously been officials at the U.S. Federal Bureau of Narcotics,[692] it is not terribly surprising to learn that, not only does Mallinckrodt possess the lone U.S. license to purify the cocaine base into cocaine hydrochloride (powder), but it also is one of only three U.S. importers legally permitted to import opium. If this were not enough, this secret government asset has a marijuana privilege as well. Dr. Mahmoud El Sohly's of the University of Mississippi is the only lab contracted by the National Institute on Drug Abuse (NIDA) to grow tons of marijuana for research. Dr. El Sohly sells the THC extracted from his marijuana to Mallinckrodt.[693] This Coca-Cola affiliate thus has its hands in – actually *on* - all of the illicit drug goodie bags – legally. What happens to all of this cocaine that Mallinckrodt produces? Henry Berger informs us:

> As the sole legitimate source for cocaine use in the United States, Mallinckrodt had a substantial lock on the substance from which it made byproducts sold to pharmaceutical companies, soft drink producers, and medical enterprises. Unintended as it *may* have been, the proliferation of cocaine, the ease with which it could be illicitly manufactured, sold relatively inexpensively, and easily ingested, contributed to an addictive culture and trade that flourished in the streets of American cities like St. Louis (emphasis added).[694]

Indeed, a massive amount of cocaine likely "disappears" out of the back door – intentionally - and finds its way into the

---

[691] Keith Schneider, "Mountain of Nuclear Waste Splits St. Louis and Suburbs," *The New York Times* March 24, 1990.
[692] Henry W. Berger, *St. Louis and Empire: 250 Years of Imperial Quest and Urban Crisis* (Carbondale: Southern Illinois University, 2015) 204.
[693] Gardiner Harris, "Researchers Find Study of Medical Marijuana Discouraged," *The New York Times* January 18, 2010; Dave Stancliff, "There's a monopoly on marijuana growing and research in America," *Times-Standard News* August 8, 2009.
[694] Berger, *St. Louis and Empire*, 205.

streets, contributing to the 1970s "rediscovery" of cocaine recreational use. So when the *Executive Intelligence Review* reports that "Coca-Cola is involved in drug-smuggling as well as other CIA-type covert operations," we have some context.[695]

During World War II the U.S. seized cocaine from her prewar rivals, the Axis powers Germany and Japan. This is partly how the U.S. gained control of the global cocaine trade in the postwar era.[696] Coca Cola assisted the Allied war-effort. Cocaine was used during the war as a salve to war-wounds. There is circumstantial evidence that Coca Cola helped get the cocaine to the soldiers.

> Although Coca-Cola began to expand overseas during the 1920s, it was World War II which gave the company its biggest boost. At the outbreak of the war company chairman Robert Woodruff vowed that no American GI would be without Coke no matter where he was fighting. To fulfill his pledge, Woodruff, with help from the War Department, got the U.S. government to subsidize the construction of more than 60 Coca-Cola plants in various parts of the world. More than five billion bottles of Coke were distributed to American soldiers during the war.
> There is strong circumstantial evidence that the Coke dispensed to U.S. soldiers at this time contained cocaine. For one thing, the War Department went to great lengths to insure that GIs had access to Coke at all times. In fact, mobile units were specially devised to permit soldiers fighting in jungle areas access to Coke. For another, cocaine was first popularized by a German army doctor in the 1870s who found that the drug enabled soldiers to march longer and endure greater physical hardships.[697]

Thus, while the government successfully eradicated the cocaine epidemic within U.S. borders it was still importing and producing large amounts of coca and cocaine through its corporate ally Coca Cola and affiliates. Why is this detour into Coca Cola relevant here? For almost thirty years America was effectively cocaine clean. In 1970, America started getting cocaine dirty again. What precipitated this "rediscovery" of cocaine? Since we *know* that the U.S. government and its agencies are well capable of sealing its borers from cocaine imports, where did all of

---

[695] "Mr. Carter's Coca-Cola Connection," 23.
[696] Gootenberg, "Secret Ingredients," 256-257.
[697] "Mr. Carter's Coca-Cola Connection," 23-24.

the cocaine that flooded the streets during the Seventies and the Eighties come from? Much of it, we suggest, was probably domestically manufactured. There is reason to believe that the "rediscovery" of cocaine in the 1970s on the streets of America was aided by the U.S. government through its corporate ally Coca Cola and its affiliates.

## II. The CIA's Tailor-made Cocaine Ravages Argentina

*the CIA, which has always been at the cutting edge of developments in psychopharmacology, continues to conduct secret research aimed at creating more sophisticated forms of chemical control...Some of the drugs – such as "designer heroin" and "designer cocaine" – have already moved from the laboratory to the street, and the consequences have been fatal.* Martin A. Lee and Bruce Shlain, **Acid Dreams: The Complete Social History of LSD, the CIA, the Sixties, and Beyond** (1992)

*through molecular architecture we can mold these drugs to do exactly what we want: put them in vehicles that control themselves, like time release capsules...We developed many years ago cocaine chewing gum, which we did some early tests with and is now for sale in another country.* Dr. Ronald K. Siegel, psychopharmacologist, Department of Psychiatry and Biobehavioral Sciences, University of California, Los Angeles, 2013.

Michael Levine was a soldier in the War on Drugs for 25 years. He is the most decorated undercover agent in the history of the Drug Enforcement Administration (DEA), having worked deep cover for 10 years from Bangkok to Buenos Aires. He has infiltrated drug organizations in Asia, the U.S. and Latin America and is responsible for the imprisonment of 3000 criminals. Today he is a whistle blower, having discovered that "The CIA is America's primary supplier of cocaine" and that "The war on drugs was only an illusion that I had been fool enough to believe in."[698] Levine's disillusion came in 1979. He was sent undercover

---

[698] Michael Levine, **Deep Cover: The Inside Story of How DEA Infighting, Incompetence and Subterfuge Lost Us the Biggest Battle of the Drug War** (New York: Delacorte Press, 1990); idem, **The Big White Lie: the CIA and the Cocaine/Crack Epidemic** (New York: Thunder's Mouth Press, 1993); Richard Stratton, "The Metamorphosis of Michael Levine: from gung-ho narc to drug war

to Argentina. While there Levine had succeeded in penetrating into the heart of a global drug network that produced an enhanced form of cocaine called *La Reina Blanca*, the White Queen. This drug was so potent it made heroin and cocaine "look like powdered sugar." One evening he and a small group of DEA and CIA agents as well as Argentine police gathered for a drinking party at the home of a CIA agent. There he learned, much to his shock and dismay, that the CIA itself was responsible for the White Queen hitting the Argentine streets. During the course of a conversation the CIA host said to Levine:

> Make *La Reina Blanca* available in a country and within weeks a significant and predictable portion of the population is turned into murderous, uncontrollable zombies doomed to a slow, expensive death. You destroy that nation's economy, its faith in its government. The nation implodes on itself. You win a war and you never fire a shot.[699]

The CIA agent described *La Reina Blanca* as "The Ultimate Chemical Weapon." According to a fellow DEA informant to Levine, as part of its ongoing post-MK-ULTRA mind/behavioral control research the CIA investigated the 200 variants of the coca plant and genetically engineered a type of cocaine that would specifically target the sex centers of the brain.[700] Grafting coca and a hallucinogen together they produced *La Reina Blanca*. Appalled, Levine chides his CIA host: "What I don't understand is how...you, a so-called American, can put that [drug] on our streets."[701] They put the drug on the streets in Argentina

---

dissident. A *Prison Life* interview," in Richard Stratton, **Altered States of America : outlaws and icons, hitmakers and hitmen** (New York: Nation's Books, 2005)

[699] Michael Levine with Laura Kavanau, *Triangle of Death* (New York: Delacorte Press, 1996) Chapter 43.

[700] "Michael Levine Speaks about Triangle of Death on The Melanin Chronicles" https://www.youtube.com/watch?v=I9cr2XN60so @ 34:30-39-37 and 40:30-43-56.

[701] Levine recounts this story in his fictional novel *Triangle of Death*, which is based on his many undercover drug cases. He explained to William Norman Grigg of **The New American** that the above scenario and conversation was not fiction but actually transpired. See William Norman Grigg, "Battle Lines in the Drug War," @ http://www.theforbiddenknowledge.com/hardtruth/fake_war.htm. Levine speaks about the factual basis of this book and why he wrote it in the "Tom

specifically to create "murderous, uncontrollable zombies doomed to a slow, expensive death."

This was neither the first nor the last time the CIA will deliberately produce a potent cocaine variant that turns people into living zombies which they (the CIA) released onto unsuspecting urban streets.

III. *Prototype in Peru: The Zombie Test Run*

Commensurate with the sudden reappearance of cocaine on the streets (or rather, in the high rises) of America in the 1970s and with the CIA-spawned *La Reina Blanca* outbreak in Argentina, a new, deadly form and use of cocaine mysteriously appeared in Lima, the capital city of Peru. Coca paste is the intermediate stage in the process of manufacturing cocaine hydrochloride. Coca leaves are first soaked in kerosene and acid in order to extract the cocaine alkaloid. This produces a gooey paste – *pasta basica* – that is then converted through a complex chemical process into cocaine powder. But starting in the early 1970s poor people in Peru started doing something no one had ever done: smoking the paste! They would lace a cigarette stick or marijuana joint with this dried toxic paste and smoke it. This cigarette laced with coca paste is called a *pastillo*. This is the first case of cocaine *smoking*. It is the prototype and the sibling of the cocaine smoking that will appear in the 1980s in America – freebase and crack cocaine. And I will suggest below that as it was a U.S. covert operation that lay behind the deadly coca paste epidemic of 1970s Peru, it is equally a U.S. covert operation that lay behind the crack cocaine epidemic of the 1980s South Central Los Angeles. Just as the CIA manufactured *La Reina Blanca* and unleashed it onto the streets of Argentina, the CIA probably innovated and introduced the *pastillos*, the cigarettes of tobacco laced with coca paste, into the slums of Peru.

The first seven smokers were "discovered" in 1972. They were Peruvian military and police offices. They were "discovered" and studied by Dr. Raul Jeri, a military police psychiatrist and

---

Clancy" way that he did during his interview on The Melanin Chronicles here https://www.youtube.com/watch?v=I9cr2XN60so.

professor of clinical neurology at the National University of San Marcos.[702] By 1974 there was an epidemic. This smoking habit produced a patient profile not seen before: a walking dead or "coke zombie," totally enslaved to the drug. Dr. Jeri reported:

> When seen these patients were generally very thin, unkempt, pale and looking suspiciously from one side to the other (...) These movements were associated, as manifested by the patients, with visual hallucinations (shadows, light or human figures) which they observed on the temporal fields of vision...the same person experienced tactile and auditory hallucinations...They were, however, very rapidly, interpreted as menacing images because of the intense paranoid tendency in these reactions. On physical examination many had dilated pupils, rapid pulse, psychomotor excitement (instability, tremors, myoclonus, marked anxiety). A good proportion had scratch marks on the skin. The scratches observed on users were related to the tactile hallucinations felt under the skin (= the "bugs" that latter crack users hallucinated were crawling under their skin – WM). On questioning, some admitted having visual hallucinations, coloured or dark, on the temporal fields mainly, elementary or complex (from points or stars to men or women), giving them the impression that they were being followed by persons or shadows that seemed to want to catch, attack or kill them...Some patients developed paranoid psychoses, which lasted up to two weeks. Others showed long lasting pathological jealousy. The somatic acute disturbances documented were tachycardia, high blood pressure, temperature increase, hyperhydrosis and bowel hypermotility (diarrhea). Motor manifestations, indicating an acute encephalopathy were tremors, myoclonic jerks, limbic seizures and generalized convulsions (rare). When the intoxication was not reversed it progressed to cardiac arrythmias, neurogenic hyperventilation, coma, respiratory and cardiac arrest. Three patients died in this series, two by acute intoxication and one by suicide. The pathological reports of the two who died from intoxication showed extensive lung damage and no brain lesions on section or routine staining (hematoxylin eosin).[703]

This is in many ways the precise pathologic profile of the later crackhead. The *paste*head is his prototype. It gets worse.

---

[702] F.R. Jeri et al., "Consumo de Drogas Peligrosas por Miembros de la Fuerza Armada y de la Fuerza Policial Peruana ("Consumption of Dangerous Drugs by Members of the Armed Forces and the Police in Peru")," *Revista de la Sanidad del Ministerio del Interior* 37 (1976): 104-112.

[703] F.R. Jeri et al., "The Syndrome of Coca Paste," *Journal of Psychedelic Drugs* 10 (1978): 361-370; idem, "Further experience with syndromes produced by coca paste smoking," *Bulletin on Narcotics* 30 (1978): 1-11.

When the habit soon caught fire in the more well-to-do communities as well, it had devastating social effects: thousands of users were dropping out of medical school and college and turning into raging addicts. Good young people instantly abandoned their whole lives and turned to stealing from their grandmothers and others to get money for their enslaving high.

> The social consequences of coca paste smoking in the group studied were very serious indeed. These individuals became so dependent on the drug that they had practically no other interest in life. They became completely deficient at work, had serious marital problems and the students failed courses or dropped out of school. When they held a job they were frequently absent from work because they felt ill or were searching for the drug. They needed money to pay for coca paste, which is not very expensive when bought in one gram packages, but becomes prohibitive when a man consumes 40 or 60 grams a day...As money becomes scarce they resort to swindling, theft, non-payment of debts, or become drug pushers. It is hard to believe to what extremes of social degradation these men may fall, especially those who were brilliant students, efficient professionals, or successful business men.[704]

Edmundo Morales describes "the extremes of social degradation" that victims of this new drug use fell into.

> Theft, robbery, prostitution, and homosexual activities are the most common methods of getting cash to buy ketes (Peruvian coca paste). The younger addicts usually get their daily dosages by way of homosexual services or exchange of sexual gratification for coca paste. Non-addict homosexual and heterosexual individuals also trade coca paste for sexual gratification.
> David is a fourteen-year old Caucasian boy. He has been smoking coca paste for the last four years. On his long hair, black lice (hair lice) run about like ants on an ant-hill and white lice (body lice) are all over David's neck. "How did you become an addict, Dave?" "Like everyone else" [he replied]... Next morning I find David sleeping on the porch of a state office building along with two other addicts. I sit on the sidewalk to hear their morning conversation. The three of them scratch their bodies permanently while they talk... Yesterday he traded his asshole for ten ketes. The owner of the bodega, that old man who likes kids, came and gave him [coca] paste. "Let me check him out," says David. He gets up and leaves for downtown. He stands by the market street for a few minutes. He goes to the back of a bank only to find empty paper "beds." Then he walks along the main street and turns left towards Chicago.

---

[704] Jeri et al. "Further experience."

> David's portrait is just one of the many hopeless children who now wander around in Peru and their desperation to satisfy their craving for drugs may even cause violent deaths.[705]

A chemical monster was let loose in the capital city of Peru, and it quickly spread to the main Peruvian cities and then to Peru's neighbors, Ecuador and Bolivia.[706] Who let it loose? Probably the same people who let loose *La Reina Blanca* in Argentina – the CIA. There is reason to suspect that this epidemic is the result of a Cold War covert operation.

On October 2, 1968 General Juan Velasco Alvarado, chief of the Peruvian Armed Forces Joint Command, led a military coup overthrowing the U.S.-friendly government of centrist Fernando Belaúnde Terry. The Revolutionary Government of the Armed Forces of President Juan Velasco was the lone left-wing government in a continent full of right-ring governments supported by the U.S. The objective of Velasco's revolution was to challenge U.S. hegemony in Latin America and break "the country's political, economic and military dependence on North America." Like Castro in Cuba, Velasco sought to raise the economic condition of the masses of the indigenous people at the expense of the traditional, exploitative elites, mostly foreign. He therefore nationalized the industries and expropriated U.S. investments. Velasco ignited a wave of U.S. fear that a second, Andean "Cuba" would emerge in the Western Hemisphere. The fears were well-founded. Velasco expelled the U.S. Peace Corps

---

[705] Edmundo Morales, "Coca Paste and Crack: A Cross National Ethnographic Approach," in *Drugs in Latin America.* **Studies in Third World Societies, Publication Number Thirty-seven**, ed. Edmundo Morales (Williamsburg, VA.: College of William and Mary, 1986) 185-186 [art.=179-200].

[706] See further F. Raul Jeri, "Coca-paste smoking in some Latin American countries: a severe and unabated form of addiction," *Bulletin of Narcotics* 36 (1984): 15-31; idem, "Coca Paste and Cocaine Abuse in Peru: Associations, Complications and Outcomes in 389 Patients," in *Drugs in Latin America.* **Studies in Third World Societies, Publication Number Thirty-seven**, ed. Edmundo Morales (Williamsburg, VA.: College of William and Mary, 1986) 149-162; idem, "The Impact of Cocaine Abuse in Some Developing Countries," in *Medicine: Proceedings of the Scientific Meeting of Cocaine. Luxembourg, 14 to 16 January 1987*, ed. Commission of the European Communities (Luxembourg, 1988) 3-15.

and abandoned the U.S. as primary arms supplier, negotiating an arms deal with the Soviet Union.[707]

Velasco's stance "earned Lima the enmity of American officials".[708] The National Security Council therefore deliberated over a set of possible hardline and softline responses. Military action was not feasible with Vietnam in full swing and barely enough military forces in West Germany and South Korea. But a CIA covert operation could be effective. So the CIA turned a highly placed official in Velasco's government.

Under President Velasco was his Prime Minister General Edgardo Mercado Jarrín. Mercado's personal aide and advisor was Vladimir Montesinos. In 1965 Montesinos was trained at the U.S. Army School of the Americas, the same school from which future Panama leader and CIA asset General Manuel Noriega had just graduated.[709] After the revolution, the CIA approached Montesinos and he was happy to oblige. The *Los Angeles Times* reports: "Montesinos...is said by the U.S. and international press to have begun a relationship with the CIA in the 1970s."[710] As aide to the Prime Minister, Montesinos had access to classified documents, which it is believed he sold to the CIA. We are told that Montesinos regularly met with the CIA station chief in Lima and also conveyed the weekly presidential agenda to the U.S. embassy.

Montesinos will outlive the Revolutionary Government of the Armed Forces, which was overthrown in 1975, and become the most powerful man in Peru under President Fuijimori (1990-2000) and the CIA's chief asset in the area. Most important is that Montesinos was the CIA's local drug-lord. It is the case that he

---

[707] See Hal Brands, "The United States and the Peruvian Challenge, 1968–1975," *Diplomacy & Statecraft* 21 (2010): 471-490; Noel Maurer, "Much Ado About Nothing: Expropriation and compensation in Peru and Venezuela, 1968-75," Harvard Business School Working Paper 11-097, 2011: 1-17.
[708] Brands, "United States and the Peruvian Challenge," 471.
[709] Alfonso W. Quiroz, *Corrupt Circles: A History of Unbound Graft in Peru* (Washington D.C. and Baltimore: Woodrow Wilson Center Press and Johns Hopkins University Press, 2008) 361.
[710] "The CIA Owes One to Peru," *Los Angeles Times* July 5, 2001. See also Cynthia McClintock and Fabian Vallas, *The United States and Peru: Cooperation at a Cost* (New York and London: Routledge, 2003) 55: "by virtually all accounts a that time [i.e. the early 1970s] he (Montesinos) became a spy for the CIA."

was "a key ally of the U.S. government in the so-called war on drugs,"[711] but as Pedro Moreno Vasquez points out:

> the government anti-drugs campaign was only a form of theatrics...While the government promised coca eradication, Montesinos truly promoted cocaine trade with cartels from all over the world.[712]

According to Peruvian journalist Gustavo Gorriti the anti-drug unit headed by Montesinos was fathered in Washington, not in Peru, and according to Maximo San Roman, former Vice President under Fujimori, Montesinos and the intelligence apparatus that he lorded over directly organized the drug trade. This is precisely the CIA's *modus operandi*: in both Venezuela and Haiti the CIA set up anti-drug units that in fact trafficked in drugs.[713] Thus, the same man that directed the Peruvian illicit drug trade during the 1990s received at the same time $10 million from the CIA to assist him in his efforts.[714]

U.S. hegemonic intervention in Latin American countries came and comes under the cover or pretext/pretense of the War on Drugs.[715] In order to justify such a pseudo-war, there needs to be a drug crisis. Where no such crisis naturally exists, it must be deliberately fabricated. No such drug crisis existed in Peru at the time – until the mysterious coca paste epidemic broke out in 1972-74. It is my contention that the CIA through its assets in Lima created the Peruvian coca-paste epidemic of the 1970s as both a Cold War covert op against the military junta of General Velasco and as an MK-ULTRA experiment with a new form of cocaine: smokable coca paste.

---

[711] Coletta Youngers, "Peruvian President Fujimori's Right-Hand Man Was a Gun Runner and Drug Dealer," **Foreign Policy In Focus** September 3, 2010.
[712] Pedro Moreno Vasquez, "Pablo Escobar's Secret CIA Connections," **XPat Nation** July 9, 2015.
[713] Tim Weiner, "Anti-Drug Unit of C.I.A. Sent Ton of Cocaine to U.S. in 1990," **The New York Times** November 20, 1993. See also Phil Davison, "Peru stunned by military aid to drug cartels," **Independent** July 21, 1996.
[714] On Montesinos getting $10 million from the CIA while engaging in drug trafficking see "The CIA Owes One to Peru," **Los Angeles Times** July 5, 2001.
[715] On the case of Peru see Cynthia McClintock, "The War on Drugs: The Peruvian Case," **Journal of Interamerican Studies and World Affairs** 30 (1988): 127-142.

The smokable coca paste that ravaged Lima in the 1970s is related to the smokable crack cocaine that ravaged South Central Los Angeles in the 1980s. As Morales notes, "crack and freebased cocaine are processes of 'stepping back' from cocaine hydrochloride to the impurity-laden coca-paste-type of substance."[716] He also reveals that coca paste users and the crack users were both "underground guinea pigs."[717] Indeed, the coca-paste outbreak among the poor (and then middle-clash) Brown neighborhoods of Lima was the precursor and prototype of the crack outbreak among the Black neighborhoods in L.A. Both communities were "guina pigs" of the American CIA, just as the Argentines were guinea pigs of the CIA in the late 1970s when they unleashed *La Reina Blanca*. According to Michael Levine an important DEA Agent told him that crack would hit six years before it actually did hit.[718]

---

[716] Morales, "Coca Paste and Crack," 189.
[717] Morales, "Coca Paste and Crack," 194.
[718] "Michael Levine Speaks about Triangle of Death on The Melanin Chronicles" https://www.youtube.com/watch?v=I9cr2XN60so @ 34:30-37:37.

# 17 The Crack Conspiracy: The Confessions

> As I have stated throughout the years: Crack cocaine is from the government of the United States of America. And when I have said this, some of you thought I was paranoid...Brother Dr. Cornell West, a really brilliant brother, said to me, "Farrakhan, do you hold to some conspiracy theory?" I said "It's not a theory, it's a fact!" The Honorable Minister Louis Farrakhan, "Crack Cocaine: The Great Conspiracy to Destroy the Black Male" (1996).
>
> **Dark Alliance** *does not propound a conspiracy theory; there is nothing theoretical about history. In this case, it is undeniable that a wildly successful conspiracy to import cocaine existed for many years, and that innumerable Americans – most of them poor and black – paid an enormous price as a result.* Gary Webb, **Dark Alliance** (1998)

I. *Who Created Crack?*

Mark Osler, Professor of Law at the University of St. Thomas, suggests:

> As with many of history's greatest innovations, we don't know the name of the person who first created what we now call "crack cocaine" (a moniker that was created a decade later). We do know, however, that his or her invention probably arose in Southern California in the mid- 1970's. Whoever it was who created crack seems to have had a strong understanding of how narcotics are used and their physiological effects.[719]

On the other hand, in 1991 Witkin and Mukenge said regarding "The Men Who Created Crack":

> Crack was not invented; it was created by a sharp group of sinister geniuses who took a simple production technique to make a packaged, ready-to-consume form of the product with a low unit price to entice massive numbers of consumers.[720]

---

[719] Mark Osler, "Learning from Crack," **Ohio State Journal of Criminal Law** 10 (2013): 665-678.
[720] Gorden Witkin and M. Mukenge, "The Men Who Created Crack," **U.S. News & World Report** vol. 111, Issue 8, August 19, 1991, pp. 44ff.

We will differ with both of these etiological theories. While we do agree with Osler that, *contra* Witkin and Mukenge, crack probably *did* have an inventor who had a strong understanding of narcotics, we disagree with Osler in his cynicism regarding the possibility of knowing the identity of such a Johnny Appleseed of Crack. We believe that the evidence points *strongly* to an easily identifiable individual and institution.

II.     *Crack as a Legacy of Dr. Jolly West*

In 1974 Dr. Jolly West was the first to warn of a major ensuing epidemic of cocaine abuse in the U.S.[721] One wonders how he surmised this, given that cocaine use had been successfully controlled for decades. One also wonders - but only rhetorically – if it is a coincidence that, at West's own institution (UCLA) that same year (1974) the very first victim of a *new form* of cocaine use was documented in the United States: a *smokable* cocaine called *freebase* that was similar to but distinct from the smokable cocaine (coca paste) that was appearing in Lima, Peru *at the same time* (1972-1974). As we hope to show, this is far from a coincidence.

Freebase cocaine is produced through a chemical process which converts cocaine hydrochloride (powder cocaine) into a smokable form. The procedure involves mixing cocaine hydrochloride with an alkali such as sodium hydroxide and boiling it with a solvent such as ether, a dangerously volatile liquid. When dried, the base cocaine crystals are left over, "freed." These are then smoked in pipes. This smoked cocaine, like its Peruvian counterpart, was profoundly addictive. In the late 1970s and 1980s there were five common methods or techniques to "free" the cocaine base, such as The California Clean-up Method that uses ether as the solvent and The Baking Soda Method which uses baking soda and water to form a paste. Crack cocaine is freebase made via The Banking Soda Method.[722]

---

[721] Louis Jolyon West, "Cocaine Abuse," *Western Journal of Medicine* 120 (1974): 294.
[722] Edith Fairman Cooper, *The Emergence of Crack Cocaine Abuse in the United States: A Public Health Perspective*, (CRS Report for Congress, 1998) 4-5.

In 1974, the year West issued his warning about an ensuing cocaine epidemic, a 31-year-old male was admitted into the emergency room of the hospital of West's own UCLA. He had a fright and panic reaction after his first episode of freebase smoking or "freebasing." He had smoked 100 mg of cocaine freebase in a tobacco-free cigarette, similar to the Peruvian *pastillo* (but without the tobacco).[723] This John Doe is the very first documented freebaser. A coincidence? Hardly.

## THE JOHNNY APPLESEED OF CRACK

> The role of drugs in the exercise of political control is also coming under increasing discussion. Control can be through prohibition or supply. The total or even partial prohibition of drugs gives the government considerable leverage for other types of control. An example would be the selective application of drug laws permitting immediate search, or "no knock" entry, against selected components of the population such as members of certain minority groups or political organizations. But a government could also supply drugs to help control a population. This method, foreseen by Aldous Huxley in Brave New World (1932), has the governing element employing drugs selectively to manipulate the governed in various ways.[724]

This Huxlian vision of using drugs as a tool of social control, such as supplying drugs to a minority group as a means of controlling that group, was articulated, as we saw above, by the CIA doctor himself, Dr. West. These words appeared in a 1975 publication, ***Hallucinations: Behavior, Experience and Theory***, which West co-edited with Dr. Ronald Siegel, psycho-pharmacologist now at the School of Medicine, UCLA. Siegel is West's protégé. West personally invited Siegel to UCLA's

Dr. Ronald K. Siegel

---

[723] Ronald K. Siegel, "Cocaine Smoking," *Journal of Psychoactive Drugs* 14 (1982): 288-289 [art.=271- 359]; Cooper, *Emergence of Crack Cocaine Abuse in the United States*, 9.
[724] R.K. Siegel and L.J. West (edd.), ***Hallucinations: Behavior, Experience and Theory*** (New York: John Wiley, 1975).

Neuropsychiatric Institute (NPI), over which West was suzerain, and gave Siegel his own lab for his studies,[725] studies which followed up on West's own investigations.[726] Siegel sought to bring design experiments to West's theories. That's a problem right there, given the anti-Black male, draconian nature of many of West's theories. Siegel drafted a proposal to do formal analysis of drug-induced hallucinations in humans, with a focus on cocaine.[727] Indeed, Siegel became distinguished as America's leading scientific authority on cocaine and its effects, particularly freebase cocaine.[728] This is because Siegel literally pioneered the study of freebase, and more...

Edith Fairman Cooper informs us: "The earliest known research that explored the impact of smokable freebase cocaine began in 1972. It was conducted by Ronald Siegel and his associates at UCLA."[729] The *first* research done on freebase was done at the *same* institution that two years later received the very

---

[725] Ronald Siegel, "Hallucinations and West's Perceptual Release Theory," in *The Mosaic of Contemporary Psychiatry in Perspective*, ed. Anthony Kales, M.D., Chester M. Pierce, MD., and Milton Greenblatt, M.D. (New York: Springer, 1992) 191-199.

[726] See e.g. Siegel's follow-up of West's most famous and infamous experiment that killed a famous Bull Elephant from an Oklahoma zoo with an over-dose of LSD: Ronald Siegel, "LSD-induced effects in elephants: Comparisons with musth behavior," *Bulletin of the Psychonomic Society* 22 (1984): 53-56.

[727] See also Ronald K. Siegel, "Cocaine Hallucinations," *The American Journal of Psychiatry* 135 (1978): 309-314.

[728] Ronald K. Siegel, "Cocaine: Recreational Use and Intoxication," in *Cocaine: 1977*, ed. Robert C. Petersen and Richard C. Stillman (NIDA Research Monograph #13; Rockville, Maryland: Department of Health, Education, and Welfare, 1977) 119-136; idem., "Long-Term Effects of Recreational Cocaine Use: A Four Year Study," in *Cocaine 1980: Proceedings of the International Seminar on Medical and Sociological Aspects of Coca and Cocaine*, ed. F.R. Jeri (Lima, Peru: Pacific Press, 1980) 11-16; idem., "Changing Patterns of Cocaine Use: Longitudinal Observations, Consequences, and Treatment," in *Cocaine: Pharmacology, Effects, and Treatment of Abuse*, ed. John Grabowski (NIDA Research Monograph 50, 1984; Rockville, Maryland: National Institute on Drug Abuse, 1984) 92; idem., "Repeating Cycles of Cocaine Use and Abuse," in *Treating Drug Problems.* **Volume 2:** *Commissioned Papers on Historical, Institutional, and Economic Contexts of Drug Treatment*, ed. Dean R. Gerstein and Henrick J. Harwood (Washington, D.C.: National Academy Press, 1992) 289-316

[729] Cooper, *Emergence of Crack Cocaine Abuse in the United States*, 61.

*first* victim of freebase use? Yes. Coincidence? No. And Ronald Siegel, West's protégé, conducted that pioneering research. And what was the nature of this pioneering freebase research in 1972, two years before the first freebase patient appeared in the UCLA emergency room?

Siegel and his UCLA associates performed preclinical laboratory studies with rhesus monkeys. They taught the monkeys both how to *chew* a gum-type form of cocaine and how to *smoke freebase*. The investigators trained the monkeys how to puff on a cigarette made of .03 grams of freebase and .07 grams of lettuce placed in cigarette paper.[730] This connects not only to the *pastillos* of Peru that had been introduced in Peru around 1972, probably by the CIA; but this connects also to the freebase *cigarette* that was smoked by the 31-year-old John Doe that was admitted to UCLA hospital in 1974. Siegel indicated that these feebase smoking monkeys "were good predictors of human behavior."[731] As we have consistently seen, the lab money is often only the temporary substitute for a human, a Black male human. This rhesus monkey research was published in 1976,[732] *the exact same year* that Dr. Raul Jeri's research on Peru coca paste smokers was published.[733] The fact that Siegel joined Jeri and other scientists in July, 1979 in Lima for an international symposium on cocaine is thus no surprise.[734] They probably were covert cooperators all along.

---

[730] Cooper, *Emergence of Crack Cocaine Abuse in the United States*, 61-62.
[731] Cooper, *Emergence of Crack Cocaine Abuse in the United States*, 62.
[732] R.K. Siegel et al., "Cocaine Self-Administration in Monkeys by Chewing and Smoking," *Pharmacology Biochemistry & Behavior* 4 (1976): 461-467. See further Ronald Siegel and Mary E. Jarvik, "Self-Regulation of Coca-Chewing and Cocaine Smoking by Monkeys," in *Cocaine 1980: Proceedings of the International Seminar on Medical and Sociological Aspects of Coca and Cocaine*, ed. F.R. Jeri (Lima, Peru: Pacific Press, 1980) 1-10; Idem., "DMT self-Administration by monkeys in isolation," *Bulletin of the Psychonomic Society* 16 (1980): 117-120.
[733] A "co-incidence" (not coincidence) that Siegel drew attention to: Ronald K. Siegel, "Historical Calendar of Cocaine Smoking," *Journal of Psychoactive Drugs* 14 (1982): 274.
[734] Webb, *Dark Alliance*, 34.

Illustration used in Ronald Siegel's 1982 article, "Cocaine Smoking," [p. 307] depicting one of the rhesus monkeys that he taught to smoke freebase in the basement laboratory at UCLA in 1972.

## CRACK CONFESSIONS

In 2005 Siegel was an expert witness for the defense in the murder trial of actor Robert Blake, testifying on the long-term effects of hard-core drugs like methamphetamines and cocaine. During his testimony Siegel makes what in retrospect is a quite earth-shattering confession. *The New York Times* reports:

> Earlier in the trial, a professor from the University of California, Los Angeles, testified as an expert witness about the psychotropic of cocaine.

He said that *he had smoked crack cocaine himself* and sat in a cage with monkeys to teach them how to smoke cocaine as well.[735]

Less we assume that there is a mistake here, the ***Los Angeles Times*** reported as well:

> UCLA professor Ronald Siegel is an expert on the sustained use of hardcore drugs, which several key witnesses for the prosecution admitted using. He drew laughs when he described some of the research on which his credentials are based: tending a cage with *crack-smoking monkeys* in a basement on campus.
>
> "I crawled into the cage with the monkeys and played monkey to make sure that the smoking tube was working," Siegel said. "I didn't become a crazy monkey from any of that. I do like bananas."[736]

Here is Dr. Siegel, protégé of the "Mr. CIA doctor" himself Dr. Jolly West, confessing under oath that he smoked and taught monkeys how to smoke crack cocaine in the basement laboratory of UCLA. CNN provides a profoundly important detail that allows us to put this confession in historical context. We are told that Siegel

> delved into his background studying drug-induced behavior, including training monkeys in the basement of UCLA to smoke crack cocaine *some 13 years before the term 'crack' became part of the lexicon.*[737]

"Crack" became a part of our lexicon in 1985. The term was first used in the November 17 edition of ***The New York Times*** in a story about a cocaine-abuse treatment program.[738] 13 years prior was 1972, the precise year of Siegel's rhesus monkey studies. We thus have a confession under oath that in 1972, over a decade before *anyone else in the world* knew about crack cocaine and before it

---

[735] Charlie Leduff, "Actor's Trial, Complete With Pulp Novel Characters, Draws to a Close," ***The New York Times*** March 5, 2005.
[736] Andrew Blankstein, "Court Bears Witness to Comic Relief," ***Los Angeles Times*** March 04, 2005.
[737] Lisa Sweetingham, "Witness says vomited all the time," ***CNN Monday February*** 21, 2005.
[738] Donna Boundy, "Program for Cocaine-Abuse Under Way," ***The New York Times*** November 17, 1985.

mysteriously popped up in the Black neighborhoods of South Central Los Aneles, this UCLA scientist was training monkeys how to smoke it, and was himself smoking some (at least trying it). This is amazing, in a horrifying kind of way. Edith Cooper's words quoted above thus take on added significance: "The earliest known research that explored the impact of smokable freebase cocaine began in 1972. It was conducted by Ronald Siegel and his associates at UCLA." Crack *is* freebase, the product of one of the five techniques of freebase production (The Banking Soda Method). So in 1972 crack was being tested on monkeys in a basement lab at UCLA. And Ronald Keith Siegel was *the first* to test it. Wow. We have found the Johnny Appleseed of crack.

On June 1, 2013 Siegel was interviewed for an hour by Bela Johnson, host of "Alternative Currents" (WERU Radio, Blue Hill, Maine).[739] Siegel's confessions were nothing short of jaw-dropping. He says:

> through molecular architecture we can mold these drugs to do exactly what we want, put them in vehicles that control themselves, like time release capsules...We developed many years ago cocaine chewing gum, which we did some early testing with and is now for sale in another country...
>
> We're in touch with a lot of the underground chemists who are synthesizing new compounds and they send a lot to us for testing. We don't give them any feedback but we like to monitor what's out there in the street. Uh, and by the way *our lab was the one that **discovered** (!) the crack epidemic and we **discovered** crack 13 years before the word was even introduced into the lexicon.* We had monkeys smoking crack cocaine in the basement labs of UCLA 13 years before the word was invented. Thus *we knew it* (or: *what*) *was coming* and we wanted to know that we understood everything. We're working on the next ones already. Drugs that are out there now on the street that not leg-, not illegal, that people are at...
>
> I came out here from New York because it's one of the few places I could do LSD research at the time and we were giving LSD and marijuana and all kinds of other drugs to volunteers in the laboratory and I wanted to move away from animal research and move into people who could give informed consent and volitionally agree to the conditions of the experiment. And it was also an exciting time because lots of new

---

[739]    http://belajohnson.com/wp-content/uploads/2013/06/01-Ronald-Siegel-10_05.m4a

epidemics started here in California. The psychedelic revolution started here, the methamphetamine epidemic in '69, '70 started here. The crack epi-, um, the crack epidemic in the form of cocaine freebase started here in 1971 and hit New York in 1985. So we were always on the cutting edge of things so it was an exciting place to be and it still is.

There are several startling confessions here.

1. By manipulating the molecular architecture of a drug that drug can be *mechanized*, made a mechanical device that will do precisely what the scientists want it to do, a self-controlled time release capsule, for example. These are tailor-made agents. Siegel reveals that they have created cocaine chewing gum – remember the cocaine *chewing* experiments that Siegel did with the rhesus monkeys in 1972. We see where these experiments lead to. While we know nothing about such cocaine gum here in America, Siegel discloses that it "is now for sale *in another country*," which country Siegel refuses to identify. This reveals to us a particular *modus operandi* of these wicked scientists: they send their evil concoctions out to cause havoc in *other nations,* mainly (if not exclusively) so-called Third World nations.
2. These UCLA scientists are in contact with "underground" or "street" chemists. While Siegel only mentions what the street chemists send to him, we can imagine that this relationship is connected by a two-way lane and that the scientists can send their concoctions to the street chemists as well, which will covertly introduce their new designer drugs into the community.
3. Siegel makes the startling disclosure that, not only did his lab *discover* the crack epidemic, but his lab *discovered crack cocaine itself in 1971-1972*! How was crack cocaine "discovered" in a basement lab at UCLA? "Discover" is clearly a euphemism here for "created": Siegel, the protégé of Mr. CIA Doctor Jolly West, here confesses that *his* lab "discovered" and tested crack cocaine over a decade before the world knew what was coming. But, Siegel confesses, *he* and his associates at UCLA *knew what was*

coming on the streets of Black Los Angeles 13 years before it struck. This is by any measure an institutional confession.
4. The same wicked scientist who "discovered" crack confesses that "We're working on the next ones already." The next what? The next psychochemical *weapons* like crack cocaine at UCLA.

We have apparently discovered our Johnny Appleseed of Crack Cocaine: Dr. Ronald Keith Siegel and the David Geffen School of Medicine.

Remember the words of Major General William Creasy describing the psychochemical weapon covert operation he wanted to conduct against American cities:

> I was attempting to put on, *with a good cover story*, to test what would happen in subways, for example, when a cloud was laid down on a city.[740]

It is a covert operation protocol that *there be a cover story* to hide the true source of a psychochemical that is tested or released on the American public. We know that the release of crack cocaine in the streets of Southern California was a covert operation because Siegel is caught red handed peddling an obvious cover story. "[C]cocaine free base [was] created, apparently, by some furtive southern California alchemist in 1974,"[741] Siegel claimed in 1982. But we have leanered that he was personally testing – and even smoking – cocaine free base (crack) in 1971-1972 in his basement lab at UCLA! Siegel is caught in a lie. He further elaborates this cover story, claiming that an unnamed drug trafficker told him that he (the drug trafficker) had travelled to South America and tried Peru's coca paste, called *basé*. This is pronounced *bah-say*, but the American trafficker mistook it to be simply base. Then he came back to California and:

> I went to a chemist friend of mine in January [1974] and told him about smoking *base*. He looked it up in Merk [Index] and said it was the free base and he could make it...We started with one ounce of [cocaine]

---

[740] Lee and Shlain, **Acid Dreams**, 40.
[741] Siegel, "Cocaine Smoking," 287.

hydrochloride, baking soda, ether, and ended up with about a half ounce of *base*.[742]

In other words, a 1974 *mistranslation* (confusing *basé* with cocaine "base") by an unnamed drug dealer and his unnamed California chemist friend is the origin of crack, even though by his own admission Dr. Siegel and his associates at UCLA had already "discovered" freebase cocaine three years prior to the alleged return of the drug trafficker from South America. This is clearly a fabricated cover story, and you *only* need a cover story if you have something to hide.

The crack cocaine that mysteriously appeared in South Central's black neighborhoods in 1981 originated or at least was first tested in the UCLA basement lab of Dr. Ronald Siegel, maybe the lab that was giving to him specifically by his mentor and his boss at the time, the CIA's own Dr. Jolly West. And remember, UCLA is home of the sociopharmacology and Dominance Hierarchy studies we looked at earlier.

III.    *The White House and Black America's Crack Epidemic*

> For the better part of a decade, a San Francisco Bay area drug ring sold tons of cocaine to the Crips and Bloods street gangs of Los Angeles and funneled millions in drug profits to a Latin American guerrilla army run by the U.S. Central Intelligence Agency, a Mercury News investigation has found.
>
> This drug network opened the first pipeline between Colombia's cocaine cartels and the black neighborhoods of Los Angeles, a city now known as the "crack"' capital of the world. The cocaine that flooded in helped spark a crack explosion in urban America and provided the cash and connections needed for L.A.'s gangs to buy automatic weapons.

Thus did "Dark Alliance," the 1996 three-part series by *San Jose Mercury News* Pulitzer Prize-winning staffer Gary Webb, infamously begin.[743] The series documented the CIA's link, through the funding and management of the Nicaraguan Contras, to the explosion of crack cocaine and its concomitant violence in

---

[742] Siegel, "Cocaine Smoking," 288.
[743] The series matured into his book, *Dark Alliance: the CIA, the Contras and the Crack Cocaine Explosion* (New York: Seven Stories Press, 2004 [1998]).

the Black neighborhoods of South Central Los Angeles in the 1980s. As the *Huffington Post* reported: "Webb's investigation sent the CIA into a panic."[744]

> Many reporters [before Webb] had written about the CIA's collusion with *contra* drug smugglers, but nobody had ever discovered where those drugs ended up once they reached American soil...The connection Webb uncovered between the CIA, the *contras* and L.A.'s crack trade was real – and radioactive.[745]

So the CIA went into panic mode. To manage that nightmare, the Agency employed their *psyc-op* called "perception management": the CIA used its contacts in the media to influence public opinion and vilify Webb, discrediting his investigation.[746] So Webb was attacked viciously and unjustly by the major media such as **The New York Times**, the **Los Angeles Times** and the **Washington Post**. Today, Webb has the last laugh. Disclosures since his series was first published – and since his untimely death either by suicide or by murder - have allowed several investigators to vindicate Webb's controversial research. Thus, in the words of award-winning investigative journalist with the **Orange County Weekly** Nick Schou, Gary Webb is "Pariah No More."[747]

---

[744] Ryan Grim, Matt Sledge and Matt Ferner, "Key Figures in CIA-Crack Cocaine Scandal Begin to Come Forward," *Huffington Post* October 10, 2014.
[745] Nick Schou, **Kill The Messenger: How the CIA's Crack-Cocaine Controversy Destroyed Journalist Gary Webb** (New York: Nation Books, 2006) 8, 10.
[746] Robert Perry, "The CIA/MSM Contra-Cocaine Cover-up," *Consortium News* September 26, 2014. See further Carl Bernstein, "The CIA and the Media," *Rolling Stone* October 20, 1977, pp. 55-67.
[747] Lawrence Christopher Skufca, "Gary Webb: The Suppression of Uncomfortable Inquiries," *NJToday.net* January 22, 2016; Nick Schou, **Kill The Messenger: How the CIA's Crack-Cocaine Controversy Destroyed Journalist Gary Webb** (New York: Nation Books, 2006); idem, "Gary Webb: Pariah No More," **OC Weekly** October 15, 2014; Ryan Grim, "Kill The Messenger: How the Media Destroyed Gary Webb," *Huffington Post* October 10, 2014; Ryan Grim, Matt Sledge and Matt Ferner, "Key Figures in CIA-Crack Cocaine Scandal Begin to Come Forward," *Huffington Post* October 10, 2014; Alexander Cockburn and Jeffrey St. Clair, *White Out: The CIA, Drugs and the Press* (London and New York: Verso, 1999); Peter Kornbluh, "The paper trail to the top: Crack and the contras," *The Baltimore Sun* November 17, 1996.

There was one glaring deficiency in Webb's reconstructed narrative, however.

> The *San Jose Mercury* series, written by Sacramento-based reporter Gary Webb, failed to mention Vice President Bush, or his role as "commander in chief" of the secret war in Central America, and focused instead on the CIA as the principal culprit. But by the end of 1981, through a series of Executive Orders and National Security Decision Directives, many of which have been declassified, Vice President George Bush was placed in charge of all Reagan administration intelligence operations (...)[748]. All of the covert operations carried out by officers of the CIA, the Pentagon, and every other federal agency, along with a rogue army of "asteroid" former intelligence operatives and foreign agents, were commanded by Vice President Bush.[749]

The Contra guns and drugs operation was *not* a "CIA" operation. The CIA were only foot soldiers. It was rather run at a higher level, by a "secret government" apparatus operating out of the office of Vice President George Bush and the National Security Council and supervised by Bush's national security advisor and former CIA official Donald Cregg.[750] It was thus a *White House*

---

[748] Edward Spannaus, "Mena drug scandal will soon hit North, Bush," *Executive Intelligence Review* 22 (1995): 57: The Contra guns and drugs operation was "an operation which was run out of Bush's office under the nominal authority of National Security Decision Directives Nos. 2 and 3. NSDD-2 created the National Security Council structure, including that covering Central America. NSDD-3, entitled "Crisis Management," created the Special Situation Group (SSG), headed by the vice president; soon after, the Crisis Pre-Planning Group was created under the SSG, as an inter-agency coordinating body whose staff coordinator was Oliver North. Under NSDD-2 and -3, taken together with Executive Order 12333, (which gave the National Security Council staff, i.e., the White House, direction of all covert operations, as well as "privatizing" certain intelligence operations), George Bush was in charge of the entire "secret government" apparatus. "
[749] Jeffrey Steinberg, "The Contras and the crack epidemic," *Executive Intelligence Review* 23 (1996): 12-14.
[750] Edward Spannaus, "New Evidence links George Bush to Los Angeles drug operation," *Executive Intelligence Review* 24 (1997); idem, "CIA report may revive Bush Crack cocaine scandal, "*Executive Intelligence Review* 25 (1998): 28-33. On Bush and the "Secret Team" see Joel Bainerman, *The Crimes of a President: New Revelations on Conspiracy & Cover-Up in the Bush & Reagan Administrations* (New York: S.P.I. Books, 1992); "George Bush: The Company Man," *Covert Action Information Bulletin* 33 (1990): 1-72; Howard Kohn and

operation. The Honorable Minister Louis Farrakhan was thus on point:

> I held a press conference in Washington, D.C. during the time that George H.W. Bush was in the White House, and I charged the government of the United States-this is on record-with declaring war on the Black community, and the Black man in particular...The order did not originate in the C.I.A...This order came directly out of the *White House* because the C.I.A. is not "Pharaoh"; "Pharaoh" is the head of government.[751]

The drug trafficking operation managed by the White House via the CIA (and other agencies) was run by two Nicaraguan exiles: CIA collaborator Juan Norwin Meneses, known in Nicaragua as *El Rey de Drogas*, "The King of Drugs," who operated in Northern California and his protégé Oscar Danilo Blandón who, having close ties to the U.S. Department of Commerce and the U.S. State Department, operated in Southern California.[752] They answered to CIA agent Col. Enrique Bermúdez who had trained at the U.S. National Defense College outside Washington, D.C., had served from 1976 to 1979 as the Nicaraguan military attaché in Washington, and was given $300,000 in 1981 by the CIA to take command of the main Contra force, the Fuerza Democrático Nicaraqüense (FDN).

With Bermúdez the CIA installed Adolfo Calero as the FDN's civilian head. Calero embodies the nexus between the CIA, Coca Cola, the drug trade, and Black suffering. When the Sandinistas took over Nicaragua in 1979 Calero, already a CIA informant, was a Coca Cola executive managing the Managua bottling plant in Nicaragua. Appointed by the CIA as the FDN's political head, Calero administered the funds that came to the

---

Vicki Monks, "The Dirty Secrets of George Bush: The Vice President's illegal operations," *Rolling Stone* November 3, 1988.
[751] The Honorable Minister Louis Farrakhan, "Crack Cocaine: The Great Conspiracy to Destroy the Black Male," *The Final Call* November 11, 2014, p. 21.
[752] In a declassified 1986 CIA cable Meneses is described as "the kingpin of narcotics traffickers in Nicaragua prior to the fall of Somoza," i.e. before the CIA organized the rebel Contras. Yet, Meneses told the Justice Department that shortly after the Sandinista takeover he met CIA agents in order to teach them how to cross his country's borders undetected. U.S. government agents, the King of Drugs boasted, escorted him across American borders. Webb, *Dark Alliance*, 52, 58. See further Cockburn and St. Clair, *White Out*, 2-3.

Contras – the drug money raised largely through the spawning of the cocaine-crack holocaust in Black South Central L.A. His brother Mario Jose Calero was a drug trafficker and Senator John Kerry, who chaired the Senate Foreign Relations subcommittee that investigated the role of drug tracking in the Contra war, said in a closed session statement (later released): "It is clear that there is a networking of drug trafficking through the contras, and it goes right up to Calero, Mario Calero, Adolpho Calero, Enrique Bermúdez. And we have people who will so testify and who have."[753]

## RICK ROSS DID NOT INTRODUCE CRACK

One of Blandón's men, Nicaraguan exile Ivan Arquellas, was supplying cocaine to a local skills center teacher in Venice who hustled the powder white on the side. That teacher had a young mentee named Rick Ross, a one-time aspiring tennis player whose illiteracy cut his dream short. Eventually he will initiate young Ross into the drug trade, with Blandón covertly watching Ross from afar. Soon all middle-men would be cut out and Ross will get his cocaine directly from Blandón. By 1983 Blandón was supplying Ross with over 100 kilos of CIA-protected cocaine per week, which converted into $3 million of crack sold per day.

Ross did *not* introduce crack to Los Angeles. Ronald Siegel's smokable freebase mysteriously *found Ross*. At first Ross was slowly selling his high-priced cocaine to only about fifteen moneyed customers a day who came to the hood from the suburbs. This was personally profitable for Ross, but not sufficient to fund a Latin American war. But few people actually *in* the hood could afford Ross's cocaine. Then, out of the blue remarkably cheap cocaine "rocks" started popping up among some of Ross's customers. No one really knows where the new form of cocaine came from. Ross and the other dealers were suspicious of it and were having nothing to do with it – "Nobody wanted to mess

---

[753] Stephen Rosskamm Shalom, *Imperial Alibis: Rationalizing U.S. Intervention After the Cold War* (Boston: South End Press, 1993) 177; Elisabeth Malkin, "Aldolfo Calero, Contra Leader in Nicaragua, Is Dead," *The New York Times* June 3, 2012; Cockburn and St. Clair, *White Out*, 278-279.

with cocaine that didn't look like cocaine...[and] the price was too low. How could anything claiming to be cocaine cost only $25? It had to be a rip off."[754] So we *know* that it was *not* the Black dealers who introduced crack to the Los Angeles scene. "Know what I got in chemistry in school," Ross asked Webb. "An 'F'."[755] And he was among the more brilliant of the hood dealers.

Tootie Reese, a South Central drug dealer of the 1960s and 1970s (mainly heroin and marijuana) says he first encountered crack in 1976 when he was visiting a friend in the Bay Area. His friend had learned the mechanics of converting powder cocaine into crack from chemists, "white guys at Cal Berkley." These whites taught Tootie and his friend how to substitute baking soda for ether, the hood way of making freebase.[756] Back in Los Angeles the rocks just started appearing among Ross's customers. Then one day one of Ross's customers came to him – or was *sent* to him – and asked Ross if he had any rock to sell. Ross finally bit. Because he could not make crack himself he paid outsiders to do so. This rest is history. As Webb states:

> What happened next was just what the scientists had been predicting since 1974. As *basé* (coca paste) had done in Lima and La Paz eight years earlier, rock caused a sensation in South Central...A 1985 study by two University of South California social scientists[757] provides some of the only existing documentation of crack's progression in South Central in the early 1980s, where Ross and others began selling it. It is like reading the origin of Black Death.[758]

## BLACK PEOPLE WERE SPECIFICALLY AND EXCLUSIVELY TARGETED, AGAIN

In 1984 Blandón and Meneses paid a visit to a San Francisco cocaine dealer named Rafael Cornejo, a long time

---

[754] Webb, ***Dark Alliance***, 140.
[755] Webb, ***Dark Alliance***, 141.
[756] Jesse Katz, "Tracking the Genesis of the Crack Trade," ***Los Angeles Times*** October 20, 1996.
[757] Malcolm Klein and Cheryl Maxson, "Rock Sales in South Los Angeles," ***Sociology and Social Research*** 69 (July 1985): 561.
[758] Webb, ***Dark Alliance***, 142.

cocaine wholesaler for Meneses. They met at Cornejo's commercial building. Cornejo recounted to Gary Webb:

> Blandón starts telling me he'd been doing lots of things with the black people down there [in L.A.]...And he said I should get into the black thing. *No one cares about them, he tells me. When they start killing themselves no one cares.*[759]

Webb reflects:

> Blandón's own experience had taught him that no one cared about the cocaine that he was pouring into South Central in 1984. By then, he'd been dealing ever-increasing amounts to Ricky Ross for two years and received *no interference from the police whatsoever*. The only media in L.A. that seemed alarmed by the spread of crack in the black neighborhoods was the African-American press. The white newspapers didn't even know what crack was.[760]

The Blandón-Ross drug empire was at its zenith in 1984-85, but they were unobstructed by law enforcement of any kind. Blandón and Ross had "one long cop-free party"[761] because this drug operation that targeted Black people was federally protected. With all of this crack cocaine moving in the hood and all of the military grade weapons proliferating, the police almost totally stood down, giving Ross's mammoth crack operation free reign. "The LAPD didn't mess with us at all," Ross says.[762] Not because the police driving around the hood were unaware. Police would stop the dealers, hand cuff them, find the crack and then let the dealers go, we are told.[763] "Fed by an unending supply of cocaine from Danilo Blandón, Ricky Ross's crack trafficking organization prospered and grew unhindered by law enforcement in the ghettos of Los Angeles."[764]

On July 2, 1990 drug dealer and San Diego DEA informant John Arman wore an undercover wire and, together with DEA

---

[759] Webb, *Dark Alliance*, 160.
[760] Webb, *Dark Alliance*, 160.
[761] Webb, *Dark Alliance*, 277.
[762] Webb, *Dark Alliance*, 142.
[763] Webb, *Dark Alliance*, 142-143.
[764] Webb, *Dark Alliance*, 151-152.

agent Judy Gustafsin, met with Blandón at the lobster restaurant Old Bonta Store. Caught on undercover DEA tapes is Blandón talking shop with fellow drug dealer Arman, trying to convince Arman to sell his weight to Blandón's buyers.

> Arman: "It ain't the Japanese guy you were telling me about?"
>
> Blandón: "No, it's not him. These [buyers] are the black people."
>
> Arman: "Black?!"
>
> Blandón: "Yeah. They control L.A..."
>
> Arman: "I don't like niggers..."
>
> [A little later Blandón comes back to the point and reassures Arman]
>
> Blandón: "Don't worry. *I don't do with anybody else, just with black people.*"[765]

The CIA-protected asset and later paid DEA informant Danilo Blandón, who was the point man for the White House drugs-for-guns operation in Southern California, specifically confesses that he *targets* Black people with his CIA-approved cocaine, and *only* Black people. There can thus be no doubt whatsoever that, as the Honorable Minister Farrakhan had declared for several years before these disclosures came to light:

> Crack cocaine is from the government of the United States of America...[T]he government of the United States [is] declaring war on the Black community, and the Black man in particular...The order did not originate with the C.I.A...This order came directly out of the *White House*...[766]

---

[765] Webb, ***Dark Alliance***, 403.
[766] The Honorable Minister Farrakhan, "Crack Cocaine: The Great Conspiracy to Destroy The Black Male," ***The Final Call*** Volume 34 Number 5, November 11, 2014, p. 21.

*Excursus*
*Strawberry: The Crack Holocaust's Greatest Victim*

>There's another girl in the Dopeman's life.
>Not quite a bitch but far from a wife.
>She's called The Strawberry and everybody know
>Strawberry! Strawberry! Is the neighborhood hoe.
>
>Do anything for a hit or two.
>Give the bitch a rock and she'll fuck the whole damn crew.
>It might be your wife and it might make you sick.
>Come home and see her mouth on the Dopeman's dick.
>
>Strawberry, just look you'll see her.
>But don't fuck around, she'll give you gonorrhea.
>If people out there not hip to the fact
>Strawberry is a girl selling pussy for crack to the...
>
>Dopeman! Dopeman! - "Dopeman" by N.W.A. (1988)

Ice-cube did not do justice here to the so-called Strawberry. He did not tell her full story and help us to see her for who she truly is: the greatest victim in this government-produced Crack Holocaust.

James Inciardi was a Miami drug research investigating the new crack phenomenon as it migrated from South Central to South Beach in the late 1980s. In 1987 he published an investigative report on the emergence of the crack phenomenon.[767] Inciardi wrote that, while he was a streetwise observer with tough skin, nothing prepared him for the horrors he observed in the newly emerging 'crack houses', a phenomenon that began in South Central and in Pacoima, a San Fernando Valley suburb, a few years earlier. The crack house or rock house of the 80s was not just the place where the rock was "cooked" in the kitchen. It was also where the crack was sold in the dining room and smoked in the living room. This is because the crack customers would smoke on site, re-up, smoke, and repeat, until their money was exhausted. But in the crack house there was also the bedroom where the "Strawberry" was. She was the "house girl," the

---
[767] James Inciardi, "Beyond Cocaine: Basuco, Crack and Other Coca Products," *Contemporary Drug Problems* 14 (Fall 1987): 461-492.

woman – but too often the minor girl – who "serviced" the day's house guests for the dealers and in return got food, clothing, a roof over her head in the crack house and, most importantly, crack. The daily fate of a crack house "Strawberry" is one of the sights that horrified Inciardi, who reported:

> I observed what appeared to be the forcible gang-rape of an unconscious child. Emaciated, seemingly comatose, and likely no more than 14 years of age, she was lying spread-eagled on a filthy mattress while four men in succession had vaginal intercourse with her.

The White House-spawned Crack Epidemic was nothing less than a holocaust - Black America's third great *Maafa* (Holocaust). The "Strawberry" would become a signature feature of the crack phenomenon, and thousands of women and young girls have been so abused over the course of the life of this *White Plague* in Black America. And as Jim Newton of the **Los Angeles Times** pointed out: "No drug is more closely associated with race than crack cocaine. Those convicted of powdered cocaine are often Anglo, but crack offenders...are overwhelming black."[768] It is, in my opinion, not the millions of Black men who over the course of this Maafa ended up dead or, if alive, are the victims of the government's mass incarceration program. *She* – Strawberry - is the greatest of the Crack Holocaust victims because she was the most vulnerable, the most defenseless, with the absolute least to gain from it all. Many of the men enjoyed short term gains – money, status, women - which they purchased with our people's long term pain. But the young girls who were turned out on this awful, laboratory-produced drug – no doubt turned out by some man for his own gain – she got nothing for her terrific victimization but more crack which only cyclically perpetuated her enslavement to her abusers: crack and the crack dealer. She and her egregious victimization have been quite marginal to the "crack narrative," Cube's lyrics notwithstanding. But she should be central to the crack narrative.

---

[768] Jim Norton, "Harsh Crack Sentences Criticized as Racial Inequality," **Los Angeles Times** November 23, 1992.

For me, *the* signature representation of the Crack Holocaust - that which we should automatically envision when we hear the word "crack" - is not the flash of the D-Boy or the Trapper, or even the walking dead crake head. The first and most enduring image that should come up in our mind's eye when we hear anything "crack related" should be, in my opinion, the image of the crack house "Strawberry." But "Strawberry" should never again be seen as simply a catchy hook from an ill N.W.A. track. She should be "seen" as a 14 year old girl strung out on government-supplied crack cocaine suffering multiple rapes daily. While we bounce to B.I.G.'s "10 Crack Commandments," we should think of her, comatose and spread-eagled on a filthy mattress.

The glorification, romanticization, or justification of the crack trade or any of its profits in any of our cultural media - music, television, cinema, etc. - should be considered by us and treated as a cultural crime. There's nothing redeeming or laudatory about the crack culture that has been imposed on us, regardless of the short term gains that many Black men did and do enjoy from it. To offer it any sort of applause or to valorize it in any way is to sanction the fate of the many comatose "house girls." And *that* should be considered a cultural crime. If I knew her name I would ask us to #SayHerName. But we don't know her name, because she has thousands of names. "Strawberry" is not one of them though.

Part Six

# Killing God In The Black Man's Brain

## AND RESURRECTING HIM

# 18. Autism and the Chemical War against the Black Male Mind (God)

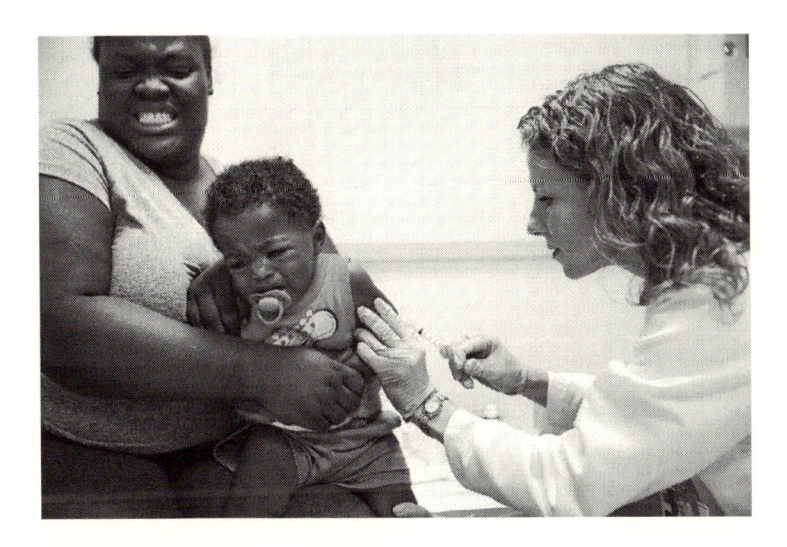

India Ampah holds her son, Keon Lockhart, 12 months old, as pediatrician Amanda Porro administers a measles vaccination during a visit to the Miami Children's Hospital on June 2, 2014. Photo: Getty Images

### I. *From White Boys' Disease to Black Boys' Disease*

Carrie Arnold reports:

> For years, the medical community has studied and treated autism as a "white person's" disease, and, today, research and therapy remain geared toward affluent, white people and families-leaving people of color in the lurch.[769]

It makes sense that autism was once widely believed to be a white person's disease. The first cases diagnosed in the 1940's were patients from that very demographic – white and affluent - and this pretty much remained the case for a long time. But something very dramatic happened in the late 1980s and early 1990s. We get

---

[769] Carrie Arnold, "Autism's Race Problem," *Pacific Standard* May 25, 2016.

a chilling picture of this new thing from Patti White, a school nurse and R.N. of Missouri Central District School Nurse Association. On May 17, 1999 White testified on behalf of school nurses of her district before the Committee of Government Reform, Subcommittee on Criminal Justice, Drug Policy, and Human Resources, U.S. House of Representatives, Hepatitis B Vaccine Hearings. Her testimony was alarming and read in part:

> As nurses we continually see more and more damaged children entering our schools, and we are very concerned that a major portion of that damage may be due to the hepatitis B vaccine's assault on the newborn neurological and immune system...For the past three or four years (i.e. since 1995-1996) our school district has noted a significant increase in the number of children entering school with developmental disorders, learning disabilities, attention deficit disorders and/or serious chronic illness such as diabetes, asthma and seizure disorders. Each of the past four years has been worse than the year before. There is only one common thread we have been able to identify in these children: they are the children who received the first trial hepatitis B injections as newborns in the early 1990s...The elementary grades are overwhelmed with children who have symptoms of neurological and/or immune system damage: epilepsy, seizure disorders, various kinds of palsies, autism, mental retardation, learning disabilities, juvenile-onset diabetes, asthma, vision/hearing loss, and a multitude of new conduct/behavior disorders.
>
> We have come to believe the hepatitis B vaccine is an assault on a newborns developing neurological and immune system. Vaccines are supposed to be making us healthier, however, in twenty-five years of nursing I have never seen so many damaged, sick kids. Something very, very wrong is happening to our children. The census of ill children treated in our health rooms each day has increased by 300% in only four years...

Universal hepatitis B (Hep B) vaccination was instituted for U.S. newborns in 1991. Patti White was accurate in what she described and the cause that she suspected. A 2010 study on the association of Hep B vaccination of boys 3-17 born before 1999 and the incidence of autism concluded: "Boys vaccinated as neonates (newborns) had a threefold greater odds for autism diagnosis compared to boys never vaccinated or vaccinated after the first month of life."[770] There was something about that vaccine that was causing great mental dysfunction in babies, including autism. But the authors make another important observation: "Non-Hispanic white boys were 64% *less likely* to have autism diagnosis relative to nonwhite boys."[771] Whatever that "something" was that was in the vaccine that caused or contributed to the onset of autism also discriminated: it affected Black and Brown boys much more than it affected white boys. A study of boys from the metro-Atlanta area born between 1986 and 1993 showed that, among those vaccinated for Hep B, Black boys had a statistically significant risk ratio of 5.53 versus a statistically insignificant risk ratio of 1.87 for white boys.[772] This increased risk for Black boys vs. white boys proved true in Patti White's Missouri as well. A 2000 study reported a dramatic *30 fold* increase in autism incidence between 1988 and 1995 in Missouri in boys 5-9 years old.[773] The hardest hit were poor Black boys. The study said:

> The apparent prevalence of autism was consistently higher in African-Americans than in Caucasians throughout the period studied and decreased only slightly with increased diagnosis. The ratio of African-Americans to Caucasians with autism was 1.9:1 in 1988 and 1.7:1 in 1995. The ratio of African-Americans to Caucasians with autism did not differ in rural areas vs. inner cities.[774]

The same results were found in California among children with autism born between 1989 and 1994 in a 2002 study.[775] Black males

---

[770] Carolyn M. Gallagher and Melody S. Goodman, "Hepatitis B Vaccination of Male Neonates and Autism Diagnosis, NHIs 1997-2002," *Journal of Toxicology and Environmental Health, Part A* 73 (2010): 1665-1677.
[771] Gallagher and Goodman, "Hepatitis B Vaccination of Male Neonates," 1665.
[772] Brian S. Hooker, "Measles-mumps-rubella vaccination timing and autism among young African American boys: a reanalysis of CDC data," *Translational Neurodegeneration* 3 (2014): 5 [art.=1-8].
[773] Richard E. Hillman et al, "Prevalence of Autism in Missouri: Changing Trends and the Effect of a Comprehensive State Autism Project," *Missouri Medicine* 97 (May 2000): 159-162.
[774] Hillman et al, "Prevalence of Autism in Missouri," 161.
[775] Lisa A. Croen, Judith K. Grether and Steve Selvin, "Descriptive Epidemiology of Austin in a California Population: Who Is at Risk?" *Journal of Autism and Developmental Disorders* 32 (June 2002): 217-224.

were at higher risk.[776] In a 2014 study of autistic children born between 1995 and 2006, those born to U.S. Black women and foreign-born Black women (Africa and the Caribbean) were observed to be at higher risk of the severe phenotype (form of autism) than U.S. born whites.[777]

What was an affluent white person's disease in the 1940s became a disproportionately poor Black and Brown disease in the 1990s. How did that happen? It happened the same way that AIDS started as a white gay disease and is now a Black gay man/straight man/straight woman disease: the disease was *migrated* (causative verb) from the white community to the Black and Brown communities. A 2010 nationwide study of the CDC's Autism and Developmental Disability Monitoring Network showed the prevalence of autism among Black children to be nearly 25% higher than that of whites.[778] By May, 2014 *Autism Speaks* reported:

> Reports of regressive autism – in which young children lose early language and social skills – *are twice as common* for African American children as for white children, according to new research. The same study found reports of regression 50 percent higher for Hispanic children than for whites... In her study, Dr. [Adiaha Spinks] Franklin [development behavioral pediatrician at the Autism Speaks Autism Treatment Network (AS-ATN)] looked at reports of regression among 1,353 children seen at AS-ATN centers from 2008 through 2011. Of these, 120 were African American and 150 were Hispanic... She found a rate twice as high among African American children as Caucasian children. It was 1.5 times higher among the Hispanic children than white children. The difference remained after Dr. Franklin adjusted her analysis to exclude differences in health insurance and parent education. These differences warrant urgent investigation, Dr. Franklin says (emphasis added).[779]

---

[776] "Increased risks were observed for males, multiple births, and children born to black mothers"; "we observed a dramatic male excess for autism overall"; "our findings of an elevated risk for blacks"; Croen, Grether and Selvin, "Descriptive Epidemiology," 217, 221, 222.

[777] Tracey A. Becerra et al., "Autism Spectrum Disorders and Race, Ethnicity, and Nativity: A Population-Based Study," *Pediatrics* 134 (2014): 63-71.

[778] Maureen S. Durkin et al, "Socioeconomic Inequality in the Prevalence of Autism Spectrum Disorder: Evidence from a U.S. Cross-Sectional Study," *PLoS One* 5 (2010): 1-8.

[779] "Regressive Autism Reported Twice as Often among African American Children," *Autism Speaks* May 06, 2014.

The UCLA study that same year found the same thing:

> Researchers have long thought that autism was more common among white children in the U.S. than other ethnic or racial groups. But a new study of birth records in highly diverse Los Angeles County suggests that children whose mothers emigrated from certain countries may be particularly at risk. Children of foreign-born mothers who are black, Central or South American, Vietnamese or Filipino were more likely to be diagnosed with autism disorder than children of white U.S.-born mothers, according to the study, published online Monday in the journal Pediatrics. The study also found that children of Hispanic and African-American mothers born in the U.S. have a higher risk of autism than white children whose mothers were born in the U.S.[780]

Not only is autism prevalence apparently higher among African Americans today than among whites, it is a more severe phenotype or form characteristic of Black children with the disorder than white children.[781] If autism is still popularly seen as a white disease, this is only because all of the *assistance* for autism still privileges affluent white families and penalizes poor Black families.[782] But the question remains: how did the formerly white disease all of a sudden so dramatically become a disproportionately *Black disease*? How was it *migrated* to the Black community? There is an answer to this urgent question.

---

[780] Melinda Beck, "Autism Rates Higher Among Certain Immigrants, Minorities: Condition Was Long Believed More Prevalent Among White Children in U.S.," *The Wall Street Journal* June 23, 2014.

[781] Michael L. Cuccaro et al., "Autism in African American Families: Clinical-Phenotypic Findings," *American Journal of Medical Genetics Part B (Neuropsychiatric Genetics)* 144B (2007): 1022-1026; Saime Tek and Rebecca J. Landa, "Differences in Autism Symptoms between Minority and Non-Minority Toddlers," *Journal of Autism Development Disorder* 42 (2012): 1-13; Areva Martin and Ashya Vahabzadeh, "Children of Color and Autism: Too Little, Too Late," *The Huffington Post* January 10, 2015.

[782] Carrie Arnold, "Autism's Race Problem," *Pacific Standard* May 25, 2016; Areva Martin and Ashya Vahabzadeh, "Children of Color and Autism: Too Little, Too Late," *The Huffington Post* January 10, 2015; Ruby M. Gourdine and Carl L. Algood, "Autism in the African American Population," in *Comprehensive Guide to Autism* ed. V.B. Patel et al. (New York: Springer Science and Business Media, 2014) 2455-2467; D.S. Mendell et al., "Racial/ethnic disparities in the identification of children with autism spectrum disorders," *American Journal of Public Health* 3 (2009): 493-8; idem., "Disparities in diagnosis of autism spectrum disorder," *Journal of Autism Development Disorder* (2006).

II.     *Blowing the Whistle on the CDC's Conspiracy Targeting Black Boys*

In August 2014 Dr. Brian Hooker, biology professor and epidemiologist from Simpson College, Redding California, published a reanalysis of some CDC data that had been provided to him by Dr. William Thompson, senior scientist in the vaccine safety division of the CDC. The reanalyzed data showed a "very strong" signal seen exclusively in Black boys born in metro-Atlanta between 1986 and 1993 indicating a clear relationship between receiving the measles-mumps-rubella (MMR) vaccination before 36 months of age (as insisted by the CDC) and high autism incidence in these Black boys.[783] Dr. Hooker noted:

> When comparing cases and controls receiving their first MMR vaccine before and after 36 months of age, there was a statistically significant increase in autism cases specifically among African American males who received the first MMR prior to 36 months of age. Relative risks for males in general and African American males were 1.69 (p=0.0138) and 3.36 (p=0.0019), respectively...The present study provides new epidemiological evidence showing that African American males receiving the MMR vaccine prior to 24 months of age are more likely to receive an autism diagnosis...The results show a strong relationship between child age at the administration of the first MMR and autism incidence exclusively for African American boys which could indicate a role in the etiology of autism within this population group.[784]

A role in the etiology of autism within this population group? So both the hepatitis B vaccine *and* the MMR vaccine are causing autism in children, disproportionately Black boys. What is

---

[783] Brian S. Hooker, "Measles-mumps-rubella vaccination timing and autism among young African American boys: a reanalysis of CDC data," *Translational Neurodegeneration* 3 (2014): 1-8.
[784] Hooker, "Measles-mumps-rubella vaccination timing and autism among young African American boys," 1-2, 4.

the connection? This question can be answered in one word: thimerosal. Both vaccines have in them a chemical that does great damage to infant neurodevelopment.

## THE THIMEROSAL CONSPIRACY

Thimerosal is a mercury-based preservative and sanitizing agent used in the U.S. in multi-dose vials of vaccines. Mercury is a potent brain poison that is hundreds of times more toxic than lead. Thimerosal is 49.6% ethylmercury, an organic mercury compound. Ethylmercury is a neurotoxin. Once the vaccine is injected into the body thimerosal decomposes to release the ethylmercury. And as Robert F. Kennedy Jr. points out: "Its undisputed that exposure to mercury in infancy reduces a child's intelligence, with boys suffering the most dramatic injury (testosterone tends to amplify mercury's damage, while estrogen seems to moderate it."[785] Undisputed indeed. Prior to 1989 school children were given three vaccinations spread out over up to eleven injections. In 1990-1991 the U.S. government dramatically increased the vaccination load and schedule: by 2 years old children now received *twenty four* vaccinations (vs. 3) over *twenty* injections (vs. 11). Many of these were thimerosal-laced vaccines.

Thimerosal was developed in 1929 by the pharmaceutical corporation Eli Lilly who registered it under the name Merthiolate. The only safety investigation done of this toxic chemical compound was done by Eli Lilly's own sponsored doctors, who failed to prove the non-toxicity of the chemical. Twenty-two terminal meningitis patients were administered the thimerosal-containing serum, all of whom died within weeks of being injected. Yet the doctors deceptively claimed its safety in scientific journals.[786]

---

[785] Robert F. Kennedy, Jr. "Tabaco Science and the Thimerosal Scandal," paper dated July 22, 2005, pp.1-66 @ http://www.robertfkennedyjr.com/docs/ThimerosalScandalFINAL.PDF. On Thimerosal see further *Thimerosal: Let The Science Speak*, ed. Robert F. Kennedy, Jr. (New York: Skyhorse Publications, 2014).

[786] K.C. Smithburn et al. "Meningococcic meningitis – a clinical study of one hundred and forty-four epidemic cases," *Journal of the American Medical*

As early as July 1935, Lilly was warned by the Director of Biological Laboratories at the Pitman-Moore Company that Lilly's claims about thimerosal's safety "did not check with ours." Pitman warned that half the dogs it had injected with thimerosal-containing vaccines became sick and concluded, "[T]himerosal is unsatisfactory as a serum intended for use on dogs." When thimerosal was used by the army in the 1940s and 1950s (in vaccines), Lilly was required by the Defense Department to label the preservative "Poison." It was well established by the 1940s in peer-reviewed scientific and medical literature that injecting thimerosal into sensitive individuals could cause serious injury. In May of 1967, a study published in Applied Microbiology found that Lilly's thimerosal killed mice when it was added to injectable vaccines. Four years later, in 1971, Lilly's own tests found that thimerosal was "toxic to tissue cells" in concentrations of less than 1 in 1,000,000. Typical vaccine concentrations are 1 in 10,000, one hundred times the levels that Lilly knew to be dangerous. Yet Lilly continued to promote thimerosal in vaccines as "non-toxic when injected." When on April 27, 1976, Rexall, which sold thimerosal under license from Lilly, asked Lilly's permission to add a toxicity warning to thimerosal labels, Lilly ordered Rexall not to add the warning and purposely misstated the potential hazards of a product it knew to be toxic: "the mercury in the product is organically bound ethyl mercury and has a completely non-toxic nature."[787]

The first cases of autism in the U.S. were diagnosed in 1943 among young people who had been born a month after Eli Lilly began adding mercury to baby vaccines in 1931. Retired chemistry professor from the University of Kentucky Dr. Boyd Haley makes an important point:

> You couldn't construct a study that shows thimerosal is safe. It's just too darn toxic. If you inject thimerosal into an animal, its brain will sicken. If you apply it to living tissue, the cells die. If you put it in a Petri dish, the culture dies. Knowing these things, it would be shocking if one could inject it into an infant without causing damage.[788]

In 1991 – the very same year the U.S. government introduced a massive amount of thimerosal to American children through a new vaccine schedule – an internal memo of pharmaceutical giant Merck, who manufactures the vaccines, indicates that they were

---

*Association* 95 (1930): 776-80; H.M. Powell and W.A. Jamieson, "Merthiolate as a germicide," *American Journal of Hygiene* 13 (1931):296-310.
[787] Kennedy, Jr. "Tabaco Science and the Thimerosal Scandal," 3-4.
[788] Boyd Haley Telephone Interview with Robert F. Kennedy Jr., April 9, 2005 quoted in Kennedy, Jr. "Tabaco Science and the Thimerosal Scandal," 2022.

well aware of the potential damage being done to American children by their product. As the *Los Angeles Times* reports:

> A memo from Merck & Co. shows that, nearly a decade before the first public disclosures, senior executives were concerned that infants were getting an elevated dose of mercury in vaccinations containing a widely used sterilizing agent...The memo was prepared at a time when the U.S. health authorities were aggressively expanding their immunization schedule by adding five new shots for children in their first six months. Many of these shots as well as some previously included on the vaccine schedule, contained thimerosal.[789]

The memo in question is from Dr. Maurice Hilleman, a father of Merck's vaccination program, to the company president Dr. Gordon Douglas. Hilleman warned that six-month old children administered shots with thimerosal suffer mercury exposure 87 times the existing safety standards: "When viewed in this way, the mercury load appears rather large," Hilleman said. He recommended the use of thimerosal in the vaccines be discontinued "especially where use in infants and young children are anticipated." Hillman affirmed that the industry was aware of non-toxic alternatives to thimerosal and urged their consideration to replace the neurotoxin. Merck refused. This refusal is the more curious because it is known that thimerosal is not terribly effective as an anti-bacterial agent and is not stable as a preservative. It dissolves in aqueous environments such as vaccines. So the insistence on the use of thimerosal must have a different motivation.

So at the time U.S. health authorities were *assaulting* American children with an overload of a proven neurotoxin, they *knew* exactly what they were exposing the county's children to. Why did they do it, then? What was their objective, since surely the *health* of the American public could *not* have been it? In the 1990s 40 million children were injected with thimerosal-laced vaccines. In 1975, before the new vaccine schedule, one in 5000 children had autism. In 2016, following the new schedule, one in 68 have autism. Why was this done to the American people, the

---

[789] Myron Levin, " '91 Memo Warned of Mercury in Shots," *Los Angeles Times* February 8, 2005.

damaged children and their devastated parents? We will proffer an answer shortly.

## THE THIMEROSAL COVER UP

The correlation between autism and the MMR vaccine was first uncovered by Dr. Andrew Wakefield, a gastrointestinal surgeon and researcher in the United Kingdom. In the February 1998 edition of the British medical journal *The Lancet* Wakefield and twelve co-authors published a report of twelve case histories of damaged children and raised the possibility of a connection between autism incidence and the MMR.[790] In 2001 Wakefield testified before the U.S. Congress regarding the possible link. But the backlash was sure to come, and it did. The U.K.'s General Medical Council alleged and ruled that Wakefield committed ethical violations and his medical license was revoked. His article was retracted by *The Lancet* in 2010. But the cover up that occurred across the sea in the U.S. was far, far more astounding.

A large number of reports filed into VAERS (The Vaccine Adverse Event Reporting System) compelled the CDC in the autumn of 1999 to turn to one of their epidemiologists Tom Verstraeten to conduct an analysis of the health agency's massive database containing medical records of 100,000 children. The Verstraeten Study indicated that thimerosal appeared responsible for a dramatic increase in autism and other neurological disorders in children: "The harm is done in the first month of life by thimerosal vaccines," he concluded.[791] The results sent agency officials and industry executives quietly into panic.

By June 2000 Verstraeten prepared for publication his study showing this causative relationship. But before it could go to publication a high-level group of top government scientists and health officials (CDC, Food and Drug Administration [FDA], and

---

[790] Dr. A.J. Wakefield et al, "Ileal-lymphoid-nodular hyperplasia, non-specific colitis, and pervasive developmental disorder in children," *The Lancet* 351 (February 1998): 637-641.
[791] Robert F. Kennedy, Jr., "Vaccinations: Deadly Immunity. Government Cover-up of a Mercury/Autism Scandal," *Rolling Stone.com* July 20, 2005/February 14, 2015.

World Health Organization [WHO]) plus pharmaceutical industry bosses secretly gathered that month in the isolated Simpswood Conference Center in Norcross, Georgia and, according to the transcript of the meeting released via the Freedom of Information Act, spent days trying to figure out how to cover-up the damning results of the Verstraeten Study. Dr. Richard Johnston, immunologist and pediatrician from the University of Colorado, whose grandson was born that day, declared after discussing the Study: "Forgive me this personal comment – I don't want my grandson to get a thimerosal-containing vaccine until we know better what is going on."[792]

But instead of going public with the information and allowing *other* parents and grandparents to make that same informed decision for their children, the gathered scientists and officials "embargoed" and buried the study (as is), hatching a plan to hide the dangers of thimerosal. The CDC and NIH contracted the Institute of Medicine (IOM) for $2 million to conduct a new study whitewashing the thimerosal risk, ordering researchers to "rule out" the chemical's links to autism. The Verstraeten Study findings were withheld, and the CDC reportedly lied to inquiring scientists stating that Verstraeten's data were lost and therefore his study could not be replicated.[793] But at the CDC the light was already beginning to shine much deeper down into the rabbit hole.

## THE CRIMINAL ASSAULT ON THE MIND OF BLACK BOYS AND THE CRIMINAL COVER UP

Dr. William Thompson, a senior scientist in the CDC's vaccine safety division, also crunched some numbers in November, 2001. But his numbers uncovered the *darkest* secret of this thimerosal/vaccination conspiracy. His data showed an effect found "exclusively" on Black boys. What Thompson discovered is today called the "African American Effect."[794] His data indicated that, while MMR-vaccinated children in general have a 69%

---

[792] Kennedy, Jr., "Vaccinations: Deadly Immunity."
[793] Kennedy, Jr., "Vaccinations: Deadly Immunity."
[794] ***Vaxxed: From Cover-Up to Catastrophe*** (2016). Film.

elevated risk of autism, Black boys specifically have an unbelievable elevated risk of 236%! "The relative risk of [Black boys] receiving an autism diagnosis was astronomical," said Dr. Hooker, who first received Dr. Thompson's raw data sets after others' sets were destroyed.[795] There is something about the thimerosal in the MMR (and the Hep B) vaccine that is dangerous for all children but, for some reason, is more dangerous to Black boys than it is to *any* other demographic. It causes a level of neurological carnage that is "exclusive" to Black males.

It was normal practice for Thompson to have regular weekly meetings at the CDC with four colleagues: Dr. Frank Destefano (M.D.), director of Immunization Safety; Dr. Colleen Boyle (Ph.D), head of the Disabilities Division; Dr. Marshalyn Yeargin-Allsop (M.D.), Thompson's direct supervisor; and Tanya Bhasin, a post-doc Research Associate. In one November meeting Thompson brought his findings up. His analysis of the African American Effect "was the 8 on the rector scale earthquake that just shook through the CDC,"[796] Hooker reports. On orders from CDC higher-ups the five of them colluded to cover up the relationship between the MMR and this neurological assault on Black Boys. "It was five of us behind closed doors for two years" searching for a way to hide this data," says Thompson who turned whistleblower in 2014: "The CDC knew about the relationship between the age of first MMR vaccine and autism in African American boys...but chose to cover it up."[797]

Thompson and his colleagues committed scientific misconduct to cover up this meaningful link between vaccines and autism in Black boys.

---

[795] *Vaxxed: From Cover-Up to Catastrophe* (2016). Film.
[796] Words of Hooker in *Vaxxed: From Cover-Up to Catastrophe* (2016). Film.
[797] Thompson quoted in "Fraud at the CDC uncovered, 340% risk of autism hidden from public," *CNN iReport* August 24, 2014.

Dr. Williamd Thompson; Dr. Frank Destefano; Dr. Colleen Boyle; Dr. Marshalyn Yeargin-Allsop

In the words of Thompson, they

> scheduled a meeting to destroy documents related to the study. The remaining four co-authors all met and brought a big garbage can into the meeting room, and reviewed and went through all the hardcopy documents that we had thought we should discard, and put them in a huge garbage can...[B]ecause I assumed it was illegal and would violate both FOIA (Freedom of Information Act) and DOJ (Department of Justice) requests, I kept hardcopies of all documents in my office, and I retain all associated computer files.[798]

This "Garbage Can" meeting was held in the fall of 2002. Over two years the CDC scientists searched for an adequate "bleach" to make the data on the "African American Effect" disappear. They decided to manipulate data from the original study by eliminating some of the population studied and this made the African American Effect invisible. The product of these two years of wrestling to get these damning data under control was the 2004 "Destafano Study," which became the industry proof-text that there is no connection between the MMR vaccine and autism.[799] But the study was the product of scientific misconduct, data suppression and manipulation, and fraud.[800]

---

[798] See Kevin Barry, Esq., *Vaccine Whistleblower: Exposing Autism Research Fraud at the CDC* (New York: Skyhorse Publishing, 2015); Robert F. Kennedy, Jr. "African American Autism and Vaccines," *New York Amsterdam News* July 9, 2015; Malen Grgodjaian, "Vaxxed: Smoking Gun on Autism," *California Black Media* May 14, 2016; "Fraud at the CDC uncovered, 340% risk of autism hidden from public," *CNN iReport* August 24, 2014.

[799] Frank Destafano et al., "Age at first measles-mumps-rubella vaccination in children with autism and school-matched control subjects: a population-based

Turning whistleblower, Thompson released thousands of documents to Hooker and to Congressman Bill Posey of Florida. On August 27, 2014 Thompson issued a statement through his whistleblower attorney Richard Morgan, Esq., stating in part:

> My name is William Thompson. I am a Senior Scientist with the Centers for Disease Control and Prevention, where I have worked since 1998.
>
> I regret that my coauthors and I omitted statistically significant information in our 2004 article published in the journal *Pediatrics*. The omitted data suggested that African American males who received the MMR vaccine before age 36 months were at increased risk for autism. Decisions were made regarding which findings to report after the data were collected, and I believe that the final study protocol was not followed.
>
> I want to be absolutely clear that I believe vaccines have saved and continue to save countless lives. I would never suggest that any parent avoid vaccinating children of any race. Vaccines prevent serious diseases, and the risks associated with their administration are vastly outweighed by their individual and societal benefits.
>
> My concern has been the decision to omit relevant findings in a particular study for *a particular sub group* for *a particular vaccine*. There have always been recognized risks for vaccination and I believe it is the responsibility of the CDC to properly convey the risks associated with receipt of those vaccines.[801]

On July 29, 2015 Rep. Posey addressed the U.S. House of Representatives and urged an investigation into the CDC for fraud, misrepresentation, and manipulation of data linking vaccines to autism. As Kennedy, Jr. elaborates:

---

study in metropolitan Atlanta," *Pediatrics* 113 (2004): 259-66; **Vaxxed: From Cover-Up to Catastrophe** (2016). Film; Robert F. ennedy, Jr. "Forward," in Barry, Esq., *Vaccine Whistleblower*, xiv.

[800] "Fraud at the CDC uncovered, 340% risk of autism hidden from public," **CNN** *iReport* August 24, 2014.

[801] "Statement of William W. Thompson, Ph.D., Regarding the 2004 Article Examining the Possibility of a Relationship Between MMR Vaccine and Autism," @
http://morganverkamp.com/statement-of-william-w-thompson-ph-d-regarding-the-2004-article-examining-the-possibility-of-a-relationship-between-mmr-vaccine-and-autism/

> Those data show that Black boys who received the MMR vaccine before 3 years of age, as the CDC recommends, were 3.36 times more likely to receive an autopsy diagnosis than those who received the vaccine after 3 years of age. *This effect was not observed in other race categories...*[W]hen the CDC scientists published their results in the journal *Pediatrics* in 2004, they omitted the damaging data, fraudulently declaring there was no risk of autism from the MMR vaccination (emphasis added).[802]

> When Thompson discovered that the MMR vaccine was causing dramatic rises in autism in African American boys, his CDC bosses ordered him to keep his mouth shut...his team fraudulently withheld data demonstrating a 340 (sic) percent higher risk of autism in African American boys *who received that vaccine on time* compared to boys who delayed the vaccine...On the basis of all the population data and the CDC's most recent autism incidence estimates, at least *100,000 African American male children* (!) could have been spared debilitating neurological injury if the CDC scientists had told the truth when Thompson and his team first discovered the increased risk in 2001 (emphasis added).[803]

In the light of our earlier discussion of Fred Goodwin and the Bush Administration's Violence Initiative targeting young Black boys for mind and behavior control through pharmacological interventions, two things really stand out in this quote: 1.] the figure 100,000 unnecessarily injured Black boys, the exact same number desired by Fred Goodwin for his target population! 2.] the CDC's insistence on the *timetable*: Black boys getting the vaccination before 36 months are the ones *most* at risk for injury and the CDC *insists* on this schedule.

The issue of timing is a key component of thimerosal's effect so the age of exposure to MMR is significant. The CDC insists that the MMR be administered to a child between 12 and 18 months. Now we know why. "In the hidden data [omitted by the CDC]...it is clear that for African Americans *this is actually the most dangerous time*," affirms medical journalist Del Bigtree.[804] The "Stick to the Schedule" campaign thus takes on a different coloring. We are also reminded here of the words and prediction of Dr. Ned Kalim and Ronald Kotulak quoted above:

---

[802] Kennedy, Jr. "African American Autism and Vaccines."
[803] Robert F. Kennedy, Jr. "Forward," in Barry, Esq., ***Vaccine Whistleblower***, xvi-xvii.
[804] ***Vaxxed: From Cover-Up to Catastrophe*** (2016). Film.

> We're going to be able to identify these (brain-impaired) children (i.e. uncontrolled Black children) within the first five years of life and make interventions to change their brains right then...exposure to the right drug *at the right time* may reset the development of the brain in a positive way.[805]

Not positive for the Black boys victimized by such brain "interventions," but positive for the dominant male group: white males. But in order for the intervention to be effective, the right drug must be administered at *the right time*. The thimerosal-laced MMR vaccine is most devastating in its "African American Effect" when children receive it before 36 months – the *right time* - and this is exactly what the CDC insists on. So we are haunted by Kotulak's words in 1993: "Children someday may be *immunized* against stunted brains."[806] As stated above, these words must be read as: "Our brain-damaging drugs are and will be administered to Black male children through immunizations." And that is *exactly* what is happening. It was all planned and executed.

Renowned French virologists Dr. Luc Antoine Montagnier who won the 2008 Noble Prize for co-discovering the AIDS virus (HIV) himself confessed:

> The vaccine-autism interaction is a worldwide problem. Not only in this county (France), in Europe – but also in Asia, even in Africa. The MMR vaccination in very early stage of infancy, before the age of two, was more prominent in Afro-American children and this was hidden for some time. This fraud, of course, ranks, very high, to my opinion, in the ethics of medicine and science. CDC, in the past, has done very good work on the discovery of AIDS. So I'm very disappointed to see a different situation with the CDC and autism.[807]

Dr. Luc Antoine Montagnier

---

[805] Kotulak, "Reshaping Brain For a Better Future."
[806] Kotulak, "Reshaping Brain For a Better Future."
[807] ***Vaxxed: From Cover-Up to Catastrophe*** (2016). Film.

Robert F. Kennedy, Jr. is a longtime environmental activists and attorney for the Natural Defense Council as well as professor at Pace University in White Plains, New York. He travels the country giving 200 speeches a year on renewable energy and sits on the boards of several green tech companies.[808] It was his uncle, Senator Edward Kennedy who convened the Senate hearings to allow whistleblower Peter Buxton to testify about the 40 year Tuskegee Experiment and terminate it. Robert F. Kennedy, Jr. sees this MMR-autism "African American Effect" as the CDC's "Latest Tuskegee Experiment."[809] He notes:

> The most reliable studies in the scientific literature indicate that African-Americans are more susceptible to vaccine injury and may also have increased susceptibility to neurological disorders such as autism.[810]

What makes Black people more susceptible to injury? Is it something about Black people, something about vaccines, or both (ethnic weapons)? Kennedy, Jr. draws our attention to a particularly egregious case of vaccine injury inflicted on Black people by the CDC. Beginning in 1989 the CDC secretly experimented on 1500 mainly Black and Brown infants in Los Angeles using an unlicensed measles vaccine.[811] The parents were not informed that their child was being exposed to a high potency experimental drug designed to overwhelm the baby's maternal immune system. The CDC halted the experiment in 1991 after it was discovered that in the companion clinical trials being conducted in Africa and Haiti female infants were showing severe immune-system disorder and increased death rate. Within two years all of the inoculated infants in the African/Haiti study died. The CDC claims that none of the Los Angeles children were injured in any way, but as Kennedy points out: "CDC denies that

---

[808] Keith Kloor, "Robert Kennedy's belief in autism-vaccine connection, and its political peril," *The Washington Post* July 18, 2004.
[809] Robert F. Kennedy, Jr. "CDC Latest Tuskegee Experiment: African American Autism and Vaccines," 2015 paper @ http://www.robertfkennedyjr.com/articles/tuskegee.html
[810] Kennedy, Jr. "African American Autism and Vaccines."
[811] Marlene Cimons, "CDC Says It Erred in Measles Study," *Los Angeles Times* June 17, 1996.

any Los Angeles black children were injured by the unlicensed vaccine, but has not produced any studies to confirm that claim."[812] For very good reason he also disputes the claim of the CDC that thimerosal has been removed vaccines.

> The common canard that US autism rates rose after the drug makers removed thimerosal from pediatric vaccines in 2003 is wrong. That same year, CDC added flu shots containing massive doses of thimerosal to the pediatric schedule. As a result, children today can get nearly as much mercury exposure as children did from all pediatric vaccines combined in the decade prior to 2003. Worse, thimerosal, for the first time, is being given to pregnant women in flu shots. Further, CDC's *current autism numbers are for children born in 2002, when kids were still getting thimerosal in their pediatric vaccines.*[813]

> The industry now claims to have removed thimerosal, but there is no independent checking and parents and pediatricians must take the word of the some companies that have behaved deceitfully on this subject in the past.[814]

### III. *Autism and the Assault on Serotonin (Just What The Government Ordered)*

Autism is a neurodevelopmental disorder characterized by three main behavioral symptoms: impaired reciprocal social interactions, language and communication deficits, and stereotypic repetitive behaviors. The etiology or cause of autism is complex and believed to be heterogeneous, i.e. there is not one cause to one disorder but several causes to a "spectrum" of disorders. This is why today we speak of "Autism Spectrum Disorder (ASD)" rather than simply "autism." One cause or at least characteristic of some of this "spectrum" of neurological disorders is clear: disruption of the serotonergic system. "[H]umans undergo a period of high brain serotonin synthesis capacity during childhood, and…this developmental process is

---

[812] Kennedy, Jr. "CDC Latest Tuskegee Experiment."
[813] Robert F. Kennedy, Jr. "Thimerosal: Let the Science Speak." @ http://www.robertfkennedyjr.com.
[814] Kennedy, Jr. "Tobacco Science and the Thimerosal Scandal," 10.

disrupted in autistic children."[815] In the Central Nervous System (CNS) serotonin plays the role of neurotransmitter and serotonergic neutrons are among the earliest developing neurotransmitter systems in the brain of mammals. Assaulting this system has devastating neurological effects.

> The disruption of the serotonergic system is one of the most consistent and well-replicated findings in autism...The early appearance of the serotonergic system, as well as its intense activity during the first stage of development, indicates its role in the developmental process...The early disturbance of the serotonergic system disrupts the developmental process and contributes to several of the neuropathological changes in autism...Neuroimaging, neuropathological and genetic studies have added to the evidence for the large-scale involvement of serotonin in pathogenesis...of autism...The normal process of high brain serotonin synthesis and synaptogenesis during preschool years is highly disrupted in children with autism...The serotonergic disruption during development is involved in some of the most consistent neuropathological findings in the autistic brain.[816]

Neuroimaging has shown a decrease in brain serotonin synthesis in autistic children between 2 and 5 years old. When TPH-2 (the enzyme that metabolizes brain serotonin) has been depleted in some mice they displayed the same behavioral characteristics of autistic children: severely impaired social interaction and communication, repetitive behaviors, and aggression and behavioral disinhibition.[817] A 2013 study

---

[815] Diane C. Chugani, "Pharmacological Intervention in Autism: Targeting Critical Periods of Brain Development," *Clinical Neurological* 2 (2005): 346 [art.=346-353]. See further George M. Anderson, "Serotonin and Autism," *Journal of the American Academy of Child and Adolescent Psychiatry* 41 (2002): 1513-1516. Serious consideration of the role of serotonin in autism dates back to 1961: R.J. Shain and D.X. Freedman, "Studies on 5-hydroxyindole metabolism in autism and other mentally retard children," *Journal of Pediatrics* 58 (1961): 315-320.

[816] D.I. Zafeiriou, A. Vereri and E. Vargiami, "The Serotonergic System: Its Role in Pathogenesis and Early Developmental Treatment of Autism," *Current Neuropharmacology* 7 (2009): 150-151 [art.=150-157]. See also C.-J. Yang et al, "The Developmental Disruption of Serotonin Signaling May Be Involved in Autism During Early Brain Development," *Neuroscience* 267 (2014): 1-10.

[817] Michael J. Kane et al., "Mice Genetically Depleted of Brain Serotonin Display Social Impairments, Communication Deficits and Repetitive Behaviors: Possible Relevance to Autism," *PLoS One* 7 (2012): 1-14: "Defects in function within the

suggested that decreased tryptophan metabolism was a unifying biochemical basis for all Autism Spectrum Disorders.[818] And as we would expect, this serotonergic disruption characteristic of children afflicted with autism is likely caused by the thimerosal within the MMR vaccines. Japanese scientists in 2011 and 2014 demonstrated that exposing pregnant rats to thimerosal impaired early serotonergic development: "a single prenatal exposure to thimerosal causes irreversible and critical effects to the brain serotonergic systems."[819]

Remember, there is precedent for the deliberate and organized chemical assault on the serotonergic system of young Black boys. For example, the hideous fenfluramine "experiment" conducted by the New York State Psychiatric Institute and Columbia University (and other universities and hospitals) between 1992 and 1996 where 34 Black boys with good serotonin levels were cherry picked from 100 Black boys examined and their healthy serotonergic systems were purposefully assaulted with a massive dose of a very dangerous, known serotonin antagonist, the drug fenfluramine.[820] This was being done at the same time U.S. health authorities were assaulting American children through a new (1991) vaccine schedule with a massive dose of another

---

serotonin (5HT) neuronal system have long been suspected of involvement in ASD...[I]ndividuals with ASD have decreased levels of 5HT receptor binding in brain. Short term reduction in the levels of tryptophan, the precursor of 5HT, exacerbates repetitive, compulsive behaviors (e.g., flapping, rocking, whirling) in drug-free adults with ASD. Children with ASD also show decreases in 5HT synthesis in brain areas important for language production and sensory integration."

[818] Luigi Boccuto et al, "Decreased tryptophan metabolism in patients with autism spectrum disorders," *Molecular Autism* 4 (2013): 1-10; Eileen Daly et al., "Response inhibition and serotonin in autism: a functional MRI study using acute tryptophan depletion," *Brain* 137 (2014): 2600-2610.

[819] Michiru Ida-Eto et al, "Embryonic exposure to thimerosal, an organomercury compound, causes abnormal early development of serotonergic neurons," *Neurosci Lett* 505 (2011): 61-64; idem, "Primate exposure to organomercury, thimerosal, persistently impairs the serotonergic and dopaminergic systems in the rat brain: Implications for association with developmental disorders," *Brain & Development* 35 (2013): 261-264. See also Hiroaki Nishio et al., "Effects of Thimerosal, an organic sulfhydryl modifying agent, on serotonin transport activity into rabbit blood platelets," *Neurochem. Int.* 29 (1996): 391-396.

[820] See above.

chemical that can damage the serotonergic system, thimerosal. While American children in general were being exposed, the thimerosal-laced vaccines were having a particularly brutal effect on Black boys, as did fenfluramine in that "experiment."

IV.     *"Operation Ferdinand" and Autism: Creating Docile Black Males*

Another cause of one or more disorders on the autism spectrum is damage done to the amygdala, the almond-shaped bundle of neurons on the inner side of the temporal lobe. The amygdala is believed to be the switchboard for emotions. It is involved in sending motivational signals related to fear, reward and punishment and social and sexual functions. The amygdala has been strongly implicated in autism pathogenesis: "Another well replicated finding in autism is the alteration of the amygdala, affecting its volume, cellpacking density and activation during processing."[821] In autistic children the amygdala has two abnormalities: enlargement through increased volume but also reduction in the number of actual neurons.[822] S. Baron-Cohen and colleagues proposed an "amygdala theory of autism," suggesting that the amygdala is one of the several neural regions that are necessarily abnormal in autism.[823] In animal studies thimerosal-laced vaccine exposure was shown to damage the amygdala.[824] This is chillingly significant.

---

[821] Zafeiriou, Vereri and Vargiami, "The Serotonergic System," 152.
[822] Cynthia Mills Schumann and David G. Amaral, "Stereological Analysis of Amygdala Neuron Number in Autism," *The Journal of Neuroscience* 26 (2006): 7674-7679.
[823] S. Baron-Cohen et al., "The amygdala theory of autism," *Neuroscience and Biobehavioral Reviews* 24 (2000): 355-364. Cf. D.G. Amaral, M.D. Bauman and C. Mills, "The amygdala and autism: implications from non-human primate studies," *Genes. Brain and Behavior* 2 (2003): 295-302.
[824] Laura Hewitson et al, "Influence of pediatric vaccines on amygdala growth and opioid ligand binding in rhesus macaque infants: A pilot study," *Acta Neurobiol. Exp.* 70 (2010): 147-164.

Amygdalotomy is a form of lobotomy (destructive brain surgery) where the amygdala is deliberately damaged. The Harvard "Operation Ferdinand" operatives Vernon Mark and Frank Ervin who initially were granted over a million dollars from the U.S. government to research and to do psychosurgery on inner city Black males who agitate for social justice, described in their book ***Violence and the Brain*** how amygdalotomy will successfully pacify an aggressive or a frightened animal, making it tractable and easy to handle, specifically their designs for Black males. As Breggin points out: "Amygdalotomy is *the* pacification operation *par excellence* (emphasis added)."[825] It's a "sedative neurosurgery." As far back as 1966 Arthur Kling studied amygdalotomies in cats, rats, and monkeys and noted a "marked taming" and a "relative docility" in some of the animals. After damaging the amygdala of two Canadian lynxes, "There was a dramatic taming effect in these wild cats" and the surgery done on the rhesus monkey produced "a change in the direction of docility toward man."[826]

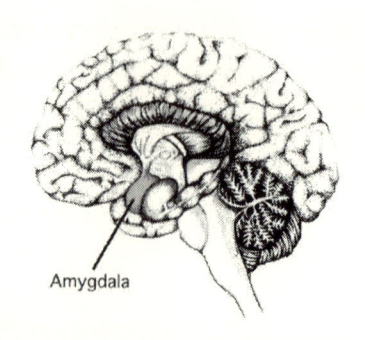

The amygdala proved relevant in dominance hierarchy studies as well. Animal studies showed that amygdalotomies effect dominance. Monkeys fell from the top to the bottom of the social hierarchy after the destructive operation and dogs who usually won out in competition for bones began to lose out. Among hooded rats the operation had the effect of "obscure[ing] the dominance-subordination relationship."[827] And *this* is

---

[825] Breggin, "Psychosurgery for the control of violence," 359.
[826] Arthur Kling, "Ontogenic and Phylogenetic Studies on the Amygdaloid Nuclei," ***Psychosom Med*** 28 (1966): 155-161.
[827] J.L. Fuller, H.E. Rosvold and K.H. Pribaum, "The effect on affective and cognitive behavior in the dog of lesions of the pyriform-amygdala-hyppocampal complex," ***Journal of Comparative and Physiological Psychology*** 50 (1957): 89-96; H.E. Rosvold, A.F. Mirsky and K.H. Pribaum, "Influence of amygdalectomy on social behavior in monkeys," ***Journal of Comparative and Physiological Psychology*** 47 (1954): 173-178; B.H. Bunnell, "Amygdaloid lesions and social dominance in the hooded rat," ***Psychonomic Science*** 6 (1966): 93-94.

precisely why this particular brain mutilation was considered as an option to be used on Black males. As Mason noted in his *Ebony* exposé of the government's psychosurgery plans for Black men: "Since they believe it moderates emotions and drives, brain specialists agree that removing the amygdala curbs aggressive behavior and makes the patient docile,"[828] and makes some Black youth docile. Thimerosal does exactly that. It damages the amygdala and autism victims tend to be socially subdued. Today's syringe with the thimerosal-laced vaccine is thus yesterday's "ice pick" of the psychosurgens.

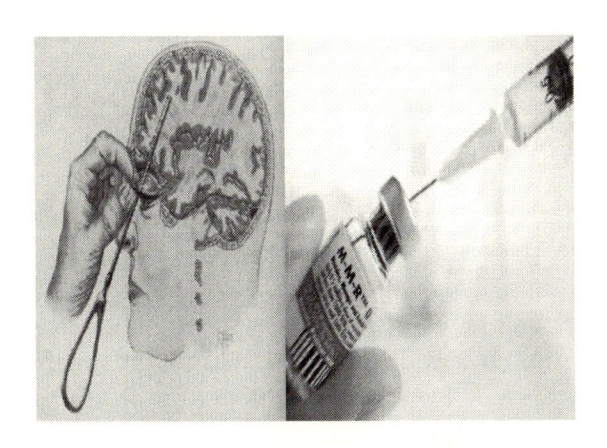

The characteristic behavioral symptoms of autism are easily seen in Ferdinand, the docile bull of Munro Leafe's children's story. He fails to engage with his peers (lack of social reciprocity) but instead stays alone under a tree all day obsessively smelling flowers (stereotypic repetitive restricted behavior). When he is agitated by a bee's sting, Ferdinand has a complete meltdown and reacts in an overly aggressive manner and then returns to his docile self, as many autistic patients do.[829]

---

[828] Mason, "Brain Surgery," 63.
[829] Alison Presmanes Hill et al., "Aggressive behavior problems in children with autism spectrum disorders: Prevalence and correlates in a large clinical sample," *Research in Autism Spectrum Disorders* 8 (2014): 1121-1133; Micah O. Mazurek et al., "Physical aggression in children and adolescents with autism spectrum disorders," *Research in Autism Spectrum Disorders* 7 (2013): 455-465.

Scott and Tara Shade are therefore insightful: "I think Ferdinand in not like other bulls because Ferdinand has autism."⁸³⁰ Ferdinand the (Black) Bull is the Black Autistic Boy. The unleashing of the autism epidemic on American children through the thimerosal-laced vaccines was part of what we have throughout this book called "Operation Ferdinand": the government's effort to transform socially aggressive Black males – Ernst Rodin's inner city Black Bulls - into brain damaged docile oxen –Ferdinand.

### V. Eli Lilly, Thimerosal and the Biomedical Social Control of Black Males

Eli Lilly developed thimerosal back in 1929. The company has been deeply involved in the Bush Administration's "Violence Initiative" aimed at Black boys. "As the first company in America to market a drug aimed specifically and exclusively at influencing brain serotonin (i.e. Prozac), Eli Lilly has a special investment in the outcome of programs for biomedical social control."⁸³¹ Eli Lilly advocated for the use of their drug Prozac in the government's "treatment of violence,"⁸³² and this was accepted. In the disclosed 1992 NIMH document discussed above, "Preventing Youth Violence," the government noted the use of the drug Depo-Provera *and Eli Lilly's Prozac* in their program to control inner city Black males.⁸³³ So we should not be surprised that their other product – thimerosal – is also being used by the government in its biomedical social control efforts. Indeed, the relationship between Eli Lilly and the Bush Administration is

---

[830] Scott and Tara Shade, "BCFR, the Bee that Empowers the Bull," *Columbia Daily Tribune* June 31, 2012.
[831] Breggin and Breggin, *War Against Children of Color*, 29.
[832] Breggin and Breggin, *War Against Children of Color*, 200.
[833] Breggin and Breggin, *War Against Children of Color*, 12.

actually perverse. Not just because Steve M. Paul, the scientific director of the NIMH moved to become a vice president at Eli Lilly in 1993. That's the tip of the iceberg.

> Eli Lilly directly funds researchers and major 'educational' programs at NIMH and ADAMHA and now has hired away Steven Paul, one of the men most responsible for directing federal mental health research. Is it a coincidence that Fred Goodwin, as the head of ADAMHA, came vigorously to the defense of Eli Lilly and Prozac when the controversy over drug-induced murder and suicide hit the press? Is it chance that NIMH is now spending tax-payer money on research that could end up supporting the use of Prozac for violence control, in effect conducting drug testing on behalf of Lilly...Perhaps most significantly, NIMH is providing Lilly with the priceless imprimatur of federal research aimed at supporting broader sales, opening what could be the greatest market ever for any drug-violence and prevention and control.[834]

But it's Eli Lilly's long and close association with President Bush and Vice President Quayle that is most unsettling. "Critics say the Bush family and the administration have too many ties to Eli Lilly. There's President Bush's father, who sat on the company's board in the 1970's; White House budget director Mitch Daniels, once an Eli Lilly executive; and Eli Lilly CEO Sidney Taurel, who serves on the president's homeland security advisory council."[835]

> After he left the C.I.A. and before he began to run for the 1980 Republican nomination, Bush worked for Lilly. Later he dropped the Lilly directorship from his resume and failed to disclose his holdings in Lilly stock. As Vice President, Bush continued to lobby on behalf of Lilly, whose Washington lobbying office was set up by Dan Quayle's uncle, back in 1959.[836]

So consider these facts:

---

[834] Peter R. Breggin, M.D. and Ginger Ross Breggin, *The War Against Children of Color: Psychiatry Targets Inner City Youth* (Monroe, Maine: Common Courage Press, 1998) 31.
[835] Joel Roberts, "The Man Behind the Vaccine Mystery," *CBS Evening News* December 12, 2002.
[836] "Paradigm of Power The Case of Eli Lilly," *The Nation* December 7, 1992, p. 160.

In the early 1990s the Bush Administration, through its Department of Health and Human Services, launches a $400 million program of biomedical social control which targeted inner-city Black male youth for pharmacological interventions – brain damage and brain control through drugs. In 1991, U.S. health officials of the Bush Administration drastically changed the vaccine schedule, overloading American children with a known chemical neurotoxin – thimerosal – which had the most devastating effect specifically on the brain of Black boys, the same population targeted for mind destruction by the Bush Administration's health department. The chemical weapon that is causing the damage to these young Black boys – thimerosal – is the specific creation of Eli Lilly, whom George Bush and many in his Administration had very long and very close ties to, politically, financially, and personally. So coming full circle: the Bush Administration planned to use Eli Lilly's other chemical creation, Prozac, to manipulate the serotonergic system of inner-city youth as part of the government's Violence Initiative targeting Black males.

None dare call it conspiracy?!

But we still have not yet gotten to the *deepest* aspect of this conspiracy; we still have not penetrated the *darkest* depths of this rabbit hole. Because all the while, the assault was never simply against the brains of some marginalized inner-city juveniles. Rather, this thimerosal conspiracy specifically targets *the Power of God* within the *Black Male Mind*. Black people in general and Black males in particular are peculiar biological vessels that most optimally and efficiently conduct the power of God on earth. White scientists a long time ago discovered the biological mechanisms that made Black people and the Black male so uniquely conductive of this divine power, and these scientists have targeted those mechanisms. Autism is really just a side effect of the thimerosal conspiracy. The real aim is disconnecting the Black male from the power of God that is literally residing in his own brain.

# 19 Putting Out The Black God's Light

I. *The Light of God in the Body of Man*

*God is light. In Him there is no darkness.* Book of John 1:5, ca. 1st century AD

*He (God) created Himself and was Light of Himself. He emitted light from the live atom of Self.*
*How could man be a self-light?...[T]he lightning bug is in their own light. The God did that to give you a sign.* Messenger of Allah, the Honorable Elijah Muhammad, 1972

*We now know, today, that man is essentially a being of light.* German biophysicists Fritz Albert Popp, ca. 1974-

*The human body literally glimmers...[T]he human body directly and rhythmically emits light...Human body is glimmering with light of intensity weaker than 1/1000 times the sensitivity of naked eyes.* Japanese Scientists Masakai Hobayashi et al., 2009

As we discussed above, according to the ancient "Theology of the Black God" God first had a body of light which he subsequently concealed within a more material, aqueous black body, i.e. the human body which is 70% water. The Honorable Elijah Muhammad taught us that Allah the Original Man, that original god, was a light of himself, a self-luminous man who emitted light from his own being like the lighting bug. And from his own light he mattered the Sun into existence. This self-luminous Man-God of the Beginning is at the root of the religions of the world. Brahma, the Self-Luminous Man-God of India; Yahweh or Jehovah, the Self-Luminous Man-God of Biblical tradition[837]; and Ra or Heru, the Self-Luminous Man-God of

---

[837] On the luminous body of the Biblical Yahweh see Wesley Williams, "A Body Unlike Bodies: Transcendent Anthropomorphism in Ancient Semitic Tradition and Early Islam," *Journal of the American Oriental Society* 129 (2009): 19-44 (esp. 25-28); H. Wheeler Robinson, "Hebrew Psychology," in *The People and the Book: Essays on the Old Testament*, ed. Arthur S. Peake (Oxford, 1925), 367: "Yahweh's body is shaped like man's, but its substance is not flesh but 'spirit,'

Ancient Egypt (Plate 11). These are not three different Gods: they are three different cultural depictions of that one Self-Luminous Man-God from the Beginning.[838] Western scholars erroneously call him the Sun God, but he created the sun and his bodily light was believed to be greater than that of the sun.

The Honorable Elijah Muhammad says further that this Self-Luminous Man-God, Allah, became pitch black like the black matter that existed before the creation of the world. I have not read or heard the Honorable Elijah Muhammad explain or describe how the Self-Luminous Man-God became the pitch black or "totally dark" God. The ancient religious texts and traditions however are pretty consistent in suggesting that the Man of Light made and wrapped himself within a black material body made from that original pitch black matter of the universe. These texts and traditions also tell us that when the Self-Luminous Man-God wrapped his body of pure light in the pitch black material body, the now internal light passed through the hair pores of the black (outer) body. What is for us today *hair* pores were originally, these traditions suggest, *light* pores. And as the white or gold light passed through the hair/light pores of the pitch black body, a blue glow was produced. This is why the King of the Gods in ancient religions is depicted as both pitch black and at other times as sapphire blue. The sapphire blue body of the god represents the blue glow around the black body that results from the gold or white light interacting with the black body. When you see the blue body or blue glow, you know that the light is

Black corpse of Egyptian deity Osiris being raised by words of lamentation and glorification form his wife Isis and sister-in-law Nephthys.

---

and spirit seen as a blaze of light. It is true that the imageless worship of prophetic religion repudiates the making of any likeness of God, and no form was seen in the storm-theophany of Sinai (Deut. iv. 12). But it is one thing to shrink from the vision of the form, and another to deny that a form exists, though a form wrought out of *ruach*-substance"

[838] See True Islam, **The Book of God: An Encyclopedia of Proof that the Black Man is God** (Atlanta: A-Team Publishing, 2007).

"on" inside because it's passing through the light-pores of the black body. When the blue glow is missing as in the case with the dead black God Asar or Osiris, this means that the light has "gone off" or has severely dimmed.

Science has once again caught up to the wisdom of the Honorable Elijah Muhammad. In the 1970's German biophysicist from the University of Warburg Fritz Albert Popp and his co-workers demonstrated the reality of coherent light radiating from the cells of all living organisms.[839] This cellular light has been called *biophotons*: quanta or elementary particles of light of non-thermal origin. As Marco Bischof informs us:

> All living organisms, including humans, emit a low-intensity glow that cannot be seen by the naked eye, but can be measured by photomultipliers that amplify the weak signals several million times and enable the researchers to register it in the form of a diagram. As long as they live, cells and whole organisms give off a pulsating glow with a mean intensity of several up to a few ten thousand photons per second and square centimeter. This corresponds to a candle-light seen from 15 miles distance and is tens of hundreds of millions times weaker than daylight. This glow can also be made visible by means of a CCD camera whose input of differences in brightness is then transformed by a computer into colors displayed on a video screen. Because of its low intensity, this cellular glow, also known as biophoton emission, is often referred to as ultra-weak cell radiation, or ultra-weak bioluminescence. Its spectral range of frequencies (colors) extends from 200-800 nanometers, i.e. from UV-C and UV-A through the whole visible range of the infrared part of the spectrum.[840]

---

[839] Fritz-Albert Popp, "Properties of biophotons and their theoretical implications," *Indian Journal of Experimental Biology* 41 (2003): 391-402; S. Cohen and F.A. Popp, "Biophoton emission of human body," *Indian Journal of Experimental Biology* 41 (2003): 440-445. For a fuller bibiliography see Marco Bischof, "A tribute to Fritz-Albert Popp on the occasion of his 70th birthday," *Indian Journal of Experimental Biology* 46 (2008):267-72.

[840] Marco Bischof, "Biophotons – The Light in Our Cells," *Journal of Optometric Phototherapy* (March 2005): 1 [art.=1-5]. On Biophoton emission and the biofield see further: Chang Jiin Ju (Zhang Jinzhu), "Physical properties of biophotons and their biological functions," *Indian Journal of Experimental Biology* 46 (2008): 371-377; Roeland Van Wijk and Eduard P.A. Van Wijk, "An Introduction to Human Biophoton Emission," *Forschende Komplementärmedizin Klassische Naturheilkunde* 12 (2005): 77-83; Jonathan Tennenbaum, "The Biophoton Revolution: Beyond Molecular Biology," *21st Century* (Winter 1998-1999): 38-40; M. Pitkänen, "Are dark photons behind biophotons?" *Journal of Nonlocality* 2

A very important characteristic of this bio-light is its profound laser-like *coherence*. "Biophotons consist of light with a high degree of order, in other words, *biological laser light*. Such a light is very quiet and shows an extremely stable intensity, without the fluctuations normally observed in light (emphasis added)."[841] The human body is thus believed to be permeated with and enveloped by a coherent biophoton field.[842] "Every portion of live human skin emits photons".[843] This high level of quantum coherence is elsewhere only observed in very cold laboratory conditions a few degrees above absolute zero. This contrasts radically from the wet, hot and messy environment ("surrounding heat bath") of the biological cell. The fact that such "cold" coherence can exist and operate in such "hot" biological conditions is a testament of the divinely paradoxical nature of DNA, where the bio-light is said to be stored.

> In quantum physics, quantum coherence means that subatomic particles are able to cooperate. These subatomic waves or particles not only know about each other, but also are highly interlinked by bands of common electromagnetic fields, so that they can communicate together. They are like a multitude of tuning forks that all begin resonating together. As the waves get into phase or synch, they begin acting like one giant wave and one giant subatomic particle. It becomes difficult to tell them apart. Many of the weird quantum effects seen in a single wave apply to the whole. Something done to one of them will affect the others.
>
> Coherence establishes communication. It's like a subatomic telephone network. The better the coherence, the finer the telephone network and the more refined wave patterns have a telephone. The end result is also a bit like a large orchestra. All the photons are playing together but as individual instruments that are able to carry on playing individual parts.

---

(2013): 1-48; Beverly Rubik, "The Biofield: Bridge Between Mind and Body," *Cosmos and History* 11 (2015): 83-96; Shamini Jain et al., "Indo-Tibetan Philosophical and Medical Systems: Perspectives on the Biofield," *Global Adv Heath Med.* 4 (2015): 16-24.

[841] Bischof, "Biophotons – The Light in Our Cells," 2.

[842] Van Wijk and Van Wijk, "An Introduction,"78: "an envelope of radiation surrounding living organisms".

[843] Rajendra P. Bajpai, "Biophotonic Route for Understanding Mind, Brain and the World," *Cosmos and History* 11 (2015): 192 [art.=189-200].

Nevertheless, when you are listening, it's difficult to pick out any one instrument.[844]

In 2009 Japanese scientists successfully imaged the biophoton emission of five healthy male volunteers in their 20s using a cryogenic change-coupled device (CCD) camera (Plate 14). They affirmed that "the human body directly and rhythmically emits light" and "literally glimmers."[845] But these researchers found something more: the intensity of the emissions coordinates with the sun's daily journey.

> the photon emission intensity on the face and upper body appeared to display time-dependent changes. We plotted total photon emission intensity over the body and face against time, averaged across the 5 volunteers (…). Photon emission was weak in the morning, increased in the afternoon and peaked in the late afternoon (ca 16:00) (…). These data strongly suggest that there is a diurnal rhythm of photon emission from the human body…Photon emission formed a peak at late afternoon, then gradually decreased and stayed low at 1:00–7:00 AM in a constantly exposed light condition (400 lux), indicating the diurnal rhythm of photon might be caused by endogenous circadian mechanism.[846]

There is thus an association between our bio-light and sunlight. We will look deeper into this relationship below. But we are reminded of the "Sun God" of ancient religions with His body of light. The strength of our bio-light is described as ultra weak. That's the difference between humanity on the one hand and the Sun God (Ra, Brahma, Allah The Original Man) on the other hand: God's biophoton emission was and is Ultra Strong, but because of the Fall of Man our biophoton emission is today Ultra Weak.[847] The strengthening of our biophoton emissions from ultra weak to

---

[844] Lynne McTaggart, *The Field: The Quest for the Secret Force of the Universe* (HarperCollins e-books, 2001) 43.
[845] Masaki Kobayashi1, Daisuke Kikuchi, Hitoshi Okamura, "Imaging of Ultraweak Spontaneous Photon Emission from Human Body Displaying Diurnal Rhythm," *PLoS One* 4 (2009): 1-4.
[846] Masaki Kobayashi, Daisuke Kikuchi and Hitoshi Okamura, "Imaging of Ultraweak Spontaneous Photon Emission from Human Body Displaying Diurnal Rhythm," *PLoS one* 4 (2009): 1-4.
[847] On this Fall of Man (The Black God) see True Islam, *The Book of God: An Encyclopedia of Proof that the Black Man is God* (Atlanta: A-Team Publishing, 2007) 162-173.

Ultra Strong has been equated with the rising of the *kundalini* "serpent fire" from the first (base) chakra to the seventh or brain chakra spoken of in Yoga tradition and the realization of our coherent lightbody.

> active kundalini means an "increase" in bio-light. Thus we can play around with the idea of activated DNA giving off increased biophotons and how *alchemical transmutation of the flesh might proceed from the physics of coherent biophoton radiation to biochemistry*. The transmuting body has a higher rate of cell growth and division and so photon emissions are higher. Yet, unlike illness or cancer (where the photon emissions lose coherence - WM) this higher frequency of emissions is likely to be more coherent and exhibit a particular morphic resonance...Regarding biophotons and spiritual luminosity, researchers found that extra biophotons are released from damaged, diseased or dying lifeforms and they explained this as an attempt by the organism to heal itself (photo repair – WM). The higher metabolism generated from this healing resulted in an observable increase in biophoton emissions. Since the metamorphic biology of kundalini constitutes greatly amplified healing (wholing), this increased metabolism is the reason for the brightening of the lightbody and the "glow" of transmuting individuals. (Hence the Shining Ones).[848]

It has been suggested that this bio-light shines light - pun intended – on the purpose of so-called "Junk DNA":

> From all these investigations it can be concluded, that merely a minuscule portion (nearly 2%) of the hereditary, genetic material (DNA) in the cell nucleus was needed for the build-up and regulation of cell processes. All the experiments and computations performed unravel the major task of junk DNA. It seems obvious that these genetic structures, which were believed to be functionless until now, are in charge of the supervision of

---

[848] Jana Dixon, **Biology of Kundalini: Exploring the Fire of Life** (Lulu Publishing, 2008) 321, 326. On *kundalini* see also Thomas McEvilley, "The Spinal Serpent," **RES: Anthropology and Aesthetics** 24 (1993): 67-77. On the relation between the biophoton field and the Chinese *Qi*/Japanese *Ki* see Roeland van Wijk, Jan van der Greef, and Eduard van Wijk, "Human Ultraweak Photon Emission and the *Yin Yang* Concept of Chinese Medicine," **Journal of Acupuncture Meridian Studies** 3 (2010): 221-231; Majid Avijgan and Mahtab Avijgan, "The Infrastructure of the Integrative Human Body; Qi/Dameh, Qi Movement/*Rouh* and Zheng/*Mezadj* – Scientific Base," **International Journal of Integrative Medicine** 1 (2013): 1-9; idem, "Can Primo Vascular System (Bong Han Duct System) be a Basic Concept for Qi Production?" **International Journal of Integrative Medicine** 1 (2013): 20-.

the highly complex machinery inside the cell by biophotonic action of DNA as proposed by Herbert Fröhlich almost fifty years ago.[849]

There is good evidence that this bio-light plays an important – some say vital – role in biological processes including brain function. Some believe that this light is the "conductor" of the chemical orchestra that is the human organism: this bio-light regulates and coordinates life processes by transmitting signals at the speed of light, activating the biochemical processes and organizing matter.[850] According to Popp, "Biological phenomena like intracellular and intercellular communication, cell growth and differentiation, interaction among biological systems...and microbial infections can be understood in terms of biophotons."[851] The *MIT Technology Review* summarizes the state of things in 2010:

> it looks very much as if many cells use light to communicate. There's certainly evidence that bacteria, plants and even kidney cells communicate in this way...[I]nteresting evidence is beginning to emerge that light may well play an important role in neuronal functions.[852]

---

[849] Hugo J. Niggli, "Biophotons: Ultraweak Light Impulses Regulate Life Processes in Aging," *Journal of Gerontology & Geriatric Research* 3 (2014): 5 [art.=1-7]; Maricela Yip and Pierre Madl, "The Light of Life – Biophotonics," Paper, December 2006, pp.1-10 (3).

[850] Bischof, "Biophotons – The Light in Our Cells," 3: "This coherent biophoton field which permeates and envelops the solid body is assumed to regulate and control all the life processes in the organism. It is a holographic field of standing waves which is able, through a broad spectrum of frequencies and polarisations and in close interplay with all material structures, to transmit signals with the speed of light to any place in the organism and activate or to inhibit biochemical processes, to organize matter, and much more."

[851] Fritz-Albert Popp, "Properties of biophotons and their theoretical implications," *Indian Journal of Experimental Biology* 41 (2003): 391-402 (391).

[852] S.N. Mayburov, "Photon emission and quantum signalling in biological systems," *EPJ Web of Conferences* 95 (2015): 1-8; idem, "Photonic Communication in Biological Systems," *Vestn. Samar. Gos. Tekhn. Univ. Ser. Fiz.-Mat. Nauki* 2 (2011): 260-265; n.a. "The Puzzling Role of Biophotons in the brain," *MIT Technology Review* December 17, 2010. On the role of biophotons in cellular communication see also Yan Sun, Chao Wang and Jiapei Dai, "Biophotons as neural communication signals demonstrated by *in situ* biophoton autography," *Photochemical & Photobiological Sciences* 9 (2010): 315-322; F. Grass, H. Klima, and S. Kasper, "Biophotons, microtubules and CNS, is our brain a 'Holographic computer'? *Medical Hypotheses* 62 (2004): 169-172.

## II. The Science of the Power of God in the Black Man's Brain

The biophotons of the human brain and their role in neural functioning are of particular significance for our discussion. There is evidence suggesting that, while biophotons are stored in the cell's DNA, this bio-light actually originates within the brain's microtubules, the major part of the cytoskeleton or skeletal structure of the cell. The cytoskeleton is like the scaffolding within and the structural support of the brain cell. It is also the cell's nervous system. The cytoskeleton of brain cells is made up of hollow tube-like structures called microtubules. Microtubules are themselves composed of connected protein sub-units called tubulins. The tubulin is an intrinsically fluorescent molecule, the fluorescence originating with the eight tryptophan residues that each tubulin contains.[853] Yes, the same tryptophan that metabolizes serotonin! "Tryptophan is the most highly suited amino acid for transferring electrons and exchanging photons, as it has the greatest electron resonance and is thus the most fluorescent..."[854] This network of eight tryptophan residues, spatially arranged within each tubulin geometrically similar to the seven chromophores in photosynthetic proteins, gives tubulin a chlorophyll-type architecture similar to that observed in light harvesting complexes.[855] In fact Tryptophan is quite plant-like.

> Tryptophan's ancient story can be traced back to plants. In fact, tryptophans always played a critical role in life processes, because of its ability to convert solar energy (photons) into biological energy... The conversion of electromagnetic energy (photons) derived from the Sun, requires capturing a light wave and the loss of a valence electron: the indole ring is the most efficient molecule for doing exactly this and the most sensitive to blue light (450 nm)... [I]n plants, tryptophan does not

---

[853] P.S. Sardar et al., "Luminescence studies of perturbation of tryptophan residues of tubulin in the complexes of tubulin colchicine and colchicine analogues," *Biochemistry* 18 (2007): 14544-56;

[854] Travis J.A. Craddock, Avner Priel and Jack A. Tuszynski, "Keeping time: Could quantum beating in microtubules be the basis for the neural synchrony related to consciousness?" *Journal of Integrative Neuroscience* 13 (2014): 293-311 (300).

[855] Travis John Adrian Craddock et al., "The Feasibility of Coherent Energy Transfer in Microtubules," *Journal of the Royal Society – Interface* 11 (2014): 1-9.

only convert solar electromagnetic energy into biological energy but provides serotonin (or auxin, etc.) in order to carry out movements toward the source of energy[856].

It is tryptophan's signature structure, the indole ring (a six-sided ring fused to a five-sided ring), which is the source of its photosynthetic properties.

> The indole ring structure of tryptophan and serotonin captures light energy and converts it to biological energy by loss of an electron (oxidation)... The creation of the indole structure served an important function in the start of aerobic life on the earth. The conversion of energy (photons) derived from the sun into biological energy requires capturing a light wave and the loss of an electron. Interestingly, the indole ring is the most efficient molecule for doing exactly this and most sensitive to blue light (450 nm) (...). Most proteins are endowed with an intrinsic UV fluorescence because they contain aromatic amino acids, specifically phenylalanine, histamine, tyrosine, and tryptophan. Of these aromatic amino acids, tryptophan has the highest fluorescence quantum yield overshadowing markedly the emissions of the other two. Tryptophan emission maxima in proteins can vary from 332 to 342 nm depending on the protein. Free tryptophan has a characteristic fluorescence emission at 350–360 nm (...). Absorption of blue light waves is able to excite the indole structure so that it loses one of the electrons from its indole ring structure, it becomes oxidized... Tryptophan's ability to capture light is used by nearly all proteins (e.g., chlorophyll, rhodopsin, and skin pigment cells) which capture light and convert it to biological energy...Tryptophan was always a key to life because of its ability to convert solar energy into biological energy... Plants are extremely efficient at capturing light because they were extremely efficient at making tryptophan. [857]

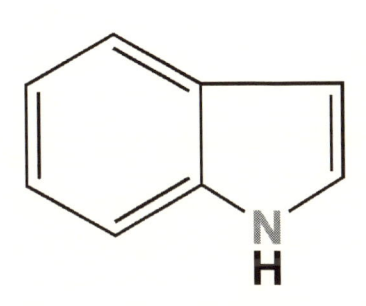

Because serotonin possesses a similar indole ring structure it is suggested that it is capable of the same photosynthesizing

---

[856] Lucio Tonello et al., "On the possible quantum role of serotonin in consciousness," *Journal of Integrative Neuroscience* 11 (2015): 1-14 (5-6).
[857] Efrain C. Azimitia, "Serotonin and Brain: Evolution, Neuroplasticity, and Homeostasis," *International Review of Neurobiology* 77 (2007): 32, 33-35 [art.=31-56].

function as tryptophan.[858] This makes the scientific assault on the serotonergic system of Black boys even more significant. In any case, the tubulins with their networks of intrinsically fluorescent tryptophans might make microtubules a natural source of luminance. It has already been argued that the brain's microtubules play an important role in the transfer of electrical signals and energy.[859] Recent research suggests however that microtubules are also involved in the creation and transference from cell to cell of bio-light as well.[860] A number of investigators believe that the hollow core of microtubules act as a QED (quantum electrodynamic) cavity.[861] Majid Rahmana of Shahid Bahonar University of Kerman, Iran and colleagues suggest that microtubules act as wave guides channeling light from one part of a cell to another. Light channeled by microtubules can help co-ordinate activities in different parts of the brain, they suggest.[862] "It's certainly true that electrical activity is synchronized over

---

[858] Tonello et al., "On the possible quantum role of serotonin" 5-6, 10 suggests "serotonin...could be an important player in the photon dynamics in biological systems" and "Serotonin's chemical structure, in particular its indole rings, is very analogous to that of tryptophan and hence a similar form may lead to similar functions."

[859] Travis John Adrian Craddock et al., "The Feasibility of Coherent Energy Transfer in Microtubules," *Journal of the Royal Society - Interface* 11 (2014): 1-9.

[860] Maricela Yip and Pierre Madl, "The Light of Life – Biophotonics," Paper, December 2006, pp.1-10 (4): "the microtubules of the cytoplasm plays a vital role in the propagation of the biophotonic emissions originating from the cell nucleus, and...they conduct biophotonic pulses to neighboring cells and to the extra-cellular matrix."

[861] N. E. Mavromatos and D. V. Nanopoulos, "On Quantum Mechanical Aspects of Microtubules," *International Journal of Modern Physics B*, 12 (February 1998): 517-542; Majid Rahnama et al., "Emission of Mitochondrial Biophotons and their Effects on Electrical Activity of Membrane via Microtubules," *Journal of Integrative Neuroscience* 10 (March 2011): 65-88; A. Nistreanu, "Collective Behavior of Water Molecules in Microtubules," in *3rd International Conference on Nanotechnologies and Biomedical Engineering*, ed. Victor Sontea and Ion Tiginyanu (Volume 55 of the series IFMBE Proceedings; Singapore: Springer, 2016) 473-477.

[862] Majid Rahnama et al., "Emission of Mitochondrial Biophotons and their Effects on Electrical Activity of Membrane via Microtubules," *Journal of Integrative Neuroscience* 10 (March 2011): 65-88.

distances that cannot be easily explained. Electrical signals travel too slowly to do this job, so something else must be at work."[863]

Within each of the microtubule subunits, the tubulins, there are reportedly uniquely ordered super-conductive water molecules (it is said that these ordered water molecules increase conductivity 1000 times).[864] Together with these unique water molecules within these nanotubes (tubulins) is said to be a *superradiance*, defined as a quantized electromagnetic radiance or electromagnetic field inside the microtubules.[865] The tryptophan in the tubulins might be involved in this radiance. This quantum system of ordered water molecules and superradiance confined within the hollow core of the tubulin subunits gives the microtubules the ability to transform any incoherent energy into coherent photons, it is believed.[866]

> the quantum dynamical system of water molecules and the quantized electromagnetic field confined inside the hollow microtubule core can manifest a specific collective dynamic called superradiance by which the microtubule can transform any incoherent, thermal and disordered molecular, electromagnetic or atomic energy into coherent photons inside the microtubule... Neurons (and other cells) may contain microscopic coherent optical supercomputers with enormous capacity like the fictional but famous HAL 9000 of '2001: A Space Odyssey' with holographic memory manipulation...each microtubule in the cytoskeletal structure of brain cells, that is, neurons and astrocytes, may play an important role in the optical information processing regimen of brain function as a superradiant device which converts the macroscopic disordered

---

[863] "The Puzzling Role of Biophotons in the Brain," *MIT Technology Review* December 17, 2010.

[864] Satyajit Sahu et al., "Atomic water channel controlling remarkable properties of a single brain microtubule: Correlating single protein to its supramolecular assembly," *Biosensors and Bioelectronics* 47 (2013): 141-148; Nistreanu, "Collective Behavior."

[865] Mari Jibu et al., "Quantum optical coherence in cytoskeletal microtubules: implications for brain function," *BioSystems* 32 (1994): 195-209.

[866] Jibu et al., "Quantum optical coherence," 199-200; Nistreanu, "Collective Behavior"; Elsevier, "Discovery of quantum vibrations in 'microtubules' inside brain neurons supports controversial theory of consciousness," *Science Daily* January 16, 2014; Stuart Hameroff and Roger Penrose, "Consciousness on the Universe: A review of the 'Orch OR' theory," *Physics of Life Review* 11 (2014): 39-78; Stuart R. Hameroff, "Quantum Coherence in Microtubules: A Neural Basis for Emergent Consciousness," *Journal of Consciousness Studies* 1 (1994): 91-118

dynamics of water molecules and protein molecules into the long-range ordered dynamics of water molecules and a quantized electromagnetic field involving a pulse mode emission of coherent photons. In other words, each microtubule is a coherent optical encoder in a dense microscopic optical computing network in the cytoplasm of each brain cell, if such a network is realized in actual cytoplasmic structure... the brain is essentially a dense assembly of microscopic and elaborated optical computing networks of microtubules in the cytoskeletal structure of brain cells... the quantum dynamical system of water molecules and the quantized electromagnetic field confined inside the hollow microtubule core manifests a specific collective dynamics called superradiance by which coherent photons are created inside the microtubule.[867]

The case is thus made that biophotons are originated inside the quantum cavity of the hollow tubulins of the microtubules, and these quantum mechanics are "eerily similar" to plant photosynthesis.[868] In these quantum cavities incoherent energy is belived to be transformed into coherent bio-light that carries information throughout the organism and regulates biological processes. It has even been argued strongly that *consciousness* is also a product of quantum processes that occur in the microtubules.[869]

---

[867] Mari Jibu et al., "Quantum optical coherence in cytoskeletal microtubules: implications for brain function," **BioSystems** 32 (1994): 195-209 (199-200, 205, 208). On the possible role of photons transmitting information stored in the tubulins throughout the organism see Mohsen Ostovari, Abolfazi and Alireza Mehdizadeh, "Entanglement Between Bio-Photons and Tubulins in Brain: Implications for Memory Storage and Information Processing," *NeuroQuantology* 3 (2014): 350-355. On the suspected "powerful light absorbing system in cells in order to convert light energy into biochemical signals" see Hugo J. Niggli, "Temperature dependence of ultraweak photon emission in fibroblastic differentiation after irradiation with artificial sunlight," *Indian Journal of Experimental Biology* 41 (2003): 419-423.
[868] Craddock et al., "Feasibility of Coherent Energy Transfer in Microtubules."
[869] Stuart R. Hameroff, "Quantum Coherence in Microtubules: A Neural Basis For Emergent Consciousness?" **Journal of Consciousness Studies** 1 (1994): 91-118; idem, "Consciousness, Microtubules, & 'Orch OR': A Space Odyssey," *Journal of Consciousness Studies* 21 (2014): 126-53; Stuart Hameroff and Roger Penrose, "Consciousness on the universe: A review of the 'Orch OR' theory," **Physics of Life Reviews** 11 (2014): 39-78; Elsevier, "Discovery of quantum vibrations in 'microtubules' inside brain neurons supports controversial theory of consciousness," *Science Daily* January 16, 2014.

There is scientific evidence that this bio-light is the material agent through which the power of God in man is realized. Dr. Ernesto Bonilla, neuroscientist from the Venezuelan Institute for Scientific Research, published an important paper in 2008 entitled, "Evidence about the Power of Intention."[870] What is intention? Intension is Will, which the Honorable Brother Minister Farrakhan describes in the Study Guide "Building the Will" as: "the faculty of conscious and deliberate action." The Minister teaches us that this is *the* Divine Faculty within humans that distinguishes us from all other creation because the Will of God is the Power of God behind the creation and maintenance of the universe, and the human will is God's essence in us, his gift to us. Look at what the science now says about Will and Intention. Dr. Bonilla's neurological investigations revealed:

> Intention is defined as a directed thought to perform a determined action. Thoughts targeted to an end can affect inanimate objects and practically all living things from unicellular organisms to human beings. *The emission of light particles (biophotons) seems to be the mechanism through which an intention produces its effects.* All living organisms emit a constant current of photons as a mean to direct instantaneous nonlocal signals from one part of the body to another and to the outside world. Biophotons are stored in the intracellular DNA. When the organism is sick changes in biophotons emissions are produced. *Direct intention manifests itself as an electric and magnetic energy producing an ordered flux of photons. Our intentions seem to operate as highly coherent frequencies capable of changing the molecular structure of matter.* For the intention to be effective it is necessary to choose the appropriate time. In fact, living beings are mutually synchronized and to the earth and its constant changes of magnetic energy. *It has been shown that the energy of thought can also alter the environment.* Hypnosis, stigmata phenomena and the placebo effect can also be considered as types of intention, as instructions to the brain during a particular state of consciousness. Cases of spontaneous cures or of remote healing of extremely ill patients represent instances of an exceedingly great intention to control diseases menacing our lives. The intention to heal as well as the beliefs of the sick person on the efficacy of the healing influences promote his healing.

Other studies have shown as well that focused mental intention increases the level of biophontons: "Preliminary

---

[870] Ernesto Bonilla, "Evidence about the power of intention," *Investigación clinica* 49 (2008): 595-615

evidence...suggests that human focused intention triggers biophotons emission that could represent the carrier of the interaction with electronic apparatuses."[871] Biophotons then, as the carriers of our intentions that can affect the physical environment around us, are the *executers of the power of God* deposited in man. As the Honorable Elijah Muhammad explained, the ability to have an idea and bring it into existence *is God* in Man:

> Everything that we think is necessary, we can produce it and bring it to reality. If this house is sitting in my mind, but not yet built, I can bring it out of my mind into reality. That's the God.[872]

And this power to conceive (intend) and achieve through the imposing of our will makes us God: "You are walking around looking for a God to bow to and worship. You are the God!"[873] "the God is Yourself,"[874] Muhammad teaches. So these biophotons, which carry our intention to the outside world, would be the agents of the power of God in Man.

---

[871] Patrizio Tressoldi et al., "Mental interaction at distance on a Photomultiplier: a pilot study," Paper. October 24, 2014; Joey M. Caswell, Blacke T. Dotta and Michael A. Persinger, "Cerebral Biophoton Emission as a Potential Factor in Non-Local Human-Machine Interaction," **NeuroQuantology** 1 (2014): 1-11; William T. Joines, Stephen B. Baumann, and John G. Kruth, "Electromagnetic Emission From Humans During Focused Intent," **Journal of Parapsychology** 76 (2012): 275-293; B.T. Dotta, K.S. Saroka and M.A. Persinger, "Increased photon emission from the head while imagining light in the dark is correlated with changes in electroencephalographic power: Support for Bókkon's biophoton hypothesis," **Neuroscience Letters** (2012): 1-4; idem, "Bright light transmits through the brain: Measurement of photon emissions and frequently-dependent modulation of spectral electroencephalographic power," **World Journal of Neuroscience** 3 (2013): 10-16.
[872] Elijah Muhammad, *100 Answers to the Most Uncommon 100 Questions*, compiled by Nasir Makr Hakim (Phoenix: Secretarius MEMPS Publications, 2012) 3.
[873] Muhammad, *Our Savior Has Arrived*, 35.
[874] Muhammad, *Our Savior Has Arrived*, 180.

III.     *Melanin and the Power of God: The Black Man as Apex*

Melanin transforms ultraviolet (UV) light energy into heat, a process known as ultrafast internal conversion. Over 99% of the UV radiation is converted from potentially genotoxic (DNA damaging) UV light into harmless heat. But there is evidence that melanin also mediates the direct conversion of thermal energy into electric field energy. Thus, not only is melanin a sunscreen shielding light-sensitive tissue from the damaging effects of UV light, it is also a natural solar panel helping to convert light into metabolic energy. "In other words, melanized tissue within our body may be capable of 'ingesting' sunlight, and not unlike plants, using the 'harvested' light in biologically useful ways."[875] Chlorophyll is the light-harvesting molecule in plants. We now know that chlorophyll's real counterpart in humans is the melanin molecule. In a ground breaking article Arturo S. Herrera and colleagues showed that, in contrast to the classical ATP-focused and glucose- and mitochondria-centric view of cellular bioenergetics, it is *melanin* that is responsible for generating most of the body's energy: over 90% of cell energy requirements are met by the chemical energy released through the dissociation of water molecules by melanin. Melanin seems to be the body's chlorophyll and like it can absorb electromagnetic radiation and use the energy:

> the intrinsic property of melanin to transform photon energy into chemical energy through the dissociation of water molecule, a role performed supposedly only by chlorophyll in plants…Our body is made up of trillions of energy dependent cells, thanks to the intrinsic property of melanin to transform light energy into chemical energy. The energy that emanates from the melanin in the form of molecular hydrogen and high energy electrons is able to account for the energy required for every single biochemical reaction that cell's life requires.[876]

---

[875] Sayer Ji, "Does Skin Act Like A Natural Solar-Panel?" *The Sleuth Journal* December 19, 2015.
[876] Arturo S. Herrera, "Beyond Mitochondria, What Would be the Energy Source of the Cell?" *Central Nervous System Agents in Medical Chemistry* 15 (2015): 32-41 (32, 40).

But melanin is even more extraordinary than this, it turns out. Not only does it absorb and transform visible light to our benefit, but melanin is radioprotective (protects against ionizing radiation, i.e. X-rays and gamma rays) and it absorbs ionizing radiation and makes it useful. A most amazing experiment was conducted by A. Kunwar et al.: they administered doses of melanin to mice and then exposed them and a control group to 6-7 Grays of gamma radiation. The mice with melanin increased their 30-day survival by 100%![877] Melanin is thus an effective radioprotector protecting organisms from radiotoxicity, but it also transforms some of this ionizing radiation into metabolically useful energy. This is proved by the melanin-rich fungi species (such as *Cryptoroccus neoformans*) that have colonized the walls and surrounding soil of the still radioactive Chernobyl meltdown reactor site. These black fungi use their melanin to absorb and transform the radiation to use as food for growth.[878] This melanin-mediated process is thus described as an "alternative to photosynthesis," "with melanin playing the role of chlorophyll and ionizing radiation the role of visible light."[879]

With this realization that melanin is analogous to human chlorophyll which is capable of converting light and radiation into useful energy, it should come as no surprise that UV and visible light seem also to activate melanin to *induce the production of biophotons*.[880] This means that melanin facilitates the production of

---

[877] A. Kunwar et al. "Melanin, a promising radioprotector: Mechanisms of actions in a mice model," *Toxicology abd Applied Pharmacology* 264 (2012): 202-211.

[878] Ekaterina Dadachova et al., "Ionizing Radiation Changes the Electronic Properties of Melanin and Enhances the Growth of Melanized Fungi," *PLoS One* 5 (2007): 1-13.

[879] David Ewing Duncan, "Eating Radiation: A New Form of Energy?" *MIT Technology Review* May 29, 2007.

[880] Ankush Prasad and Pavel Pospíš, "Ultraweak photon emission induced by visible light and ultraviolent A radtion via photoactivated skin chromophores" *Journal of Biomedical Optics* 17 (2012): 1-8; Geoffrey Goodman and Dani Bercovich, "Melanin directly converts light for vertebrate metabolic use: Heuristic thoughts on birds, Icarus and dark human skin," *Medical Hypotheses* 71 (2008): 190-202; Masaki Kobayashi, Daisuke Kikuchi and Hitoshi Okamura, "Imaging of Ultraweak Spontaneous Photon Emission from Human Body Displaying Diurnal Rhythm," *PLoS one* 4 (2009): 1-4 (3); Yan Sun, Chao Wang and Jiapei Dai, "Biophotons as neural communication signals demonstrated by *in*

this bio-light and the more melanin an organism possesses, the more bio-light potential they have. And vice versa: the less melanin an organism has, the *less* bio-light potential they have. The lack of melanin means the inability to convert sunlight into metabolic energy. As Ekaterina Dadachova et al. note: "the ability of melanin to capture electromagnetic radiation combined with its remarkable oxidation-reduction properties may confer upon *melanotic organisms* the ability to harness radiation for metabolic energy (emphasis added)."[881] This makes *melanotic organisms* the dominant lifeforms:"Melanized microorganisms are often the dominating species in certain extreme environments."[882] But not just melanized microorganisms but human melanotic organisms as well. This puts the Black man at the apex and the white man at the nadir in terms of access to this Power of God, light.

This explains how it is that the Black Man is naturally the dominant human group on the planet and it explains white supremacy's obsessive assault on the Black Man. In this regard the experiment with melanin-fed mice led to a realization with frightening implications for Black people. Kunwar et al. conclude that study with this: "diets rich in melanin may be beneficial to overcome radiation toxicity in humans."[883] In other words: organisms that don't naturally possess sufficient melanin can eat melanin – *or eat melanotic organisms* – and by so doing benefit from the radioprotective properties of the melanin. It is impossible to not consider in this light the fact of America's *consumptive culture* vis-à-vis the Black male. The phenomenon of the *Paracelcian corpse* and European Christian cannibalism and spirit vampirism; the phenomenon of consumptive homoeroticism that characterized the American institution of slavery; and the ritual cannibalism that defined the Jim Crow lynchings of Black men in the American South; all of this takes on new meaning in the light of the *dietary value of melanin and melanotic organisms*.

---

*situ* biophoton autography," ***Photochemical & Photobiological Sciences*** 9 (2010): 315-322.
[881] Dadachova et al., "Ionizing Radiation Changes," 11.
[882] Dadachova et al., "Ionizing Radiation Changes," 1.
[883] Kunwar et al. "Melanin, a promising radioprotector," 21.

What I am suggesting – that whites cannibalized Black people hoping to harvest their spirit by harvesting their melanin and thus their bio-light potential – is not farfetched. We know that in order to strengthen our bio-light we must literally *eat* and *ingest light*. Unprocessed green leaf foods are great stores of bio-light as a result of the photosynthesis process. As Jane Dixon explains:

> Light, of course, was present in plants, the source of energy used during photosynthesis. When we eat plant foods, it must be...that we take up the photons and store them. Say that we consume some broccoli. When we digest it, it is metabolized into carbon dioxide ($CO_2$) and water, plus the light stored from the sun and present in photosynthesis. We extract the $CO_2$ and eliminate the water, but the light, an electromagnetic wave, must get stored. When taken in by the body, the energy of these photons dissipates so that it is eventually distributed over the entire spectrum of electromagnetic frequencies, from the lowest to the highest. This energy becomes the driving force for all the molecules in our body.[884]

Melanin may provide a similar scenario. Hugo Niggli suggested that melanin may absorb and store biophotons.[885] It is conceivable that whites who cannibalized Black men did so (and do so) believing that they are drawing benefit from the melanin they are consuming.

## THE THIMEROSAL CONNECTION

What does this have to do with autism or the thimerosal conspiracy? The MMR vaccine is more than an attack on the mental health of Black boys. Thimerosal disrupts more than the serotonergic system. It can be viewed as a specific assault on the Godhood of the Black male, which has its seat in the Black male's brain. The mercury in the MMR vaccine causes neuron degeneration. But that is only half of the story. Mercury specifically assaults and deconstructs that part in our brain cells - the tubulins/microtubules - that is believed by a number of

---

[884] McTaggart, *The Field*, 43.
[885] Hugo J. Niggli, "Biophoton Re-emission. Studies in Carcinogenic Mouse Melanoma Cells," in *Recent Advances in Biophoton Research and its Applications*, ed. Fritz Albert-Popp and Qiao Gu, K.H. Li (Singapore: World Scientific, 1992): 231-243.

scientists to be the "factory" in which human biophotons or bio-light is produced. Mercury vapor (Hg⁰) inhibits the tubulins from binding together to form the necessary microtubules – it prevents polymerization.[886] Mercury exposure also causes disintegration or "disassembling" of the microtubules.[887] Mercury ions attach to neurons and cause microtubules to disassemble. Less microtubules means less bio-light produced. The mercury in the MMR vaccine specifically disrupts the production of Divine Light in the brain and disrupts the transmission of that Divine Light from cell to cell.

It should not be assumed that this specific targeting of tubulins/microtubules is incidental or accidental. As far back as 1984 – six to seven years before the new vaccination schedule unloaded an enormous amount of microtubule-degenerative thimerosal on American children - scientists were experimenting with various chemical agents and testing their effectiveness in inhibiting tubulin polymerization. Paul Horowitz and colleagues from the University of Texas in 1984 studied the compound Bis-ANS, a common contaminant of commercial supplies, as a "novel and potent inhibitor of microtubule assembly."[888] This chemical

---

[886] Polymerization is the chemical process in which relatively small molecules, called monomers, combine to produce a large chainlike or network molecule, called a polymer. In this case it means tubulin molecules polymerize or chemically combine into microtubules.

[887] Adam Askew, "The Effects of Mercury on Microtubule Polymerization in Axons of *Gallus gallus* neurons," **Wheaton Journal of Neurobiology Research** 5 (2013): 1-4; S. Chitra and K. Jayaprakash, "Effect of Mercury on microtubular protein in brain cells of fish *Labeo rohita*," **Journal of Academia and Industrial Research** 2 (2013): 50-52; M. Lawton et al. "Reduced tubulin tyrosination as an early marker of mercury toxicity in differentiating N2a cells," *Toxicology in Vitro* 21 (2007): 1258-1261; C.C. Leong, N.I. Syed, F.L. Lorscheider, "Retrograde degeneration of neurite membrane structural integrity of nerve growth cones following in vitro exposure to mercury," *Neuroreport* 12 (2001):733-7; James C. Pendergrass et al., "Mercury Vapor Inhalation Inhibits Binding of GTP to Tubulin in Rat Brain: Similarity to a Molecular Lesion in Alzheimer Diseased Brain,"*NeuroToxicology* 18 (1997): 315-324.

[888] Paul Horowitz, Veena Prasad and Richard F. Luduena, "Bis(1,8-anilinonaphthalenesulfonate): A Novel and Potent Inhibitor of Microtubule," **The Journal of Biological Chemistry** 259 (1984): 14647-14650.

binds strongly to tubulin sites and blocks microtubule assembly.[889] The next year mercury itself was studied. In 1985 Daryl Vogel et al. studied methylmercury's (MeHg) role in the polymerization (assembly) and de-polymerization (disassembly) of microtubules and concluded: "These results show MeHg *in vitro* to be a potent microtubule assembly inhibitor."[890] Polly R. Sager and Tore L.M. Syversen's 1986 study affirmed: "one cellular insult caused by methylmercury in *developing brain* involves the disruption of microtubules."[891]

But not just methyl mercury but thimerosal (ethyl mercury) as well ill-effects the brains tubulins.[892] Thimerosal also prevents the polymerization or assembling of microtubules. Martin Brunner et al. in 1990 studied the effects of ten suspected spindle poisons (Colchicine, vinblastine, thimerosal, cadmium chloride, thiabendazole, chloral hydrate, hydroquinone, diazepam and econazole).[893] A spindle poison is a poison that disrupts cell division by affecting the protein threads that connect the centromere regions of chromosomes. Thimerosal not only proved to be a spindle poison but a microtubule inhibitor as well. In fact, M. Wallin and B. Hartley-Asp divided these ten suspected spindle

---

[889] See also Manjari Mazumdar et al., "Bis-ANS as a specific inhibitor for microtubule-associated protein-induced assembly of tubulin," *Biochemistry*, 31 (1992): 6470–6474 and further Shalini Srivastava et al., "C1, a highly potent novel curcumin derivative, binds to tubulin, disrupts microtubule network and induces apoptosis," *Bioscience Reports* 36 (2016): 1-15.

[890] Daryl Vogul, Robert L. Margolis and N. Karle Mottet, "The effects of methyl mercury binding to microtubules," *Toxicology and Applied Pharmacology* 80 (1985): 473-86; idem, "Analysis of methyl mercury binding sites on tubulin subunits and microtubules," *Pharmacol Toxicol* 64 (1989): 196-201.

[891] Polly R. Sager and Tore L. M. Syversen, "Disruption of microtubules by Methylmercury," in *The Cytoskelaton: A Target for Toxic Agents*, ed. Thomas W. Clarkson, Polly R. Sager, Tore L.M. Syverson (New York and London: Plenum Press, 1986) 97-116.

[892] M. Lawton et al. "Reduced tubulin tyrosination as an early marker of mercury toxicity in differentiating N2a cells," *Toxicology in Vitro* 21 (2007): 1258–1261; H. Alexandre et al., "Effect of taxol and okadaic acid on microtubule dynamics in thimerosal-arrested primary mouse oocytes: a confocal study,"*Biol Cell* 95 (2003): 407-414,

[893] Martin Brunner, Silvio Albertini and Friedrich E. Würgler, "Effects of 10 known or suspected spindle poisons in the *in vitro* porcine brain tubulin assembly assay," *Mutagenesis* 6 (1990): 65-70.

poisons into two categories: strong inhibitors and weak inhibitors. Three of those, including thimerosal, are a strong inhibitor of microtubule assembly.[894]

The thimerosal-laced MMR vaccine - and the thimerosal-laced flu vaccine given to pregnant women! - assaults the Black male brain, which is the greatest potential source of Divine Light on Earth. White Supremacy through its science is attacking the Black male brain in a myriad of ways, including at birth and before three years of age through vaccine injections that contain poisons which target these Black boys' serotonin and microtubules, both of which - when left alone - facilitate male dominance, social and divine.

---

[894] M. Wallin and B. Hartley-Asp, "Effects of potential aneuploidy inducing agents on microtubule in vitro," ***Mutat Res.*** 287 (1993): 17-22.

# 20 Creating the "Lady of the Races": Science and Black Homosexuality

I. *The Black "Sissy"*

"Men on Film" from the early 1990s comedy series *In living Color* (Fox)

University of Maryland professor Patricia Hill Collins' discussion of images and caricatures of Black masculinity in the media observes in her book, **Black Sexual Politics** (2005), that the now common "Black sissy" is a relatively new media phenomenon:

> This "punk," "sissy," or "faggot" may have its roots in an emasculated Uncle Tom, but it also operates as a new representation in the post-civil rights era. Given the virtual absence of representations of gay Black men in the past, these new representations enjoy a visibility within contemporary Black popular culture that is surprising...[895]

"a new representation in the post-civil rights era". The post-civil rights era saw the birth of "Operation Ferdinand," our term for the government's program to turn Black males

---

[895] Patricia Hill Collins, **Black Sexual Politics: African Americans, Gender, and the New Racism** (New York and London: Routledge, 2005) 172.

involved in social protests and racial riots into docile dullards through psychosurgery and pharmacological interventions. The Black docile dullard is a non-threat to the dominant white male. The Black Sissy is also. As Collins remarks:

> the sexual practices attributed to the Black 'sissy' do not constitute a credible threat to White heterosexual men because the presence of Black gay sexuality constitutes a feminized and therefore non-threatening Black masculinity. Representations of Black gay sexuality operate as further evidence that Black men are 'weak,' emasculated, and 'feminized' in relation to White men. Black gay sexuality is depicted as reflecting male submission or capitulation, especially those men who are penetrated like women. When joined to the broader theme of the Black buddy or sidekick, "faggots," "punks," and "sissies" constitute the extension of the seeming symbolic emasculation of middle-class Black men associated with images of Uncle Tom and Uncle Ben...
> On the other hand...[w]ithin the universe of Black masculinity, gay Black men pose a threat to a beleaguered Black male heterosexuality that strives to claim its place at the table dominated by representations of White-controlled masculinity. Within popular Black culture, the widespread caricature of Black gay men, thus making this sexuality visible, works to uphold constructions of authentic Black masculinity as being hyper-heterosexual...and protects hegemonic White masculinity.[896]

The media popular Black Sissy is just a modern version of the Negro as "Lady of the Races" propaganda. There is a key difference here though: The "Lady of the Races" claim was purely a propagandistic construction with no basis in reality, while the modern Black Sissy is not just a media construction but – as we shall show - is also a real *scientific creation*. That is to say, the Black Sissy - or the *actual* feminized Black male and even the Black homosexual - are likely phenomena born from the same sociopharmacological research that focused on serotonin manipulation that we have been discussing. The Black Sissy is a form of "Operation Ferdinand's" docile Black male who poses no threat to the current dominance hierarchy in America.

---

[896] Collins, *Black Sexual Politics*, 172-174.

II.     *A Horrendous Scientific Study of Sodomy and Black Boys*

Elizabeth Harrington of the ***Washington Free Beacon*** broke deplorable story in 2015:

> The National Institutes of Health (NIH) has spent over $400,000 studying the satisfaction levels of the first sexual experiences of young gay men. The four-year study, being conducted by Johns Hopkins University, is examining the "meaning and function" of first "penetrative same-sex sexual experiences"...
>
> "The goal of this project is to understand the meaning and function of first same-sex sexual experience and to prospectively be able to assess its impact on subsequent sexual experiences, young adult sexual health and health protective behaviors," the grant said.
>
> The project has cost taxpayers $410,265 so far, with funding not set to expire until May 2016. The study is also examining the satisfaction levels of young gay men during their first time...The study will also look at the amount of time between the first and second partner, depending on the "sexual satisfaction" of the first "PSSE."[897]

The study is entitled, "First and Subsequent Same-Sex Sexual Satisfaction and Behavior in Young AAMSM." The acronym "AAMSM" stands for "African American Men who have Sex with Men." But it is *not men* whose satisfaction with anal penetration is being "studied" here. The grant proposal reads:

> Little is known about the meaning and function of first same-sex experience in *AA adolescent men* and whether satisfaction with first penetrative same-sex experience impacts sexual trajectories.[898]

What exactly is an *adolescent man*? It is an oxymoron and an impossibility. The age group that is subsumed under this

---

[897] Elizabeth Harrington, "Feds Spent $410,265 Studying 'Satisfaction' Levels of Young Gay Men's First Time," *Washington Free Beacon* April 17, 2015.
[898] Renata A, Sanders, "First and Subsequent Same-Sex Sexual Satisfaction and Behavior in Young AAMSM." Project Information @ https://projectreporter.nih.gov/project_info_description.cfm?projectnumber=5 K23HD074470-03.

ridiculous designation seems to be either 15-19 or 15-24.[899] But the specific interest of the lead researcher Dr. Renata Arrington-Sanders, assistant professor of pediatrics at Johns Hopkins and a Black woman, seems to be with the younger age group: the adolescents rather than the men. Elsewhere (a parallel study?) she investigated Black boys who were sexually penetrated by older men (at least five years older).[900] Age 15 is reportedly the mean age Black boys tend to be penetrated/sodomized.[901] Johns Hopkins University invested over $400,000 to study how *satisfied* these Black boys were the first and second time they were *penetrated/sodomized* by a (older) man. Dr. Arrington-Sanders says further in her grant proposal:

> The research phase of the award is to explore the reasons for and satisfaction with first and subsequent penetrative same-sex sexual experiences (PSSE) and to examine the role of first PSSE on second and subsequent PSSEs in AA men (Study 1) and how social context impacts sexual satisfaction with first PSSE; how sexual satisfaction during first PSSE impacts time to second partner and satisfaction with second PSSE; and engagement in young adult sexual health protective behaviors during most recent sex (Study 2). Specific aim 1 is to identify the reasons for and satisfaction with first penetrative same-sex sexual experiences (PSSE) in 45 African American adolescent males in an in-depth baseline qualitative interview.

Why in the world is Johns Hopkins University so interested – almost a half million dollars of interest – in how "satisfied" adolescent Black boys are being anally penetrated by an older man the first, second or third time? One point of this study is the promotion of Black homosexuality: Dr. Arrington-Sanders et al want to combat "homonegativity" in the Black community and remove the stigma around homosexual anal sex. Why? This study

---

[899] Renata Arrington-Sanders et al, "The Role of Sexually Explicit Material (SEM) in the Sexual Development of Black Same-Sex-Attracted Men," **Arch Sex Behav** 44 (2015): 597-608; Jessica L. Oidtman, "Satisfaction at Sexual Debut and Sexual Risk Among Young Black Men Who Have Sex With Men," Masters thesis, Johns Hopkins University. Baltimore, Maryland. May 2015.

[900] Renata Arrington-Sanders, "Older Partner Selection in Young African American Men Who Have Sex with Men," **Journal of Adolescent Health** 52 (2013): 682-688.

[901] Oidtman, "Satisfaction at Sexual Debut," ii.

is no doubt anchored in the "The Man vs. Sodomized Boy" culture which began in ancient Greece and Rome and which also characterized the culture of the American slave master and slave. This country uses every means to reinforce the Black Man's "proper" place and role in the society: America's "Boy," i.e. the anally penetrated non-man, feminized and neutralized. This horrible "study" by Johns Hopkins University is designed to reinforce that, and the fact that the "study" is led by a Black woman no anomaly at all, unfortunately.

The promotion of homosexuality and the combating of "homonegavtivity" in the Black community have very harmful effects.

> Young Black men who have sex with men (YBMSM) living in the United States acquire human immunodeficiency virus (HIV) at a rate 3 times higher than their White male counterparts (Koblin et al., 2013), despite reporting comparable rates of condomless anal intercourse, substance use, and number of sex partners with unknown HIV serostatus (Millett et al., 2012). Stall et al. (2009) suggest that given the high HIV incidence and prevalence rates in YBMSM, approximately 60% of uninfected 18-year-old YBMSM living in the United States will become HIV-positive by the age of 40.[902]

In 2010 72% of all incident HIV infections in young people aged 13-24 were among men who had sex with men and 55% of those are young Black males.[903]

> Black men who have sex with men (MSM) are disproportionately affected by the HIV epidemic in the United States (US). Approximately one quarter of all new HIV infections in the US occur among Black MSM. Moreover, the Centers for Disease Control and Prevention (CDC) reports a 48% increase in HIV incidence among young black MSM between 2006 and 2009.[904]

---

[902] Renata Arrington-Sanders et al, "Context of First Same-Sex Condom Use and Nonuse in Young Black Gay and Bisexual Males," *Journal of Research on Adolescence* (2016): 1 [art.=1-16].

[903] Oidtman, "Satisfaction at Sexual Debut," 1.

[904] Risha Irvin, "Examining Levels of Risk Behaviors among Black Men Who Have Sex with Men (MSM) and the Association with HIV Acquisition," *PLoS ONE* 10 (2015): 1-8.

The promotion of young Black men having sex with other men is a health hazard. But that is precisely White Supremacy's point. After all, HIV is as much a product of American science as is the Black Sissy.[905] And the face of the AIDS victims changed – or *was changed* – from exclusively gay white to predominantly straight and gay Black. That is not an accident.

This puts into alarming perspective a 2012 Gallup poll study which showed that today, "Poor blacks and Asians are more likely to be gay than wealthier whites".[906] In the largest single study of the distribution of the lesbian, gay, bisexual and transgender population in the U.S. on record, Gallup found that a third of all who identified as LGBT were non-white, and the highest single percentage were African American or Black:

| | |
|---|---|
| Black | 4.6% |
| Asian | 4.3% |
| Hispanic | 4% |
| Caucasian | 3.2% |

---

[905] Leonard G. Horowitz, D.M.D., M.A., M.P.H., *Emerging Viruses. AIDS & Ebola: Nature, Accident or Intentional?* (Standpoint, Idaho: Tetrahedron, Inc., 1999); Alan Cantwell Jr, MD, "Gay Cancer, emerging viruses, and AIDS," *New Dawn* (Melbourne), September 1998, pp. 1-12; idem, *Queer Blood: The Secret AIDS Genocide Plot* (Los Angeles: Aries Rising Press, 1993); idem, *AIDS and the Doctors of Death: An Inquiry into the Origin of the AIDS Epidemic* (Los Angeles: Aries Rising Press, 1988); T. Curtis, "The Origin of AIDS" *Rolling Stone* Issue 626, March 19, 1992, pp. 54-63; Wesley Muhammad, *AIDS: The Genocide Project*, unpublished, 1997.

[906] Tom Leonard, " 'White people are less likely to be gay': Poll reveals African-American community has highest percentage of 'LGBT' adults in U.S.," *Daily Mail* October 19, 2012; Gary J. Gates and Frank Newport, "Special Report: 3.4% of U.S. Adults Identify as LGBT," *Gallup* October 18, 2012, 1-10.

They were mostly *young* (18-29). And while the percentage of young women (8.3%) doubled that of young men (4.6%), these percentages and the disproportionately higher representation of Black self-identifiers are startling. This study documented the *complete reversal* of the American homosexual profile: "This survey – based on interviews with more than 120,000 people – contradicts the perception that lesbians and gays are mostly white, urban and affluent..."[907] But this perception *was reality* until recently. However, somehow the profile of the American homosexual morphed from affluent white into poor black. But we don't have to search far to find the "somehow." This demographic shift in the American homosexual population can no doubt be attributed to the methods of sociopharmacology.

*Excursus: History of Johns Hopkins Nazi-like Experiments*

The context in which we are to understand this most heinous "study" of sodomy and satisfaction among young Black boys conducted by Johns Hopkins University is surely this institution's long history of racist experimentation and scientific "study" which had damaging effects on Black and Brown people, especially males. Johns Hopkins University in Baltimore has a long history of conducting racist and dangerous research on Black and Brown people. Starting in 1946, while the U.S. Public Health Service was conducting its infamous "Tuskegee Experiment" on unsuspecting Black men in Alabama, it was conducting a very similar experiment on our Brown family in Guatemala. Under its auspices Johns Hopkins worked with the Rockefeller Foundation and Bristol-Myers Squibb pharmaceutical group and they intentionally infected 1600 Guatemalans – orphans, prostitutes, prisoners, mental health patients – with sexually transmitted diseases: syphilis (696 infected), gonorrhea (772 infected) and chancres (142 infected). The stated purpose was to test the effectiveness of penicillin (made by Bristol-Myers Squibb). Prostitutes were infected with the STDs in order to spread them. Syphilis spirochetes were injected into the spinal fluid of some

---

[907] Leonard, " 'White people are less likely to be gay'"; Gates and Newport, "Special Report," 2.

subjects and gonorrhea pus from a male subject was injected into the eyes of a female psychiatric patient. Many subjects died while others passed the disease to their spouses and children.[908]

Equally abusive and racist was the Lead Abatement, Repair and Maintenance Study conducted between 1993-1995 by the Kennedy Krieger Institute (KKI) affiliated with Johns Hopkins University. The stated purpose of this study was to find cheaper and less hazardous ways to get rid of the lead that contaminated more than 100 000 homes in Baltimore city. But in the process the researchers deliberately exposed mainly Black children to high levels of lead, causing lead poisoning and even brain damage. Harriet Washington explains:

> Researchers approached black families in 108 units of decrepit housing encrusted with crumbling, peeling lead paint. Lead paint is a notorious cause of acute illness and chronic mental retardation in young children, who inhale the lead borne on the air and nibble the peeling paint chips, drawn by the appealing sweet taste of the lead...But the agenda of the KKI scientists did not include removing children from lead exposure, because they planned to use these children to evaluate new, cheaper lead-abatement techniques-of unknown efficacy-in old homes with peeling paint. Because scientists wanted to explore cheaper ways of eliminating the lead threat in the future, they purposely arranged with landlords to have children inhabit lead-tainted housing so that they could monitor changes in the children's lead levels as well as the brain and developmental damage that resulted from different kinds of lead-abatement programs. Scientists offered parents of children in these lead-laden homes incentives such as fifteen-dollar payments to cooperate with the study, without divulging that it placed their children at risk to lead exposure...KKI researchers simultaneously encouraged landlords of approximately 125 tainted housing units to rent to families with young children by paying for the lead abatement if the landlords rented to such families.[909]

The researchers identified lead-infested hotspots in the homes and concealed that information from the parents, allowing children to

---

[908] Sarah Gantz, "Judge dismisses $1 billion Guatemalan syphilis experiment case against Hopkins, others," *The Baltimore Sun* October 11, 2016; Ralph Ellis, "Guatemalans deliberately infected with STDs sue Johns Hopkins," *CNN* April 14, 2015; CNN Wire Staff, "Researchers infected Guatemalans with STDs, commission affirms," *CNN* September 1, 2011.
[909] Washington, *Medical Apartheid*, 291-292.

be exposed is such spots.[910] Regarding the incentives for the landlords Deborah Josefson of the *British Medical Journal* reported:

> Landlords were paid (largely by a government grant) from $1650 (...) to $7000 to partially remove lead paint by scraping off peeling paint, to paint over existing paint, or to add coverings. Residents were allowed, and in some cases encouraged, to remain in their homes while these techniques were going on. Lead levels of children living in the homes were periodically tested to monitor the efficacy of the various techniques.[911]

This experiment by Johns Hopkins was so callous and racist that the judge in the suit brought against KKI by some of the victimized families, Judge Dale Cathell, went so far as to compare this lead study to the Nazi experiments on concentration camp victims and even the Tuskegee Experiment, saying the study

> presents similar problems as those in the Tuskegee Syphilis Study conducted from 1932 until 1972...the intentional exposure of soldiers to radiation...the secret administration of LSD to soldiers by the CIA and the Army in the 1950s and 60s...and notorious use of "plague bombs" by the Japanese military in World War II.[912]

Indeed, Johns Hopkins University's history is replete with Nazi-type scientific racism and abuse.

### III. Lab Homo: The Scientific Manipulation of Sexuality

> *The Black male is being feminized...What about the rise of homosexuality and lesbianism? Is that a natural phenomenon? Are we born that way? Or is it a chemical reaction that makes us susceptible to ideas like that? We gotta think now, because we are dealing with a scientist of evil that is called in Scripture "Satan," and he's out to get us...I think if we check what we eat and check the pills that we use, we'll find out that some of us are absolutely being chemicalized as we are being feminized.* The Honorable Minister Farrakhan on The Breakfast Club, May 24, 2016.

---

[910] Washington, *Medical Apartheid*, 292.
[911] Deborah Josefson, "Johns Hopkins faces further criticism over experiments," *BMJ* 323 (September 2001): 531. See also Leiter and Herman, "Guinea Pig Kids" 32-33.
[912] Leiter and Herman, "Guinea Pig Kids" 33.

The "Negro as the Lady of the Races" propaganda and the thinking underpinning it fueled deliberate and consistent attempts from that day till this to transform the Black male into the actual "lady" of the races: to literally feminize him. These attempts were social (the disempowerment of the Black male in the home and the deliberate creation of the Black Matriarchy), cultural (the promotion of feminized Black male images such as Black actors and athletes in dresses), as well as scientific. Scientists have been inducing sexual inversion in many species since the 1950s and they now have mastered several methods to artificially feminize males and masculinize females physiologically, psychologically and behaviorally.

As far back as 1987 Lee Ellis and M. Ashley Ames published a remarkably candid and revealing article in which they discuss "Experimental Induction of Sexual Inversions," i.e. artificially causing sex reversal in both nonhumans and humans.[913] They report:

> In the past 30 years, a large array of sexual inversions have been experimentally induced in laboratory animals... Five basic methods for inducing sexual inversions of a neurological-behavioral nature have been documented in laboratory animals: (a) direct perinatal[914] androgen manipulation, (b) pharmacologically blocking or augmenting the perinatal effects of androgens, (c) maternal and neonatal exposure to androgen depressing emotional stress (d) the induction of immunity responses to androgens or other hormones involved in sexual differentiation, and, possibly, (e) sexual segregation during childhood...[A]ll aspects of mammalian anatomy, physiology, and behavior can be sexually inverted. Most, if not all, of the methods for causing sexual inversion involve altering androgen and/or other sex hormone levels while the various parts of the body are sexually differentiating...Even though sexual inversions are not induced in humans for *experimental* purposes, evidence has accumulated that many of the experiments conducted with laboratory animals have close parallels in humans...[A]though the kinds of *controlled* experiments carried out with a variety of other mammalian species have not been replicated in humans, "natural and inadvertent experiments" relevant to

---

[913] Lee Ellis and M. Ashley Ames, "Neurohormonal Functioning and Sexual Orientation: A Theory of Homosexuality-Heterosexuality," *Psychological Bulletin* 101 (1987): 233-258.
[914] Perinatal refers to the time period from a few weeks before birth to a few weeks after birth.

the process of sexual differentiation have been documented. Recent studies of these "experiments" point toward the same general conclusions as have been reached for other mammals: Sexual orientation is mainly the result of neurological factors that are largely determined prenatally, even though they do not fully manifest themselves until adolescence or adulthood (emphasis added).[915]

It must be pointed out here that, as it relates to the experimental induction of sexual inversion in humans, the authors are hedging. Such human experiments would of course be a violation of international law and thus could not be openly admitted, so we are informed only of "inadvertent experiments," whatever that means. The language smacks of "plausible deniability." Nevertheless, Ellis and Ames suggest to us that these nonhuman experiments point toward conclusions for humans too.

Among the methods enumerated by Ellis and Ames to experimentally invert or reverse sexuality and sexual behavior, they list the exposure of mothers and newborns to emotional stress that depresses androgen production (c). Androgen is the hormone that controls the development and maintenance of male characteristics in men, the opposite of estrogen which controls and maintains feminine characteristics in women. By manipulating the social environment and thus creating environmental stressors the scientists can alter androgen biosynthesis and induce homosexual behavior. In monkeys "inverted tendencies to mount and present (their rear end to other males) appear to have been either induced or at least augmented by manipulating social environments,"[916] and manipulating social environments and artificially inducing depression are among the methods of sociopharmacology.

Scientists have succeeded in weaponizing the immune system against a male fetus' masculinity. They induced an immunity response to androgens and other hormones involved in sexual differentiation (d). Ellis and Ames report on this particularly insidious method, developed in 1987. The method tricks the immune system into targeting for repression the hormones responsible for sex differentiation:

---

[915] Ellis and Ames, "Neurohormonal Functioning," 240, 247, 248.
[916] Ellis and Ames, "Neurohormonal Functioning," 243.

*Immunity* refers to the tendency for an organism's white blood cells to chemically attack foreign substances by building antibodies to those substances. A recently developed method for inverting sexual orientation in laboratory animals involves the induction of an immune response to one or more of the biochemicals necessary for sexual differentiation of the brain. Either the mother's or the individual animal's own immune system is induced to regard one of the biochemicals required for sexual differentiation as a foreign substance. The immune system then prevents sexual differentiation from taking place (or at least from taking place completely) by breaking down the "foreign chemicals" required to carry it out.[917]

The artificially induced antibodies that target the androgen/testosterone appeared to cross the placenta and saturate the fetus' blood system. In an experiment with rabbits who were mated and became pregnant after this procedure, "The male offspring of these mothers had genital structures, both internally and externally, that were distinctly [feminized/demasculinized], with the exception of the testes themselves, which were well formed and fully capable of producing male-typical levels of testosterone."[918]

The most enduring method to artificially invert sexuality is perinatal androgen manipulation [(a) and (b)], i.e. altering the androgen levels of a male fetus or newborn during the perinatal period (from a few weeks before birth to a few weeks after birth). Two tested methods of androgen manipulation were castration and pharmacological intervention (using drugs to manipulate androgen).[919] These two methods will evolve into a *single* and a *legal* method in the United States: chemical castration. There are many drugs, including marijuana, which proved effective as *anti*androgens "that partially divert or block masculinization of

---

[917] Ellis and Ames, "Neurohormonal Functioning," 242.
[918] Ellis and Ames, "Neurohormonal Functioning," 242.
[919] Ellis and Ames, "Neurohormonal Functioning," 247: "the evidence that drugs can cause sexual inversion, including inverted sexual orientation, is strong…The list of drugs that can induce sexual inversion is already fairly extensive and is bound to lengthen as new drugs are developed and more is learned about how they affect various bodily processes."

the nervous system during neuro-organization."[920] And these drugs can induce homosexual behavior: "They have "[feminizing/demasculinizing] effects on the sexual behavior of male rats after the onset of puberty (e.g. presenting and elevating the rear to other males accompanying a failure to mount females."[921]

A particularly effective type of drug in inducing sexual inversion is the progesterone drugs. Progesterone is a sex hormone involved in the menstrual cycle, pregnancy and embryogenesis. Progestin is a synthetic form of progesterone. Progesterone/progestin drugs can cause feminization in males and masculinization in females.[922] A progesterone drug that will later be especially targeted at Black males is medroxyprogesterone acetate (MPA), known popularly as Depo-Provera (DePro). MPA/DePro is an antiandrogen drug that blocks testosterone effects. "When administered to a pregnant mother while her fetus' brain is being sexually organized, offspring are likely to have their postpubertal sexual behavior affected."[923] This is true of lactating mothers as well. Currently DePro is used as a female contraceptive, and breastfeeding mothers are not restricted from using it so the demascilinizing effects are conveyed in the breastmilk.

### CHEMICAL CASTRATION AND THE FEMINIZATION OF THE BLACK MALE

This antiandrogen drug MPA/DePro is the same agent used today in the legal procedure of *chemical castration*, which, as Marques P. Richeson has well argued, threatens to be used as a tool to legally dehumanize and demasculinize Black men in the

---

[920] Ellis and Ames, "Neurohormonal Functioning,"241. Also Elaine M. Hull, J. Ken Nishita and Daniel Bitran, "Perinatal Dopamine-Related Drugs Demasculinize Rats," *Science* 224 (June 1, 1984): 1011-1013.
[921] Ellis and Ames, "Neurohormonal Functioning," 241.
[922] Ellis and Ames, "Neurohormonal Functioning," 241.
[923] Ellis and Ames, "Neurohormonal Functioning," 241.

service of white domination.[924] Chemical castration is the chemical suppression of a man's sex drive through the injection of antiandrogen drugs that reduce testosterone levels. The first to do chemical castration was Dr. Fred Berlin of John Hopkins Hospital in Baltimore – remember this institution – in 1981. In 1996 California was the first state to legalize the compulsory chemical castration of certain categories of sex offenders. The treatment may continue on an individual for as long as the State determines is necessary and there is no requirement for medical personnel involvement. Six other states soon followed California in enacting legislation providing for chemical castration of offenders: Florida, Iowa, Louisiana, Montana, Oregon, and Wisconsin. The preferred agent for chemical castration is DePro, which has devastating effects on male physiology over the long run:

> Studies have proven that prolonged use of MPA, in such doses (i.e. 300-500 milligrams), can reduce testosterone to the level of a prepubescent boy. Furthermore, MPA suppresses erections, ejaculations, and erotic thoughts. Male reproductive side effects of MPA include impotence, abnormal sperm, lowered ejaculatory volume, loss of body hair, and shrinkage of the prostate and seminal vessels. The physical, neurological, and sexual effects of MPA upon the male body thus prove devastating.[925]

But here is the catch: it does not work! As Richeson notes:

> Despite pervasive medical evidence that MPA is ineffective in preventing recidivism in most cases involving sex offenders, its use has persisted. If the benefit of chemical castration is not rooted in the prevention of recidivism or other rehabilitative or therapeutic purposes, however, then its value must lie in its retributive function. In this retributive function, nonetheless, the ugly head of eugenics has reemerged. Aside from the punishment for the harm done to the alleged victim, the primary act of retribution lies in the State's temporary (or permanent) deprivation of the capacity to procreate amongst particular segments of society deemed "unfit" – a cornerstone of eugenics.[926]

---

[924] Marques P. Richeson, "Sex, Drugs, and…Race-to-Castrate: A Black Box Warning of Chemical Castration's Potential Racial Side Effects," *Harvard BlackLetter Law Journal* 25 (2009): 95-131.
[925] Richeson, "Sex, Drugs, and…Race-to-Castrate," 122-123.
[926] Richeson, "Sex, Drugs, and…Race-to-Castrate," 100-101.

Though it is ineffective in terms of its stated objective, the value of chemical castration and another justification for its continued use by the U.S. legal system is also clear: it *feminizes* Black men, the main target of this procedure.[927] Prolonged treatment with MPA/DePro and other antiandrogens has been suspected of physically feminizing males, as certain appellate court cases show: "pumping massive doses of female hormones into the male body assists the construction of a feminine identity," Richeson argues rightly.[928] And in the hands of the American legal system – an instrument of the white dominant male group - chemical castration is but another tool to un-man the Black male and keep him subordinate. While Black men suffer most under these chemical castration regimes, Black men *are not* this country's chief sex offenders, the prison records notwithstanding. The Innocence Project, which works to free wrongfully convicted inmates through DNA, report that "There are thousands upon thousands of [innocent people] languishing in prisons" and "In most cases, the innocent man is an African American – wrongfully convicted...of raping a white woman."[929] As Stan Simpson of the *Hartford Courant* notes:

> The chilling data [the Innocence Project is] compiling is an indictment of our public-safety and judicial systems and a reminder that we haven't really evolved much when it comes to race and criminal justice. Sixty percent of the men exonerated by the Innocence Project are blacks wrongly convicted of raping white women. To appreciate the disparity, understand that, according to the Justice Department, black men attacking white women make up only 15 percent of sexual assault cases nationwide... ``It's definitely institutional racism. There's no question. It's systemic because it's happening with such frequency.''[930]

---

[927] Richeson, "Sex, Drugs, and...Race-to-Castrate," 116: "Black men are more likely to face punishment under chemical castration statutory regimes because of the racialized criminalization of rape and sexual assault. Historically, courts have consistently applied statutory penalties for rape and sexual assault in a discriminatory manner."
[928] Richeson, "Sex, Drugs, and...Race-to-Castrate," 123.
[929] Stan Simpson, "Injustice Heaped on Black Men," *Hartford Courant* April 7, 2007.
[930] Simpson, "Injustice Heaped on Black Men."

This systemic targeting of Black men with false charges of a sex crime feeds right into the targeting of Black men for un-manning through chemical castration.

> The legal system...has served as a primary instrument of oppression, carving out the racialized sphere of subordinate masculinity...[T]he phenomenon of chemical castration, in turn, treatens to serve as a tool of white domination insofar as it possesses the kinetic energy to perpetuate and further entrench black male subordination...
> 
> When applied to the particular positionality of black men, chemical castration can thus undercut notions of black masculinity insofar as the drug possesses the potential to effectively demasculinize and effeminize the consumer. In light of the historical effeminization of the black male slave as a method of deconstructing the black family, this possibility becomes even more troublesome. In a courtroom setting predominated by the white male presence of prosecutors, judges, and juries, one could conceptualize the chemical castration sentence as a reassertion of white male hegemony and a modern-day repackaging of physical castration. From this analytical framework, the burgeoning chemical castration regimes could prompt the devolution of courtrooms into modern-day lynch mobs.[931]

Chemical castration as a legal procedure is a tool used by America in the construction of the Black Sissy. It is not an accident that the main drug used in this legal procedure, MPA/DePro, is the very drug previously preferred as a sex inverting agent.

### IV. Serotonin and the Scientific Spawning of Homosexuality

Serotonin is an impulse inhibitor and among the many impulses that it modulates or regulates is the sexual impulse. Laboratory research indicates that an appropriately high level of brain serotonin is the lid on sexual urges: it calms and checks the sex drive. On the other hand, reduced levels of serotonin increases sexual urges and behavior.[932] But more than that: reducing

---

[931] Richeson, "Sex, Drugs, and...Race-to-Castrate," 96, 97, 123.
[932] Berend Oliver et al, "Differences in Sexual Behavior in Male and Female Rodents: Role of Serotonin," in *Biochemical Basis of Sex Differences in Psychopharmacology*, ed. J.C. Neil and J. Kulkarni (Current Topics in Behavioral Neurosciences 8; Berlin and Heidelberg: Springer-Verlag, 2011) 15-26; Elain M. Hull, John W. Muschamp, and Satoru Sato, "Dopamine and serotonin: influences on male sexual behavior," *Physiology & Behavior* 83 (2004): 291-307.

serotonin enough induces *hyper*-sexuality that crosses over to *homosexuality*. This is demonstrated by laboratory studies as far back as the 1970s. Recall that the UCLA researchers used two drugs in particular to target serotonin for reduction or depletion: fenfluramine and *p*-chlorophenylalanine (p-CPA). The latter is a selective tryptophan inhibitor; it therefore disrupts the production of brain and whole blood serotonin. As far back as 1985 G. Vanitha Kumari could report

> p-Chlorophenylalanine (p-CPA) has been the pharmacological drug of choice in studies on sexual behaviour and associated aggressive behaviour in animals *for the past two decades*. p-CPA has been shown to induce hypersexuality in male rats and cats...The drug acts by selectively inhibiting serotonin synthesis in the brain, pineal and other tissues by inhibiting tryptophan conversion to 5-hydroxytryptophan, the precursor of serotonin.[933]

The hypersexuality caused by serotonergic dysfunction or depletion of brain serotonin is coupled with heightened aggression.[934] This hypersexuality included homosexual behavior: injection of p-CPA induced male-on-male mounting in rats and in cats.[935] By 1977 scientists were able to produce this same effect – male-on-male mounting – by *manipulating the diet of the lab animals*. By imposing a diet depleted of the amino acid that produces serotonin when ingested, tryptophan, Italian scientists produced laboratory homosexuality or homosexual behavior.

> The ingestion of a diet containing all amino-acids but tryptophan causes a marked depletion of brain serotonin, tryptophan and 5-hydroxyindoleacetic acid both in rats and rabbits...At the time of maximal

---

[933] G. Vanitha Kumari, "Effect of Para-Chlorophenylalanine on Male Rats: Histopathological and Biochemical Changes in the Testes," *Indian Journal of Physiology and Pharmacology* 30 (1986): 223-224 [art.=223-231].

[934] Elizabeth E. Shillito, "Effect of parachlorophenylalanine on behaviour of castrated male rats," *British Journal of Pharmacology* 41 (1971): 404P; James Ferguson et al, " 'Hypersexuality' and Behavioral Changes in Cats caused by Administration of p-Chlorophenylalanine," *Science* 168 (1970): 499-501.

[935] Anthony M. Gawienowski and Gary D. Hodgen, "Homosexual Activity in Male Rats after *p*-Chlorophenylalanine: Effects of Hypophysectomy and Testosterone," *Physiology &Behavior* 7 (1971): 551-555; M. Del Fiacco et al, "Lack of Copulatory Behaviour in Male Castrated Rats after *p*-Chlorophenylalanine," *British Journal of Pharmacology* 51 (1971): 249-251.

serotonin depletion, a marked increase in male to male mounting behavior both in rats and rabbits was observed. This response was prevented by the administration of 5-hydroxytrypotophan, the direct serotonin precursor.[936]

Feeding a confined, caged or colonized population who depends on you for their food a diet that is purposely depleted of tryptophan reduces brain serotonin in that population and increases hypersexuality (because the "lid" is off the impulses and primitive drives) and that can lead to homosexuality. Diet manipulation is thus as effective as pharmacological intervention in this regard. Adding tryptophan to the diet later or injecting 5-hydroxytrypotophan directly into the lab animal reverses this effect: the male-to-male mounting was suppressed or inhibited.[937]

A study published in 2003 in *General and Comparative Endocrinology* is relevant here. Dr. Earl T. Larson of the University of Colorado and colleagues studied the role of serotonin and noradrenalin, the two "brain buttons" that scientists push and determine futures, in the process of sex reversal in the Hawaiian saddleback wrasse (*Thalassoma duperrey*) fish.[938] In certain social conditions the saddleback wrasse naturally undergoes sex reversal. When there are a greater number of smaller female fish in a population than there are larger male fish, a female will convert to a male. The researchers used pharmaceutical agents – drugs – to manipulate serotonergic activity and artificially induce sex reversal in the fish. They discovered that serotonin and noradrenalin play a key role in sex reversal in the saddleback wrasse.

> Noradrenergic signaling appears to be an important stimulator and 5-HT an important inhibitor of both the initiation and completion of the process...Manipulations of serotonergic activity were...effective in

---

[936] Walter Fratta, Giovanni Biggio and Gian Luigi Gessa, "Homosexual Mounting Behavior Induced in male Rats and Rabbits by a Tryptophan-Free Diet," *Life Sciences* 21 (1977): 379-384.
[937] Fratta, Biggio andGessa, "Homosexual Mounting Behavior," 383.
[938] Earl T. Larson et al, "Monoamines stimulate sex reversal in the saddleback wrasse," *General and Comparative Endocrinology* 130 (2003): 289-298.

altering the process of sex reversal...Increasing synaptic 5-HT...seemed the most effective method for arresting the process at an early stage.[939]

Just as increasing noradrenalin in humans increases aggression, it likewise facilitates sex reversal in lower species. And just as elevated serotonin inhibits impulsive aggression, hypersexuality and even homosexual behavior in humans, it also inhibits sex reversal in lower species.

But not just saddle wrasse fish. Scientists have demonstrated that in mammals also the manipulation of serotonin induces sexual inversion or at least homosexual behavior. In a number of studies on mice scientists demonstrate that serotonin impacts sexual preference.[940] Through either pharmacological intervention with p-CPA or through a tryptophan-free diet these scientists produced mice that lack TRP-2, the amino acid that metabolizes brain serotonin. These TRP-2-deficient male mice initiated sexual and courtship behaviors with both males and females, showing no sexual preference. This indicated that "5-HT and serotonergic neurons in the adult brain regulate sexual preference"[941] and scientists have successfully inverted this preference, admitting: "A genetic alteration made *in the laboratory* has reversed sexual preference without changing sex hormones."[942] And this *deliberate* production of sexual inversion in the laboratory is not to be under-emphasized. As Hull, Nishita and Bitran acknowledge:

---

[939] Larson et al, "Monoamines stimulate sex reversal," 294-295.

[940] Shasha Zhang, Yan Liu and Yi Rao, "Serotonin signaling in the brain of adult female mice is required for sexual preference," *PNAS* 110 (2013): 9968-9973; Yan Liu et al, "Molecular regulation of sexual preference revealed by genetic studies of 5-HT in the brains of male mice," *Nature* 472 (2011): 95-99; Bradley G. Leypold et al, "Altered sexual and social behaviors in trp2 mutant mice," *PNAS* 99 (2002): 6376-6381; Lisa Stowers et al, "Loss of Sex Discrimination and Male-Male Aggression in Mice Deficient for TRP2," *Science* 295 (2002): 1493-1500. For studies that got the opposite results see Mariana Angoa-Pérez et al, "Brain Serotonin Does Not Determine Sexual Preference in Male Mice," *PLOS* February 23, 2015: 1-16; D. Beis et al, "Brain serotonin deficiency leads to social communication deficits in mice," *Biology Letters* 11 (2015): 20150057. For a cogent harmonization of the divergent studies see Bethany Brookshire, "Serotonin and the science of sex," *Science News* April 10, 2015.

[941] Liu et al, "Molecular regulation of sexual preference," 95.

[942] Zhang, Liu and Rao, "Serotonin signaling," 9971.

Alterations in monamergic[943] activity may also play a role in the developmental demasculinizing effects noted above. Because [dopamine] is the only monoamine shown to facilitate masculine behavior in adulthood, *we investigated the effects of several perinatatally administered drugs that effect [dopamine] transmission* (emphasis added).[944]

What is most important here for our discussion is this: scientific attention to serotonin manipulation or the pushing of our two "brain buttons" was not solely focused on the increase or decrease of aggression and violence; it was also focused on the inversion or reversal of sex and/or sexuality. The sociopharmacological methods did not solely produce the hyper-aggressive, impulsively violent urban *thug*. Those methods also produce hypersexuality, homosexuality and gender inversion. Sociopharmacology's most important investigative question was: what are the social consequences of drug-induced behavioral changes? Scientists succeeded in inducing sexual changes through drugs like p-CPA and others and through diet manipulation. Homosexual behavior has been artificially induced in laboratories for several decades now, and scientists have mastered the process. Their focus on serotonergic dysfunction as a pathway to homosexual behavior and sex reversal puts the insidious fenfluramine studies that targeted Black boys in cities across this country in a new perspective.

V.     *Chemically Feminizing the American Public*

Syngenta is the largest chemical company in the world. They produce atrazine, a weed-killer, which is Syngenta's top-selling product. Atrazine is used on American corn, the largest crop in the U.S. Exposure to Atrazine had been known since the 1990s to cause androgen reduction and estrogen elevation in wildlife, and in 1997-1998 the Ecorisk Atrazine Endocrine Ecological Risk Assessment Panel invited and then funded Dr. Tryone Hayes, biologist from the University of California Berkley, to examine the effects of atrazine on amphibians. Subsequently

---

[943] Monoamines are neurotransmitters like serotonin, dopamine, etc.
[944] Hull, Nishita and Bitran, "Perinatal Dopamine-Related Drugs," 1011.

Syngenta contracted with his lab to do the same examination. They did not like what Dr. Hayes uncovered.

Dr. Hayes has demonstrated that atrazine is an endocrine disrupter.[945] Endocrine disruption is: interference with hormone synthesis and/or secretion, interference with receptor binding or activity and/or receptor degradation. The endocrine disruption caused by atrazine demasculinizes and feminizes males of various species. In fish, amphibians, reptiles and mammals atrazine decreases and inhibits androgen activity in males and increases estrogen production.[946] In fish, amphibians and reptiles atrazine exposure induces partial and/or complete feminization: 10% of exposed males when adults develop into functional females that copulated with unexposed males and produced visible eggs.

Dr. Tyrone Hayes, biologist and professor of Integrated Biology at the University of California, Berkley

---

[945] The endocrine system is the collection of glands of an organism that secretes hormones directly into the circulatory system.

[946] Tyrone B. Hayes, "There Is No Denying This: Defusing the Confusion about Atrazine," *BioScience* 54 (2004): 1138-1149; Tyrone B. Hayes et al, "Atrazine induces complete feminization and chemical castration in male African clawed frogs (*Xenopus laevis*)," *PNAS* 107 (2010): 4612-4617; Tyrone B. Hayes et al, "Demasculinization and feminization of male gonads by atrazine: Consistent effects across vertebrate classes," *Journal of Steroid Biochemistry and Molecular Biology* 127 (2011): 64-73.

Atrazine completely sex-reverses some lower species.[947] Atrazine is, in Dr. Hayes' words, an "assault on male sexual development."[948]

Why is the chemical feminization of African clawed frogs relevant to us? Because, not only is atrazine used on the U.S.'s largest crop, but it is the most commonly detected pesticide contaminant of ground, surface and drinking water.[949] Humans are thus highly exposed to this endocrine disrupter. In a human cell line atrazine induces the production of the enzyme aromatase, which converts androgen to estrogen.[950] This ubiquitously present contaminant thus puts the general public at risk of its feminizing effects. However, I am willing to bet that the highest presence of this contaminant is in and around urban areas where Black people are the most exposed. The Flint lead crisis gives us ample reason to be suspicious. However, we have evidence that urban areas are indeed more at risk, as if they are "targeted."

Between 1999 and 2009 Dr. Larry Barber, research geologist with the U.S. Geological Survey, tested the water and the fish of the Great Lakes and Upper Mississippi River regions for contaminants and found that over this ten-year period there was a constant discharge amount into the Great Lakes of alkylphenols, which are hormone disrupting compounds.[951] These compounds are used widely both commercially and residentially in products such as detergents, cleaning products and adhesives. They slip through in wastewater treatment plants to contaminate the water. Thus, these "compounds pervade the Great Lakes basin."[952] They accumulate in the tissue of local invertebrates and act estrogenically in fish, birds, and mammals. Alkylphenols are endocrine disrupters causing female machinery to shut down and males to produce estrogen. It has demasculinized fish, fish that we

---

[947] Hayes et al, "Atrazine induces complete feminization."
[948] Hayes, "There Is No Denying This," 1140.
[949] See also World Health Organization, *Atrazine and Its Metabolites in Drinking water* (World Health Organization, 2011).
[950] Hayes, "There Is No Denying This,"1139.
[951] Brian Bienkowski, "Hormone-Mimicking Chemicals Found throughout Great Lakes," *Scientific American* March 23, 2015.
[952] Bienkowski, "Hormone-Mimicking Chemicals Found throughout Great Lakes."

eat. As Brian Bienkowski reports "both contaminated fish and water represent yet another route of estrogen exposure for people," and this exposure can lead to endocrine disruption in humans. And Bienkowski makes an important acknowledgment: "concentrations [are] higher in sediments near larger cities." Duluth and St. Paul, Minnesota; Chicago; Detroit; Indianapolis; and Akron, Ohio are at higher risk. So males in such large cities – mainly Black males – are at great risk of exposure through the water and through the consumption of fish to a hormone-mimicker with demasculinizing capacity. There is thus no mystery why today more Black people identify as LGBT than whites, a remarkable demographic shift given the history.

# 21   Concluding Reflections: "Arise, O God!"

> *I said, "You are Gods";*
> *Sons of the Most High, all of you*
> *But you will die like mere mortals;*
> *You will fall like every ruler*
> *Arise, O God, judge the earth,*
> *For you shall inherit all nations.* Psalm 82:6-8.

In every place the white man succeeded in dominating, the architecture of that dominance was built on the mandate and the strategy to feminize the local male population. The white man always must be the *only* man in town. He did everything he could to stomp out all signs of manhood in the Black man, but he failed. There were always men among us. But when men show up, like Nat Turner, they pay a severe price. After hanging Turner, they skinned his body and made an infamous "money purse" from his skin; they boiled his body and from the liquefied flesh made grease, and they may very well have ingested it as tonic. Nat Turner's skull circulated among aristocratic and wealthy whites up to the late 20th century. American White Supremacy comes down hard or any display of non-domesticated Black manhood.

The Black man in America represents the carcass of the dead Black God and murderous police officers like Darren Wilson (killer of Michael Brown), Daniel Pantaleo (killer of Eric Garner), Michael Slager (killer of Walter Scott), etc., as well as the whole US justice system, are vultures feeding off of the already dead body of the God, the God that White Supremacy has been fighting now for a very long time.

The whole point of the Nation of Islam is to restore or resurrect the Black God. Most people do religion in order to *worship* God; in the Nation of Islam we do religion in order to *be* God. That's the purpose of life in Muhammad's Mosque. The Honorable Elijah Muhammad said "You are walking around looking for a God to bow to and worship. You are the God!"[953] and: "the God is Yourself";[954] But the Black man in America after centuries of slavery and ill-treatment is a *dead* god. The purpose of *this* Islam is restoration of our Godhood. Muhammad says:

---

[953] Elijah Muhammad, ***Our Savior Has Arrived*** (Chicago: Muhammad's Temple of Islam No. 2, 1974) 35.
[954] Muhammad, ***Our Savior Has Arrived***, 180.

God and I love you so well that He sent me to tell you these things to make Gods out of you. This is just what it is for: to make Gods out of you. You say, "Oh, I know I will never be a god." Don't say that, because you are already a god...Every one of you...will be Gods... we lost our power and knowledge...We had knowledge and we will be powerful when we are restored to what we originally were. But we have been robbed of power through depriving us of the Knowledge of Self. You are the Brother of the Creator and you should be able to create too. Allah taught me that He would like to restore you....back to Self. He didn't come here just to show us who He was. He came here to show us who He was, who we are, and then make us rulers.[955]

In America the resolve to possess and display authentic Black Manhood is a declaration of war. And that's why we the Fruit of Islam (FOI) wear military uniforms: because we have declared *war* on the white man's project of unmanning and feminizing the Black man. This is the official uniform of Black Manhood in America, because it represents Resurrected Black Godhood that can result from living the life that this uniform represents and requires (Plate 8). The gold trimming or the white trimming of the uniform can signal the divine light within you and I – like the gold in the garment of Amun or Yama seems to represent their internal divine light - and the blue of the uniform, like the blue glow around the black body of Amun and Yama, can signal that the light is *on* inside of our black body. That's what the life of Elijah Muhammad's Islam aims to do. And that's why we talk about the FOI *glow*. But the FOI Glow is only a hint of what this life can do.

Do you know how the Most Honorable Elijah Muhammad succeeded and succeeds through the Honorable Brother Minister Farrakhan in re-manning the unmanned Black male? He first restored in us what slavery deliberately and systematically took from us: the Black man's self-respect. There is no manhood for the Black man without first having non-negotiable self-respect. I said *non*-negotiable. Once you got it, you don't negotiate your self-respect with anyone: not your employer, not your landlord, not your wife or girlfriend; not your husband or your superior officer. No one.

---

[955] Elijah Muhammad, *Theology of Time* (Hampton, VA: U.B. & U.S. Communications Systems, 1992) 80, 118-119.

The Oromo people of East Africa have a proverb that says, "In a land with lots of hunchbacks, a straight-backed person looks ugly." The Black community has been made a land with lots of hunchbacks: Black men broken and domesticated. This is what the white man expects and, unfortunately, this is what the Black woman has become used to and has too come to expect from us. Any Black masculinity that is not domesticated by White Supremacy has a hard time in America, particularly with the white male but also with the Black female. The Black man with true self-respect is a menace to white society and is often a headache for the Black woman. Yet, *she* is the critical piece to the Black man's restoration.

What is the solution? "How, Bro Dr. Wesley, can the Black man possibly avoid being consumed by the machinery of America's project of domination?" I am suggesting that the Black woman is *the* agent of his salvation. She is not the source of his salvation – Allah is - but she's the agent. The Black woman is Aset or Isis through whom the dead Black God Asar or Osiris was and is restored to life. How does she restore Osiris?

In the below detail from an Egyptian coffin we see the corpse of the Black God Osiris being raised back to life through the recited words of Isis his wife and Nephthys her sister. As it is written in Egyptian legend, "Isis the Healer, the Mistress of Magic, in whose mouth is the Breath of Life, whose words destroy disease and awake the dead." The Divine Widow Isis is the Mistress of Magic because she heals with words of power. Through the power of her tongue she can restore the dead to life, at least her dead husband. Isis and her sister are called the Wailing Women of Osiris because the words that they recite to the dead body of the God are lamentations and glorifications. A lamentation is the sorrowful bewailing of a death or tragedy. Isis and Nephthys recite over the divine corpse words of love, grief and loss and it is these words of lament or lamentation that actually bestows life and prosperity on the dead Osiris. See, dear Sisters, part of the problem today is you don't weep for your dead man anymore. You have little sympathy these days

"Isis the Healer, the Mistress of Magic, in whose mouth is the Breath of Life, whose words destroy disease and awake the dead." "Legend of Ra and Isis"

for his dead condition, and so many of you have hardened to him, even as a wife. Many have lost your femininity with us Black men and find it only when you're in the presence of white men. But you are the Blcak man's restorer.

Isis and Nephthys recited to the divine corpse words of lamentation *and* glorification: They glorify their man even in his dead state. And it is the combination of words lamenting the god's condition of death and glorifying him in his condition of death that restores her husband to life and power. The Black woman is the Mistress of the Magic that restores the Black man, and the magic is in your mouth. Just as the words that come from the Black woman's mouth can dismantle him and aide the white man's project of domination over him, her words are the Magic, the Power, that restores the Black man to life and to manhood, engendering in him the strength to overcome his enemies.

We in the Nation of Islam have a manhood training class called FOI Class that meets every Monday evening. In this class we are given military training and manhood training. Men are *trained* in this class; however, men are *rebuilt* in his home. Our captains train the men but our wives rebuild the man. And you rebuild your man Sister in large part with your mouth, with your powerful words of healing and glorification. In the home you rebuild him back brick by brick or you dismantle him brick by brick: you can do both with your tongue. Some of our Sisters talk to their husbands as if you are a party to the white man's project of domination, feminization and disempowerment of the Black man. Only a disempowered man can be feminized. An empowered Black man cannot be unmanned. In order for the Black man to have power in such a hostile society as this that has for 461 years been literally at war with his manhood he *has* to be empowered in his home. If he is disempowered and unmanned in his home, how can he go out in this hostile society and be strong and empowered? *You*, Sisters, have to empower him in his home. After 461 years as a target and a victim of America's Project of Domination, he can't just "be" a man. He has to be rebuilt as a man and you, Sisters, are one of the chief architects. You have to be a*ctive* and not passive in the process and you have to be patient with the process.

You say: "Bro Dr Wesley, I hear you but it's hard to glorify my man in such bad shape. He aint got no job so I'm paying all of the bills. Our children are being slaughtered and abused all over this country by white men and by Black men because he has not stood up to protect us," etc. etc. You are right. Too many of us Black men are guilty of all of that. We are dead. You are married, Sister, to a corpse; a divine corpse, a handsome corpse, maybe even a corpse with some swagger. But we're still a corpse. But like Isis, you should not curse the corpse. It was over the corpse of Osiris that Isis and Nephthys recited words of lamentation and glorification.

You know what you must do Sisters in order to, with sincerity and a clear conscience, glorify a man who by most objective measures *is not worthy of glorification*? You have to be like the Apostle of God who is often styled in scripture as a woman in relation to God. Despite the undeniable cultural savagery that we Black people continue to descend into (by scientific design), the Honorable Brother Minister Farrakhan never treats or handles us as savages. He always treats us as fellow Gods. Why? Because he stays looking through our human condition to see the God in us languishing there and the Minister invariably treats us according to the God that he sees rather than according to the human condition that he found us in.

This is why when the Minister met the rapper Young Thug, who *has* wittingly or unwittingly be conscripted into the war against Black masculinity, Young Thug was genuinely impacted by his encounter with the Minister. And when he said to the Minister, "I want to be great like you," the Minister replied in all sincerity to Young Thug: "You are *greater* than me." The Minister looked underneath our Brother's victimized and manipulated human condition and saw God. That's how you must be, Sisters. You have to be able to look through – not look *past* but look *through* – the human condition of the man and love him and glorify him based on the God in him trying to come out rather than according to the miserable human condition that you found him in when you married him or that unfortunate circumstance may have latter forced upon him. And by doing that, Sisters, you help to excavate the God out from underneath the dirt of the Black man's human condition. You bring God out of him and you make a man of him. The Bible says "Let Us Make Man," because only God and the Woman can remake a Man today. The Black woman – Isis – is the Black man's hope; she helps determine his ability to effectively challenge this assault on his manhood and masculinity, an assault that is deeply entrenched in this society.

# Appendix

## "The Black Man and the White Fear"

Interview with Sis Ebony Muhammad and *Hurt2Healing Magazine*
July 12, 2016

# HURT2HEALING

*Ebony S. Muhammad (EM): With your recent messages, "What Happened to Black Manhood and Masculinity", what sparked that subject? What was it like for you preparing and delivering that message?*

**Wesley Muhammad (WM):** I'll answer the last (question) first. It was difficult delivering it, and as I said in the first lecture, I knew it would be difficult (for the people) receiving it.

What sparked it? I cannot say, Sister Ebony, that those two lectures or my crusading on the subject, if you will, were born from any event. You cannot be a follower, in my opinion, of the Honorable Brother Minister Farrakhan; you cannot be a Muslim in the Nation Of Islam, and not see the un-manning of the Black man in America and not feel the sense of urgency about the un-manning of the Black man in America. So with those two lectures, the issue has been an issue that I've spoken out against and [spoken] on for the longest.

What brought those two lectures together at this time? I resist being put in the normal (speaking) rotation at Mosque Maryam. I don't want to be put in the regular rotation. I only want to speak when Allah gives me something and puts a subject on my heart to speak on. So each of the four times that I have spoken [at Mosque Maryam], it was because Allah put those subjects on my heart to speak on.

Yes, the preparation was difficult. I knew it would be difficult to deliver, because I knew it would be received with great difficulty. And indeed it was [received with difficulty] because of the controversy.

**EM: Yes sir, thank you. That goes right into the next question. What was the feedback like, especially from other Black men?**

**WM:** Well, the Black men loved it. The number of Black men who came to me, literally in tears, was humbling. It spoke to, by Allah's grace, the soul of our Black males. We knew [something was happening to us], but we could not really ... articulate precisely [what was happening]. We feel the un-manning. We can't necessarily spot or spy the methods of it, but we live it, we feel it and we're burdened by it. Therefore, to hear it articulated and the methods laid out, it brought tears to [to the eyes of] so many Black men.

There was also mixed feelings and controversy. There were Black men who were burdened and are burdened by that knowledge now, because they have to go home. The sisters received it with mixed views and reviews, especially the younger sisters.

**EM: Wow...**

**WM:** Oh absolutely. Two things a non-domesticated manhood is a threat to in American society: white men and Black women [unfortunately]. Black women have become accustomed to domesticated Black men [or his overcompensating opposite: the super macho Black men]. That's what most Black women have in the home [to one degree or another], and that's what they have become accustomed to. So when I put that out there that the Black man is to be a man first in his home and he does not ask permission from his Black woman, a lot of brothers went home and sisters were like, "Don't bring that s___ here". [LOL] Therefore, there was some conflict, but it is necessary conflict. The terms of our arrangement up to this point must be renegotiated. The Black woman is the critical piece to the re-manning of the Black man.

Many sisters absolutely received it [well]. Either sisters appreciate Dr. Wesley [for it] or they don't like Dr. Wesley anymore. The reason I say it was the young sisters [who received it with the most difficulty] is because it's this young generation of sisters who are very different. It's really the young generation of sisters who have no real vision of real Black manhood. [With] the older generation at least they had a vision in their mind. Masculinity was sold on television. Even if you didn't live with it [personally], you had Black masculinity in the media. Now, the media today [crusades for the femininity of the Black male]. So the younger sisters are raised on that arch-type. They're raised on men [in the media] who … nine times out of ten [are] men whose emasculation is all but complete.

[I said:] "You have the Black matriarchy over here with the sisters and you got skinny suits over here with the brothers." Well a lot of the brothers in skinny suits, those sisters put them in skinny suits. That's the "now" thing. You don't see the older brothers in skinny suits. It's the younger brothers, and it's the younger sisters who co-signed those skinny suits.

So when the brothers go home and say, "I'm gonna get rid of this skinny suit", the younger sisters have problems with that. So yes, there have been mixed feelings and controversy especially with the sisters. Black men reasserting themselves seems confrontational, it seems arrogant, it seems all of that *ugly* stuff. Not that it [actually] *is* that [ugly stuff]. But in the Oromo tribe in East Africa, they say that in a land of many hunchbacks, a straight back is ugly…

**EM:** *There was a Final Call tweet that quoted the Honorable Minister Louis Farrakhan stating, "There are efforts to feminize the Black male and plant seeds of homosexuality". This tweet has three images of Black men, two of which are pro-athletes in tight fitted capri pants and loafers with no socks, and the third brother is on the runway with an actual dress on!*

**The Final Call News**
@TheFinalCall

There are efforts to feminize Black men, and plant the seed of homosexuality
finalcall.com/artman/publish...
#Farrakhan

**WM:** Yes ma'am, Dwayne Wade...

**EM:** *Right! So these images gave an illustration to the words Minister Farrakhan was speaking on about the feminization of the Black man. There have been over 200 retweets and countless comments. A lot of those comments were in such opposition to the concept of Black men being feminized even with having those* *images. There were many comments stating that none of those men are homosexual and asking how can clothes feminize a man. How would you respond to those comments to show and prove that feminization is taking place with that example of clothing?*

**WM:** Absolutely, yes ma'am.

One of my objectives in the first two lectures was to help our people and the world to see that the feminization of the Black man in America is not an isolated phenomenon. It is specifically a local manifestation of a global project. This global project of unmanning the Black man, White supremacy has engaged in it all over the Earth. American media has become so savvy in creating a virtual reality for most Americans. American media has become so savvy in hiding or concealing the reality of life in America for those who are living here. But outside of America things are clearer, things are more stark. Therefore, by seeing the method that White supremacy uses all over the world, we can recognize those methods here in America.

One of the methods that White supremacy uses everywhere they go to achieve the objective is there can never be two men in any town. The white man must be the only man in town. Everywhere White supremacy goes, the white male must be the only man in town. So the local males are always feminized. The local gods are feminized, and they're put in a dress. So skinny suits, skinny jeans appeared in South Africa before they appeared in the cities in America.

*EM: Interesting...*

**WM:** Skinny jeans were imposed upon the Zulu male, because Zulu masculinity, before the rise of the Nation Of Islam, was *the* number one enemy to White Supremacy. The British colonial officers stated that the Zulu is the number one obstacle to White domination in Africa. It wasn't just Zulu military skill that was at the root of their humiliating victory over Queen Victoria's army. It was Zulu masculinity, because Zulu warriorhood was one part of the Zulu masculinity. Wisdom with Martial (Art) skills, morality with integrity. It was that Zulu masculinity that the British were determined to break. They were determined to un-man the Zulu man.

One of their methods was 1) Impose an economic system that reverses the roles in the home 2) Redress the male in feminine clothing. So they imported the skinny jeans, and the ones who were caught in the skinny jeans were specifically the ones who were forced to fall victim to the new economic system, which meant they were forced into the gold and diamond mines of the British colonial capitalist system. So economic depression, role reversal in the home and redressing of the male is part of the process.

When we see an obsession with putting Black men, in particular Black men of fame, in dresses it is not an accident. Our brother, Dave Chappelle... HBO tried to assassinate his character when he walked away from $50 million. They made a concerted effort to put Black males in a dress. The dress was forced upon the Black male by the industry. In order to make the feminization of the Black male mainstream, mainstream people had to visualize it. So you see it on the big screen, our heroes feminized.

So now they suggest that a man wearing a dress is not necessarily a homosexual. Well that is true, but homosexuality is [only] one part of the process of the feminization of the Black male. White supremacy's objective is the *un-manning* of the Black male, the domesticating of the Black male. Homosexuality [is not the best term for what this is about]. We are talking about sodomy and the nature of *power politics* in this society. That is part of the method of White Supremacy to dominate the Black male. [But] White Supremacy doesn't have a need to sodomize *every* individual male. What they have a need of is *un-manning* every individual Black male. [And they do that in multiple ways.]

The methods range from the literal sodomizing of Black boys, for example there was the National Institutes of Health that dedicated $400,000 for a project conducted by John Hopkins University to study the satisfaction of under-aged Black boys that were being sodomized. That's one method. The other method is putting chemicals in the water supply that literally reverses gender in mammals. Other methods are making men present themselves before the world as women. That's what we see in the tweets [under discussion]. When we see our men present themselves to the world as women, and we applaud it, the un-manning is successful.

*EM: The comedian Dave Chappelle ...*

**WM:** Yes Dave Chappelle! That's critical, because he blew the whistle on the conspiracy when they tried to force him to put on a dress. He said, "No". He said that one executive after another, came in his trailer to force him to put on that dress. One of them says, "Well Dave, all of the greats have done it". What that exec was really saying was, "All of your greats are great, because they complied with our demands to put on a dress and we allowed them to be great. If you, Dave, want to be great like them, you need to comply with this demand to put on a dress". He would not do it.

When [Dave] first got in the industry, he didn't know [about the conspiracy] and he put on the dress. However, he said when he got in the industry and he started reflecting and seeing and putting the facts together, he said, "Oh, why are they putting all of us in a dress?" That day he stood up and resisted. The industry assassinated his character and his career. So we have a Brother Dave Chappelle, [who is a] whistle blower, if you will, on the inside of the industry that [is letting] us know that [there's] a concerted effort [to] dress our men of noted fame in a dress.

*EM: I would like to go back to the younger Black females as well as the young Black males; if you could give more subtle ways that they are aiding in the un-manning that they can see better. I'm thinking in terms of the music and with some of the artists.*

**WM:** The rise of the Frank Oceans...it's not subtle when there's [almost no] Black reality show or any other kind of show that's currently on television where there's not a prominent Black flaming homosexual. There's [almost] not one. It's not an accident that within music there's the embracing of gay artists. It's not an accident, [and] it's not subtle. They are overt with it. They are open with it. It's subtle [only] if we don't pay attention.

Sister Nicki Minaj busted on the scene as this great lesbian except she's not a lesbian! However, she was crafted [as] the artist "Nicki Minaj" as this big promoter of homosexuality. So the industry is pushing homosexuality in our music and is pushing homosexuality in sports and entertainment. Every avenue to stomp out any vestige of Black manhood, America is [pursuing]. They will leave no stone unturned.

One subtle method, we spoke on last night on Sister Cassandra's show about White supremacy. I was asked about Black boys in the public school system. I spoke on the experience of the Black boy in the public school system and the un-manning experience. The number one authority figure, for the most part, are Black females [with white males]. Allah deposited in the Black women His attributes. So the Black woman, as the first teacher of the child, is qualified to teach our boys. However, that's not what we have in the public school system. We don't have too much of *that* Black woman. We have the Black female that's the spawn of American slavery, like we Black males are the spawn of American slavery. The Black female in American society is a Black female that was shaped by White supremacy and its agenda of un-manning the Black male. [I'm sorry, but that's true.] So that's what Black boys run up against in the public school system. It's in our Black homes too.

So one asks why there are so few Black males in the public school system. Yes you hear the cries for more Black men in the school system, but the public school system does not accommodate the presence of Black males, and so there's the subtle effort to maintain the public school system dominated both by white men and Black women, the two elements that are most threatened by the non-domesticated Black male. Black boys who are coming through the public school system, that's all they have [in front of them]. If they don't have strong Black male figures in their life, then not only is the public school system the pipeline to jails, it's the pipeline to the un-manning of the Black male.

*EM: My last question is: How can men honestly begin taking inventory of themselves to counter this effort against them?*

**WM:** Black men: not only is it necessary to do an inventory of ourselves... The problem has been that we feel it, we live it but we can't define it. We can't visualize exactly what's happening to us. Therefore, we have an enemy that we can't see. We have a problem that we feel but we can't identify. My hope is that my two lectures helped us see the enemy more clearly and see the problem more clearly. There are many ways we fall victim to this global project and not even know it.

The sagging pants: It literally signals to the White man that his boy has been or is ready to be appropriately sodomized. When a Black man is aware of the architecture of White Supremacy's domination of us, then we can make changes. When we know better, we can do better. Now that we know the context of the sagging pants and what it signals, now we can do better. So it's critical for Black men to get the fuller picture of this process of our domination in order for us to be inspired to really fight it.

It is necessary for a Black man to have a genuine desire to be a man. In America, to [insist on being] a real man is actually a declaration of war in American society. It will be an arduous process and will make way more enemies than friends, both Black and white, both male and female. Unless our desire is very deep, Black men will not carry through with the process. We will have to fight everybody; our bosses, our mommas, our wives everybody! That's real. Everything in this society makes a non-domesticated Black man an enemy. Most of our sisters, our mothers and our wives; they mean well. They don't know they are a victim of this system as well. Therefore, they need to hear and know. But it starts with the Black male having the desire to be a man. When we declare that, all of the forces of this society will come against us. So our desire must be strong enough to withstand all of that.

> "Every man, in order to be a man, must be a man of God or he's not a man at all!" - The Honorable Minister Louis Farrakhan

It will make life more difficult, but once the Black man finds his self-respect he must fight like hell, anybody and everybody and everything, to preserve it. Unfortunately that first fight, most often, starts in the house. Not a physical fight, of course, but the Black woman has not been raised on that. The Black woman or Black female, the Black matriarch has to get used to non-domesticated black manhood. It's going to be a process and it won't be easy.

What's critical is that when the Black man finds his self-respect, he never ever negotiates it; not with his boss, not with his wife not with his superior officer. Never negotiate a new found self-respect.

The sisters: I cannot stress this enough, there is no resurrected Black man except the Black woman is the agent of that resurrection. The Honorable Minister Louis Farrakhan said this on the Breakfast Club. A man cannot be a man without a woman. In fact he said that a man doesn't even know that he is a man without a woman. A woman will test us, and if her heart and mind is right, she will test us in a way that will bring out the God in us. It is absolutely necessary. The Black woman is the Isis. Your Black man is the dead god, Osiris. There is no resurrection for Osiris except through Isis. Isis' source of power in raising up her dead god is through the power of her words. The Black woman's tongue can literally bestow life on her man.

The Black woman must save her role, her critical role, her central role in the process of resurrecting the Black man.

*EM: Thank you very much, Brother Wesley, for your words and for your work! May Allah continue to bless you and strengthen you.*

**WM:** All praise is due to Allah. Thank *you* Sister Ebony.

*Ebony S. Muhammad is the Publisher of Hurt2Healing (H2H) Magazine, a digital publication that has been described as inspiring, life-saving and cutting-edge. Known for its penetrating exclusive interviews, H2H holds to the principle that there are no subjects too heavy for discussion. A trail-blazer of its time that believes in taking a direct approach to topics that are intellectually and spiritually stimulating as well as issues that many choose to ignore exist. Here is your front row seat to a space that is sure to rearrange the way you think and see the world around you. Visit Hurt2HealingMag.com*

# Select Bibliography

"(U) White Supremacist Infiltration of Law Enforcement," Federal Bureau of Investigation Intelligence Assesment 17 October 2006.

Abdur-Rahman, Aliyyah I. "'The Strangest Freaks of Despotism': Queer Sexuality in Antebellum African American Slave Narratives." *African American Review* 40 (2006): 223-237.

Achenbach Joel and Lenny Bernstein. "Prestigious medical journals rejected stunning study on deaths among middle-aged whites," *The Washington Post* November 3, 2015.

Aldrich, Robert. *Colonialism and Homosexuality.* London and New York: Routledge, 2003.

Alexander, Michele. "Where Have All the Black Men Gone?" *The Huffington Post* April 24, 2010.

Idem. *The New Jim Crow: Mass Incarceration in the Age of Colorblindness* Revised Edition. New York: The New Press, 2010, 2011.

Anderson, Carol. *White Rage: The Unspoken Truth of Our Racial Divide.* New York: Bloomsbury, 2016.

Arondekar, Anjali. "Without Trace: Sexuality and the Colonial Archive." *Journal of the History of Sexuality* 14 (2005): 10-27.

Baruti, Mwalimu K. Bomani. *Homosexuality and the Effeminization of Afrikan Males.* Atlanta: Akoben House, 2003.

Berglund, A. *Zulu Thought-Patterns and Symbolism.* Bloomington and Indianapolis: Indiana University Press, 1976.

Bernal, Martin. *Black Athena: The Afroasiatic Roots of Classical Civilization*, **Volume II:** *The Archaeological and Documentary Evidence.* New Brunswick, NJ: Rutgers University Press, 2002.

Berne, Eric. "The Mythology of Dark and Fair: Psychiatric Use of Folklore." *The Journal of American Folklore* 72 (1959): 1-13.

Bhattacharji, Sukumari. *The Indian Theogony: A Comparative Study of Indian Mythology From the Vedas to the Purāṇas.* Cambridge: Cambridge University Press, 1970.

Binns, C.T. *The Warrior People.* London: Robert Hale, 1975.

Bleek, Wm. H.I. *Zulu Legends.* Pretoria: J.L. van Schaik, Ltd., 1952.

Boone, Joseph A. "Vacation Cruises: Or, the Homoerotics of Orientalism." *PMLA* 110 (1995): 69-107.

Breggin, M.D., Peter Roger. "Psychosurgery as Brain-disabling Therapy," in *Divergent Views in Psychiatry*, ed. M. Dongier and E. Wittbower (Hagerstown, MD: Harper and Row, 1981): 302-326.

Idem. "Psychosurgery for the Control of Violence: A Critical Review." in *Neural Bases of Violence and Aggression.* Edited by W. Fields and W. Sweet. St. Louis. MO: Warren H. Green, Inc., 1975. 350-378.

Brown, Elaine *The Condemnation of Little B: New Age Racism in America.* Boston: Beacon Press, 2002..

Callaway, H. *The Religious System of the Amazulu.* Springvale, Natal, 1868-1884 [reprint: Cape Town, 1970].

Capehart, Jonathan. "Hillary Clinton on 'superpredator' remarks: 'I shouldn't have used those words'." *Washington Post* February 25, 2015.

Carton, Benedict and Robert Morrell. "Zulu Masculinities, Warrior Culture, and Stick Fighting: Reassessing Male Violence and Virtue in South Africa." *Journal of Southern African Studies* 38 (2012): 31-53.

Case, Anne and Angus Deaton. "Rising morbidity and mortality in midlife among white non-hispanic Americans in the 21st century," *Proceedings of the National Academy of Sciences* 112 (December 8, 2015) 15078-15083

Cassidy, John. "Why did the Death Rate Rise Among Middle Aged White Americans?" *The New Yorker* November 9, 2015.

Carol Christ, "Whose history are we writing? Reading feminist texts with a hermeneutic of suspicion." *Journal of Feminist Studies in Religion* 20 (2004): 59-82.

Craig, Maureen A. and Jennifer A. Richeson. "More Diverse Yet Less Tolerant? How the Increasingly Diverse Racial Landscape Affects White Americans' Racial Attitudes." *Personality and Social Psychology Bulletin* 40 (March 2014): 750-761.

Idem. "On the Precipice of a "Majority-Minority" America: Perceived Status Threat From the Racial Demographic Shift Affects White Americans' Political Ideology." *Psychological Science OnlineFirst*, April 3, 2014:1-9.

Daniélou, Alain. *The Myths and Gods of India.* Rochester, Vermont: Inner Traditions International, 1985 [1964].

Danquah, J.B. *The Akan Doctrine of God: A Fragment of Gold Coast Ethics and Religion*. Second Edition. London: Frank Cass & Co. ltd., 1968.

Davie, Maurice. *Negroes in American Society.* New York: McGraw, 1949.

Dexter, Jim. "Fact Check: Do U.S. Food Policies Contribute to Haiti's Poverty?" *CNN* January 27, 2010.

DiIulio, John J. "The Coming of the Super-Predators." *the Weekly Standard* Nov 27, 1995.

Idem. "My Black Crime Problem, and Ours." *City Journal* Spring 1996.

Diop, Cheikh Anta. *the Cultural Unity of Black Africa: The Domains of Matriarchy & of Patriarchy in Classical Antiquity.* London: Karnak House, 1989 [1963].

Douglas, Christopher. *A Genealogy of Multiculturalism.* Ithaca and London: Cornell University Press, 2009.

Douthat, Ross. "The Dying of Whites," *The New York Times* Nov. 7, 2015.

Drizin, Steve. "The Superpredator Scare Revisited." *The Huffington Post* June 9, 2014.

Edsall, Thomas B. "The Great White Hope." *The New York Times* May 20, 2014.

Eliade, Mircea. *Patterns in Comparative Religion*, translated by Rosemary Sheed. Lincoln and London: University of Nebraska Press, 1996 [1958].

Emery, Frank. *The Red Soldier – The Zulu War 1879.* London, 1977.

Ehrenhaus Peter and A. Susan Owen. "Race Lynching and Christian Evangelicalism: Performances of Faith." *Text and Performance Quarterly* 24 (2004): 276-301.

Fandos, Nicholas. "Joe Biden's Role in '90s Crime Law Could Haunt Any Presidential Bid." *The New York Times* August 21, 2015.

Fandrych, Ingrid. "Between tradition and the requirements of modern life: Hlonipha in Southern Bantu societies, with special reference to Lesotho." *Journal of Language and Culture* 3 (2012): 67-73.

Fanon, Frantz. *A Dying Colonialism*, tr. Haakon Chevalier. New York: Grove Press, 1967.

Faria Jr., Miquel A., "Violence, mental illness, and the brain – A brief history of psychosurgery: Part 1 – From trephination to lobotomy." *Surgical Neurology International* 4 (2013): 1-23.

Foster, Thomas A. "The Sexual Abuse of Black Men Under Slavery." *Journal of the History of Sexuality* 20 (2011): 445-464.

Gates, R. Ruggles. "The Asurs and Birhors of Chota Nagpur." In *Indian Anthropology. Essays in Memory of D.N. Majumdar*. Edited by T.N. Madan and Gopāla Śarana New York: Asia Publishing House, 1962. 163-184.

Gonda, J. "Vedic Gods and the Sacrifice." *Numen* 30 (1983): 1-34.

Grier William H. and Price M. Cobbs. *Black Rage.* New York: Basic Books, 1968.

Griffin, John Howard. *Black Like Me.* New York: Sugnet, 1963.

Grump, James. "The Subjugation of the Zulus and Sioux: A Comparative Study," *Western Historical Quarterly* 19 (1988): 21-36.

Hadene, Lindani. "Zulu Masculinity: Culture, Faith and the Constitution in the South African Context," MA thesis, University of KwaZulu-Natal, 2010.

Hanretta, Sean. "Women, Marginality and the Zulu State: Women's Institutions of power in the Early Nineteenth Century." *Journal of African History* 39 (1998): 389-415.

Hasenfratz, Hans-Peter. "Patterns of Creation in Ancient Egypt." In *Creation in Jewish and Christian Tradition*. Edited by Henning Graf Reventlow and Yair Hoffman. JSOTSup 319; Sheffield: Sheffield Academic Press, 2002. 174-178

Herbert, Robert K. "Hlonipha and the Ambiguous Woman." *Anthropos* 85 (1990): 437-455.

Hernton, Calvin C. *Sex and Racism in America.* New York: Grove Press, Inc., 1965.

Hexham, Irving. *Texts on Zulu Religion: Traditional Zulu Ideas About God.* Lewiston, NY: Edwin Mellen, 1987.

Idem, "Lord of the Sky-King of the Earth: Zulu traditional religion and belief in the sky god." *Sciences religieuses/Studies in Religion* 10 (1981): 273-285.

Hillebrandt, Alfred. *Vedic Mythology*. 2 vols. Delhi: Motilal Banarsidass Publishers, 1999. Reprint.

Hodgson, Dorothy L. "Women as Children: Culture, Political Economy, and Gender Inequality Among Kisongo Maasai." *Nomadic Peoples* NS 3 (1999): 115-129.

Hokanson, Jack E. and George Calden. "Negro-White Differences on the MMPI." *Journal of Chemical Psychology* (1960): 32-33.

Horgan, John. "The Forgotten Brain Chip: The work of Jose Delgado, a pioneering star in brain-stimulation research four decades ago, goes largely unacknowledged today. What happened?" *Scientific American* (October 2005): 66-73.

Hornblower, G.D. "Min and His Functions," *Man* 46 [1946]: 113-121.

**Hornung,** Erik. *Conceptions of God in Ancient Egypt: the One and the Many*. Ithaca: Cornell University Press, 1982.

Hunter, Mark. "Fathers without amandla: Zulu-speaking men and fatherhood." In *Men and Fatherhood in South Africa*. Edited by R. Morrell and L. Richter. Cape Town: HSRC Press, 2006. 99-117.

Hyam, Ronald. *Empire and Sexuality: The British Experience*. Manchester, 1990.

Hymowitz, Kay S. "The Black Family: 40 Years of Lies." *City Journal* Summer 2005

Kaelber, Walter O. "'Tapas,' Birth, and Spiritual Rebirth in the Veda." *History of Religions* 15 (1976): 343-386.

Katz, Jonathan M. "The King and Queen of Haiti." *Political Magazine* May 4, 2015.

Kenosian, David. "The Colonial Body Politic: Desire and Violence in the Works of Gustav Frenssen and Hans Grimm." *Monatshefte* 89 (1997): 182-195.

Kessler, Dieter. "Bull Gods." In *The Ancient Gods Speak: A Guide to Egyptian Religion*. Edited by Donald B. Redford. Oxford: Oxford University Press, 2002.

Krisberg, Barry. "Youth Violence Myths and Realities: A Tale of Three Cities." Testimony before the House Subcommittee on Crime, Terrorism, and Homeland Security. Youth Violence: Trends, Myths, and Solutions. February 11, 2009.

Lang, Graeme. "Correaltions Versus Case Studies: The Case of the Zulu in Swanson's *The Birth of the Gods*." *Journal for the Scientific Study of Religion* 28 (1989): 273-282.

Laurent, Oliver. "Haiti Earthquake: Five Years After." *Time* January 12, 2015.

Lewis-Williams, D. *Believing and Seeing: Symbolic Meanings in Southern San Rock Art.* London, 1981.

Lincoln, Bruce. Idem. "The Lord of the Dead." *History of Religions* 20 (1981): 224-241.

Idem. *Priests, Warriors, and Cattle: A Study in the Ecology of Religion.* Berkley: University of California Press, 1980.

MacClintock, Anne. *Imperial Leather: Race, Gender and Sexuality in the Colonial Context.* New York: Routledge, 1995.

Mason, B.J. "New Threat to Blacks: Brain Surgery to Control Behavior." *Ebony* February (1973): 62-74

Masubelele, M.R. "Missionary Interventions in Zulu Religious Practices: The Term for the Supreme Being." *Acta Theologica Supplementum* 12 (2009) 76ff.

Masuku, Norma. "Perceived Oppression of Women in Zulu Folklore: A Feminist Critique." Doctoral dissertation, University of South Africa, 2005.

Mayeri, Serena. "Historicizing the 'End of Men': The Politics of Reaction(s)," *Boston University Law Review* 93 (2013): 729-744.

Merritt, Keri Leigh. "Men without Pants: Masculinity and the Enslaved." *African American Intellectual Historical Society* September 11, 2016.

Monteiro-Ferreira, Ana Maria. "Reevaluating Zulu Religion: An Afrocentric Analysis." *Journal of Black Studies* 35 (2005): 347-363.

Moriearty Perry L. and William Carson, "Cognitive Warfare and Young Black Males in America." *The Journal of Gender, Race & Justice* 15 (2012): 281-313.

Muhammad, Elijah. *The Divine Sayings of The Honorable Elijah Muhammad, Messenger of Allah.* Volumes 1,2 & 3 . Secretarious Publications, 2002.

Muhammad, Wesley. *The Book of God,* **Volume II:** *Allah and the Sacred Science of the Black God in African Traditional Religions.* Atlanta: A-Team Publishing, forthcoming.

Idem. "Color struck: America's White Jesus is a global export and false product," *The Final Call* 32 (January 1, 2013) 3, 8.

Idem., "As the image of God: Adam and the Original Black Man." *The Final Call* 32 (January 8, 2013) 24, 32.

Idem. "The God of Israel is a man, a Black man." *The Final Call* 32 (January 29, 2013) 24.

Idem. *Religion of the Black God: Indic Sacred Science and the Black God.* Atlanta: A-Team Publishing, 2013.

Idem. *Egyptian Sacred Science and Islam: A Reappraisal.* Atlanta: A-Team Publishing, 2012.

Idem. "Who is the Original Man." *The Final Call* 32 (December 25, 2012) 24.

Idem. *Take Another Look: The Qur'an, the Sunna and the Islam of the Honorable Elijah Muhammad.* Atlanta: A-Team Publishing, 2011.

Idem. *Black Arabia and the African Origin of Islam.* Atlanta: A-Team Publishing, 2009.

Idem. *Who Is God? The Debates.* Atlanta: A-Team Publishing, 2009.

Idem (True Islam). *The Book of God: An Encyclopedia of Proof that the Black Man in God.* Atlanta: A-Team Publishing, 2007.

Idem (True Islam). *The Truth of God: the Bible, the Qur'an and the Secret of the Black God.* Atlanta: A-Team Publishing, 2007.

Nairn, Allan. "Our Man in FRAPH: Behind Haiti's Paramilitaries." *The Nation* October 24, 1994, pp. 458-461.

Idem. "Haiti Under the Gun: How U.S. Intelligence has been exercising crowd control." *The Nation* January 8/15, 1996, pp. 11-15.

Idem. "Haiti: Different Coup, Same Paramilitary." *Democracy Now!* February 26, 2004.

O'Conner, Maura R. "Subsidizing Starvation: How American tax dollars are keeping Arkansas rice growers fat on the farm and starving millions of Haitians." *Foreign Policy* January 11, 2013.

Parpola, Asko. *The Sky-Garment: A Study of the Harappan religion and its relation to the Mesopotamian and later Indian religion.* SO 57; Helsinki, 1985.

Idem, "The Harappan 'Priest-King's' Robe and the Vedic Tārpya Garment: Their Interrelation and Symbolism (Astral and Procreative)." *South Asian Archaeology* 1983, vol. 1, 385-403.

Idem. "New correspondences between Harappan and Near Eastern glyptic art." *South Asian Archaeology* 1981. 178ff.

Patterson, James T. "Moynihan and the Single-Parent Family: The 1965 Report and its Backlash." *Education Next* Spring 2015: 6-13.

Patterson, Orlando. *Rituals of Blood: Consequences of Slavery in Two American Centuries.* New York: Basic Civitas, 1998.

Idem. "Rituals of Blood: Sacrificial Murders in the Postbellum South." *The Journal of Blacks in Higher Education* 23 (Spring 1999): 123-127.

Petrella, Christopher. "On Stone Mountain: White Supremacy and the Birth of the Modern Democratic Party," *Boston Review* March 30, 2016.

Petrosyan, Armen. "Armenia and Ireland: Myths of Prehistory." In *Ireland and Armenia: Studies in Language, History and Narrative.* Edited by Maxim Fomin, Alvard Jivanyan and Séamus Mac Mathúna. Washington D.C.: Institute for the Study of Man, 2012. 113-131.

Idem, *The Indo-European and Ancient Near Eastern Sources of the Armenian Epic.* Washington D.C.: Institute for the Study of Man, 2012.

Idem. "Armenian Traditional Black Youths: the Earliest Sources." *The Journal of Indo-European Studies* 39 (2011): 342-354.

Idem. "The Indo-European *$H_2ner(t)$-s and the Dānu Tribe." *The Journal of Indo-European Studies* 35 (2007): 297-310.

Pettersson, Olof. "Foreign Influences on the Idea of God in African Religions." In *SYNCRETISM: based on papers read at the symposium on cultural contact, meeting of religions, syncretism held at Åbo on the 8.-10. of September, 1966.* Edited by Sven S. Hartman. Stockholm : Almqvist & Wiksell, 1969. 41-65.

Pettigrew, Thomas F. *A Profile of the Negro American.* Princeton, NJ: D. Van Nostrand Company, INC, 1964.

Philips, Michael M. "The Lobotomy Files. Part II: How one doctor steered the VA toward a lobotomy program." *Wall Street Journal* December 11, 2013.

Porterfield, Amanda. "The Impact of Early New England Missionaries on Women's Roles in Zulu Culture." *Church History* 66 (1997): 67-80.

Power, Samantha. "Bystanders to Genocide." *The Atlantic* September 2001.

Rich, Jeremy. "Torture, Homosexuality, and Masculinities in French Central Africa: The Faucher-d'Alexis Affair of 1884." *Historical Reflections* 36 (2010): 7-23.

Ricketts, Erol. "The origin of black female-headed families." *Focus* 12 (Spring-Sumer 1989): 32-37.

Ringgren, Helmer. "Light and Darkness in Ancient Egyptian Religion." In *Liber amicorum. Studies in honour of Professor Dr. C.J. Bleeker. Published on the occasion of his retirement from the chair of the history of religions and the phenomenology of religion at the University of Amsterdam.* SHR 17; Leiden: E.J. Brill, 1969. 140-150.

Robinson, Nathan J. *Super Predator: Bill Clinton's Use & Abuse of Black America.* W. Somervillw, MA, 2016.

Rudwick, Stephanie and Magico Shange. "Hlonipha and the Rural Zulu Woman." *Agenda* 82 (2009): 66-75.

de Santillana, Georgia and Hertha von Dechend. *Hamlet's Mill: An essay on myth and the frame of time.* Boston: Gambit, Inc., 1969.

Schmidt, Heike. "Colonial Intimacy: The Rechenberg Scandal and Homosexuality in German East Africa." *Journal of the History of Sexuality* 17 (2008): 25-59.

Schou, Nick. *Kill The Messenger: How the CIA's Crack-Cocaine Controversy Destroyed Journalist Gary Webb*. New York: Nation Books, 2006.

Sciolino, Elaine. "Clinton Says U.S. Will Continue Ban on Haitian Exodus." *The New York Times* January 15, 1993.

Sedensky Matt and Norman Merchant. "Hundreds of Cops Kicked Off Force For Committing Sex Crimes." *The Huffington Post* November 1, 2015.

Sharma, Ram Sharan. *Sūdras in Ancient India. A Social history of the lower order down to circa A.D. 600*. Delhi: Molilal Banarsidass, 1980.

Shaw, John. "A Gaelic Eschatological Folktale, Celtic Cosmology and Dumézil's 'Three Realms'." *The Journal of Indo-European Studies* 35 (2007): 249-273.

Shendge, Malati J. *The Aryas: Facts Without Fantasy and Fiction*. New Delhi: Abhinaw Publications, 1996.

Idem. *The Civilized Demons: The Harappans in Ṛgveda*. New Delhi: Abhinav Publications, 1977.

Shope, J. H. "'Lobola is here to stay': rural black women and the contradictory meaning of lobolo in post-apartheid South Africa." In *Agenda Empowering Women for Gender Equality*. Durban: Agenda Feminist Media Company, 2006. 64-72.

Sinha, Mrinaline. *Colonial Masculinity: The "Manly Englishmen" and the "Effeminate Bengali" in Late Nineteenth Century*. Manchester, UK: Manchester University Press, 1995.

Smith, Andrea. "Not an Indian Tradition: The Sexual Colonization of Native Peoples." *Hypatia* 18 (2003): 70-85.

Soga, John Henderson. *The AmaXhosa Life and Customs.* Alice: Lovedale Press, 1931.

Spencer, Paul. "The Transfiguration of Samburu Religion." In idem, *Youth and Experiences of Ageing among Maa: Models of Society Evoked by the Maasai, Samburu, and Chamus of Kenya* (Berlin : Walter De Gruyter, 2014) 111ff.

Staples, Robert. "The Myth of the Impotent Black Male." *The Black Scholar* 2 (1971): 52-59.

Straight, Belinda. "Killing God: Exceptional Moments in the Colonial Missionary Encounter." *Current Anthropology* 49 (2008): 837-860.

Idem. *Miracles and Extraordinary Experience in Northern Kenya.* Philadelphia: University of Pennsylvania, 2007.

Stoks, Hans. "A Perception of Reality within an East-Nilotic People: point of departure for a philosophy of perception." in *I, We and Body: Writings in Philosophy of Difference*, vol. 3. Amsterdam: Verlag B.R. Grüner, 1989. 79-92.

Suggs, Richard. *Mummies, Cannibals and Vampires: The History of Corpse Medicine from the Renaissance to the Victorians.* London and New York: Routledge, 2011.

Tetreault, Mary Ann. "The Sexual Politics of Abu Gharib: Hegemony, Spectacle, and the Global War on Terror." *National Women's Studies Association Journal* 18 (2006): 33-50.

Tule, James E. *E. Franklin Frazier and Black Bourgeoisie.* Colombia and London: University of Missouri, 2002.

Uchendu, Egodi. "Introduction: Are African Males Men? Sketching African Masculinities." In *Masculinities in Contemporary Africa*. Edited by Egodi Uchendu. Dakar: CODESRIA, 2008. 1-17.

Velakazi, A. *Zulu Transformations: A Study of the Dynamics of Social Change.* Pietermaritzburg: University of Natal Press, 1962.

Vos, René L. "Varius Coloribus Apis: Some Remarks of the Colours of Apis and Other Sacred Animals." in *Egyptian Religion: The Last Thousand Years*, **Part 1**. *Studies Dedicated to the Memory of Jan Quaegebeur.* Edited by Willy Clarysse, Antoon Schoors and Harco Willems Leuven: Uitgeverij Peeters en Departement Oosterse Studies, 1998.

Walther, Daniel J. "Sex, Race and Empire: White Male Sexuality and the 'Other' in German Colonies, 1894-1914." *German Studies Review* 33 (2010): 45-71.

Idem. "Racializing Sex: Same-Sex Relations, German Colonial Authority, and Deutschtum," *Journal of the History of Sexuality* 17 (2008): 11-24.

Webb, Gary. *Dark Alliance: The CIA, the Contras, and the Crack Cocaine Explosion.* New York: Seven Stories Press, 2004 [1998].

Weiner, Tim. "Key Haiti Leaders Said to Have Been in the CIA's Pay." *The New York Times* November 1, 1993.

Weir, Jennifer. "Chiefly women and women's leaders in pre-colonial southern Africa." In *Women in South African History: They Remove Boulders and Cross Rivers.* Edited by Nomboniso Gasa. Cape Town: HSRC Press, 2006. 3-20.

Idem. "Whose *uNkulunkulu?*" *Africa* 75 (2005): 203-219.

White, Vernon Franklin. "An analysis of the Race Relations Theory of Robert E. Park." Master's thesis, Atlanta University, 1948.

Witzel, Michael. *The Origins of the World's Mythologies.* Oxford: Oxford University Press, 2012.

Idem. "Vedas and Upaniṣads." In *The Blackwell Companion to Hinduism*. Edited by Gavin Flood. Blackwell Publishing, 2003: 68-98.

Idem. "The Development of the Vedic Canon and its Schools: The Social and Political Milieu." In *Inside the Texts, Beyond the Texts: New Approaches to the Study of the Vedas*. Edited by Michael Witzel. Cambridge, 1997. 257-345

Wohlstein, Herman. *The Sky-God An-Anu.* Jericho, New York: Paul A. Stroock, 1976.

Woodard, Vincent. *The Delectable Negro: Human Consumption and Homoeroticism within U.S. Slave Culture.* New York and London: New York University Press, 2014.

York, Michael. "Toward a Proto-Indo-European vocabulary of the sacred." *WORD* 44 (August, 1993): 235-254.

Young, Harvey. "The Black Body as Souvenir in American Lynching." *Theatre Journal* 57 (2005): 639-657.

Zandee, J. "The Birth-Giving Creator-God in Ancient Egypt." In *Studies in Pharaonic Religion and Society, in Honour of J. Gwyn Griffiths.* Edited by Alan B. Lloyd. London: The Egypt Exploration Society, 1992. 168-185.